SOU

ROYAL HISTORICAL SOCIETY

STUDIES IN HISTORY 55

LAW AND POLITICS
IN EIGHTEENTH CENTURY GERMANY

LAW AND POLITICS
IN EIGHTEENTH CENTURY GERMANY

The Imperial Aulic Council in the Reign of Charles VI

Michael Hughes

THE ROYAL HISTORICAL SOCIETY

THE BOYDELL PRESS

© Michael Hughes 1988

First published 1988

A Royal Historical Society publication
Published by The Boydell Press
an imprint of Boydell & Brewer Ltd
PO Box 9 Woodbridge Suffolk IP12 3DF
and of Boydell & Brewer Inc.
Wolfeboro New Hampshire 03894-2069 USA

ISBN 0 86193 212 9

ISSN 0269-2244

British Library Cataloguing in Publication Data

Hughes, Michael
    Law and politics in eighteenth century
    Germany. — (Royal Historical Society studies in
    history, v. 55).
    1. Germany. Politics 1711-1740
    I. Title II. Series
    320.943
    ISBN 0-86193-212-9

Library of Congress Cataloging-in-Publication Data

Hughes, Michael
    Law and politics in eighteenth century Germany : the Imperial Aulic Council
in the reign of Charles VI / Michael Hughes.
        p. cm. — (Royal Historical Society studies in history, ISSN 0269-2244 ; 55)
    "A Royal Historical Society publication" — T.p. verso.
    Bibliography: p.
    Includes index.
    ISBN 0-86193-212-9 (alk. paper)
    1. Holy Roman Empire. Reichshofrat — History. 2. Charles VI, Holy Roman
Emperor, 1685-1740. 3. Mecklenburg (Germany : State) — Politics and
government. 4. East Friesland (Germany) — Politics and government. I. Title. II.
Series: Royal Historical Society studies in history ; no. 55.
JN3285.H85 1988
943'.052—dc19   88-14123
                                                                      CIP

∞ Printed on long life paper
made to the full American Standard

Printed in Great Britain by
St Edmundsbury Press, Bury St Edmunds, Suffolk

Contents

The Society records its gratitude to the following whose generosity made possible the initiation of this series: The British Academy; The Pilgrim Trust; The Twenty-Seven Foundation; The United States Embassy's Bicentennial funds; The Wolfson Trust; several private donors.

Acknowledgements

Many people have earned my deep gratitude for their help and encouragement in the preparation of this work. The order in which I list them is arbitrary and I apologise for any omissions. Professor R. F. Leslie first steered me towards the study of German history. Professor F. L. Carsten has been unstinting with his help and encouragement over many years. I am most indebted to the directors and staffs of the Haus- Hof- und Staatsarchiv, Vienna, the Lower Saxon State Archives at Hanover and Aurich, the Mecklenburg State Archive at Schwerin, the State Archive Depository at Göttingen and the university libraries at Göttingen and Vienna. It is invidious to mention individuals but I feel I must single out in particular Dr Anna Coreth of the Haus- Hof- und Staatsarchiv, who gave me invaluable advice. Dr Harm Wiemann of the East Frisian *Landschaft*, Aurich, also gave me valuable guidance. To the University College of Wales, Aberystwyth, I am grateful for financial assistance which enabled me to visit archives in Germany and Austria. I must also thank Peter Michael Heinecke, Professor T. A. Watkins of University College Dublin, Mrs Janet Godden and Mrs Christine Linehan of the Royal Historical Society and my wife, Yvonne Hughes, for their help and advice during the long gestation of this work.

M. Hughes
Aberystwyth 1988

Abbreviations

EHR   *English Historical Review*
Fr HS   *French Historical Studies*
HZ   *Historische Zeitschrift*
JMH   *Journal of Modern History*
MIÖG   *Mitteilungen des Instituts für österreichische*
           Geschichtsforschung
TRHS   *Transactions of the Royal History Society*

Introduction

This is a study of two cases in the imperial aulic council (*Reichshofrat*) during the reign of the Emperor Charles VI. Although involving those comparatively small and insignificant states of the Holy Roman Empire, Mecklenburg and East Frisia, this litigation became a significant element in German politics and European diplomacy and was considered in the inner councils of the Austro-imperial government. Detailed analysis of the course of the litigation can illuminate the constitutional development of the Holy Roman Empire, in particular the tension between imperial authority and princely rights and the struggle of German rulers to destroy the power of their parliamentary Estates and to establish an absolutist system of government; it can provide insights into the changing role of the Austrian state in European diplomacy after Austria's establishment as a great power; it can describe the functioning of one of the supreme tribunals of the Empire as an illustration of the exercise of judicial authority in what had become a federalistic political system; and it can contribute to knowledge of the reign of Charles VI, an important yet neglected period.

The Holy Roman Empire was then in the last century of its existence. Its reputation has suffered much from the fact that historians, German and non-German, have tended to ignore it and concentrate on 'living and constructive forces' in German history, the growth of strong states, especially Prussia.[1] It has suffered from the belittling phrase, the clever aphorism, only half understood and taken out of context: it was of course neither holy, Roman nor an empire and perhaps the only part of Pufendorf's work widely

---

1 G. Barraclough, *The Origins of Modern Germany*, 2nd ed. (Oxford, 1949), p. 397: 'The historians's only interest in this stultifying ossification lies in the process by which it was brought to an end and in its durable effects on the people who underwent it.' The historians of the so-called 'Borussian legend' sought to portray Brandenburg-Prussia after 1648, if not before, as the bearer of the true German spirit: U. Scheuner, *Der Staatsgedanke Preussens* (Cologne/Graz, 1965), p. 5.

quoted is the description of the imperial constitution as irregular and like a monster.[2] This old-fashioned view is currently being revised as a result of a number of works which have appeared in the last fifteen years.[3]

The imperial aulic council, like other aspects of the Empire as an institution after 1648, has scarcely been touched by modern scholarship.[4] This study seeks to show how it worked and to examine its impartiality, corruptibility and the extent to which it was subject to external political pressures, questions which were the object of much public debate in the eighteenth century. Incidentally it illustrates the conflict between law and reason of state and the difficulties produced in Germany and Europe by the Emperor's dual role as ruler of the Empire and head of the house of Austria.

Moreover an examination of the cases of Mecklenburg and East Frisia supplements work already done on constitutional developments within the individual states of the Empire, although to date, the events in East Frisia have not been dealt with in English and a modern history in German has only recently appeared.[5] East Frisia is of particular interest as its constitutional forms and the political theories underlying them were unique in Germany, while Mecklenburg too stood aside from the mainstream of the constitutional developments of eighteenth century Germany. The imperial aulic

---

[2] K. von Raumer, 'Préfecture Francaise: Monteglas und die Beurteilung der napoleonischen Rheinbundpolitik' in *Spiegel der Geschichte. Festgabe für Max Braubach* (Münster, 1964), p. 647.

[3] G. Benecke, *Society and Politics in Germany 1500 – 1750* (London, 1974), p. xi. The author attempts 'a new interpretation of the Holy Roman Empire' and 'a long overdue revision of the real nature of early modern German society and politics'. M. Hughes, 'The Imperial Aulic Council ("Reichshofrat") as Guardian of the Rights of Mediate Estates in the Later Holy Roman Empire: Some Suggestions for Further Research' in R. Vierhaus (ed.), *Herrschaftsverträge, Wahlkapitulationen, Fundamentalgesetze* (Göttingen, 1977), pp. 192 – 204. J. A. Vann and S. W. Rowan, (eds.), *The Old Reich. Essays in German Institutions 1495 – 1806* (Brussels, 1974), pp. ix – xii.

[4] The only modern work on it is O. von Gschliesser, *Der Reichshofrat* (Vienna, 1942). This is rather limited in its coverage of the activity of the council but is immensely valuable for biographical details of the councillors. W. Sellert, *Über die Zuständigkeitsabgrenzung von Reichshofrat und Reichskammergericht insbesondere in Strafsachen und Angelegenheiten der freiwilligen Gerichtsbarkeit*, (Aalen, 1965) is a detailed study of the competence of the two imperial supreme courts and is valuable for its clear exposition of complex legal points.

[5] H. Wiemann, *Die Grundlagen der landständischen Verfassung Ostfrieslands: die Verträge von 1595 bis 1622* (Aurich, 1974). B. Kappelhoff, *Absolutistisches Regiment oder Ständeherrschaft? Landesherr und Landstände in Ostfriesland im ersten Drittel des 18. Jahrhunderts* (Hildesheim, 1982).

council was the source of decisions of far-reaching importance in the two states for over a century and the development of both might have been different had the aulic council not existed or if its verdicts had been different.[6] This fact alone indicates that, after 1648, the Empire was by no means as defunct as its critics would have us believe. To Charles VI, to many of his ministers and to most of the princes and rulers of the Empire the imperial title was far more than an empty show.

---

[6] This has been underlined by recent historians of Mecklenburg: P. Wick, *Versuche zur Errichtung des Absolutismus in Mecklenburg in der ersten Hälfte des 18. Jahrhunderts* (Berlin, 1964) and E. Hofer, *Die Beziehungen Mecklenburgs zu Kaiser und Reich* (Marburg, 1956), pp. 61, 88. R. Vierhaus, 'Land, Staat und Reich in der politischen Vorstellungswelt deutscher Landstände im 18. Jahrhundert', *H.Z.*, vol. 223 (1976), pp. 40 – 60.

PART ONE
THE CONTEXT

1

Charles VI, the Empire
and the supreme judicial office

Charles VI, ruler of the Austrian Habsburg lands and Holy Roman
Emperor from 1711 to 1740, is not one of the more colourful figures
of European history. Distinguished neither by great ability nor
spectacular vice, he was in many respects an unremarkable
eighteenth-century monarch, whose main claim to historians'
attention has been that he was the father of Maria Theresa.[1] He is
little known. For long periods he kept sketchy diaries mainly
recording the movements of his court but, unfortunately, revealing
little about the man. The rare occasions when he did allow his
feelings to show perhaps modify slightly the view of a man long
regarded as cold, arrogant, formal and unapproachable.[2] He had
the deformed jaw typical of his house and the resulting speech
defect made him hard to understand: this certainly increased his
apparent remoteness.[3] He was hard working, intelligent and
concerned for the welfare of his subjects and had a high sense of
morality and duty: he abolished the sale of titles which Leopold I
had made into a lucrative business.[4] His knowledge, judgement and
humanity are revealed in his correspondence with his chancellor

---

[1]   A modern scholarly account of his reign has yet to be written.
[2]   O. Redlich, 'Die Tagebücher Kaiser Karls VI' in *Gesamtdeutsche Vergangen-
      heit: Festgabe für Heinrich von Srbik* (Munich, 1938), pp. 141 – 5.
[3]   There are several examples of diplomats reporting that the Emperor had
      spoken to them but that they had not understood what he said: Göttingen,
      State Archive Depository [hereafter Göttingen], Aw 474, no. 54, report of
      the Mecklenburg diplomat Eichholtz 31 May 1719. T. Gehling, *Ein
      europäischer Diplomat am Kaiserhof zu Wien: Francois Louis de Pesme, Seigneur
      de Saint-Saphorin, als englischer Resident am Wiener Hof 1718 – 1727* (Bonn,
      1964), pp. 8, 50 – 1, suggests that Charles deliberately mumbled when he
      wished to avoid committing himself. W. Michael, *Englische Geschichte im
      achtzehnten Jahrhundert* (Berlin, 1934), part 2, vol. 3, p. 491 quotes a report of
      the Austrian resident in London, Palm, to the effect that George I mumbled
      at an audience and he had no idea what the king had said.
[4]   A. Fauchier-Magnan, *The Small German Courts in the eighteenth century* (tr.
      M. Savill, London, 1958), p. 54.

Sinzendorff while the latter was representing him at the congress of Soissons in 1728.[5] In May 1722 George I's envoy St Saphorin reported that Charles was the best intentioned of men, neither a bigot nor a persecutor, but that he had the vice of putting off decisions in the hope that the need for them would disappear.[6] It was also known that he preferred to come to decisions alone rather than in close consultation with his ministers.

At the beginning of his reign conditions favoured the revival of imperial power and influence. Austria's prestige was high after years of war against the Turks and France, from which she gained substantial increases in territory. In 1720 the Emperor's position in Germany and Europe was stronger than for ninety years.[7] This was almost entirely the result of the strength and prestige of the Habsburgs rather than of any change in the Emperor's influence in the Reich or anything more than a temporary halt in the loosening of the bonds holding the Empire together. Austria continued to grow away from the trellis of the Empire.

Charles brought to his office an elevated concept of his imperial position, to him far more than a collection of empty titles, and a determination to use his remaining powers and influence to the full.[8] A movement for the revival of imperial power, the so-called imperial reaction of the early eighteenth century, had begun under Charles' brother Joseph I (1705 – 11), who determined to wield a tighter control over the Empire than his father and predecessors had done. His reign was seen as the beginning of a brilliant period in Austrian history; Joseph was the Austrian sun-king, his court graced with a galaxy of talented advisers. Two years before his father's death, Joseph had presided over a great shake-up at the top of the Austrian government, bringing in men like prince Eugene of

5   G. Mecenseffy, *Karls VI Spanische Bündnispolitik 1725 – 9* (Innsbruck, 1934), p. 108.

6   K. Borgmann, *Der deutsche Religionsstreit der Jahre 1719 – 1920* (Berlin, 1937), pp. 70 – 3. The Emperor had the habit of trying to please everyone; it was said that anyone who spoke to him came away with the impression that Charles VI thought exactly as he did: Schwerin, Mecklenburg Provincial Archive, Landständisches Archiv, E.III P.1.5., Behr to Bernstorff 10 July 1717.

7   M. Naumann, *Österreich, England und das Reich* (Berlin, 1936), pp. 9, 14.

8   K. Perels, 'Die allgemeinen Appelationsprivilegien für Brandenburg-Preussen' in *Quellen und Studien zur Verfassungsgeschichte des deutschen Reichs im Mittelalter und in der Neuzeit*, vol. 3, no. 1 (Weimar, 1908), pp. 85. B. Erdmannsdörfer, *Deutsche Geschichte vom Westfälischen Frieden bis zum Regierungsantritt Friedrichs des Grossen* (2 vols., Berlin, 1880 – 93), vol. II, pp. 375 – 6

Savoy.[9] Under Joseph there was a new tone in the statements of imperial representatives at the imperial diet and the pronouncements of the imperial aulic council and a new emphasis on the imperial dignity,[10] which culminated in the imperial ban against Bavaria and Cologne, allies of Louis XIV. This was combined with a policy of internal reform within the Austrian lands, especially in finance, in which the Habsburgs were perennially weak.[11]

In 1711 Charles was elected Emperor without serious difficulty under the influence of the French threat to Germany, which seemed temporarily to have united the princes of the Empire, and the patronage of the maritime powers, which had supported his candidature from the beginning.[12] Habsburg prestige was at a pinnacle. Austrian arms had been successful against the French and the Turks, although the Empire fought on after 1713 in a fruitless campaign in the Rhineland which gained nothing, and the ardently desired restoration of Strasburg and the firm 'Imperial barrier' against France were both denied to Germany.[13] Many of Austria's gains from the Spanish empire were legally incorporated into the Holy Roman Empire. German national feeling, however, was little satisfied by reflected glory.

Contemporary commentators and later historians, often relying excessively on the reports of the French, English and Prussian agents in Vienna, have portrayed Charles VI as an arrogant and

---

[9]   H. von Srbik, *Österreichische Staatsverträge. Niederlande.* vol. I (Vienna, 1912), pp. 393, 419 notes Joseph's determination to prevent foreign interference in the Empire. K. O. von Aretin, 'Kaiser Joseph I zwischen Kaisertradition und österreichische Grossmachtpolitik', *HZ*, vol. 215, p. 606.

[10] R. Koser, 'Brandenburg-Preussen in dem Kampfe zwischen Imperialismus und reichsständischer Libertät', *HZ*, vol. 96, (1906), p. 202. H. R. Feller, *Die Bedeutung des Reichs und seiner Verfassung für die mittelbaren Untertanen und die Landstände im Jahrhundert nach dem Westfälischen Frieden* (Diss. Marburg, 1953), p. 23.

[11] J. W. Stoye, 'Emperor Charles VI: The Early Years of the Reign', *TRHS*, 5th series, vol. 12 (1962), pp. 63–84. During the war of Spanish Succession Austria's war effort was dependent on subsidies from the Maritime Powers.

[12] J. Ziekursch. *Die Kaiserwahl Karls VI (1711)* (Gotha, 1902), pp. 22 ff. R. Place, 'The Self-Deception of the Strong. France on the eve of the War of the League of Augsburg', *FrHS*, vol. 6, pp. 459–73.

[13] M. Braubach, 'Um die Reichsbarriere am Oberrhein' in *Diplomatie und geistiges Leben im 17. und 18. Jahrhundert* (Bonn, 1969), pp. 231–67. Stoye, p. 64 describes the decade 1711–20 as the most acquisitive in Austria's history.

stiff-necked ruler intent on restoring imperial power in Germany.[14] In 1718 the Prussian resident in Vienna confirmed an earlier warning that Charles was very sensitive in matters touching *point d'honneur*, imperial authority and jurisdiction and in 1721 the English minister reported that he had ambitions to 'imitate Caesar Augustus and the grandeur of the first Roman Empire'.[15]

These and similar views grossly exaggerated the Emperor's power and influence in Germany. Certainly Charles inherited from his brother a vigorous and even aggressive policy in the Empire; in prince Eugene of Savoy and the imperial vice-chancellor von Schönborn he also inherited two ministers anxious to see a revival of imperial authority within Germany and to break the power of the rising states, particularly the north German Protestant states, Hanover and Brandenburg-Prussia.[16] In the case of Eugene this policy was certainly designed to further purely Austrian aims but Schönborn was convinced that only Habsburg power in Germany could save it from dismemberment, foreign domination and the devouring of the weak by the strong. Charles' experience as king of Spain during ten of his formative years is also said to have influenced his policy as Emperor.[17] Some writers have found evidence of the 'imperial reaction' in architecture; Joseph I had plans for a German Versailles, more spectacular than the original, at Schönbrunn and Charles VI began the construction of an Austrian Escorial at Klosterneuburg near Vienna.[18]

[14] Typical is A. McC. Wilson, *French Foreign Policy during the Administration of Cardinal Fleury 1726 – 43* (Cambridge, Mass. 1936), pp. 108 – 10. He describes Charles's German policy as 'tantamount to a revolution . . . The policy of Charles VI was indubitably an invasive and aggressive one and Chavigny [the French representative at the imperial diet] reported in 1727 that the German situation was comparable not to that which existed in the time of Louis XIV but to that of the period before the Treaties of Westphalia'.

[15] H. Hantsch, *Reichsvizekanzler Friedrich Karl von Schönborn* (Augsburg, 1929), pp. 226 n62, 275.

[16] Schönborn's dislike of these states was returned undiminished. Frederick William I saw him as a malign influence set on thwarting Prussia at every turn. Many weaker princes were frightened of antagonizing a man with such great influence: Naumann, pp. 15, 40 n53, Mecenseffy, p. 14n, Hantsch, *Schönborn*, p. 63.

[17] Redlich, 'Die Tagebücher', p. 147. Stoye, p. 74 argues that the after-effects of the Spanish period have been exaggerated by historians. Certainly Charles brought back with him to Vienna many Spaniards and Italians to form distinct Spanish, Italian and Flemish councils to run former Spanish possessions. This produced great jealousy among Austrian ministers.

[18] H. Sedlmayr, 'Die politische Bedeutung des deutschen Barocks (Der "Reichsstil")' in *Gesamtdeutsche Vergangenheit*, pp. 126 – 40, esp. p. 136.

If these varied ingredients did amount to a concerted new policy towards the Empire, an imperial reaction, it failed to halt the loss of imperial power in Germany and may even have quickened it. The brilliant promise of the first decade of Charles VI's reign turned into the era of failures and decline of his last years. Extensive possessions were to prove a curse for the Habsburgs. Great lands brought them great commitments and great ambitions which their sparse resources and politically exposed position in Europe made dangerous. Austria was always too weak and too poor for the role it tried to fill, as was revealed during Charles's reign.

By the reign of Charles VI the Holy Roman Empire was more a vacuum than a state, characterized as it was by a weak central monarchy, virtually sovereign local rulers and diplomatic impotence, especially noticeable after and, it is still believed by many, largely as a result of the treaties of Westphalia. The treaties have been portrayed[19] as a great turning point in the history of Germany: before them it had possessed a real existence as a state but after them it existed in name only. In fact, the decline of the Empire into the impotence and division which marked it in the eighteenth century had begun long before 1648 as had the loss of German power in Europe.

In spite of this, the Empire survived into the nineteenth century and this survival in a state of advanced decay demonstrates the power of an idea. The Empire was strongly rooted in memories of the Christian Roman Empire, taken over by the Frankish empire and transmitted in part to the later German kingdom. The translation of this idea into a concrete state structure was a major preoccupation of medieval German rulers but, although some German commentators of the seventeenth and eighteenth centuries habitually portrayed the medieval Empire as a powerful state, it is hard to find any lengthy period in its medieval history when the strong centrifugal forces at work within it were effectively controlled or reversed by German monarchs.[20] In the last centuries of its existence there was a considerable debate as to whether the Empire was a state at all and, if it was, what kind of state. It was perhaps the abstract quality of the concept of the Empire which made it hard to fit its constitution neatly into any accepted category and which

[19] H. Holborn, *A History of Modern Germany*, vol. II (London, 1965), p. 4. Huber, E. R., 'Reich, Volk und Staat in der Reichsrechtswissenschaft des 17. und 18. Jahrhunderts', *Zeitschrift für die gesamte Staatswissenschaft*, vol. 102 (1942). A. Wandruszka, *Reichspatriotismus und Reichspolitik zur Zeit des Prager Friedens von 1635* (Cologne/Graz, 1955), pp. 113–14.

[20] J. B. Gillingham, *The Kingdom of Germany in the High Middle Ages*. Historical Association pamphlet 1971, *passim*.

led Pufendorf to describe it as a monstrosity in his frequently quoted passage.

The sheer size of the Empire and its fluid borders to the south and east were among the main enemies of strong monarchy and this was made worse by the obsession of many medieval German kings with recovering authority in Italy. The growth of feudalism in Germany compounded the weakness of the monarch; royal servants had their offices converted into hereditary fiefs conveying ownership of large areas of land and a growing collection of deputed royal rights and powers. This process began early and was actively fostered by Emperors like Frederick I and Charles IV, often later portrayed as among the strongest medieval Emperors.[21] Power in Germany passed increasingly into the hands of a number of noble families while the allegiance they owed to the crown remained vague. Not only was the power taken from the German kings; they also gave it away. Barbarossa used this proliferating feudalism to buy the financial and military support of his established feudatories for his campaigns in Italy. Whether or not *Lehnzwang*, the obligation on the king to regrant vacant or sequestered fiefs, was in operation by the end of the twelfth century, the king could not afford to alienate potential supporters by retaining these fiefs.[22] Barbarossa was unable to use the lands confiscated from Henry the Lion to construct a solid block of royal land across Germany.[23] Feudalization also cut the Emperor off from the mass of his subjects who became subjects of the nobility and only mediate subjects of the crown. The Emperor lost his military

[21] A. Randelzhofer, *Völkerrechtliche Aspekte des Heiligen Römischen Reiches nach 1648* (Berlin, 1967), p. 35. P. Munz, *Frederick Barbarossa: a study in medieval politics* (London, 1969), pp. 318 ff. Munz' first chapter is an interesting analysis of the development of the Barbarossa legend.

[22] Gillingham, pp. 24 – 5. K. Hampe, *Deutsche Kaisergeschichte im Zeitalter der Salier und Staufer* (Leipzig, 1929), pp. 170 – 1. German monarchs also leased territory and rights as a reward for service or to raise ready cash. The proverb 'Pfand gibt oft Land' suggests the difficulty experienced in recovering such rights once leased.

[23] Munz, pp. 323 – 5: 'Frederick decided no more and no less than to become a feudal king, stretching the network of feudal allegiances over as wide a field as possible . . . With this development [the destruction of Henry the Lion's power and the distribution of his duchies among the Emperor's supporters as fiefs] Frederick had actively assisted in the abolition of the old order, in which the German monarchy had, in theory, been an association of tribes and, in practice, an association of a limited number of princely families whose standing and power were rooted in the remnants of tribal law. This constitutional transformation was the most far-reaching and constructive change the German monarchy had ever undergone.' Whether this amounted to a conscious and consistently pursued policy is questionable.

power; not he but his vassals called out the people in arms. Although Frederick defeated the overmighty subject Henry the Lion, the struggle between the two weakened the Germany monarchy and made the final triumph of other overmighty subjects all the more likely.[24]

Henry VI tried to complete the process by seeking from the nobility the recognition of an hereditary monarchy over hereditary fiefs. But by then the king had nothing to offer to make the bargain worthwhile to them and the offer was rejected. Henry died too soon and the last Hohenstaufen Emperor, Frederick II, saw Germany as an adjunct of an empire based in southern Italy. He was ready to recognise formally that the princes ruled as well as held their fiefs. It could be argued that, from this point on, the Holy Roman Empire had no chance of developing into a unitary state. The elective principle, a succession of different dynasties, short reigns, minorities, double elections, friction with the Church and the imperial preoccupation with the non-German, especially Italian, interests had by the fifteenth century robbed the German kings and Emperors of much of their power. Virtually all the king's *regalia* or rights of sovereignty were lost or given to the princes in the thirteenth and fourteenth centuries. By the time of Emperor Frederick III (1415 – 93) the territorial princes could coin money, take tolls, issue safe conducts, maintain roads and waterways, draw the revenues from forests and fisheries, exploit mines, establish monopolies, take treasure trove, extend their protection to Jews, dispose of lordless land and take possession of objects washed up on their shores, all of which had been royal rights and prerogatives. The whole nature of the German constitution changed from a monarchy, in which certain powers were devolved downwards to sub-rulers, to a loose federation in which the sub-rulers claimed these powers as a birthright.[25]

From the fifteenth century onwards there were voices loud with warnings of the weakness of the Empire and its threatened dissolution and offering programmes for its recovery. In the late fifteenth century the imperial diet became the platform for a vocal

---

[24] O. Engels, *Die Staufer* (Berlin/Stuttgart, 1972), ch. 8 *passim*. In 1156 Frederick set up the highly privileged duchy of Austria for Henry Jasomirgott of Babenberg. This was the first fully-fledged territorial state and was soon to be followed by others: Munz, pp. 105 – 7.

[25] H. Conrad, *Deutsche Rechtsgeschichte. Ein Lehrbuch* (Karlsruhe, 1954), pp. 370 – 6. I. Bog, *Der Reichsmerkantilismus im 17. und 18. Jahrhundert* (Stuttgart, 1959), p. 43. For the debates on the imperial constitution see A. Rauch, *Kaiser und Reich in dem Jahrhundert nach dem Westfälischen Frieden* (Ochsenfurt/Munich, 1933), ch. I *passim*.

reform party.[26] The majority of these reform schemes involved a strengthening of the central authority in some form or another and some permutation of the following: an imperial standing army, the codification of imperial law, a permanent universal peace and a strong imperial judicial apparatus to enforce it.[27] These movements often gained impetus from brief revivals of imperial patriotism such as that associated with the person of Emperor Maximilian I, whose reign saw a slowing down in the erosion of imperial power.[28] In one respect, the fact that after the reign of Frederick III the Habsburgs achieved what amounted to hereditary possession of the somewhat rusted inheritance of Charlemagne, the power of the Emperor had increased. The imperial title continued to bring a large measure of esteem to the man who held it, especially when that authority was permanently backed by the strong *Hausmacht* of Austria. Further, the external threat from France and the Turks and the German Humanist movement produced a short-lived reawakening of German national enthusiasm, during which Maximilian planned a reform of the Empire from the centre to strengthen it for war to east and west. Against this the archbishop elector of Mainz, Berchtold von Henneberg, and his party put forward counter-proposals which, if they had been put into effect, would have subjected Empire and Emperor to an aristocracy of the great princes, too often concerned with their own particular interests.[29]

The reform movement eventually came to nothing. Rulers below the rank of elector opposed a new constitution which proposed to give the electors a more powerful position and there was an important group of princes opposed to any reform which involved a

---

[26] By this time the procedure and membership of the imperial diet had become regularized. For much of the fifteenth century attendance at diets was often small as the Emperor could summon representatives selectively. As a result the absent could refuse to be bound by the decisions of the present.

[27] For the imperial reform movement see F. Hartung, 'Imperial Reform 1485 – 95: its course and its character' in G. Strauss (ed.), *Pre-Reformation Germany* (London, 1972), pp. 73 – 135 (An article originally published in 1913).

[28] Randelzhofer, ch. V.

[29] P. Joachimsen, (ed.), *Der deutsche Staatsgedanke von seinen Anfängen bis auf Leibniz und Friedrich den Grossen* (Munich, 1921), pp. 24 – 5. Hartung, 'Imperial Reform', pp. 92 – 3: 'While the reform party among the Estates strove to obtain the greatest possible control over the Emperor's exercise of power, Maximilian countered with the idea of a monarchical reform of the empire which, while consolidating the imperial union, would also strengthen the political and financial resources of the sovereign.' See also Rowan in Vann and Rowan, *The Old Reich*, p. 53 on Maximilian I's skilled use of German patriotic pride in support of his own desires.

strengthening of central authority and a loss of their powers to imperial institutions. In spite of this basic failure there were tangible results; the procedure of the imperial diet was further regulated, an eternal imperial peace was established in 1495, the Empire was organized into Circles with a peace-keeping function, in 1495 the new imperial cameral court was set up as a supreme imperial tribunal, in 1532 a new criminal code for the whole Empire was passed and in 1555 an ordinance of execution (*Exekutionsordnung*) established a procedure for dealing with internal and external threats to order. In the same year the institution of the imperial deputation, a select committee drawn from the electors, princes and towns in the imperial diet, was set up to deal with urgent or special matters. The attempt to provide the Empire with a permanent administration, the *Reichsregiment*, which established a council of twenty appointed by the Estates of the Empire to govern in collaboration with the Emperor, proved a short-lived experiment and lasted only from 1500 to 1502 and from 1521 to 1530. Most of the princes of the Empire refused to cooperate with it. Conspicuously absent from the list of reforms were a viable imperial financial system and an imperial standing army.[30]

It is ironical that this period of creative legislation also saw the Reformation in Germany, which added another factor of division in the Empire and further alienated the Emperor and the princes. Had all Germany become Protestant, the outcome might have been different. As it was, Charles V's efforts to revive his imperial authority were combined with a campaign to rid Germany of heresy and thereafter attempts to increase imperial power suffered from the identification of the Emperor with the militant Counter-Reformation.[31] Charles V's reign was also of significance in that at his election in 1519 the electors obtained from him, as well as great sums of money, the first capitulation of election (*Wahlkapitulation*)

[30] The 1555 ordinance of execution provided the Circles with an executive committee and gave them extensive peace-keeping functions. The graduated poll-tax, the Common Penny and the *Reichspfennigmeisteramt* in Frankfurt never fulfilled their promise and suffered from bad payers among the larger states of the Empire from the outset: H. Mohnhaupt, 'Verfassungsrechtliche Einordnung der Reichskreise in die Reichsorganisation' in K. O. von Aretin, (ed.), *Der Kurfürst von Mainz und die Kreisassoziationen 1648 – 1746* (Wiesbaden, 1975), pp. 3 – 10.

[31] The Austrian Habsburgs' connexion with their cousins in Madrid was a valuable propaganda weapon in the hands of opponents of an extension of imperial power, which could be characterized as 'Spanish tyranny': H. H. Hofmann, 'Reichsidee und Staatspolitik. Die Vorderen Reichskreise im 18. Jahrhundert' in *Zeitschrift für bayerische Landesgeschichte*, vol. 33 (1970), p. 974. B. Gebhardt, (ed.), *Handbuch der deutschen Geschichte*, vol. II (Stuttgart, 1955), p. 101.

setting out the duties of the Emperor and the rights of the Estates of the Empire, which Charles had to swear to observe.[32] This was a clear sign of things to come.

The real power of the Emperor was barely less after 1555 than before, though the power of the princes, especially the Protestants, was increased by their acquisition of important new authority, which the Emperor could not claim to have granted as a privilege. The Reformation completed the process by which the Protestant princes gained total control over Church property and jurisdiction and became, as heads of their Churches, truly sovereign in one facet of government. Conversely the organized Counter-Reformation increased the powers of Catholic rulers like the dukes of Bavaria, who, as leaders of the movement, could control the personnel and resources of the Church, sometimes more competely than their Protestant fellows.[33] The attempts of Ferdinand II and his son to rescue the faith and reassert their imperial authority in the early seventeenth century were perhaps the last chance to do so[34] but it is questionable whether their victory in the Thirty Years' War could have reversed the trend of centuries; at all events the Emperor's victories in the early part of the war were nullified by foreign intervention. Foreign influence and interference were to remain major factors in German politics until the end of the Empire. It became an axiom of French, Dutch and Swedish diplomacy to deny the Habsburg Emperor the use of the resources of his Empire.[35]

In charting the decay of the Holy Roman Empire much emphasis has traditionally been placed on the results of the treaties of Westphalia, which recognized the German rulers' possession of

---

[32] G. Kleinheyer, *Die kaiserlichen Wahlkapitulationen. Geschichte, Wesen und Funktion* (Karlsruhe, 1968). Each Emperor's capitulation of election was personal and lapsed with his death. It was a contract between the Emperor and the whole *Reich*, though only the electors had a say in its formulation. Before the election of Charles VI there were serious disputes between the electors and the other princes over parts of the proposed permanent *Wahlkapitulation* under discussion since the 1640s.

[33] F. L. Carsten, *Princes and Parliaments in Germany from the 15th to the 18th century* (Oxford, 1959), pp. 393, 437. L. G. Duggan, 'The Church as an Institution of the Reich', in Vann and Rowan, *The Old Reich*, p. 153.

[34] The old view that Ferdinand II's policies represented a species of imperial absolutism should perhaps be modified in the light of H. Haan, 'Kaiser Ferdinand II und das Problem des Reichsabsolutismus. Die Prager Heeresreform von 1635', *HZ*, vol. 207 (1968), pp. 297 – 345.

[35] P. Joachimsen, *Vom deutschen Volk zum deutschen Staat*, 3rd ed. (Göttingen, 1956), p. 27. Conrad, pp. 314 – 15.

Landeshoheit, full sovereignty within each individual territory.[36] The constitutional provisions of the treatise virtually completed the edifice of 'German liberty'. The princes had gradually been acquiring the elements of *Landeshoheit* for centuries but, by awarding the right to conduct an almost sovereign foreign policy, the treaties seemed to confirm the existence of the greater princes as fully-fledged states on the European stage.

Only a small number of the states of the Empire were large and strong enough to exercise all the functions of sovereignty or even to defend themselves. One authority counts 296 more or less sovereign entitles in the Empire after 1648 though there were in all about 1,490 direct or immediate subjects of the Emperor including the numerous free imperial knights. On the other hand, the votes in the imperial diet were shared between some 160 electors, princes and towns.[37] The great majority of the Estates of the Empire, especially the free cities, all but the largest ecclesiastical states and the small counties and principalities, may have postured and pretended to be independent and self-sufficient but they needed someone to protect them against their stronger neighbours, in the face of whose ambitions they would have had little chance of survival in an open struggle or a loose confederation. The alternatives before them were some form of dependence on the Emperor, a mild lord most of the time, dismemberment, or acceptance of satellite status under a powerful neighbour. The reorganization of the Empire in 1803 showed this only too well.[38]

---

36 Koser, p. 196. K. Kormann, 'Die Landeshoheit in ihrem Verhältnis zur Reichsgewalt im alten deutschen Reich seit dem westfälischen Frieden' *Zeitschrift für Politik*, vol. 7 (1914), p. 140. Territorial sovereignty was now a right of all the Estates of the Empire, not just privileges bestowed by the Emperor on some and usurped by others.

37 S. W. Rowan, 'A Reichstag in the Reform Era: Freiburg im Breisgau 1497 – 8' in Vann and Rowan, *The Old Reich*, pp. 33 – 57. It was possible after this diet to say exactly who was and who was not an immediate Estate of the Empire. Rowan's article contains lists of those present and absent. W. Fürnrohr, *Der immerwährende Reichstag zu Regensburg. Das Parlament des alten Reichs* (Regensburg, 1963), p. 9. K. Stoye, *Die politischen und religiösen Anschauungen des Freiherrn F. von Moser und sein Versuch einer Regeneration des Reichs* (Diss. Göttingen, 1959), p. 85 n203 quotes F. C. von Moser's *Beherzigungen* (Frankfurt, 1761): 'By fatherland they understand only the province in which they live. There are now at least two hundred sovereigns in Germany'.

38 J. E. d'Arenberg, *Les princes du Saint Empire* (Louvain, 1951), pp. 63 – 72, 132 – 6. H. H. Hofmann, 'Die preussische Ära in Franken' in H. H. Hofmann (ed.), *Die Entstehung des modernen souveränen Staates* (Berlin/ Cologne, 1967), pp. 244 – 58 describes the enforced absorption of the small territories within Ansbach-Bayreuth after 1792 to create homogeneous states. The *Reich* was unable to prevent this.

These states were especially dependent on the Emperor's traditional role of protecting the weak against the strong. In 1814 it was, significantly, these small states and towns which offered a revived German imperial crown to Francis I.[39] It was in that part of Germany where small and weak states were thickest on the ground, the south west, in the last years of the Empire commonly called *das Reich*, that the imperial aulic council in the eighteenth century found the majority of its litigants and where imperial sentiment lived longest.[40]

The treaties of Westphalia did not fulfil the promise their main authors, France and Sweden, had expected of them. The great majority of the German princes had little say in their formulation and it was a source of bitter complaint from the French soon after 1648 that, in spite of all the promised advantages, they were able to find very little support among the princes for the dismemberment or dissolution of the Empire, or even for a radical reform of its constitution.[41]

As had been the case with so many 'turning points' in the constitutional development of Germany, the treaties of Westphalia only ratified established practice. In the last century and a half of its existence the Holy Roman Empire could be described as a federation which no one had intended to set up[42] and in which the powers of the federal organs, instead of being used for the good of the federation as a whole, were employed almost solely for the benefit of the individual members.[43] The abiding evil of the Empire, particularism, compounded this. As archdukes of Austria, the Habsburg Emperors were often as guilty of this as the most egotistical of the princes. Surprisingly, the actual constitution was not seen by many as the root cause of Germany's decline; there was a strong belief that it was historically necessary for Germany to have

---

[39] Hantsch, *Schönborn*, p. 90. H. Günter, 'Die Reichsidee im Wandel der Zeiten', *Historische Jahrbücher*, vol. 53 (1933), p. 426.

[40] P. Jastrow, *Pufendorfs Lehre von der Monstrosität der Reichsverfassung* (Berlin, 1882), p. 33. O. F. Winter, 'Die Wiener Reichsbehörde und die fränkischen Reichsstädte', *Jahrbuch für fränkische Landesforschung*, vol. XXIV (1964), p. 547. Rauch, pp. 9–11.

[41] G. Scheel, 'Die Stellung der Reichsstände zur römische Königswahl seit dem westfälischen Friedensverhandlungen' in *Forschungen zu Staat und Verfassung: Festgabe für Fritz Hartung* (Berlin, 1958), pp. 121–2.

[42] Randelzhofer in his concluding chapter describes the late Empire as a *Staatengemeinschaft*, a community of states. He makes interesting comparisons between the Empire and the United Nations or the E.E.C.

[43] It is unfortunate that the two German words *kaiserlich* and *Reichs-* can only be rendered in English as 'imperial'. What began as a united concept, *Kaiser und Reich*, had by the eighteenth century come to designate distinct, if not conflicting, interests.

two governments, central and local, forming an Empire over states. The German constitution in all its forms has, until this century, accommodated elements of unity and diversity. After 1648 many commentators regarded the Empire as the ideal political framework for Germany, uniting and reconciling the two characteristics in the correct proportion.[44] The German territories were bound by the legal form of the Empire until 1806, even though at the same time these territories sought a supplementary independent sphere of action. The particularist state was never the ultimate in German political life even in the eighteenth century. The Emperor remained as a symbol of German unity even when he was no longer capable of acting as its instrument. Long after 1648, however, it was a commonplace of princely propaganda that the Emperors nursed an abiding ambition to destroy 'German liberty'. No such ambition existed.

The recovery of imperial power in Germany ceased to be a primary aim of Habsburg foreign policy long before 1648; but long after 1648 the Emperors were ready to make use of what remained of imperial sentiment to serve their interests. In the later seventeenth and early eighteenth centuries there were brief periods when imperial patriotism revived and gave a little coordination to the German dinosaur.[45] This usually coincided with war against the French or Turks and the unity and enthusiasm were short-lived. Apart from this, imperial consciousness existed almost solely in cultural circles and among a number of great eighteenth century jurists who recognised the unifying functions of the body of imperial law. It is ironical that the eighteenth century saw the production of monumental works on the law of the Empire when it had almost ceased to have any practical meaning. Men like J. J. Moser (1701 – 85) and J. S. Pütter (1725 – 1807) were responsible for the collection and publication of imperial law, custom and usages, with commentary, illustrating the whole range of legal relationships within the Empire. A magnificent epitaph for the Empire had been created before its final demise.

Imperial pessimism, the belief that the Holy Roman Empire was doomed to disappear, strengthened in the eighteenth century. Commentators were amazed, not at its obvious impotence, but at the fact that it had not collapsed sooner in view of the deep mutual mistrust of head and members, the existence of a mass of effete and corrupt petty princes, chronic religious strife and the decay of old

---

[44] Joachimsen, *Der deutsche Staatsgedanke*, p. xii; Vann and Rowan, *The Old Reich*, pp. ix – x; Benecke, p. xi.
[45] Wandruszka, *passim*.

forms.[46] Writers bewailed the loss of 'old honest Germanness';[47] the German language, sprinkled with a tinsel of foreign words, was seen as a fitting symbol of a nation grown subservient to foreigners.[48]

The spirit of the age was against the Empire; its decay provided both the motive and the opportunity for the growth of self-centred absolutist states in Germany. The rise of absolutism involved growing interference by the state in every aspect of the life of the subject and close supervision of every detail of administration. The resulting barrage of edicts and decrees and the increasing emphasis on the role of the individual sovereign state further weakened imperial consciousness and promoted rival nationalisms. By the reign of Charles VI the foundations of Prussian, Saxon, Bavarian and Austrian national spirits were well laid.

The early years of Charles's reign seemed to offer conditions favourable to a revival of imperial influence. The Emperor faced no serious rivals and, as was usual in the later Empire, there was no united front of even the more powerful German princes against him. The imperial diet was always liable to split along a number of long-existing fault-lines, the deep rivalry between electors and non-electors over their respective prerogatives, between Circles and between states with and without standing armies over financial contributions to the Empire, especially towards the maintenance of the imperial cameral court and the imperial fortresses, between the three religious groups represented in the diet and between individuals and dynasties for the possession of disputed territory and ecclesiastical jobs. It was easy for the Emperor and foreign powers to build up parties in this hotbed of jealousies and antagonisms which often cut across one another producing an extremely fluid political situation.[49]

In addition the influence of the two foreign guarantors of the peace of Westphalia, Sweden and France, was slight. Sweden was busy defending her Baltic empire against concerted attack and French prestige was low in Germany after 1700 because of the cumulative effects of the revocation of the edict of Nantes, the aggressive *réunions* policy, the devastation of the Palatinate and

---

[46] Hantsch, *Schönborn*, pp. 45, 59.
[47] Joachimsen, *Der deutsche Staatsgedanke*, pp. 31–2; Rauch, pp. 28–9.
[48] C. T. Atkinson, *A History of Germany 1715–1815* (London, 1908), ch. I and II; Fauchier-Magnan, p. 30.
[49] J. Dureng, *Mission de Theodore Chevignard de Chavigny en Allemagne. Septembre 1726–Octobre 1731* (Paris, 1911), pp. 16–17. Vann and Rowan, *The Old Reich*, pp. 49–50: the bickering over precedence in the *Reichstag* was a factor of great political importance as the acknowledged leaders of the *curia* were always represented on important committees.

increasing evidence of Louis XIV's undisguised contempt for the German nation.[50] Where Leopold I had failed Louis succeeded in creating a surge of German national unity, even though it was to prove short-lived. Louis tried to exploit his role as guarantor of the 1648 settlement, seen by the French as a licence to interfere in German internal affairs.[51] France's defeat in the Spanish Succession war and the accession of a minor king in 1715 damaged French prestige further although her influence was beginning to revive by the early 1720s.

As before, the Wittelsbach rulers, especially the elector of Bavaria, acted as the main vectors of French influence. Bavarian ambition led the elector into a French alliance during the Spanish Succession war, with the result that the allies occupied his lands after Blenheim. The chastening effect of this did not last long and the Wittelsbachs remained the most serious rivals to imperial influence in the south and west of Germany. After 1715 they quickly resorted to their traditional policy of accumulating a constellation of ecclesiastical states in the hands of their family and revived links with the French.[52] A number of ambitions sharpened Wittelsbach dynasticism. They wanted the imperial crown, and Habsburg lands in the Tyrol, and the Austrian archduchies, ambitions whetted by the marriage in 1722 of the electoral prince of Bavaria to the younger daughter of Emperor Joseph I. The Emperor was expected to continue buying Wittelsbach support with ecclesiastical principalities while at the same time they maintained their traditional links with France. A nine year treaty between France and Bavaria was signed in 1714 and in May 1724 this was extended into a dynastic alliance including Bavaria, Trier, Cologne and the elector palatine.[53]

The elector palatine was the least committed to an anti-imperial policy and after 1648 drifted indecisively between a French connexion and a firm imperial alliance. The memory of the White Mountain and its aftermath lingered and the elector's role as standard bearer of anti-imperialism taken up by the unfortunate Frederick V, did not last. Under Charles VI the main concern of the elector was the future of the provinces of Jülich and Berg on the

---

50   R. Place, 'The Self-Deception of the Strong'.
51   Wilson, p. 187. Experts on German law were permanently attached to the French foreign office during Louis' reign.
52   By 1728 Clement Augustus of Bavaria had acquired the sees of Cologne, Hildesheim and Osnabrück. In 1731 the papacy forbade such accumulations. This, and the failing fertility of the Wittelsbachs, brought an end to spectacular pluralism.
53   Mecenseffy, p. 56. Wilson, p. 328 n3: Bavaria also claimed Austrian lands under the will of Ferdinand I. The Bavarian copy of this was found to be a forgery in 1740.

21

Lower Rhine, one of the major concerns of imperial politics in the first half of the eighteenth century. The ruling house of the Lower Rhenish duchies died out in 1609 and claims to the territories devolved by marriage to Brandenburg-Prussia and Palatinate-Neuburg, a line of the palatinate Wittelsbachs.[54] The elector palatine Charles Philip (1716 – 42) had only one child, a daughter, who married the Neuburg heir in 1717, creating a claim to Jülich and Berg if the Neuburg line died out. This appeared distinctly possible in the 1720s. Brandenburg also claimed the succession to the territories under an arrangement of 1666.[55] After 1718 the elector palatine was anxious to secure imperial help for his claims against the rival Hohenzollerns: this made him wary of antagonizing the Emperor.[56]

In the south and west of Germany the Emperor enjoyed three elements of strength. Imperial troops and fortresses lay close in the Austrian Netherlands, Luxemburg and the Tyrol. The Habsburg territories in the area, a scattered collection of small counties and lordships known collectively as *Vorderösterreich*, provided a focus of attention and a base for imperial influence among the little states of the area, many of them ecclesiastical. It was in the south and west that the Circle organisation was most vigorous and effective. Imperial influence on the Circles grew in importance after the Ryswick peace of 1697 which made the Rhine the border between France and the Empire and gave France the major imperial fortress of Strasburg.[57] The third and perhaps most important vehicle of imperial influence was the Schönborn family, former free imperial knights who had risen from obscurity to the highest offices and titles in Germany by a policy of consistent loyalty to the Habsburgs, the imperial idea and the Catholic Church.[58] With the help of the Emperor in elections to vacant sees, which increased as part of the 'imperial reaction', they became the most important rivals of the

---

[54] Carsten, pp. 288 ff.
[55] *Ibid.*, p. 314, Mecenseffy, p. 118: Frederick William I was not happy at the prospect of the aulic council's enquiring too closely into the matter, as Brandenburg's legal rights to the other Rhenish territories, Cleves, Mark and Ravensberg, were not spotless. The basic issue was whether Jülich and Berg could be inherited in the female line. Charles VI had a personal interest inherited from his mother, a sister of the elector-palatine.
[56] Mecenseffy, pp. 60 – 1.
[57] For details of the Circle organization see Aretin, *passim*. J. A. Vann, 'Economic policies of the Swabian Kreis, 1664 – 1715' in Vann and Rowan, *The Old Reich*, pp. 107 – 27 describes the important role of the Circles in the south and west in regulating the commercial and financial life of their area.
[58] The Schönborns were the most successful of the imperial knights. They managed to keep one of their number on the electoral throne of Mainz for all but three years between 1555 and 1806.

22

Wittelsbachs for ecclesiastical preferment. Lothar Francis Schönborn became archbishop-elector of Mainz in 1695, a title which
brought with it the important position of arch-chancellor of
Germany and director of the imperial diet. His deputy in Vienna,
the imperial vice-chancellor, was his nominee and during the
'imperial reaction' the post was held by the elector's nephew,
Frederick Charles Schönborn. Frederick Charles was a Minorist and
coadjutor of his uncle's bishopric of Bamberg, which gave him an
automatic right of succession when it became vacant in 1720.[59] His
brothers were respectively bishops of Speyer and Würzburg. With
their bases in Franconia the Schönborns played a major part in
revitalising the Circle organisation in the early years of the
eighteenth century, an important element in the 'imperial reaction'.
The relationship between the Habsburgs and the Schönborns was
not always free of tension, as the latter were sometimes more loyal
to the imperial idea than to the man who happened to be wearing
the imperial crown at the time.

It was a constant preoccupation of Austrian policy to prevent
another strong state establishing itself in this area of small states,
forced by their weakness to look to the nearby Emperor for
protection and help. One of Frederick Charles Schönborn's earliest
achievements as vice-chancellor was to sabotage Prussian attempts
to acquire Ansbach and Bayreuth from the collateral Hohenzollern
line which ruled there.[60]

Imperial influence was weakest in the north of Germany,
dominated by the Protestant states Denmark, Sweden, Hanover,
Prussia and Saxony. What little influence the Emperor possessed
centred on small states like Mecklenburg and the Hanseatic cities,
especially Hamburg, which experienced growing prosperity during
the early years of the eighteenth century. Active Emperors could
also preserve some say in the affairs of northern Germany by skilful
exploitation of the rivalries of the powerful states there.

North Germany was shot through with foreign influence. In the
north west the Dutch kept a wary eye on the bishopric of Münster, a
strongly Catholic outpost in a Protestant zone of Germany and an
old enemy of the United Provinces, and more particularly on
growing Prussian territorial power on the Lower Rhine. It was a

---

[59] On Schönborn see Hantsch's biography.
[60] *Ibid.*, pp. 63–5, 134–6, 237. See also Vienna, Haus- Hof- und Staatsarchiv,
[hereafter Vienna] Reichskanzlei *Vorträge* fasz. 6b on the attempts by
Brandenburg to secure the succession to Kulmbach and Bayreuth in
Franconia, a threat to Austria and the Empire, according to Schönborn.
Also Vienna, Staatskanzlei *Vorträge* K.22 i – v fol. 98 for details of imperial
action to prevent Hesse-Cassel taking over the important fortress of
Rheinfels from the Catholic branch of the Hessian ruling family.

Dutch ambition to extend their protective Barrier from the Netherlands into Germany[61] and they were worried by the potential threat which Prussian ambitions on Jülich and Berg seemed to represent.

The Great Northern War of 1700 – 21 demonstrated how little influence the Emperor had in the north; in spite of the congress of Brunswick held under imperial auspices and the supposed neutralisation of German territory, the war was partly fought inside the Empire and the spoils of Sweden's German lands were distributed among the nothern allies with little regard for the Emperor's wishes. Since 1630 the history of north-Germany had been determined by the fortunes of Sweden. By 1719 Sweden was finished as a German power and foreign influence began to decline. Denmark held Holstein and Oldenburg and still entertained ambitions against the cities of Hamburg and Bremen but the days of Danish power had long passed.

Imperial feeling was very low in the two Saxon Circles in the early eighteenth century, as is shown by the desultory working of the Circle organisation, the total absence of Circle meetings[62] and the patent fact that they were run only for the benefit of the leading princes of the area. Mecklenburg and East Frisia presented tempting power vacuums, which could only too easily be filled by foreign powers or by the Emperor's own overweening vassals, especially Prussia or Hanover, whose growth caused increasing disquiet in Vienna. F. C. von Schönborn was permanently afraid of the expansion of Prussia, which he called 'a gnawing worm in the bowels of the Empire'[63] and his tenure of the imperial vice-chancellorship saw determined efforts to halt the decline of imperial influence in the North.

Some of Schönborn's Austrian rivals took the view, echoed by later historians,[64] that the Empire without Austria would have been

---

61 M. Braubach, 'Holland und die geistlichen Staaten im Nordwesten des Reichs während des Spanischen Erbfolgekrieges' in Diplomatie und geistiges Leben, pp. 188 – 9. A. C. Carter, Neutrality or Commitment: the Evolution of Dutch Foreign Policy 1667 – 1795 (London, 1975), pp. 31 – 6. K. O. von Aretin, 'Kaiser Joseph I', pp. 585 – 6.

62 P. C. Storm, 'Militia Imperialis-Militia Circularis 1648 – 1732' in Vann and Rowan, The Old Reich, p. 80. Hantsch, Schönborn, p. 67.

63 Ibid., p. 217, 22. Naumann, p. 16. Prussia had long waged a guerilla war against imperial authority. A typical example was a campaign by Brandenburg and Saxony in the 1670s to destabilize the imperial coinage by unilaterally abandoning the standard silver content of the Gulden established in 1623. This led to thirty years of chaos with a rash of devaluations and rival coinages: Vann, in Vann and Rowan, The Old Reich, pp. 115 – 20. See also D. McKay, 'The Struggle for Control of George I's Northern Policy 1718 – 9', JMH, vol. 45 (1973), p. 369.

64 Hantsch, Schönborn, p. 88.

nothing, while Austria without the Empire could have sustained her position as a power and even enhanced it. The reign of Charles VI marked the high point of the struggle within the Vienna government between imperial and purely Austrian interests, symbolized by the competition for power between the imperial chancery and the Austrian aulic chancery.[65] It is the story of a steady loss of influence by the imperial chancery though when the office was in the hands of an active and aggressive politician the process could be slowed down.[66] The struggle ended in total victory for the Austrian interest in the 1730s but not without a last strong challenge for the imperial idea personified in F. C. von Schönborn.[67] Unlike his immediate predecessors in the office, he was not an Austrian and, as a *Reicher*, he faced the mistrust of a series of ministers in the aulic chancery, most notably Philip Ludwig von Sinzendorff.[68] Schönborn won a small victory in 1708 with the establishment of a regular weekly meeting of high-ranking ministers to discuss imperial affairs, the *Reichskonferenz*, separate from the Austrian *Hauskonferenz* and later he gained admittance to the privy conference, the inner cabinet, when affairs of the Empire came under discussion.[69] A system of dual diplomacy also developed; representatives at the imperial diet and at important German courts reported both to the imperial chancery and the aulic chancery.[70] Schönborn suffered a serious setback in 1719, when a reorganization of the aulic chancery gave Sinzendorff formal precedence over him and competence over all foreign and dynastic affairs.[71] Thereafter

---

[65] For examples of the many squabbles between the two bodies, see a letter of the imperial chancery to Schönborn, 11 June 1726 in Vienna, *Kleinere Reichsstände* K. 404.

[66] Hantsch, *Schönborn*, pp. 72–4.

[67] M. Braubach, 'Friedrich Karl von Schönborn und Prinz Eugen' in *Österreich und Europa: Festgabe für Hugo Hantsch* (Graz, Vienna, Cologne, 1965), pp. 113–15. Although Schönborn faced great jealousy because of his non-Austrian origins, his closer collaboration with prince Eugene after 1720 greatly improved his position.

[68] A. von Arneth, *Prinz Eugen von Savoyen* (Vienna, 1858), vol. II, pp. 97–9.

[69] Hantsch, *Schönborn*, pp. 72–4.

[70] The Austrian and Bohemian representatives in Regensburg reported to the aulic chancery and the imperial Principal Commissioner and his assistants to the imperial chancery: Naumann, pp. 84–5. G. Klingensten, 'Kaunitz kontra Bartenstein. Zur Geschichte der Staatskanzlei 1749–53' in H. Fichtenau and E. Zöllner, (eds.), *Beiträge zur neueren Geschichte Österreichs* (Vienna/Cologne/Graz, 1974), pp. 243–63.

[71] Vienna, Staatskanzlei *Vortr.* K. 23 fol. 51–63.

Schönborn's influence fluctuated but in the late 1720s his influence declined sharply with the waning of the 'imperial reaction'.[72]

Other Austrian ministers like prince Eugene saw the Empire as an important factor among many in Austria's European-wide diplomatic involvement. Eugene ran his own private intelligence network in Germany, which often excluded not only Schönborn but also Sizendorff.[73]

Throughout Charles VI's reign, loud voices urged him to turn his back on the Empire as no more than a blister on the heel of Austrian progress.[74] The idea that the Habsburgs had a choice of policy, concentration on the German *Reich* or on specifically 'Austrian' aims, has been repeated by later historians.[75] In reality no such choice existed. The Habsburgs could not abandon Germany without an unacceptable abdication of prestige and risk to Austrian security. Germany was Austria's back door. As is clear from the example of the French ever eager to deny the Habsburgs access to the resources of the Empire, her enemies did not distinguish between Habsburg dynastic, Austrian and imperial policies.

---

[72] Borgmann, pp. 68 – 9, quoting St Saphorin, who disliked Schönborn and may have exaggerated.

[73] H-J. Pretsch, *Graf Manteuffels Beitrag zur österreichischen Geheimdiplomatie von 1728 bis 1736* (Bonn, 1970), pp. 14 ff., 40 – 3. The funds which financed this system were not officially accounted for in the *Hofkammer*.

[74] Details of this so-called *Reichsmüdigkeit* in Vienna are given in Borgmann, p. 77.

[75] Mecenseffy, p. 95 argues that it was the failure to solve this 'dilemma' which led to the ultimate frustration of Austria's ambitions.

2

The Reichshofrat

Most of the organs of the Empire still operating in the eighteenth century were under the shared control of the Emperor and the representative body of the Estates of the Empire, the imperial diet.[1] This was true of the imperial cameral court *(Reichskammergericht)* and the imperial army organised under the war constitution of 1681.[2] The imperial diet was not a businesslike institution, for it was often paralysed by disputes and trivial questions of precedence. As a sounding board of German opinion it was however very important and both the Emperor and European rulers usually kept talented professional diplomats at Regensburg.[3] The diet which began in 1663 was never dissolved. It lasted for the remaining lifetime of the Empire although there were many occasions when Emperors, disgusted at the obstructionism and self-seeking of some of its members, threatened to dissolve it.[4]

Certain powers and functions remained under the sole control of the Emperor; these, the *Reservatrechte*, were jealously guarded. As supreme judge, feudal overlord, protector of the German Churches and supreme guardian of the rights of all his subjects,[5] an energetic Emperor, though lacking the armed strength to defeat and subjugate recalcitrant vassals, could exercise considerable

---

[1]   Jastrow, pp. 11, 14.
[2]   The Empire had no peace-time standing army. Under the 1681 arrangements, each Estate's obligations in men or money were laid down. The imperial contingents were, in theory, to assemble under the imperial high command on the declaration of war. In fact the military effort of the Empire was usually a source of scorn and despair. The payments for the armed forces, the Roman Months, were invariably in arrears and the greater states rarely paid anything.
[3]   Naumann, pp. 149 – 50.
[4]   J. J. Pachner von Eggenstorff, *Vollständige Sammlung . . . aller Reichsschlüsse*, (Regensburg, 1740 – 77), vol. II, p. 566: the commission decree of 23 November 1685 contained a bitter complaint by Leopold I about the diet's behaviour.
[5]   Rauch, p. 49, prints a full list of the Emperor's titles and functions.

27

influence. Of the reserved powers the imperial supreme judicial office *(kaiserliche obristrichterliche Amt)*, deriving from the Emperor's position as feudal suzerein over the whole Empire, was probably the most important source of influence left to the Emperors after 1648. It was exercised without the participation of the Estates of the Empire and was not subject to review or revision by the imperial diet.[6] This concept of the king or Emperor as the source of all justice was never abandoned. By his election the Emperor acquired the right to judge the possessions, fiefs and bodies of his subjects and to the end the Emperors claimed absolute powers in this field. The theoretical basis of the imperial judicial authority, the idea that the Emperor inherited the God-given plenitude of power possessed by his Roman forebears, remained intact in spite of the intellectual battle over the nature of the imperial constitution which raged in the seventeenth and eighteenth centuries.[7] Despite the obvious fact that the Emperor's real power within the Empire was very small, in theory he was an absolute monarch drawing his power from God by means of the voices of the electors. His power was not in the gift of the electors nor did it revert to them during the interregnum after the death of an Emperor when there was no elected king of the Romans as an automatic successor. In such cases the Empire, except the Austrian lands, was divided and ruled by two imperial vicars, the elector palatine of the Rhine and the elector of Saxony. By the same token, each surrender of power to the princes did not in theory reduce the Emperor's plenitude of power *(Machtvollkommenheit)* but was seen as the grant of a privilege or as a delegation of authority to them, revocable at will.[8] These theories were never brought together into a coherent statement which could be used to counter the numerous theoretical attacks on the Emperor's 'usurped' authority, such as the work of Hippolitus a Lapide,[9] but their vagueness was perhaps a source of strength rather than weakness. The *Kaiseridee* was protean; the Emperor's reserved powers were at one and the same time feudal and pre-feudal in

---

[6] Holborn, vol. II, p. 5, Feller, pp. 53 ff., Conrad, pp. 196, 495, 500–2, Kormann, p. 141.

[7] Rauch, pp. 14 ff., 34 ff., Koser, p. 194: in 1609 Rudolph II was baldly informed by a number of princes that he did not possess all the powers of the Roman Emperors. See H. Gross, 'The Holy Roman Empire in modern times' in Vann and Rowan, *The Old Reich*, pp. 8, 25–29 on theoretical challenges to the Emperor's claims to the powers of the Caesars.

[8] Kormann, pp. 164–5, Rauch, p. 38. On *plenitudo potestatis* see E. Schubert, *König und Reich* (Göttingen, 1979), p. 136.

[9] F. H. Schubert, *Die deutschen Reichstage in der Staatslehre der frühen Neuzeit* (Göttingen, 1966), pp. 554–62.

origin. Attempts to undermine imperial authority usually took the form of challenges to its operation rather than its source.

By the reign of Charles VI much of this debate was irrelevant to the real course of German politics but the imperial judicial authority and one of the organs through which it was administered, the imperial aulic coucil *(Reichshofrat)*, saved it from being pure fantasy. Charles VI could claim with justification that his precedessors on the imperial throne had acted as supreme judges. In 1235 Frederick II had set up the new and permanent post of *Hofrichter* or aulic justiciar *(justitiarius curiae imperialis)*, later joined by a permanent aulic chancery and secretariat.[10] There was no direct link between these institutions and the later cameral court and imperial aulic council, which were products of the great organisational activity of the reign of Maximilian I.[11] There were periods when the imperial judicial office was totally in abeyance but even during these times the imperial court at Rottweil and the *Fehmgerichte*[12] continued to dispense justice in the Emperor's name even though they were not under his control.[13]

Emperors' attempts to combat the lawlessness which threatened to become endemic in parts of Germany in the High Middle Ages met with but limited success and the intermittent jurisdiction of the imperial aulic court offered no cure for the violent self-help remedies persistently resorted to by the nobility under the graphic name of *Faustrecht* (the law of the fist).[14] Attempts to deal with this ran into a vicious circle; Emperors were unable to enforce the many *Landfrieden* issued in conjunction with the Estates of the Empire and often the feud *(Fehde)* was the only means left whereby a man could protect his interests. The Emperor needed some effective means of protecting the weak and controlling the strong even when the *Fehde*, under which, after three days' notice, one noble could unleash a little war against another, disappeared.

As a result of the paralysis of imperial peace-keeping, other forms of self-help blossomed. The towns and nobility formed armed unions to protect themselves and settle disputes among themselves in the absence of effective imperial action. Of these most successful

---

10 F. Thudichum, 'Das vormahlige Reichskammergericht und seine Schick-sale' in *Zeitschrift für das deutsche Recht*, vol. 20 (1861), p. 152. Conrad, pp. 252–3. K. Hampe, pp. 251 ff. E. Schubert, *König und Reich* (Göttingen, 1979), pp. 84–6, 90.
11 Randelzhofer, p. 51 n6. H. Wiesflecker, *Kaiser Maximilian I* (Munich, 1975), vol. II, pp. 398, 410.
12 B. Gebhardt, *Handbuch der Deutschen Geschichte* (Stuttgart, 1954), vol. I, pp. 552 f.
13 Conrad, pp. 335–7, Feller, p. 35.
14 Barraclough, pp. 336–8.

in keeping peace within its border was the Swabian League in the fifteenth century.[15] Attempts by the Emperor to offer a workable alternative were hampered by a factor which remained constant throughout the modern history of the Empire: the princes were not prepared to provide the Emperor with the armed forces which were, in the last resort, necessary to enforce decisions of any imperial court.

In 1456 the decayed *Hofgericht* was replaced by the completely reorganised *Kammergericht* which in that year received its first ordinance. The Emperor retained full control over its composition; he appointed its president, the *Kammerrichter*, and its assessors from among his councillors. Frederick III won back a little by the appointment of an imperial fiscal procurator to initiate cases and by placing limits on the immunities enjoyed by the courts of some of the princes but he soon lost interest. Between 1470 and 1475 the *Kammergericht* was leased to the elector of Mainz and soon afterwards it ceased to operate. At the diet of Frankfurt in 1486 there was strong pressure from influential princes for the re-establishment of a permanent imperial court and a perpetual imperial peace. In 1495 the imperial cameral court was established, an event of major constitutional significance. Sadly its promise was never fulfilled.[16]

The imperial aulic council was founded in 1497 and from the first it was clear that its function was to balance the cameral court[17] and to provide an alternative supreme tribunal for the Empire under the total control of the Emperor.[18] From its foundation the influence of the princes on the cameral court was paramount. The president of the court, the *Kammerrichter*, was to be a prince of the Empire or a nobleman. The judges or assessors were to be chosen by the Emperor and the Estates of the Empire[19] and the court was maintained by collections from the princes, the *Kammerzieler*.[20] At the time of its establishment at the Worms diet in 1495 the Estates of the Empire tried to take over sole control of the court as part of the general imperial reform movement. As part of the same movement a universal and eternal *Reichsfrieden* was proclaimed over the whole

---

15 F. Hartung, 'Imperial Reform 1485–95: its course and its character', pp. 91–2, 98. Thudichum, p. 156.
16 Sellert, pp. 5–6.
17 *Ibid.*, p. 8, Thudichum, p. 177.
18 T. Fellner, and H. Kretschmayer, *Die österreichische Zentralverwaltung* (3 parts, Vienna, 1925), vol. I, Abt. 1, pp. 218–19.
19 Conrad, pp. 501–2. Before 1521 the Emperor chose four, the Electors six and the Circles eight assessors.
20 For detailed accounts of the *Reichskammergericht* see Thudichum and R. Smend, *Das Reichskammergericht* (Weimar, 1911).

Empire and the beginnings of an apparatus to enforce it were seen. This peace was essentially a medieval concept, an extension of the special peace which for centuries covered certain places, persons or times, where and when a feud was illegal. The cameral court was supposed to employ the sanction of the ban of the Empire against breaches of the *Reichsfrieden* and the new ban was to be stronger than the old. In §7 of the ordinance of the 1521 *Reichsregiment* and clause 11 of the ordinance of the cameral court of 1555 the Emperor reserved to himself the right to decide whether the dynasties of banned princes were to be deprived of their fiefs in perpetuity. It was not surprising that, faced with what on paper seemed a serious threat to their power, the German princes at once began to place limitations on the competence of the *Reichskammergericht*.[21]

By the reign of Charles VI the cameral court was a paradigm of decay. Its history is a story of waste, inefficiency and corruption: the German princes allowed this, their own supreme court, to sink beneath mountains of paper and streams of empty stylized verbosity. The court was almost always understaffed because of the princes' tardiness in paying their contributions to its upkeep. In spite of this they remained most jealous of their control over it.[22] Such a contrast between eagerness to retain control and unwillingness to pay was typical. All the imperial institutions the princes laid their hands on eventually fell into decay. In 1507 Maximilian I offered to maintain the cameral court out of his own resources and did so for six years. Charles V likewise maintained it for fifteen years but the Estates of the Empire would never agree to this becoming a permanent arrangement. The *Kammerzieler* system was introduced on a permanent basis in 1548 but it provided no solution to the chronic shortage of money which afflicted the court.[23]

Perhaps the most influential feature of the cameral court was its large ordinance of 1555, setting out its aims and procedure. This was to be the model for that of the aulic council and for the high courts of many of the large states of the Empire. Under the imperial recesses of 1600 and 1654 the Estates of the Empire agreed to adopt this ordinance for their own courts of cassation as far as possible.[24]

---

[21] Thudichum, pp. 157–9.
[22] Hanover, Lower Saxon State Archive [hereafter Hanover], *Cal. Br.* 24, Österreich I no. 131, fol. 17–18 contains Hanoverian complaints that the Emperor Charles VI was attempting to usurp authority over the cameral court, which properly belonged to the imperial diet.
[23] In the 1720s much time was taken up in the imperial diet in negotiations for reductions and repartitions of the *Kammerzieler*, which were a serious burden on small states or on those fallen from their earlier prosperity: Naumann, p. 67.
[24] Thudichum, p. 174.

The court itself, however, remained a most imperfect instrument for the exercise of the Emperor's supreme judicial authority.

The need for such an instrument by no means lessened after 1648; if anything it grew steadily. The geographical, religious, political, constitutional and land-holding circumstances of eighteenth century Germany were as complex and variegated as the patchwork quilt maps of the Empire at the time. They provided ample opportunities for litigation in a litigious age.[25] The protocols of the aulic council and the cameral court contain an amazing variety of cases of different types: border and boundary disputes, disputes arising from vague points in the religious settlement of 1555 and the treaties of Westphalia,[26] complaints of breaches of contracts and agreements of all kinds, appeals by subjects and princes over breaches of constitutional agreements confirmed by the Emperor, disputes among persons of all ranks, including members of princely families and the Emperor's relatives, on widows' portions, marriages, dowries, inheritances and appanages and appeals against all manner of injustices. Every legal contract or relationship contained within itself the possibility of dispute which, if the parties were tenacious enough, might come before one of the high courts of the Empire.

The Emperors also had a deep interest in maintaining the judicial authority. One of the main troubles of the Empire before and after 1648 was the lack of an organ capable of settling the manifold disputes among the princes. The wide disparity in size and strength between the members of the Empire made necessary a power above the members and beyond their control. The ingredients of such a power existed in the Empire: the perpetual *Landfrieden*, the ordinance of execution, the ban of the Empire, the imperial cameral court and the imperial aulic council.

By giving an unfavourable verdict, by delaying the investiture of a prince with his fief or by listening with a favourable ear to the complaints of Estates against their *Obrigkeit*, the aulic council could cause considerable inconvenience and embarrassment especially to smaller princes dependent on the favour of the Emperor. Although Charles VI lacked the power to coerce, by granting or withholding these favours he was often able to make his will felt where it might well have been ignored. The aulic council had a high nuisance value and many princes were consequently eager to obtain as wide exemption as possible from its jurisdiction. During the reign of Charles VI the king of Prussia put considerable pressure on the

---

[25] *Ibid.*, p. 150.
[26] H. Hantsch, *Die Geschichte Österreichs*, 3rd ed. (2 vols., Graz etc., 1962), vol. II, p. 21.

Estates of several of his territories to make them renounce their right to appeal to Wetzlar and Vienna, the seats of the two courts. The Estates resisted this strongly.[27] The achievement of the aulic council was all the more remarkable given that it rarely had the means to enforce its decisions. Usually it could at best only try to persuade or appeal to the respect which the imperial name continued to enjoy.[28]

There are several full accounts of the history, composition and procedure of the aulic council,[29] the most important written in the eighteenth century and essentially intended for young men proposing to make a career in law. Most are theoretical and academic, concerning themselves with the set procedures of litigation, and bear little relation to the reality of conditions inside the council. They are useful in explaining the highly technical language used and for an understanding of what should have happened there but not of what did in fact happen there. Other studies of the council deal with it in the wider framework of the German legal system and also seem to have been intended for academic and informed audiences.[30]

The imperial aulic council was the highest court of the Holy Roman Empire. It dealt with all matters between the Emperor and his subjects with a few important exceptions. Under Leopold I, if not earlier, it lost all influence in *Kabinettsachen*, relations at diplomatic level between the Emperor and the larger princes powerful enough to warrant treatment as foreign powers, and it had no authority in military affairs.[31] It had no competence over other imperial organs of government. Apart from this its competence was unlimited within the non-Habsburg parts of the Empire. It was a civil court with the right to try all cases. Its competence over criminal cases of first instance, except against a direct subject of the Emperor, ended with the imperial recess of

---

27   Perels, pp. 57 – 65.
28   Feller, pp. 164 – 9.
29   Gschliesser. J.C. Herchenhahn, *Geschichte der Entstehung, Bildung und gegenwärtigen Verfassung des kaiserlichen Reichshofraths nebst der Behandlungsart der bei demselben vorkommenden Geschäfte* (3 vols., Mannheim, 1792 – 9). J. C. Uffenbach, *Tractatus singularis et methodicus de Consilio Caesareo-Imperiali Aulico* (Vienna, 1683), J. A. Reuss, *Beiträge zur neuesten Geschichte der reichsgerichtlichen Verfassung und Praxis*, vol. II (Ulm, 1786), J. J. Moser, *Von der Teutschen Justizverfassung*, vol. I, book ii/3 (Frankfurt and Leipzig, 1774) and *Einleitung zu dem Reichshofratsprozess* (3 vols., Frankfurt, 1731 – 7).
30   Typical of this are several works of the major jurists J. J. Moser and J. S. Pütter.
31   H. F. Schwartz, *The Imperial Privy Council in the Seventeenth Century* (Cambridge, Mass., 1943), pp. 16 – 19.

1530. It was the highest feudal tribunal of the Empire and was competent in the grant of a wide range of privileges, declarations of majorities, the confirmation of succession arrangements, wills, contracts, adoptions, wardships, treaties and the issue of legitimations, letter of protection and passports. The imperial fiscal procurator could also petition the council to initiate processes against immediate Estates of the Empire. A plaintiff could also petition it against a denial of justice in a lower court.[32] As a court of first instance it was only competent where one party was an immediate subject of the Emperor. Mediate subjects could appeal to the imperial courts only if a verdict in a lower court was manifestly null and void.[33]

In their earlier years the two imperial courts were in theory equal and dispensed justice in competition but by the reign of Leopold I the aulic council was definitely established as the more important of the two and, as the tribunal which dealt with rights belonging to the Emperor alone, its competence was wider than that of the cameral court. Between 1689 and 1693 and again from 1704 to 1711 the cameral court was closed, first after its flight from Speyer to escape the French and then because of a bitter and paralysing dispute among the judges and assessors.[34] During these periods the volume of business in the aulic council rose sharply. The cameral court wilted further because of a chronic shortage of money. The assessors went without salaries for years and in 1707 they and the heirs of assessors long dead petitioned the imperial diet for the payment of arrears amounting to 60,000 *Reichstaler*.[35] It is an interesting comment on the relative effectiveness of the two courts that when, in the reign of Charles VI, the count of Nassau-Weilburg attempted to turn his protectorate over the free city of Wetzlar, seat of the *Reichskammergericht*, into sovereignty, the citizens' appeal

---

[32] Thudichum, p. 159.
[33] Sellert, pp. 74–5.
[34] Thudichum, p. 186.
[35] *Ibid.*, p. 189. The currency of the Empire was very complicated, sums being expressed in *Gulden* and *Kreuzer* (*Fl.* and *Kr.*) or rixdollars (*Reichstaler, Rt.*) A *Reichsgutachten* of 23 October 1775 listed over forty different coinages in which the *Kammerzieler* could be paid: K. von Ernst, 'Geschichte des Münzwesens bis zum Jahre 1857' in *Österreichisches Staatswörterbuch*, 2nd ed. (Vienna, 1906), vol. II, pp. 248–64. F. Blaich, *Die Wirtschaftspolitik des Reichstags im Heiligen Römischen Reich* (Stuttgart, 1970), pp. 9–14, 43 ff. Austria's slowness in paying her contributions did not encourage the others: in 1739 Bohemia and the Burgundian Circle were heavily in arrears. Vienna, Reichskanzlei, *Vorträge* fasz. 6d, fol. 11-18. See Naumann, p. 67 on petitions for reductions of the *Kammerzieler*.

went to the aulic council, where they received favourable verdicts in 1720, 1722 and 1725.[36]

The aulic council was entirely at the disposal of the Emperor, who appointed its members, paid their salaries and issued regulations governing its operation without reference to the princes[37] and he resisted all attempts by them to determine its constitution or composition.[38] The common view of the council among the princes was that it was an instrument of Habsburg dynastic and religious policy, an impression strengthened by the fact that the Emperor jealously guarded it against princely attempts at interference.[39] This was, in fact, the greatest single element of its strength, as anything on which the princes laid their hands quickly declined. Given that Germany had developed into a loose confederation of states, it needed that basic element of any healthy federal system, an organ or organs beyond the control of individual member states. As long as the Emperor made an effort to preserve his supreme judicial authority uncontaminated by his political interests as a prince of the Empire, the aulic council could fulfil this need. Unwittingly, perhaps, by jealously guarding the aulic council as the one unblemished jewel in the crown inherited from Charlemagne, the Emperor was maintaining an organ which could make a reality of the Empire as a state above states.[40]

The first ordinance of the council of 13 February 1498 determined its functions as to handle 'each and every affair, case and business which in the future shall come to it from the Holy Roman Empire and our hereditary principalities and lands'. In 1518, as part of a general reform of the imperial administration, the competence of the council and its membership were further defined. At this stage the council was still regarded as within the competence of the Austrian Estates, who approved the membership.[41] The Emperor could appoint five noblemen or lawyers from the Empire while five were appointed from Lower Austria and two each from the Tirol and Further Austria.[42] Under the Emperor Ferdinand I the *Hofrat*, with competence for the Austrian lands, was merged with the aulic council but it was intended as the highest judicial authority for the

36 Thudichum, pp. 187–8.
37 There is a list of such ordinances in Vienna, RHR *Verfassungsakten*, Archivbehelf AB I/3.
38 Kormann, p. 147, Schwartz, p. 16.
39 This view has been echoed by historians: Kormann, p. 150, Holborn, p. 10, Koser, pp. 213–14.
40 Gschliesser, p. 43.
41 *Ibid.*, p. 1.
42 K. Bohm, *Der Ausschuss-Landtag der gesamten österreichischen Erbländer zu Innsbruck 1518* (Innsbruck Diss., 1906), pp. 256–8.

whole Empire and its administrative functions were soon lost to the Austrian aulic chancery.[43] By 1527 it was firmly established as part of the imperial government[44] and by the end of the sixteenth century had developed into a purely judicial body. The restrictions on the Emperor's freedom of choice of members were quickly dropped under Ferdinand II as part of his offensive against the Austrian Estates. The ordinance of 1541 contained only one restriction on the Emperor's choice, the provision that the Austrian aulic marshall (*Hofmarschall*) was to be an *ex officio* member.[45]

Before the Thirty Years' War the aulic council had already become the highest judicial organ for the Empire. In the ordinances of 1559 and 1654,[46] the first in which it was given the name *Reichshofrat*, its competence was further defined as 'to handle all common matters of justice and litigation'.[47] Clause two of the 1654 ordinance, which became the basic charter of the court, indicated the comprehensiveness of its competence:

> in our imperial aulic council shall be dealt with all affairs of the Holy Roman Empire, its soveregnty, law, lordship, jurisdiction, pledging, ransoming, rights, higher and lower fiefs, privileges, liberties, confirmations and all other matters, of whatever nature they are, in short everything which should be directed and decided according to the infallible rules of justice, especially each and every case, which by usage of the law, connexion and consequence, belong before our imperial court or may be brought before it by means of appeal, from a court of first instance and which belong within its competence. All these shall be heard, considered, decided and the necessary measures taken.

It was available to all except those under twenty-five, lunatics, deaf mutes, outlaws and those by custom excluded from recourse to the law. It was available to Jewish plaintiffs.[48] The council was to

---

43   Joachimsen, *Der deutsche Staatsgedanke*, p. 28.
44   Fellner and Kretschmayr, pp. 218 – 19. Gross, pp. 9 – 10.
45   Gschliesser, p. 5.
46   The ordinances of the council are reproduced in full in Uffenbach, *Mantissa* I.
47   Sellert, p. 10, Feller, pp. 61 ff. See Gschliesser, p. 6 for details of the wide competence of the aulic council.
48   Vienna, RHR *Protocollum Rerum Resolutarum* XVIII, 13, verdicts of 5 October 1705, 27 July 1705: 'E. Frisia and Jews of Norden, David Lazarus and Nathan Jacobs v. Norden guilds'. Jews could also be appealed before the council: *ibid*., 43, verdict of 8 March 1718; 'E. Frisia v. Jonas and Levi Goldschmidt'.

dispense justice and exercise its jurisdiction according to the prescribed laws, the imperial constitution and observance and the confirmed and extended privileges of the Electors, princes and Estates of the Holy Roman Empire so that no rights were injured.[49]

It was essentially a court of appeal as the Emperor had abandoned his *Evokationsrecht*, the right to summon cases to the aulic court from the courts of the princes without an appeal from one of the parties. This right was never regained.[50]

After 1637 the council was no longer competent in matters concerning the Habsburg hereditary lands within the Empire, as the *Revisionsordnung* of that year excused the Emperor from being appealed before his own court as archduke of Austria.[51] The Austrian lands had long claimed exemption from the jurisdiction of both imperial courts and were able to produce a long list of privileges to justify this claim. In 1530 Charles V had declared that all his Austrian subjects were forbidden to appeal to any imperial court and ordered his aulic council not to entertain any such appeals[52] but in fact the council continued to handle Austrian appeals until the establishment of the aulic chancery in 1637. After this Silesia and Bohemia were also outside the council's competence.[53] In fact there are in Vienna records of cases from the Austrian lands after 1637.[54] On 27 June 1739 the imperial conference debated whether the council was competent in a case in which one party, a prelate, held lands in the Austrian Breisgau. The conference decided that its competence was founded.[55] It was a constant complaint of the princes that Austria had exempted herself from the attentions of both imperial courts and this led them to seek further exemptions for themselves.

One method was the acquisition of the *privilegium de non appellando*, which set limits on the cases which could be transferred by appeal from the courts of a prince to the imperial courts, or the *Austräge*, agreements among princes to settle disputes themselves

---

49   Gschliesser, p. 7.
50   Conrad, p. 501.
51   Gschliesser, p. 11. There is some dispute over the exact date of this change. Erich Döhring, *Geschichte der Rechtspflege in Deutschland seit 1500* (Berlin, 1953), p. 6 gives 1559. Hantsch, *Schönborn*, p. 73 gives the date 1654, after which the aulic chancery became the supreme court for the hereditary lands.
52   Sellert, pp. 23 – 5.
53   *Ibid.*, pp. 32 – 6.
54   Vienna, RHR *Judicialia Miscellanea* O, fasz. 1-4. In RHR *Antiqua* AB I/27 there are several cases involving Austrian parties, often archdukes and arch-duchesses, as late as the 1660s and 1670s.
55   Vienna, Reichskanzlei *Vortr.* fasz. 6d fol. 19 – 24.

without recourse to imperial mediation.[56] The ordinance of the council laid down that the court was to observe both forms of privilege. The first privilege placed only limited restrictions on the aulic council's competence and may well have helped its operations by keeping away trivial cases. §112 of the 1654 imperial recess established a general limit, barring the court to any property cases of a value below 600*Fl*.[57]

Under article XX §6 of his capitulation of election Charles VI promised, as his predecessors had done, to observe great caution in granting such privileges which restricted imperial jurisdiction, injured the rights of third parties or infringed older existing rights. German rulers were anxious to obtain even a limited version of the privilege placing a minimum cash value on cases which could be appealed to an imperial court, as it would enable them to set up a supreme court for their subjects' cases. This was useful for princes whose high courts were wholly or partially under the control of the Estates, such as Mecklenburg, East Frisia and Brunswick-Lüneburg, or princes with scattered territories. The supreme court of cassation in Berlin was a valuable instrument in the unification of the Hohenzollern lands.[58] An unlimited privilege, which cut off the right of appeal of all the subjects of a prince to the imperial courts, with the important exception of cases of denial of justice, was rarely granted. The aulic council, to which requests for such privileges were often referred for comment, opposed them tenaciously, arguing that such a grant would diminish the Emperor's authority, of which it saw itself as guardian.[59] The Mecklenburg privilege was in 1651 increased to exclude all cases worth less than 2,000*Fl* but by a decision of the aulic council of 9 September 1653, this privilege was specifically not to include the rights of the Estates as guaranteed in the Mecklenburg constitution.[60] The princes considered a wide privilege highly desirable and kept up constant pressure to obtain it. The establishment of the cameral court had ended the unlimited privilege enjoyed by the Electors under the

---

[56] On the *Austräge* see Sellert, pp. 52 – 8 and Thudichum, pp. 154 – 5. It was rarely used privilege which gave the Estates concerned one year's grace in which to seek a settlement before the 'compromise tribunals' (*Austrägalgerichte*). On the various privileges see Perels, *passim*, Uffenbach, p. 13, and Moser, *Justizverfassung*, I, pp. 190 – 231. There is a full list in Vienna RHR *Privilegia de non appellando*.

[57] *Vortrag* of the imperial chancery 13 June 1768, Vienna, Reichsk. *Vortr.* fasz. 7c.

[58] Döhring, p. 5, Perels, p. 73.

[59] *Ibid.*, p. 48 n.

[60] Hofer, p. 73.

Golden Bull [61] and thereafter it lay solely in the gift of the Emperor. No privilege could exclude from the imperial courts any case involving an Estate of the Empire either as appellant or defendant. However large the armoury of privilege held by one prince, this could not prevent the aulic council hearing appeals against him from his subjects.[62] Frederick William I of Prussia tried hard to persuade the Estates of his territories to give up their rights of appeal. They replied that this would in any case be invalid without imperial confirmation.[63] The aulic council got wind of what was going on when a certain Prussian nobleman complained to Metsch, the imperial envoy in Lower Saxony. The council strongly opposed any attempts at such restraints.[64]

There were other minor exemptions. Mediate Catholic clergy were exempt from the jurisdiction of the council. After 1648 the king of Sweden enjoyed the special right of *electio foris*, the right to choose which of the two imperial courts he would answer to for Bremen, Verden, Pomerania and Rügen. The same privilege was enjoyed by Brunswick-Lüneburg.[65]

The procedure of the aulic council was similar to that of the cameral court but it was not bound to observe the 'unnecessary solemnities' of judicial procedures. It was intended to promote 'the common good and to further salutary justice'.[66] The ordinance of the aulic council was shorter, clearer and more definitive than that of the cameral court. The original ordinance of the cameral court of 1555, in itself a very important definition of law, had been so changed by the decisions of visitations and imperial recesses that it was difficult to find one's way among the resulting mass of regulations.[67] The aulic council was faster, more effective and came to handle more important cases, denied to the cameral court.[68]

[61] Sellert, p. 137.
[62] This is sometimes not appreciated: H. Gross, p. 4, Benecke, p. 16. Koser, p. 225 n 1 states that the acquisition by Frederick II of an unlimited privilege ended for ever imperial interference in Prussian justice. If this was true it was not as a result of the privilege. E. Schubert, pp. 314–15.
[63] Perels, p. 12. According to Moser, *Justizverfassung*, vol. I, p. 32, such a process would have been illegal.
[64] Vienna, RHR *Vota* K. 7, *votum* of 29 November 1717.
[65] Moser, *Justizverfassung*, vol. I, p. 319.
[66] *Reichshofratsordnung* 1654 Tit. 2 §§7 and 8.
[67] Sellert, p. 7.
[68] *Ibid.*, pp. 125–6. W. H. Bruford, *Germany in the Eighteenth Century* (Cambridge, 1965), p. 8 and Anton Faber (ps.), *Fabri Europäische Staats-Canzley* (115 parts, Nuremberg, Frankfurt and Leipzig, 1697–1760), vol. III, p. 135 state the opinion that the aulic council was the slower but this is contrary to the usual view.

In spite of this the council was very slow.[69] Its enemies claimed that this was the result of a deliberate attempt to delay justice or a sign of its inefficiency. It was in fact inherent in the nature of the council but it was not unavoidable. In cases of imminent danger or *periculum im mora* the council could issue inhibitory mandates without delay. These restrained one party provisionally while the case proceeded normally.

The council was overburdened with work.[70] The aulic council was not in theory a court of law but a council to advise the Emperor on the exercise of his judicial office. It was a court of appeal dealing in the main with civil cases between parties. Nevertheless it could deal with criminal cases brought by the imperial fiscal and leading to the ban of the Empire.[71] In cases of a denial of justice or of nullity in a lower court it could order a retrial.[72]

As in the cameral court all business in the council was conducted in writing.[73] This was true to many high courts in Europe at the time, including the courts of cassation of many princes of the Empire. In the slower cameral court, where a procurator considered himself fortunate if called upon to present a plea once a year, cases were dealt with in strict rotation; in the aulic council the president controlled the order of business. Indeed the president occupied a very important position, his direction of business being little limited by the ordinance. This simply contained provisions that certain cases, those brought by the fiscal or by poor parties, were to be handled in a set order of precedence. The Emperor could instruct the council to deal with a case more quickly or slowly by means of an aulic decree *(Hofdekret)*.

Litigating parties never saw the inside of the council, which, under Charles VI, met in the imperial chancery building in the Vienna Hofburg. All communication with it was through agents appointed by the council or, rarely, by presentation of documents to the porter *(Türhüter)* by the litigants in person. The agents were resident in Vienna and some were knowledgeable and influential men able to take over the whole conduct of a case. Their number was limited to between twenty-four and thirty and they were examined and appointed by the council. Each was usually retained

---

69   Moser, vol. I, p. 285: 'Wie langwührig und oft unsterblich und wie kostbar seynd die Processe an denen höchsten Reichsgerichten'.
70   *Ibid.*, p. 485 n 6.
71   Uffenbach, pp. 36 ff. lists crimes for which it was the highest criminal court of the Empire. These included breaches of the peace and the religious peace, fiscal cases against immediate Estates and breaches of the imperial *Polizeiordnung*.
72   Sellert, pp. 73 ff.
73   Thudichum, p. 168.

by several princes or Estates and the position passed in several cases from father to son. Two Prauns, father and son, represented the prince of East Frisia and the Mecklenburg nobility during the period of this study. The agents were often as much diplomats as advocates, having access to ministers and councillors, and their knowledge or procedure and the special *styla curiae* was a valuable aid in drafting documents for presentation in the council.[74] The agents or the parties themselves presented written *Deduktionen*, appeals or memoranda, under a variety of names, the *exhibita* or *presentata*. Oratorical displays had no place in the council's procedure and these had to be committed to paper. The exhibits had to be very detailed and to conform to established forms. All copies of documents quoted as evidence had to bear the attestation of an imperial notary. The collections of such *Beilagen* to an exhibit often ran into hundreds of pages as the parties tried to present exhaustively full evidence. These factors explain the enormous length and extreme style of many exhibits as the writers sought to combine the facts of the case with emotional appeals designed to sway the councillors.

The council's jurisdiction was free but parties had to pay their agents and for copies of the *expeditiones*, the mandates, decrees or verdicts of the council to be sent to the other party, from the imperial chancery and these were expensive.

Each exhibit had to be passed on to the opposing party to enable him to reply or to make objections to the competence of the council in the case, the latter called the *Exceptiones*. Bearing in mind the great distance from Vienna to the corners of the Empire and the difficulties of transport at the time, a long period naturally elapsed between each stage of the case. Arrears of unfinished business built up steadily but in this respect the council never fell into the state of the cameral court, where thousands of appeals awaited decision. The council was also more effective than the cameral court, which employed *Kammerboten* to deliver its verdicts. These unfortunates were on occasions supposed to take over the government of recalcitrant princes and the kings of Prussia were in the habit of having them arrested and escorted over the border.[75] The council employed imperial notaries or left the *Insinuation*, that is the legal delivery, of its edicts to the party at whose request they had been issued. A period of two months from receipt was usually granted

---

74 Hofer, p. 40. *Acta Borussica. Behördenorganisation* (Berlin, 1901), vol. III, pp. 96 – 8. King Frederick William I agreed to pay his agent Graeve more if he would exercise his influence solely on behalf of the king and enter 'a closer relationship' with him. Graeve was also agent for the East Frisian Estates.

75 Döhring, p. 2.

for reply if requested or even granted unasked. Cases often lasted years because of this, as exhibits to each stage were communicated to opposing parties. The reply to the *Exceptiones* was called the *Replik*, the reply to this the *Duplik* and so on through *Triplik* and *Quadruplik* without any limit. As each stage could take up to six months or more the slowness of the council becomes understandable.

Final verdicts in important cases often depended on a decision of the Emperor and they had to take their place in the queue of matters waiting for his attention.[76] The absence of important councillors also held up business[77] and it might further be held up by death or illness in the imperial family.[78]

The handling of business in Vienna tended to be slow and methodical. The council's recommendations, the *vota*, were passed first to the imperial vice-chancellor and then to the Emperor. Charles was hard-working and liked to reserve decisions to himself but difficult decisions tended to be put off for as long as possible.[79] The *vota* were usually debated in the privy council and, if necessary, in the conference.

The council was an imperial college and issued collegiate decisions, though the bulk of the work was done by individual councillors. When a case began the president of the council appointed a *Referent* and in important cases a second *Correferent*, to whom all *acta* in this case were passed after they had been handed in.

When the exchange of exhibits was complete and the *acta* had been enrolled in the *Inrotulation*, the *Referenten* drew up a *Relation* and *Correlation* giving a digest of the case and sometimes making recommendations. After this the president put questions to the council on points raised by the *Relation*, on which the councillors voted, a majority decision being taken. The majority of the *Relationes* have disappeared from the records of the court and the few that remain under the rubric in the Vienna archive are usually bald résumés of the evidence presented by both sides without any recommendations. Among the records of the council in the two

---

76   Göttingen, Aw. 504, no. 112, report of Verpoorten 29 July 1733: there had been no decisions as the Emperor and his court were out hunting and shooting every day.

77   *Ibid.*, Aw. 512, Vogel to duke Charles Leopold of Mecklenburg, 30 September 1739. The *Correferent* was absent from Vienna until October and the case was in suspense until his return.

78   *Ibid.*, Aw. 474, II nos. 98 and 99 on the illness and death of the dowager empress Eleanore.

79   M. Braubach, 'Eine Satire auf den Wiener Hof aus den letzten Jahren Kaiser Karls VI', *MIÖG*, vol. 53 (1939), p. 36.

cases considered in this study, the writer has found only four places where a record of the way in which each councillor voted has been preserved, and from their appearance these seem to be rough notes kept for his own purpose by a councillor.[80]

In minor cases the council could issue immediate decisions but otherwise its function was to give advice to the Emperor based on its collective knowledge of the law by means of a *votum ad imperatorem* or *votum ad Caesarem (Gutachten)*. This was obligatory in any case touching imperial rights or the state interests of the Empire or the Emperor. The laws on which the council was to base its decisions were prescribed in the ordinance of the council. Its concern was law and not right and wrong. A great disadvantage of this was that counter-arguments to its decisions could often be found in the bottomless well of imperial law. The councillors also suffered the disadvantage that they were often ignorant of conditions in the states of the Empire. This was especially true of the technicalities of administration which varied considerably from province to province.[81]

The *vota* set out the facts of the case and contained the recommendations of the council. There is internal evidence that the drafting of *vota* was left to the *Referent*, often under the supervision of the president.[82] The job of the council was to sift the voluminous material sent in by the litigating parties but, no matter now carefully the chaff was winnowed out and how fine the grain was milled, an enormous pile of papers, usually involving delicate matters of politics and diplomacy, always lay waiting for the final dispositions which only the Emperor could make. *Vota* were also sent in a case of serious division among the councillors, in which case both views were reported, or in matters too delicate to be settled by the council on the basis of law.[83] In theory justified by the Emperor's position as

---

[80] Vienna, RHR *Relationes* K. 134, 'Ostfriesland v. Ostfriesland, Commissionis in pto. div. grav.', 17 October 1726, 2 March 1730 and two undated from 1734.

[81] Aurich, Rep. 4 C III a no. 113 fasz. 1. The East Frisian ambassador reported 4 May 1726 on the ignorance of the councillors concerning technicalities of the situation in East Frisia. The councillors were faced with the additional problem that there was too much law in Germany. There was no imperial constitution as such but a protean collection of agreements and recesses and a great ill-defined body of custom. Imperial law was a bottomless pit in which the enterprising and assiduous searcher could usually find an appropriate precedent.

[82] Vienna, RHR *Denegata Recentiora* K. 700(8) no. 5, a note of aulic councillor Berger to the president, 15 November 1728. He had finished the *votum* and passed it to the president for 'his further enlightened disposition'. Berger commented that he was heavily overworked and needed a rest.

[83] Gschliesser, pp. 41 – 2.

supreme judge,[84] this was regarded by the princes as the means by which the Emperor perverted justice for his own ends.

Certainly successive Emperors resisted all attempts by the princes to loosen their control over the aulic council.[85] Several times in the course of the seventeenth century the princes tried to compel the Emperor to consult them either on the staffing of the council or on changes in its ordinance.[86] Frequently the princes appealed to the imperial diet, arguing that the imperial courts had produced verdicts based on haste, partiality, ignorance, prejudice, spite, inefficiency, disorder or a plain desire to pervert justice. Successive Emperors resisted this strongly, arguing that the function of the imperial diet was to make law and not to act as a tribunal of judicial review or to revise decisions of the imperial courts. In 1725 the Elector of Hanover raised complaints in the diet that the Emperor's decisions on *vota* of the aulic council were regarded as final and absolute verdicts (*judicata absoluta decreta*), against which there was no legal appeal.[87] The idea that the imperial diet had any judicial competence was never accepted by Vienna, except in the case of a ban of the Empire against an immediate Estate, when the diet had the right to examine the *acta* of the case and confirm or reject the verdict of the cameral court or the aulic council. In the Empire supreme judicial power belonged to the Emperor alone and was not shared with the Estates, a view consistently maintained by the aulic council and imperial ministers. A *votum* of the council of 7 January 1715 dealt with cases where the imperial diet had issued resolutions not in the form of recommendations but definitive verdicts after the council had already reached a conclusion. This the council condemned as an assault on the supreme judicial office and recommended that the Emperor take firm steps to put a stop to it. The imperial conference, in a *Vortrag* of 26 October 1727, stated that the imperial diet was not competent to deal with any case handled in the imperial courts as these were the highest instances in the Empire. In a *Vortrag* of 4 October 1730 the state conference, dealing with a proposed alliance between the Emperor and the duke of Württemberg, advised the Emperor to reject a statement in the

---

84 A decree of 4 January 1720 described the council as 'His Majestys' own person': Vienna RHR *Verfassungsakten* fasz. 1.

85 Döhring, p. 22. In 1766 the imperial vice-chancellor Colloredo described it as the sole remaining jewel in the imperial crown. The council seems to have regarded itself increasingly as the guardian of the small remnant of imperial authority: Koser, p. 214.

86 Gerstlacher, part I, p. 53.

87 Hanover, *Cal. Br.* 24 Österreich I no. 131 fol. 42. Pachner von Eggenstorff, vol. III, pp. 666 – 72, commission decree 14 August 1715 replying to claims that the *Reichstag* had the right to control the imperial courts.

Württemberg draft that the duke would help to maintain the Emperor's reserved powers 'according to the true interpretation of the laws of the Empire' as this suggested that the Emperor was in the habit of bending the imperial law. The duke was in the van of attacks on the aulic council.[88]

Apart from the Elector of Mainz's rarely exercised right of inspection of the court as arch-chancellor of Germany, the only other limitation on the Emperor's absolute control of the council was the right of the imperial vice-chancellor, an appointee of the Elector, to an *ex officio* seat in the council. Between 1708 and 1713 Schönborn acted as president of the council, as the abbot of Kempten, appointed to the post, did not take it up. He was most displeased when he lost the position on the appointment of von Windischgrätz.[89] Schönborn also acted as president when the president was unable to exercise his office.[90]

As early as 1615 the princes tried to have clauses relating to the aulic council included in the *Wahlkapitulation* of Matthias.[91] The suspicions and complaints of the princes grew as the business of the council expanded. After 1648 there was a lasting religious cold war in the Empire;[92] the Protestant Estates seem to have regarded the council as an agent of Catholicism or at least they chose to attack it as such.[93] In the course of the seventeenth century they were able to compel the Emperor to appoint a fixed number of Lutheran councillors and to agree that cases involving Protestant litigants would be handled by Protestant councillors. The *Corpus Evangelicorum* complained bitterly and frequently, with justification, that these rulings were ignored.

The basis of the organisation and procedure of the council, the *Reichshofratsordnung* of 16 March 1654, was issued hurriedly by the Emperor to forestall strong attempts by the assembled imperial diet to establish the control of the princes over it by issuing their own

---

[88] Vienna, Reichskanzlei *Vortr.* fasz. 6b fol. 584 – 6. *Ibid.*, Staatskanzlei *Vortr.* K. 27 fol. 80 – 2, K. 31 fol. 39 – 53.

[89] Hantsch, *Schönborn* pp. 171 – 6.

[90] Aurich, Rep. 4 A IV c no 245, report of 17 April 1720: Windischgrätz could not act in a case concerning Saxe-Lauenburg as he was related to one of the litigating parties.

[91] Gschliesser, p. 45.

[92] Sellert, p. 80.

[93] Naumann, pp. 30, 33. Vienna, Reichsk. *Vortr.* fasz. 5d, *votum* of the privy council 17 February 1685. K. S. Bader, 'Die Rechtssprechung des Reichshofrats und die Anfänge des territorialen Beamtenrechts', *Zeitschrift der Savigny-Stiftung für Rechtsgeschichte*, Germ. Abt., vol. 65 (1947), p. 363.

long-planned ordinance.[94] Ferdinand III adhered to his own ordinance in spite of threats by the Protestants that they would not recognise it as legal unless he considered critical memoranda and introduced a full complement of Lutherans. Added interest was provided by Brandenburg pressure for a Calvinist councillor.[95] The ordinance contained provision for the appointment of six Lutherans to act in cases concerning Lutherans. Under Leopold I the vacant Protestant places remained long unfilled but, in case of complaint, the Emperor could usually rely on an automatic Catholic majority in the imperial diet.

Protestant opposition to the aulic council came to a head under Charles VI. The complaints were the same as before: that equality of religion was not observed and that Protestant litigants were victimized in favour of Catholics. Despite this, Protestants continued to appeal to the council rather than to the cameral court.[96] During the reign of Charles VI the council contained Protestants of high reputation and several converts from Protestantism rose high. These included Wurmbrand, president of the council from 1728 to 1740 and a man of great ability, the councillors Knorr and Wucherer, Metsch, councillor and later imperial vice-chancellor, and Bartenstein, the secretary of the privy conference. Three Protestants who rose to prominence were Johann Heinrich Berger and his son Christoph Heinrich, professor of law at Wittenberg, and von Wernherr, former professor of mathematics at Wittenberg.[97]

The council also suffered attacks from princes of both religions. Hippolitus à Lapide called it the most poisonous spring for the destruction of German liberties and the tradition was continued in the pamphlets of Christian Thomasius, a Prussian councillor, who attacked the council in the reign of Charles VI and Francis I. It was, he claimed, the instrument by which the Emperor infringed the rights of the princes while pretending to dispense justice.[98]

At the electoral diet of 1711 the electors drew up a list of grievances against the council, sent to the Emperor on 23

---

[94] L. M. C. Lundorp, *Londorpii Acta Publica* . . . (19 parts, Frankfurt and Cologne, 1668 – 1721), Vol. V, cxxvi, session of the imperial diet 2 September 1641.

[95] Frederick I of Prussia made the cession of the Schwiebus Circle to Austria conditional on the appointment of the Prussian Calvinist Dankelmann to the council: Gschliesser, pp. 350 – 5.

[96] Gschliesser, p. 61. The Protestant jurist J. J. Moser was in Vienna often between 1720 and 1726 and was part-time secretary of councillor Nostitz: Döhring, p. 425.

[97] See Gschliesser, pp. 376 – 419, the chapter on the council under Charles VI, for short biographical details of the members.

[98] Sellert, p. 86.

December.[99] The projected permanent *Wahlkapitulation* of July 1711 contained clauses placing further restrictions on the council.[100] The election was the first since 1658 and the states saw it as a chance to strip the Emperor of his power to annoy them, as he had long since lost the power to do more. Many matters concerning the internal organisation of the Empire, including the reorganisation of the council,[101] had in 1648 been left over for later consideration. The Emperors were able to circumvent this and the princes in 1711 saw a chance to give vent to over fifty years' accumulated grievances. The authors seem to have been especially anxious to prevent the council's interfering, to their discomfort, in constitutional troubles between them and their Estates. The proposed Article XV read:

> The ruling Roman Emperor will protect mediate subjects and keep them in due obedience to their rulers and he will not exempt any subject from his due subordination to his ruler, from his jurisdiction or from customary taxes and other burdens and dues under any pretext.

He would further permit no unions or alliances of Estates against their rulers

> and in no way, by the grant of untimely litigation, commissions, rescripts and the like, encourage this.

and would permit rulers to maintain their rights against their subjects with the help of their neighbours if necessary.

The authority of the council was to be protected against encroachment by other organs of the Vienna government and resolutions of the council were to be debated elsewhere only with the advice of the vice-chancellor and members of the council.

---

[99] Hanover, *Cal. Br.* II E.1 no. 131: 'Acta betr. die bei dem jüngsten Wahltage zu Frankfurt erhobenen Beschwerden über den RHR.' The agitation continued into 1714, mainly under the leadership of the large Protestant princes: ibid. fol. 3–4, 22. Among the complaints which Hanover and her allies planned to bring up at the international congresses at Cambrai and Soissons was the charge that the aulic council drew to itself cases which belonged before the imperial diet: *ibid.*, E.1 no. 274m fol. 13–17.

[100] There is a copy in Hanover, *Cal. Br.* II E.1 no. 86.

[101] G. Scheel, 'Die Stellung der Reichsstände zur römischen Königswahl seit dem Westfälischen Friedenverhandlungen' in *Forschungen zu Staat und Verfassung: Festgabe für Fritz Hartung* (Berlin, 1958), p. 114.

All the above proposals were extensions of existing provisions. Article XVII of the draft was new and ruled that neither imperial court would in any way be altered without the knowledge, consent and advice of the imperial diet. A supplement to Article XVI put forward the idea that a new ordinance for the council would be worked out between the Emperor and the diet and until then the council would observe only part of Article V of the existing ordinance.[102]

Article XIX laid down that the council would issue no mandate or decree against a prince on the complaint of subjects without first hearing the case of the prince. The Emperor would also not permit the Estates of any princes to enjoy exclusive administration of the province's revenues to the exclusion of the *Obrigkeit*, nor to hold meetings without the knowledge of the prince.

Article XXV made it incumbent on the Emperor to appoint as president and vice-president of the council only a prince, count, or baron of the Empire,[103] and to instruct the president to permit no one to interfere in the conduct of the cases in the council.

The standard of the councillors appointed by the Emperors varied greatly. The ordinance laid down the rules to be observed in their selection but often councillors were appointed not for their legal ability but because of family connexions or for political reasons.[104] In the eighteenth century the council seems to have been regarded as a convenient training ground for scions of Austrian or imperial noble houses destined for government or diplomatic service. This was commented on unfavourably in the Empire[105] but did not prevent princes petitioning the Emperor and offering substantial bribes for the appointment of their servants to the council. The provisions of the ordinance on attendance, conduct, dress and procedure were often flouted under weak presidents and had to be repeated in a barrage of imperial decrees. A list of the many failings was drawn up during the first flush of reforming zeal under Joseph II but attempts at reform seem to have had little effect.[106]

The council consisted of two benches of councillors who sat down two sides of a long table, one of men of comital and baronial rank, the bench of lords *(Herrenbank)* and one of knights and learned jurists *(Ritter- und Gelehrtenbank)*. The councillors took precedence

---

[102] Gerstlacher, vol. I p. 55.
[103] This was already a provision of the *Reichshofratsordnung*.
[104] Gschliesser, p. 49.
[105] Schwerin, Mecklenburg Provincial Archive [hereafter Schwerin], E III P.1.5, Marquard to Behr, 29 April 1717.
[106] Vienna, RHR *Verfassungsakten* fasz. 12, 'Über die Gebrechen des RHRs', 1766.

over all but privy councillors[107] and a place was eagerly sought. The appointment enjoyed great prestige and influence and its holders wide privileges,[108] which passed to their widows and servants.[109] In 1706 the Lower Austrian Estates complained that prosperous men were attaching themselves to a member of the council and in this way obtaining exemption of their property from the property tax.[110] The members of the council and their dependants were subject only to the jurisdiction of the council, as were litigants, and no other court could try them. The council reacted violently when parties tried to appeal over its head to the cameral court or the imperial diet.[111] By the eighteenth century the majority on the bench of lords were Austrians[112] and many were related to those already in high positions in the imperial government. Many noblemen were appointed to the council very young and did not take up their posts until more experienced or quickly moved on to other positions, for which the council had been preparation. In 1713 Charles VI issued an ordinance that members of the bench of jurists must have served for a time in a high court in the hereditary lands or the Empire. This speeded the process by which the council was dividing into two distinct groups, those who made the council their career and did most of the work and those, mainly noble, members whose presence was decorative or who regarded the council as a stepping stone to other careers.[113] Julius Francis Xavier von Hamilton was appointed to the council in 1708 at the age of eighteen but was not admitted until 1717 after service in the Bavarian *Hofrat*. He remained until 1740.[114] Francis Wenzel von Sinzendorff sat in the council from 1722 to 1725 and was afterwards imperial ambassador in The Hague.[115] In January 1736 Joseph Balthasar, Count Dietrichstein, was given the promise of a place (*Expektanz*) on condition that

---

[107] *Londorpii Acta Publica*, vol. VII, p. 603, *Memorial* of the RHR 1654.
[108] There is a list of the *Immunitäten* of the aulic council and the imperial chancery in Vienna, RHR *Verfassungsakten* fasz. 10 – 20.
[109] Vienna, RHR *Vota* K. 66, *votum* of 29 October/17 December 1731.
[110] Vienna, Lower Austrian Provincial Archive, *Hofprotocollum pro anno 1707*, fol. 213.
[111] Sellert, p. 89.
[112] Gschliesser, p. 391.
[113] Vienna, Reichskanzlei *Vortr.* fasz. 6d fol. 155 – 72: a *Referat* of the imperial chancery of 5 June 1746 stated that it would be valuable to appoint more councillors than were needed as they would always be available for use as diplomats.
[114] Gschliesser, p. 319.
[115] *Ibid.*, p. 395.

he first obtained experience in public and civil law and the law of the Empire.[116]

The attendance of the majority of the noble councillors was often irregular and most of the serious work was done by the jurists. The Empire, with its multitude of universities and courts, provided a constant reservoir of highly trained lawyers anxious to make their career in the highest tribunal of the Empire. Potential members of the council were required to submit to examination, though this requirement was often dispensed with on the wish of the Emperor. A member of the bench of jurists was exempt if he had a law degree, had practised in a high capacity in the judiciary or administration of a state, had acted as an assessor in the cameral court or *syndicus* of a free city or had held a chair in law.[117] The abiding feature of imperial government at this time was chronic penury. The councillors' salaries were paid irregularly and under Charles the device was employed of appointing supernumeraries, councillors who sat in the court but received no salaries until a paid post fell vacant. In this way the Emperor was able to exceed the statutory number of councillors without increasing the cost. The income of the councillors from various fees was large but irregular as only those who took part in the revision of a verdict received a share.[118] On his entry into the council the councillor was obliged to give up all salaries and pensions from all other sources and to swear that he was not in any way obligated to anyone but the Emperor. There were frequent complaints that it was impossible to live in Vienna in any style on the salary of 4,000Fl a year.[119]

Understandably accusations of partiality against the council were exceeded only by charges that the councillors were prepared to sell their vote for money. Certainly the councillors took 'presents'.[120] Metternich, the Prussian ambassador in Vienna at the beginning of the reign of Frederick William I, recommended that bribery was the surest means of influencing the council's decisions. The councillors liked to be invited to dinner, flattered and presented with gifts. They enjoyed being courted and could be won by titles or offices for their friends and relatives. In February 1716 he listed the bribable councillors and it is interesting that most were on the learned

---

[116]   *Ibid.*, p. 413.
[117]   *Ibid.*, p. 72.
[118]   There are lists of these fees, under the names *Sporteln* and *Laudemien* in Vienna, RHR *Verfassungsakten* fasz. 5 no. 39.
[119]   Vienna, Reichskanzlei *Vortr.* fasz. 7c: report on a prospective councillor 28 September 1768. Droysen, vol. IV/1 p. 101 states that the post cost at least 4,000Fl a year in the obligations it entailed. When in 1694 the Emperor established a post for a Calvinist, many refused it.
[120]   Döhring, pp. 102–3.

bench: Stein, Heuwel, Kirchner, Keller, Hartig, Berger and Steiningen.[121] There is ample documentary evidence of bribery among the records preserved in Schwerin, Aurich and Hanover. In Hanover is a list of 'rewards and presents' *(Laudemien und Präsenzgelder)* to be offered for a favourable decision in the case concerning Hanover's investiture with Saxe-Lauenburg and Hadeln in 1715.[122] This listed the sums paid to various persons in and attached to the council and sums promised if the investiture were completed and the sequester on Hadeln lifted. The amounts involved were very large: the president received 4,000Fl, the vice-president 3,000Fl and participating councillors 2,000Fl each. Schönborn had been promised 30,000Fl and had received half of this. In addition the costs of the investiture and payments to the secretaries were substantial. The letter of investiture for Lauenburg cost 3,000Fl. Further, 1,500Fl were paid to the secretary of the aulic council, Menshengen, and additional presents to the chancery staff totalled 1,081Fl. There is nothing to suggest that, had these sums not been paid, Hanover would not have been invested with Lauenburg. At worst the process would have been delayed but, as Hanover was already in possession of the territory, this was not tragic. Investiture gave the stamp of imperial approval and access to extra votes in the *Reichstag* and was therefore considered desirable. The question of Hadeln was more important. This territory remained in imperial sequester in 1732 and proved an important issue of negotiation between the Elector and the Emperor for years.

There is evidence that this bribery sometimes took the form of regular pensions paid to councillors to retain their continuing good offices. On 20 October 1736 the widow of the late councillor Berger wrote to the duke Christian Louis of Mecklenburg asking for the continued payment of 'gratuities' *(Erkenntlichkeiten)* to her, as a comfort in her old age, as they had been paid to her husband during

---

[121] Perels, pp. 86 and 91. He quotes accounts in the Berlin archive of sums paid in bribes. Kappelhoff, pp. 204–15 lists the sums spent by the East Frisian litigants.

[122] Hanover, *Cal. Br.* 11 E.1 no. 144. After the death of the last native duke of Saxe-Lauenburg, Hanover bought off all rival claimants and occupied all but Hadeln, a small territory on the Elbe estuary, which was taken into imperial sequester as the last duke's daughters claimed it as an allod heritable by women. While this case was pending in the aulic council, Hanover could not be enfeoffed with the Saxe-Lauenburg lands. Hanover offered bribes to Schönborn and Wurmbrand, the *Referent* in the case, for a favourable verdict: Naumann, pp. 43–4, 47. Borgmann, pp. 86–7 describes Hanoverian plans to bribe the imperial vice-chancellor to influence other cases.

his lifetime.[123] The euphemisms used to describe these payments were numerous. An agent reported to his master, the duke Charles Leopold of Mecklenburg, in September 1725: 'Nothing can be achieved here without walking along Gold and Silver Street.'[124] Under the title *Arcana Vienensia*, the Schwerin court preserved full accounts of bribes paid to named councillors between 1696 and 1698 and 1708 to 1710.[125] These bribes were called *Qualifikationen*. Not only money was offered and accepted. The lists speak of gifts of lace, silver plate and kettles, liqueurs, horses and other valuables to the councillors and their wives. The name of von Schönborn recurs. The sums involved were immense. Councillor Binder was in 1704 offered 16,000*Rt.* for his help. A total of 25,000*Rt.* was made available to facilitate the acquisition of the Güstrow inheritance by the duke of Schwerin and was to be promised: 'If the following cases are decided favourable, saving justice.'

There is no direct evidence of bribery in the Mecklenburg litigation under duke Charles Leopold. On 3 May 1719 the Mecklenburg ambassador in Vienna, Eichholz, tried to explain away the lack of progress in the duke's great matter by his failure to pay *Douceurs*.[126]

Equally, everything was for sale in Vienna. No document appears to have been too secret to be beyond price. The chancery employees were poorly paid and had to rely for their income on a system of fees. Vienna was a very expensive city and prices continued to rise during the reign of Charles VI. In Aurich are a large number of 'secret' *vota* of the aulic council, meant for the eyes of the Emperor and his ministers alone, some bearing notes of the sums for which they had been purchased.[127] The secretaries of the council were also apparently willing to sell copies of the material which passed through their hands.[128] The number of such instances could be multiplied.[129]

---

[123] Göttingen, Aw. 501 fasz. 2.
[124] *Ibid.*, Aw. 505, Paulsen to the duke of Mecklenburg-Schwerin, 26 September 1725.
[125] *Ibid.*, Aw. 404.
[126] *Ibid.*, Aw. 474 no. 27.
[127] Aurich, Rep.4 C III a no. 17. Naumann, p. 150.
[128] Aurich, Ostfriesische Landschaft, Dep. I 4911 no. 77, report of 2 October. *Ibid.*, Rep. 4 A IV c no. 254. Brawe reported that councillor Binder was ready to reveal details of the council's business for money and that other members were useful sources of information. The Mecklenburg diplomat Eichholtz had a 'confidant', who sent him copies of all the opposition's exhibits: Göttingen Aw. 474 II no. 24, Aw. 491 no. 21.
[129] On the sale of documents see Vienna, RHR *Verfassungsakten* fasz. 27 no. 12, fasz. 30–2.

There were attempts to stop all this. Efforts were made to halt the sale of documents in the imperial chancery and one councillor, Binder, lost his post for bribery.[130] However it should be noted that, from the point of view of eighteenth-century administration, bribery was an accepted, often the only, method of bringing oneself to the notice of those in authority. During Charles VI's reign several aulic decrees were issued reminding the council that the rules were not being observed.[131] In April 1734 the imperial vice-chancellor was told to investigate many complaints against the council.[132] There was a real fear that the matter would be brought up in the imperial diet and that a movement for a visitation of the council would begin. The investigation showed 'that the order and respect of this highest imperial court for various reasons has in truth sunk into great decay' and that the president had lost great authority. Some councillors flatly refused to obey him while others had come to dominate the council, especially in political cases, in which they claimed to know imperial wishes and in this way swayed the council from purely legal recommendations. Under the ordinance of the council the president was supposed to prevent the growth of cliques in the council but this still happened. A hard-working and knowledgeable councillor could quickly achieve a dominant position.[133]

The 1734 investigation also revealed a great deal of time-wasting and absenteeism in the council. Distinct parties formed around dominant personalities. Secrecy was not respected, documents were 'lost' and *vota* were not kept confidential. The resulting aulic decree of 25 April ordered an end to these abuses. The council's opinion was to be based on law, not on what the council believed the Emperor wanted to hear. *Vota* expressing split opinions were not to be sent and there was to be no disorder, interruptions, wrangles and the like. Secrecy was to be strictly observed, especially with regard to *vota*.

By following cases through from the start it should be possible to determine the effects of bribery, if there were any. In the cases of Mecklenburg and East Frisia there is no evidence that the aulic council was influenced by any other consideration than precepts of

---

[130] Gschliesser, pp. 395–6.
[131] Vienna, RHR *Verfassungsakten* fasz. 19, packet 17.
[132] *Ibid.*, fol. 373–97, 564–70.
[133] Lyncker's *Facies judicii imperialis aulici* of March 1712 in Vienna, RHR *Verfassungsakten* fasz. 3 (manuscript copy) describes Hauwel as a 'dictator' in the council. See also Aurich, A IV c no. 249, report of 30 September 1724 and Göttingen, Aw. 501 fasz. 2, various reports, on the existence of groups within the council. Also Hofer, p. 58 n 89.

imperial law, the merits of the cases and the interests of the Emperor, the latter decided in a privy conference dominated during most of the reign of Charles VI by that notoriously incorruptible prince Eugene of Savoy and Gundacker Thomas von Starhemberg. Metsch, who succeeded Schönborn as imperial vice-chancellor apparently refused bribes.[134] Another study of litigation in the aulic council found that there was no evidence of bribery influencing the decisions of the council and suggests that, in important cases, the council observed the law and treated the case as a matter of principle.[135] If bribery had any effect, other than to speed a case's passage through the court, it was probably in minor cases of property and land without great political significance.

Thus it seems likely that the councillors happily took gifts from both sides in a case, as a kind of perquisite, without allowing this to influence their votes. 'Evidence' of the effects of bribery adduced by some writers is often no more than the unconfirmed reports of agents of the litigating parties, for whom the plea that the opposition must have paid more was an easy excuse for failure. It is interesting that in his vitriolic *Facies* of 1712, a sharp attack on the members of the council, Lyncker, while praising his own diligence and intellect, levelled every kind of charge against his colleagues, illegitimacy, low birth, ignorance and more, but never directly corruption. He stated that some of the councillors had amassed fortunes but did not reveal how.

There were many opportunities. Vienna was a hive of influence, jealousy and intrigue[136], and one of the most important features of litigation there was the practice of solliciting *(Sollicitieren)*. As is revealed by reports sent to the duke of Mecklenburg, the prince of East Frisia and the king of England a great deal of negotiation about cases in the council was carried on in personal contacts behind the scenes, although there is no evidence, and by their nature nor could there be, that such negotiations in any way influenced the outcome of cases. Discussions, solliciting, usually consisted of an exchange of information and the delivery of pleas to support a party's case,

---

134   Aurich, Rep. 4 A IV c no. 254, report of 7 December 1729.
135   E. von Ranke, *Das Fürstentum Schwarzburg-Rudolstadt zu Beginn des 18. Jahrhunderts* (Diss. Halle, 1915), pp. 96 – 9, 111, 122, 124. The conclusions are somewhat contradictory.
136   In October 1732 the city of Emden decided to send a deputation to Vienna to collect support for its case. Two lawyers and Walbrunn, a knight, were chosen, the former for their knowledge and the latter for his ability to mix easily with ministers, councillors and high-born ladies: Aurich, Rep. 4 C III a no. 128, prince of East Frisia to Brawe, 31 October 1732, including a copy of the protocol of the Emden Privy Commission dd. 10 October. See also Borgmann, pp. 23, 66 – 73 for the intrigues in the Viennese court.

and involved ambassadors, agents and representatives begging audiences with those in power. The process could also be carried on in writing, for it was considered advisable for parties to write to ministers and councillors congratulating them on promotions and the like, asking their help and a favourable ear for the verbal pleas of their agents.[137] They seem to have received little in return but vague promises of support and comforting words. On 24 September 1729 prince Eugene replied to a letter of the prince of East Frisia that his case was being conducted in the aulic council where it belonged 'and I do not make a habit of interfering in cases which belong there'. He repeated this on 19 November and advised the prince to put his trust in the Emperor's love of justice.[138] Charles VI, like his predecessors, seems to have confined himself to vague assurances that he would do what was right and just.[139] Sometimes a councillor would give helpful suggestions. Berger wrote to the prince of East Frisia on 19 May 1734 advising him not to withdraw his ambassador Gersdorff at a critical stage in the case.[140] The agents were also able to obtain useful information on the progress of the case or advance notice of pending decisions. They seem to have experienced little difficulty in obtaining audiences with ministers and this is true of the agents of the Estates of Mecklenburg and East Frisia as well as those of the rulers.[141] This solliciting and influence increased the suspicion that in Vienna justice was for sale.[142]

A major objection made by subsequent writers is that the council lacked the means to put its verdicts, however just and proper, into

---

[137] Aurich, Rep. 4 C III a no. 110 contains copies of letters from the prince of East Frisia to members of the imperial family, prince Eugene and members of the council.

[138] *Ibid.*, for the replies. If the conference, the heart of the Austro-imperial government exercised influence on the aulic council, it would seem to have been limited to holding up rather than altering verdicts. Vienna, Reichskanzlei *Vortr.* fasz. 6c fol. 682 – 711, *Referat* of 21 January 1734: the conference debated a list of cases pending in the council in which, because of political circumstances, it was questionable whether verdicts should be reached.

[139] H.-J. Ballschmieter, *Andreas Gottlieb von Bernstorff und der mecklenburgische Ständekampf, 1680 – 1720* (Cologne/Graz, 1962), p. 58 n 70.

[140] Aurich, Rep. 4 C III a no. 110.

[141] Göttingen, Aw. 492 no. 7: Eichholtz reported a long conversation with the council president, Windischgrätz. He also advised the Estates, urging their delegate, Behr, to ensure that they had a representative in Regensburg. He was described elsewhere as the 'great patron' of the Estates: Schwerin, E.111 P.1.6, Behr to Bernstorff, 1 December 1717. *Ibid.*, P.1.5, Schavius to Behr, 3 March 1717.

[142] Thudichum, p. 202.

effect.[143] It could, in the Emperor's name, issue orders, pronounce the ban, place territories under sequester, appoint commissioners to execute or investigate or to bring about a settlement between parties, order its verdicts to be put into effect by force and relieve subjects of their duty of obedience to a prince. Its usual weapons were *Mandata sine Clausula*, unconditional orders, *Conservatoria*, orders to A to protect B, *Protectoria*, orders forbidding A from taking any action against B, *Auxiliatoria*, orders to C to help A protect B or carry out imperial instructions, and commissions. Like all courts the council was ultimately dependent on armed force. After 1648 the Emperor was most unwilling to use his own forces to put verdicts into effect, barely having enough for his own military needs, and the prospect of bodies of imperial troops marching round the Empire in peace-time to enforce the decisions of a tribunal heartily disliked and suspected as a tool of Habsburg, imperialist or Catholic policies, would have been too much for the princes. The council lacked any quick way of dealing with contempt of its orders. Often it seems to have chosen to ignore the fact that a party had failed to react to its communications rather than to display its impotence by trying to do something about it. This also tended to slow up its procedure and damaged the Kafkaesque air of inaccessible authority around it. A Hanoverian *Promemoria* of 6 November 1760 stated: 'It seems as if the imperial court is making a business out of sending verdicts, rescripts, decrees and countless dispositions of the same sort, none of which can have any effect, in this way making the Emperor laughable.'[144] Certainly there was a great contrast between the rolling phrases of majesty and the threats of dire punishment in imperial patents and the ridicule with which they were often greeted.

The ultimate method employed by the council was to commission one ruler to execute verdicts against another by force. This method depended for its success on the political interest of the commissioner, whether he wished to do a favour to the Emperor and whether he could afford to offend a fellow prince who might next year be commissioned to execute against him. In the case of small princes, free knights and free cities[145] this was not serious, but it meant that a powerful prince, such as the king of Prussia, might ignore the aulic council's commands with impunity. But even Prussia could not afford to ignore the aulic council under Charles VI

---

143   Döhring, pp. 22–3.
144   [Fabri] *Europäische Staats-Canzley*, vol. V, pp. 152ff.
145   Moser, p. 1103: 'I can remember examples where the aulic council and the cameral court have completely changed the internal government of individual free cities.'

and the king thought it worthwhile to spend large sums on pensions to secure and keep the friendship of some councillors.[146] The council reached a high standard under Charles VI, containing men of talent from many parts of the Empire, an improvement which had begun under Joseph I. By the aulic decree of 3 March 1706 the Emperor ordered that those parts of the ordinance dealing with the examination of prospective councillors, which had not been observed under Leopold, were to be obeyed in full. In addition the Estates of the Empire were to be given no cause for complaint against the council.[147] Nevertheless, in practice the provisions on the examination of candidates were often ignored.[148]

In his recommendations of 27 August 1712, Schönborn put forward proposals for a reform of the council in reply to the *puncta et gravamina communa* drawn up by the imperial diet and the special grievances of the Protestant Estates.[149] Schönborn recommended that steps be taken to stop bribery, infringements of the jurisdiction of the cameral court, breaches of secrecy and the growth of groups in the council and to promote higher standards among the councillors by more careful selection. He also proposed an increase in salary to 4,000Fl a year to be paid from a regular and fixed fund, such as the yield of the Austrian salt monopoly, and that attempts should be made to persuade more non-Austrians to join the council. The trained councillors of the great German princes should also be recruited for the bench of jurists. By the decree of 14 January 1714, which consisted mainly of a repeat of the provisions of earlier decrees with some new regulations, these provisions were put into effect.[150]

No one was to enter the council who was in any way obligated to another person and a declaration on oath to this effect was to be given before a new councillor was admitted. It repeated the provisions of the ordinance on the clothing, attendance and behaviour of the councillors in the tribunal: there was to be no bright clothing, chattering or horseplay and the members were to stand respectfully to attention when Caesar's commands were read out. No one was to be admitted to the bench of jurists without prior

---

146 Döhring, pp. 102 – 3. Gschliesser, pp. 328, 330 and 381 on Kirchner, Heuwel and Berger, all said to have been in receipt of Prussian pensions.
147 Gschliesser, p. 364.
148 Hanover, *Cal. Br.* 11 E.1 no. 131 fol. 1 – 2.
149 Vienna, RHR *Verfassungsakten* fasz. 19 packet 17 fol. 447 – 560: *Monita, den RHR und dessen Besserung betr. 1711.*
150 There are copies of this in Hanover, *Cal. Br.*, 11 E.1 no. 131 fol. 5 – 16 and in Gerstlacher, vol. I, p. 57. Hantsch, *Schönborn*, p. 128 states that after the accession of Charles VI the council showed renewed energy, further encouraged by the prostration of the imperial cameral court.

experience in a high court. No councillor was to keep the documents of a case after he had finished with them but was to return them to the registry of the imperial chancery. There had been reports that many had disappeared.[151] No councillor was to remove *Relationen* from the registry without permission from the Emperor, the vice-chancellor or the president. All complaints against the conduct of imperial commissions were to be heard unless they were manifestly aimed only at delaying or hindering justice. This left the council a great deal of power in this matter. Facts contained in commission reports were to be made available to anyone who applied for them in a seemly manner but the commission's recommendations and their *relationes decidendi* were to be kept secret. There had been complaints that cases had been dealt with at the whim of the *Referent* in a haphazard fashion. The ordinance was to be observed strictly. Only in dangerous or urgent cases or those with a political content could the rules of the ordinance be relaxed at the will of the president or his deputy. The president was to ensure that councillors did not vote out of personal considerations and that parties and cliques did not grow up in the council. He was to decide with the majority or to report both opinions in case of a serious division in a vote. If a case came up for revision, the former *Referenten* were to have no vote. Councillors not present from the beginning of a *Relation* were also to lose their vote. The council was to be more sparing in the use of *Protectoria, Conservatoria* and *Auxiliatoria*; clearly the Emperor was aware of the danger in the over-zealous dispensing of unenforceable paper commands. When such mandates were issued, however, they were to be strictly enforced. This did not explain how the paper tiger was to acquire teeth. The decree ended with a homily on the duty of the council to dispense Christian justice.

Too often reforms on paper remained paper reforms. This decree, with its implied catalogue of the faults of the council, was repeated when it was reconstituted in 1745 under the name 'improved ordinance'. Some provisions were not put into effect or were quietly ignored. But the new spirit, of which it was a sign, revived a body which had gone into decline under Leopold I and heralded the short period in which it reached the pinnacle of its activity. It showed also the Emperor's genuine desire to reform the council. On 16 January 1714 he wrote to the Elector of Mainz informing him of the proposed changes and asking him to obtain details of the abuses complained of by the princes. He could do nothing if these

---

[151] In view of the gaps in the records of the council, this order seems to have had very little effect. Very few of the important *Relationes* remains.

remained vague and general but he stressed his desire to correct all faults.[152]

The decree illustrates the great responsibility placed on the president for the efficient working of the council. Under Charles VI it had two outstanding presidents, both learned jurists and experts in imperial affairs. This was particularly important as the post carried with it automatic membership of the privy council and the imperial conference. The first, Count Ernst Freidrich von Windisch-grätz, a nobleman but also a jurist of note, held the post from 1713 to September 1727. The second, Count Johann Wilhelm von Wurmbrand, a Lutheran converted to Catholicism in 1722, was president from 1728 to 1740 and again from 1745 to 1750. He was a most able man who accumulated vast experience, serving in the council for fifty-three years.[153] Von Windischgrätz had the reputation of favouring the rights of Estates and mediate subjects against their rulers[154] and there is evidence to confirm this.[155] Litigation of this sort between rulers and Estates, occupied an important place in the council's activities during the 'imperial reaction'.

---

[152] Hanover, *Cal. Br.* 11 E.1 no. 131 fol. 17 – 20.

[153] Gschliesser, pp. 326, 336 – 7.

[154] Schwerin, E. III P.1.6, Marquard to Behr, 31 March 1718. The Hanoverian government was considering employing Behr, the representative of the Mecklenburg knighthood and Mecklenburg-Strelitz *chargé d'affaires* in Vienna, to handle a case for it in the city. Marquard warned him that there was a religious element in it and he would therefore face the hostility of the whole Catholic 'interest' in Vienna and the Empire. 'However, the cause of justice can triumph in the end under the present Emperor and president of the aulic council.' See also von Ranke, p. 99.

[155] Ballschmieter, p. 115 n15.

3

Mecklenburg and East Frisia
in the imperial aulic council

The long and involved cases between the rulers and Estates of
Mecklenburg and East Frisia were among the most important in the
aulic council during the reign of Charles VI and both rapidly
acquired great importance in the diplomacy and politics of the
Empire and Europe. They typified many of the more significant
cases brought before the council during the great expansion of its
business in the late seventeenth and eighteenth centuries,[1] products
of the constitutional struggles seen in many parts of Germany.[2] The
troubles which caused the names of Mecklenburg and East Frisia to
appear so regularly in the protocols of the council were sparked off
by disputes between princes and subjects. In Mecklenburg the
council devoted its efforts to protecting Estates against attempts by
the dukes to destroy their constitutional rights; in East Frisia it
supported a prince against overmighty Estates threatening to rob
him of all power, a circumstance rare enough to make it interesting
in itself for it was more common for rulers to turn their efforts to
destroying the rights of their Estates in the cause of 'moderniza-
tion'[3], the fashion of absolutism.

Both cases reached a crisis during Charles VI's reign and in both
the aulic council took vigorous action, which can be seen as an
important element in the 'imperial reaction'. Both states lay in north
Germany, an area where imperial influence was at its weakest at the
beginning of the eighteenth century. The two cases could be
interpreted as an attempt by the Emperor to move back into a part
of the Empire where he was virtually powerless, another aspect of
'imperial reaction'. Imperial policy in the two cases has been
portrayed as part of a purely Habsburg dynastic foreign policy, a
method of keeping intact European alliances on which the security

---

[1] Gschliesser, pp. 31 – 2.
[2] For which see Carsten *passim*. E. von Ranke's work on another case is very
     much of its period, showing a distinct bias toward the princely side and
     portraying the dualist *Ständestaat* as an enemy of progress.
[3] K. Epstein, *The Genesis of German Conservatism* (Princeton, 1967), p. 261.

of the Austrian lands depended. Protagonists of this view regard the aulic council as nothing more than a tool of Habsburg ambitions and its decisions in the two cases as nothing more than temporary expedients which later got out of hand and became a source of embarrassment to those who had initiated them.[4] This view assumes that the Emperor had the desire and the ability to move the aulic council to come to any decision he required without regard for imperial law, or in the conviction that this could be bent to justify any action. The whole apparatus of the council and the mass of documentation it produced were no more than an exercise in political or diplomatic window-dressing, a fig-leaf intended to cover the nakedness of the *raison d'etat*, which, according to this interpretation, motivated Charles VI's actions. Certainly many German princes had no doubt of the Emperor's ability to influence the council by interfering with a case in progress there.[5]

However, there is little hard evidence for the conspiracy theory of imperial jurisdiction and the documents of the aulic council and the conferences which directed Austrian and imperial policy offer sparse confirmation for this unsubtle view; there are strong indications to the contrary. Charles VI wished to exercise his supreme judicial office impartially but his freedom of action was limited by political and diplomatic considerations. In seeking to maintain law and order in Mecklenburg and East Frisia he was forced to take into account the political situation in Germany and his relations with interested foreign powers. The aulic council and the imperial and privy conferences sought a climate favourable to the exercise of imperial jurisdiction, one in which it had some chance of success, while at the same time pursuing a foreign and imperial policy in line with distinct Habsburg interests. The privy or state conference, the heart of the Vienna government, had no need to express the polite fictions which in public governed the relations between rulers and states and this body frequently spoke of the Emperor's *obristrichterliche Amt* as something to be preserved intact at all cost. Even though it was politic for an astute minister to say what he knew the Lord's anointed wanted to hear, it is unlikely that, for example, prince Eugene would have given his Emperor

---

4   Naumann, pp. 17–20, 187–8, 110: 'Eine genaue Untersuchung der Reichshofratsentscheidungen dieser Jahre würde zeigen, dass diese vor 1725 im Sinne der Reichspolitik Schönborns, nach 1725 aber in steigendem Masse nach den Interessen Österreichs gefällt wurden.' So close an examination is not undertaken by Naumann.
5   Hanover, 'Cal. Br. 11 E.1 no. 410a, fol. 77–8. Subsequent historians also express this view: Benecke, p. 275: 'Vienna dealt more equitably with the cases of a dangerous political, social or constitutional nature, yet decisions there had a Habsburg bias'. See also *ibid.*, p. 332.

advice contrary to his real interests. If the maintenance of the imperial supreme judicial office was a passion of Charles VI it became, by this token, an ingredient of imperial policy which ministers had to take into consideration in making their recommendations.

In addition the maintenance of the Emperor's judicial function was a major Habsburg interest.[6] The Emperor had a better prospect of retaining the loyalty or at least the dependence of the smaller states of Germany if he could offer them impartial justice as well as protection. The movement towards absolutism and self-sufficiency among the larger states after 1648 was not seen among those states without the strength or means to build up the necessary organisation.[7] Like many others, Mecklenburg was too weak and her geographical position too exposed to provide the breathing space, the 'creative pause', during which a strong apparatus of state could be built up. For Mecklenburg and East Frisia, as for scores of others, the only real alternative was dependence on strong neighbours or on the Emperor. Larger states tried to discredit the Emperor by attacking his jurisdiction as partial and motivated only by concern for his own dynastic interests, especially when it operated against them. The sources on which the 'conspiracy theory' of the aulic council is based are mainly reports from the agents of these states in Vienna.[8] It was easy to excuse one's failure to move a case in favour of one's principals by claiming that the jurisdiction was tainted. Many of the larger states, particularly Prussia, took great trouble to try to change the aulic council and to challenge it in the imperial diet and in public pamphlets. Frederick William I of Prussia was especially fond of claiming that the council was biased against him but, if the council was dedicated to condemning breaches of law and if Prussia happened to be pursuing a policy characterized by a singular lack of regard for law, it is not likely that they would have agreed.[9]

An examination of the records of the Mecklenburg and East Frisian cases in the aulic council shows up the conflict between the imperial and specifically Austrian interests of the house of Habsburg, as Austria's diplomatic position in Europe was closely involved in both. The basic question at issue in both cases was how

---

[6]   O. F. Winter, pp. 456 – 7.
[7]   Hofer, p. 39. F. Hartung, *Deutsche Verfassungsgeschichte*, 5th ed. (Stuttgart, 1950), pp. 159 ff.
[8]   For example, those quoted by Naumann, Koser and Ballschmieter.
[9]   Hantsch, *Schönborn*, p. 225 n. 60A: at one point in the reign of Frederick William I some forty separate cases were pending against him in the aulic council.

far the Estates were to exercise control over the actions of the rulers by virtue of consitutional agreements entered centuries earlier when conditions had been different. As elsewhere in Germany, the struggles hinged on the right of the Estates, by granting or withholding taxes at will, to fetter the actions of princes who regarded themselves as sovereign. In both cases one party accused the other of seeking to set up an arbitrary regime and appealed to the Emperor for aid and protection. The two cases also present a number of interesting contrasts.

In their social, economic and constitutional conditions Mecklenburg and East Frisia were totally different. Socially, economically, politically and in agriculture the two duchies which formed Mecklenburg were one of the most backward areas of the Empire.[10] The country suffered badly in the Thirty Years' War; one estimate places the loss of population at eighty per cent, which was not recovered in 1700.[11] Mecklenburg was constitutionally one state with two dukes,[12] each with his own apparatus of government. Schwerin was the stronger and traditionally the more active of the two. The duke of Strelitz was little more than an overgrown *Junker*. Since 1621 certain institutions had been common to both, the Estates, annual diets, the national Church, the university of Rostock, the Consistory, the provincial high court (*Land- und Hofgericht*), the provincial treasury (*Landkasten*), the city of Rostock with Warnemünde and the Rostock city lands and the three convents and other church lands which belonged to the Estates.[13]

The Mecklenburg Estates were among the most highly privileged in Germany.[14] As elsewhere, the initiative for their early development came from the dukes themselves who had called the first meetings of their subjects. Their power had grown out of the poverty and disunity of the dukes and they formed a permanent Union in 1523.[15] By 1561 the Estates had acquired control of the

---

[10] In 1695 the native line of the duchy of Mecklenburg-Güstrow died out and, after a long dispute, the inheritance was divided in 1701 by the treaty of Hamburg. Most of the territory and the Güstrow vote in the imperial diet passed to the house of Schwerin while the Stargard Circle and the secularized bishopric of Ratzeburg, with its vote, passed to Strelitz.

[11] F. Mager, *Geschichte des Bauerntums and der Bodenkultur im Lande Mecklenburg* (Berlin, 1955), pp. 135, 225. It was said that only sand and air were in abundance in Mecklenburg.

[12] P. Steinmann, *Bauer und Ritter in Mecklenburg* (Schwerin, 1960), p. xviii.

[13] The convents were maintained as convenient places to which to send unmarried daughters of the nobility: Duggan in Vann and Rowan, *The Old Reich*, pp. 161–2.

[14] For the early development of the Estates see G. Hegel, *Geschichte der mecklenburgischen Landstände bis zum Jahre 1555 mit einem Urkundenanhang* (Rostock, 1856).

[15] *Ibid.*, p. 119.

grant and collection of taxes and had their own treasury, the *Landkasten*, into which these were paid. This enabled them to accumulate capital and raise loans. After 1555 they administered through committees the taxation authorised for the repayment of the ducal debts which they, like many other German Estates, had taken over. This had led to the establishment of a permanent Small Committee *(Engere Ausschuss)*, which came to organise the activities of the Estates between the annual diets. The wide powers of the Estates were enshrined in the two *Reversales* of 1572 and 1621 granted by the dukes in return for the takeover of a million Fl of ducal debt. Even after the expulsion of the native dukes in 1628, when the country came under the direct rule of Wallenstein, the constitution remained in force.[16]

The Estates of Schwerin and Güstrow[17] were dominated by a large aristocracy, the knighthood *(Ritterschaft)*, which consisted of the holders of some seven hundred knight's fees. It was the constant aim of this class to prevent the dukes buying and keeping vacant knight's fees, thus reducing the strength of the knighthood.[18] Of these the majority did not attend diets and a small number of active members conducted affairs in the name of the whole class.[19] Certain names recur frequently in documents on the history of the Estates. The most significant feature of the knighthood was its size. As a proportion of the total population of the duchies it was one of the largest nobilities in the Empire. Traditionally the poverty of the country forced the knights to seek employment in the civil or military service of princes throughout the Empire and in neighbouring states and many rose to high positions. Absolutist dukes encouraged this as it allowed them to employ foreigners in their own service. At the beginning of the troubles the knights were represented by a web of influence among their friends and relatives highly placed in a number of courts.[20]

Rostock, the one remaining sea-town after the cession of Wismar to Sweden under the treaty of Osnabrück, was also powerful in the Estates and usually acted in conjunction with the knights. The forty

---

[16] Hofer, p. 17.

[17] The secularized bishoprics of Schwerin (also called Bützow) and Ratzeburg took no part in the Mecklenburg Estates. Ratzeburg had no constitution while the Estates of Bützow met separately.

[18] W. Mediger, *Mecklenburg, Russland und England-Hannover 1706 – 1721. Ein Beitrag zur Geschichte des Nordischen Krieges* (Hildesheim, 1967), p. 17 n48.

[19] Schwerin, Landständisches Archiv, *Protocol* of 1721. At the diet of 1721 some 250 knights attended, the largest number in living memory.

[20] There were Mecklenburg knights in high positions in Hanover, Prussia, Vienna, Denmark, Sweden and many other courts in the early eighteenth century: Mediger, *Mecklenburg*, p. 13, Vienna, *Den. Rec.* K. 694(4) no. 21.

or so country towns (*Landstädte*), which formed a separate Estate, were often little more than overgrown walled villages largely dependent on the produce of the land outside their gates.[21] What little industry there had ever been had by the reign of Charles VI largely disappeared and the larger towns were almost entirely dependent on brewing for local consumption. There was also some distilling and slaughtering but the whole economy was uniformly agrarian. Quantities of grain, cattle and other agricultural products were exported. The land was poor and required heavy manuring and working. The social dominance of the large knighthood was based on the existence of a large unfree peasantry tied to the soil or evictable from it at the will of the landlord. In earlier centuries agriculture had required a large labour force; the early eighteenth century saw the growing popularity among noble landowners of the Holstein *Koppelwirtschaft*, a more efficient method of land utilization requiring fulltime labourers. Land became more valuable than peasants and the pace of evictions grew as landlords began to take peasant land and 'waste hides' into their domains. The main burden of taxation fell on the peasantry. The knights were exempt from taxation for their persons and their actual knight's fee (*alte Ritterhufen*).[22] As a body the knighthood was deeply conservative and little touched by the Enlightenment. Their stubborn adherence to their constitutional liberties and economic rights in the face of horrendous pressures was amazing.

Relations between the dukes and Estates of Mecklenburg had long been strained before the accession of the egregious duke Charles Leopold (1713 – 47). The dukes quickly found the fetters they had forged for themselves becoming irksome as they, like many of their fellows, wished to flex the new muscles which the treaties of Westphalia had given them, to take part in the exciting and possibly profitable game of power politics and diplomacy, which the peace of 1648 had in theory put within the reach of even the insignificant.[23] After a short period following Westphalia, when the dukes, chastened by their deprivation in 1628 and long dispossession, remained quiet,[24] they began again to try to win

---

[21] Mediger, *Mecklenburg*, p. 5. Rostock's trade had much declined, especially because of Sweden's possession of Warnemünde: Vienna, RHR *Den. Rec.* K. 697, exhibit of 31 October 1718, *Beitrag* B, a description of the poverty of the country and the absence of industry. At this time the towns held over a quarter of the land in the duchies.

[22] Steinmann, pp. xvi, 38 – 9, 44, 65. Mager, pp. 82 – 103, 146. The annual taxes were paid in three equal parts by the knighthood, the ducal domains and the towns.

[23] Mediger, p. 9.

[24] Hofer, p. 43.

advantage from the strategically important position of their lands. This involved a need for more revenue and a tighter control of all aspects of government so that all available resources could be husbanded to finance the new and expansive policies.

In this new theme of a state above territories, the Estates had no part to play except in the provision of money. The age of absolutism was marked by a deep interest in financial rationalisation and attempts to find new sources of money. This bred a movement for closer government control and mercantilist economics, a rash of new projects and attempts to mobilize the resources of individual territories for the benefit of the whole state.[25] In Mecklenburg the Estates proved regrettably unsympathetic to these ambitions. They resisted the idea of a state above provinces and fought hard to prevent the disappearance of their functions in the building of a state in which they had no place. They refused to grant the dukes any more than their traditional dues, stubbornly resisting ducal attempts to establish permanent and fixed annual taxation. When the dukes tried to collect taxes by force the Estates in 1660 appealed to the Emperor, initiating a complex bout of litigation which lasted, without a break, for over a century. Duke Christian I (Louis), a great admirer of Louis XIV, whose name and religion he took in 1663, tried to build up a standing army. He founded the absolutist tradition of the dukes of Schwerin[26] and in 1671 he joined the *Extendisten*, the princes who united against their Estates and proposed to use force to suppress them if necessary and to lend one another troops.[27] In 1708 duke Frederick William allied with the king of Prussia; the treaty contained a provision under which Prussia promised the duke armed aid against his nobility.[28]

The dukes ascribed the problems facing them to the factiousness of the Estates, the Estates to the fact that the dukes were trying to destroy their old-established and dearly bought liberties. The main points at issue were initially the obligation of the Estates to contribute to the imperial and Circle taxes and later, once this obligation had been established, the question of who was to decide

---

25   F. Hinsley, *Power and the Pursuit of Peace* (Cambridge, 1964), pp. 164 – 5, 177 – 8.

26   Güstrow was traditionally less active and after 1701 Strelitz was too weak to adopt anything but a passive role.

27   Feller, pp. 156, 196 – 7 quotes the preamble of the Act of Association of 1671. The founder members were Bavaria, Cologne, Brandenburg and the elector palatine. They bore the name 'Extensionists' because they wished the Emperor to extend the terms of the last imperial recess of 1654 to give them wider powers over their subjects. For Christian Louis's reign see Hofer, pp. 68 ff.

28   Mediger, pp. 19 ff.

the amount and the means of collection of the money, the *quantum et modus contribuendi*.

The detailed story of the constitutional dispute in Mecklenburg has been well told elsewhere;[29] its importance here lies in the way it was dealt with in the aulic council, the various considerations which motivated it and as an illustration of the importance of the imperial supreme judicial authority. The Mecklenburg case is especially interesting as, in the course of it, there took place one of the few examples of an imperial execution which actually achieved anything. A reigning duke was deprived of his government not simply because it was politically advantageous to the Emperor but because he behaved as a vicious tyrant and broke the laws of the Empire and Mecklenburg.

Compared with Mecklenburg, East Frisia was very progressive and in some respects unique in eighteenth-century Germany in the breadth of its democracy and the strength and influence of its Estates. In the Early Middle Ages it had been part of the Frisian nation extending from the Zuider Zee to Jutland and a tradition of 'Frisian liberty' *(Friesische Freiheit)* remained alive there though East Frisia was only a fraction of the former nation.[30] The Estates looked back consciously to a time when representatives of the people had assembled in the open outside Aurich to debate the nation's affairs.[31] This would not have been so important if it had remained only tradition and nostalgia but the Estates, according to the princes, behaved as if part of a sovereign republic subject only to God and continued to insist that the benefits of this liberty were enjoyed by all Frisians of whatever race, Christian or Jew, without distinction.[32]

---

[29]   *Ibid.*, pp. 10 ff. H. N. Witte, *Mecklenburgische Geschichte* (2 vols., Wismar, 1909 – 13), David Franck, *Alt- und neues Mecklenburg*, vols. 17 – 19 (Güstrow and Leipzig, 1753 – 8), O. Vitense, *Geschichte von Mecklenburg* (Gotha, 1920), H. H. Klüver *Beschreibung des Herzogthums Mecklenburg* (6 vols., Hamburg, 1728 – 42), G. Matthias, *Die Mecklenburger Frage in der ersten Hälfte des 18. Jahrhunderts und das Dekret von Mai 1728* (Diss. Halle, 1885), Wick, *Versuche*.

[30]   Vienna, RHR *Den. Rec.* K. 885 fasz. 2 no. vi *Beilage* 224. Hughes, M., 'The East Frisians: the Survival of powerful Provincial Estates in N.W. Germany in the 18th Century' in *Album François Dumont* (Brussels, 1977), pp. 125 – 52.

[31]   Conrad, p. 350. O. Klopp, *Geschichte Ostfrieslands* (2 vols., Hanover, 1854 – 8), vol. I, pp. 78 ff. G. Möhlmann, 'Norder Annalen' in *Quellen zur Geschichte Ostfrieslands* (Aurich, 1959), *passim*.

[32]   Vienna, RHR *Den. Rec.* K. 722(3), exhib. of Emden 8 April ;1720, *ibid.* K. 922(3), exhib. of 7 February 1718.

East Frisia had acquired a prince late, become a fief of the Empire equipped with a large body of customary law and the people continued to enjoy great personal liberty.[33] This and later constitutional agreements were collectively called the *Akkorden*, which together formed the constitution of the country.[34]

The province was quite fertile and in good years enjoyed modest prosperity. Its main income came from dairy products.[35] The population was small; the census taken in 1749 by Prussia revealed that East Frisia, with the province of Harlingerland, had 112,000 people.[36] In direct contrast with most other parts of Germany, its society was characterised by a strong peasantry and a weak nobility. There was no tradition of serfdom and unfreedom. Most land was allodial and not held under feudal tenures. All men holding a small amount of land or possessed of capital of 1,000*Rt.* were enfranchised and represented in the Third Estate (*Dritter* — or *Hausmannsstand*). There was no princely standing army; the princes traditionally employed levies of peasants under elected officers.[37] The prince's rights as supreme bishop of the East Frisian Church were very limited and his people enjoyed wide freedom in the exercise of the Protestant religion. By the concordats of 1599 the prince had virtually abdicated his powers over the resources of the church and the right of election of pastors and teachers was vested in the parishes.[38]

The nobility of the county, the First Estate, was small, weak and comparatively unprivileged. They enjoyed only limited exemption from taxation for their own lands.[39] In 1744 there were only nine nobles with the right of a seat in the diet.[40] The nobles were not feudatories of the prince. Their seats in diets were attached to the possession of a 'lordship' (*Herrlichkeit*), the largest of which carried the title 'Chief' (*Häuptling*), a relic of the time when the free Frisians had united under such men for war. Unlike many German princes, the rulers of East Frisia were unable to find natural allies among the

---

33 J. König, *Verwaltungsgeschichte Ostfrieslands bis zum Aussterben seines Fürstenhauses* (Göttingen, 1955), pp. 304 – 5.

34 The fullest printed collection of these is the two-volume *Ostfriesische Historie*, published in Aurich in 1721. The commentaries by the chancellor Brenneysen are highly polemical.

35 Vienna, RHR *Den. Rec.* K. 924 no. 48 *Beilage* 7.

36 Klopp, vol. II, p. 594.

37 *Ibid.*, p. 590.

38 H. Reimers, *Ostfriesland bis zum Aussterben seines Fürstenhauses* (Bremen, 1925), p. 189. The clergy lost their direct representation in the diet after the Reformation.

39 König, p. 312.

40 Klopp, vol. II, p. 592.

nobles in building absolutism. Princes complained that the unwillingness of these men to serve him forced him to employ foreigners,[41] a cause of complaint by the Estates.

The position of the ruler was constitutionally unusual. The prince of East Frisia was not regarded as ruling by divine right but as the representative of the people organised in Estates. The concept of *Obrigkeit*, the source and nature of the ruler's power, was quite different from that of the rest of the Empire. Sovereignty lay not with the 'prince in parliament' but with the parliament alone, which regarded the prince as its agent and the executor of its wishes. The ruling house, the Cirksenas, were a younger dynasty than many in Germany. Originally chiefs among other chiefs, they owed their position to force. After defeating his rivals, the Ulkenas and tom Brocks, Ulrich Cirksena became sole ruler of the territory in 1439 and accepted East Frisia as a fief of the Empire with the title of count, later elevated to that of prince.[42] Only in the region of Harlingerland, the villages of Esens and Wittmund and the surrounding areas, and the Frisian islands,[43] were the princes sovereign. Elsewhere they were bound to observe the constitutional arrangements theoretically in force before East Frisia became part of the Empire.

The Estates were very strong. The judicial sovereignty of the prince was subject to the supervision of the *Hofgericht*, which enjoyed equality with the prince's own chancery and whose assessors were appointed and paid by the Estates. Financial sovereignty lay with the Estates. Through their College of Administrators and Deputies, elected from all three Estates, they controlled the voting, collection and spending of all taxation. The prince was forced to live off his own revenues or to beg extraordinary subsidies from the Estates which they granted only rarely. The Estates held an annual day of account on 10 May, at which the College presented accounts to deputies of the three Estates. The presence of a princely agent was not obligatory. In addition the Estates had the right to convene if the prince refused to summon a diet at their request. All legislation required their consent, as did any agreement to hire

---

41 Vienna, RHR *Den. Rec.* K.885 fasz. 1 no. 1 §78.

42 Enno Louis was declared a prince in 1656 and the title became hereditary under George Christian in 1662.

43 Klopp, vol. II, p. 457. The prince claimed that these lands were a fief of Guelders and therefore not subject to the Empire. There was long litigation at the end of the seventeenth century as the princess-regent refused to extend the burden of imperial taxation to these lands. The loyal peasantry was often called out and civil war had more than once appeared imminent. Harlingerland gave the prince a regular income of about 32,000*Rt.*: *ibid*, p. 399.

troops. Not only at the centre was the government weak: the East Frisians enjoyed wide local autonomy through elected officials.[44] The system had an unpleasant side; the costs of administration were low and many local officials lived from fees. The administrative and judicial systems were outdated and there was definite corruption.[45]

The leading force in the Estates was the port city of Emden, which dominated the province. Its strength and wealth had reached their height in the last decades of the sixteenth century when it had been able to take advantage of the troubles in the Netherlands.[46] When the Dutch blocked the Ems river in 1599, five hundred vessels were held up at Emden.[47] Its prosperity soon declined as a result of renewed Dutch competition, the silting of the river and, it was said, the lack of a German fleet to protect its commerce.[48] The city made no secret of its poverty in the eighteenth century. In October 1723[49] it admitted that it had enormous debts and could not meet the cost of maintaining harbours, roads, bridges, fortifications and a garrison. After 1700 it ceased paying its due share of taxation levied in the country.[50] The steeper the city's ecconomic decline, the more stubbornly it clung to its political dominance of East Frisia. The Estates' treasury and the College of Administrators were located in the city and it contained the only standing army in the country, the *Landschaftstruppen*, a garrison maintained at the cost of all the Estates. In 1721 the force consisted of four companies of sixty-five men each but many were unfit.[51] Emden used these troops to strengthen her position over the other Estates, to resist the prince and to collect taxes by force. Only the Reformed religion was permitted within the city walls and if the Lutheran prince resided there, a rare event, he was compelled to attend Calvinist services. Both Protestant faiths were legal in East Frisia.[52]

The city's virtual independence originated in an urban revolt in 1595, in which the so-called Popular Party, with open Dutch

44 König, pp. 331 – 7.
45 Klopp, vol. II, pp. 587 – 8, 461 – 2.
46 Reimers, p. 166.
47 Klopp, vol. II, p. 413.
48 Reimers, p. 191. Count Enno III (1599 – 1625) had dreams of a German naval base at Emden with himself as imperial admiral.
49 Vienna, RHR *Den. Rec.* K. 925(4).
50 Klopp, vol. II, pp. 472 – 3. In 1730 its income was estimated at 147,000Fl but it had debts amounting to millions: Aurich, *Rep.* 4 C III a no. 113/2.
51 Vienna, RHR Den. Rec. K. 884(2) no. 8 fol. 379 – 85.
52 Vienna, RHR *Den. Rec.* K. 919(1), exhib. of the prince 20 December 1702. Klopp, vol. II, pp. 112 – 14.

support, overthrew the prince's city government.[53] Perhaps as a token of its new freedom, in 1604 the city invited the Herborn Law professor, Johannes Althusius, to become its *syndicus*, or chief administrative and legal official, a position he held until his death in 1638.[54] Althusius probably owed this honour to his radical political views made known in his *Politica methodice digesta*, published the year before his appointment. His experience of practical politics in Emden led him to strengthen and extend his theories. He worked on behalf of the East Frisian Estates as diplomat, legal adviser and publicist and his prestige probably did much to strengthen links between the city and the United Provinces. His doctrines are clearly discernible in the documents produced by the Estates in this period and he was able to turn his academic pen to political propaganda with ease, providing the Estates with that most valuable asset in a legalistic age, a clever polemicist. As *syndicus* he had the opportunity to put his ideas into practice and his experience led him to publish an enlarged edition of his *Politica* in 1610, in which East Frisian conditions clearly served to provide further illustrations and examples to justify his arguments. In East Frisia there seemed to exist these very conditions and phenomena which previously had appeared only in the dry paragraphs of legal treatises.

Althusius' ideas remained an active yeast in East Frisian politics well into the eighteenth century and, according to the prince, his pernicious views continued to guide and motivate Emden's policies.[55] In a letter of 7 May 1722 to the aulic council the prince set out in great detail the steps by which the city, with foreign help and in pursuit of totally false principles, had made itself virtually independent.[56]

Most significant, Emden was an important channel for foreign influence in East Frisia, a major reason for the Estates' retention of power. Situated in the extreme corner of the Empire, the province was remote and vulnerable and in its history fell prey to many states. Most important in the seventeenth and still strong in the eighteenth century was the influence of the States-General. The Dutch assumed a right of interference in the country based on the fact that they had mediated many of the agreements which formed

---

[53] Reimers, pp. 177–80.
[54] Joachimsen, *Der deutsche Staatsgedanke*, p. 48. O. von Gierke, *Natural Law and the Theory of Society* (Cambridge, 1935) and *The Development of Political Theory* (London, 1939).
[55] Vienna RHR *Den. Rec.* K. 885 fasz. 1 no. 1 §66, a letter of George Albert to the Emperor quoting Grotius' *Annales Belgicae*.
[56] *Ibid.*, I. 885 fasz. 1 no. 3.

the East Frisian constitution. At the Emden diet of 1606 representatives of England and the Dutch guaranteed an agreement between the count and the Estates, promising to act by force if necessary against any attempt by the count to break it. The *Recess* of 1606 established the College of Administrators. The Osterhusen *Accord* of 16 May 1611, mediated by the Dutch, was regarded as the East Frisian *Magna Carta* and the keystone of the country's liberties.[57] During the Dutch revolt many refugees had fled to Emden and East Frisia, strengthening the Calvinist faith and the tradition of liberty. The Dutch put a garrison into the city to prevent its capture by the Spaniards, a fate which had befallen Rees and Wesel on the lower Rhine, and it remained there.[58] There was also a small Dutch force in the border fort at Leerort. During the Dutch wars of independence and the Anglo-Dutch wars of the seventeenth century the city's commerce had been treated as belligerent by the powers at war with the States-General. The Dutch had a deep interest in preventing the growth of a strong state on their borders and regarded East Frisia as 'a province serving the welfare of their republic as a main defence wall'.[59] There was a committee of the States-General concerned with East Frisian affairs and they claimed a permanent right of inspection in the province.[60] At the beginning of the reign of Charles VI there was considerable mistrust of the Dutch in Vienna, where it was believed that they had ambitions against the whole Rhine and, having fewer enemies, were more dangerous than the French.[61]

Other states were anxious to prevent East Frisia becoming a Dutch satellite and they also found it advantageous to fish in the troubled constitutional waters of the country. Rather than run the risk of putting troops in the hands of the prince, the Estates met their military obligations to the Empire and the Circle by paying substitution money to neighbouring states. This reinforced the

---

[57] Reimers, pp. 198 – 200.

[58] Klopp, vol. II p. 569 estimates the number of the garrison, including dependants and servants, at 4,500. In 1721 there were only three companies of some twenty-eight men each and a further dozen in Leerort, but they were easily reinforceable by land or water: Vienna, RHR *Den. Rec.* K. 884(2) no. 8 fol. 379 – 85.

[59] *Ibid.*, K. 907, *votum* of the aulic council 23 October 1725, fol. 6 – 7.

[60] *Londorpii Acta Publica* vol. VII, p. 984, resolution of the States-General 28 April 1655 setting up a commission in The Hague to settle the points at issue in the country and, if necessary, to dictate a settlement to both sides. *Ibid.*, p. 1025, resolution of 23 October 1655. *Ibid.*, vol. VIII pp. 216 – 17, resolution of 18 December 1657. Aurich, *Rep.* 4 C III c no. 140 fol. 1, Dutch resolution of 10 December 1727.

[61] Hantsch, *Schönborn*, p. 130, n14.

abiding evil of the country, the readiness of both the prince and the Estates to take recourse to foreigners for help.[62] Between 1682 and 1702 the Estates paid a total of 2,088,762Fl to Brandenburg and Münster in substitution subsidies and for the maintenance of the Salva Guardia, a small force of imperial troops put into East Frisia under an imperial *Conservatorium* of 1677 and permanently stationed there.[63] This *Conservatorium*, which instructed the convening princes of the Rhenish-Westphalian Circle to preserve peace in the country, gave the bishop of Münster, an old enemy of the Dutch,[64] a legal sanction to interfere and the elector of Brandenburg a welcome opportunity to obtain a foothold in a province with access to the North Sea. In 1676 a Münster force entered East Frisia on the invitation of the princess-regent to overawe the Estates and 6,000 troops entered the country again in 1680 under a substitution agreement with the Estates.[65] Both the Estates and the princess were anxious to secure the support of Brandenburg, whose possessions on the Lower Rhine made her a power in north-west Germany. Christine Charlotte offered the elector the use of the port of Greetsiehl in return for help against her subjects but he saw more hope of lasting influence in a connexion with the Estates.[66] On 5 November 1682 a force of four hundred Prussian marines took Greetsiehl under the pretext of the imperial *Conservatorium* on the Circle.[67] Emden became the seat of the Brandenburg admiralty and the Brandenburg Africa Company under a treaty between the elector and the Estates signed on the 8 November 1682.[68] The city was also to be the base for the Brandenburg navy. This seemed to offer the impoverished and depopulated city an opportunity of recovering its former position and prosperity and, although

---

[62] Vienna, RHR *Vota* K. 44, protocol of 9 April 1677.
[63] Klopp, vol. II, pp. 396, 454, 465. There is a *Facta Species* on the Salva Guardia in Vienna, RHR *Den. Rec.* K. 924 Lit. B fol. 10 – 73. In 1678 200 men from the imperial garrison in Bonn entered East Frisia to protect the country. In 1682 it was increased to 400 out of fear of Dutch intervention but thereafter its numbers fell. At its smallest it contained only some twenty men.
[64] Reimers, p. 223, *Londorpii Acta Publica* vol. IX, pp. 416 – 18. In 1665 the bishop complained to the Dutch about their activity in East Frisia, which he regarded as a preserve of his bishopric. Münster was one of the earliest German states to build a standing army and fought against the Dutch in alliance with England in 1672.
[65] Vienna, RHR *Den. Rec.* K. 917(1), exhib. of 26 October 1676. *Ibid.*, Reichskanzlei *Vortr.* fasz. 5c fol. 52. The Estates were able to outbid the princess-regent and buy off her potential ally.
[66] Reimers, pp. 233 – 4.
[67] *Londorpii Acta Publica* vol. XI, pp. 443 – 4, memorandum to the Dutch 13 November 1682.
[68] Reimers, p. 235, Klopp, vol. II, pp. 450 – 1.

these commercial and naval ambitions died with their initiator, this agreement began a period of co-operation between the Estates and Brandenburg which lasted until the incorporation of the county into Prussia in 1744.[69] Many of the leaders of the Estates during the reign of Charles VI were in receipt of pensions from Prussia and held nominal Prussian offices.

The Brandenburg troops in the country were taken into the allegiance of the College under the treaty of 8 November and they swore to maintain the constitution. Thereafter they were always available to reinforce the Emden troops and provided the Estates with another weapon to use against the prince if required. In return the Estates paid Prussia 15,000Rt. a year.[70] In May 1702 they again entered an arrangement with Prussia for the supply of the East Frisian contingent for the imperial war against France at a cost of 20,000Rt. a year.[71]

Both East Frisia and Mecklenburg were ideal victim states: they were too small to defend themselves but were large enough or strategically or economically important enough to be coveted by their neighbours. The imperial execution in Mecklenburg and the course of imperial action in East Frisia must be viewed against the background of imperial diplomacy inside the Empire and in Europe. Both states were small and insignificant in themselves but very significant in the politics of North Germany.

After the Thirty Years' War two states had grown to a dominant position in north Germany, Brunswick-Lüneburg and Brandenburg-Prussia. Their steady territorial expansion and the eventual assumption by both of royal titles strengthened them. In retrospect it is easy to overlook the fact that it was never certain in the late seventeenth century which of the two would eventually gain hegemony in north Germany. The acquisition of the English crown by the elector of Hanover, though it brought temporary advantage, probably ruined Hanover's chances of carrying off the victory. It distracted the king-elector's attention and the so-called 'Hanoverian interest' played a part in English policy for only a short time. There had been great state-building activity in the house of Brunswick after the Thirty Years' War.[72] By a combination of luck and judicious co-operation with the Emperor, the Hanoverians built up a substantial state and obtained an electorate. There was also an established tradition of collaboration between Hanover and the

---

69 *Ibid.*, pp. 418 – 30, 565. The fleet was sold or rotted away.
70 Klopp, vol. II pp. 405 – 6.
71 *Ibid.*, p. 475. Vienna, RHR *Den. Rec.* K. 884(2) exhib. of the prince 13 January 1721 (B) fol. 256.
72 Holborn, vol. II, p. 21. R. Lodge, *Great Britain and Prussia in the 18th Century* (Oxford, 1923), pp. 5 – 6.

other Welf lines such as Brunswick-Wolfenbüttel.[73] A real chance of winning decisive advantage came with the accession to the Prussian throne of the clumsy, hesitant and fearful Frederick William I: Prussia was fortunate that both Hanover and Saxony were distracted by extra-German interests.

In the period of reorganization after the peace of Utrecht a number of smaller states were rising in Europe, their rise marked by intense egotism and ambition.[74] Brandenburg-Prussia was typical of these states. So close was the balance of strength between the larger states that, after the collapse of the Swedish empire, the rising powers could no longer hope to make large gains of territory. Prussia became especially adept at snapping up small territories whenever the chance presented itself. In Frederick William I's *Instruction* to his successor, drawn up in February 1722, the king laid down the principle that Prussia's main interest lay in the acquisition of *Land und Leute*, as these alone could strengthen the house. Prussia had legitimate claims to the succession to Jülich and Berg, Mecklenburg and East Frisia.[75]

The German portions of Sweden's empire also offered ideal areas of expansion for both Hanover and Prussia and the natural lines of expansion led in different directions: Hanover had ambitions in Bremen and Verden and Prussia in Pomerania. There was intense rivalry between them for control of Mecklenburg, strategically the most important medium-sized principality in North Germany, where their ambitions crossed, and of East Frisia with its desirable position on the Ems and its access to the North Sea.

The little state of Mecklenburg-Strelitz rapidly became a virtual tributary of Hanover, to which the duke looked for protection against his cousin in Schwerin.[76] Hanover's influence in Mecklenburg was founded on the elector's position as director of the Lower Saxon Circle. In the seventeenth century this Circle had enjoyed the reputation of being *reichspatriotisch* and *gut kaiserlich*, as the duke of Celle needed the Emperor's support to further his own ambitions

---

73 Naumann, p. 67 n35: the Brunswick-Blankenburg line had the vote for Grubenhagen in the imperial diet but it was not permitted to vote differently from Hanover.

74 Hinsley, pp. 173–6.

75 *Acta Borussica.* Behördenorganisation, vol. II, p. 461. Vienna, Reichskanzlei Vortr. fasz. 5d *Ratisbonensia* 8 November 1687 – February 1688, a Brandenburg memorandum of 14 December 1687. In return for her losses in the imperial war Brandenburg wanted the free cities of Mühlhausen, Nordhausen and Dortmund, one million *Reichstaler* and the reversionary right to East Frisia. The elector was still insisting on this in 1692: *Referat* of the Bohemian aulic chancery 8 February 1692, *ibid.*, fasz. 5c fol. 242–50.

76 Ballschmieter, p. 107. Mediger, p. 15.

and his loyalty in the French wars was rewarded with an electorate. As Circle director, Hanover often supported the dukes of Mecklenburg against their Estates, especially in the matter of the collection of Circle taxes.[77]

Brandenburg had long exercised influence in Mecklenburg, possessing an old-established *Expektanz*, right of eventual succession, on the duchies. There was also a tradition of intermarriage between the two houses.[78]

Both states also had claims in East Frisia.[79] In a letter to his agent in Vienna, dated 24 January 1689,[80] the elector Frederick III of Brandenburg claimed an *interesse radicatum* in East Frisia because of the presence there of his Africa Company. Hanover's efforts to secure influence in the country[81] were, according to Frederick, motivated solely by the desire to injure Brandenburg. In 1694 Brandenburg obtained imperial confirmation of his *Expektanz* on East Frisia.[82] This seemed to cancel the mutual succession pact between the houses of Brunswick and East Frisia entered in 1691.[83]

[77] Hofer, pp. 69, 71–2.
[78] Mediger, pp. 6, 19 ff.
[79] H. Rother, *Die Auseinandersetzung zwischen Preussen und Hanover um Ostfriesland von 1690 bis 1740* (Diss. Göttingen, 1951).
[80] Aurich, Ostfr. Landschaft Dep. I no. 3244.
[81] In 1693 Hanoverian mediation produced an agreement between the princess-regent and the Estates, the Hanover treaty.
[82] Droysen, vol. IV/1, pp. 145–56.
[83] Klopp, vol. II, p. 463.

4

The European dimension

An abiding feature of German history after 1648 was the importance
of foreign influence. No change or development in imperial policy
could be regarded with indifference by the major European powers
and the imperial supreme judicial authority could not be exercised
in a vacuum, especially when it involved areas of great interest to
the Empire's neighbours. After 1714, in a new Europe dominated
by a cluster of roughly equal powers with none in a position to claim
hegemony, the Emperor was one among the great powers.[1]
Austria's position among the powers and the weight this could give
to the Emperor's ambitions in Germany had an important role in
the 'imperial reaction', which coincided with a period when
Austria's military and diplomatic successes masked, briefly, her
inherent weaknesses.

In 1719 the Emperor seemed in a stronger position than for many
years, having fought two victorious wars and won great gains in
territory and prestige. The peace, however, was unsatisfactory and
many Austrian and German statesmen were left with a bitter taste
of desertion and unfulfilled hopes in their mouths. The French
candidate retained the Spanish throne and France kept most of the
territory she had taken from the Empire during Louis XIV's reign.
The Empire fought on after the peace of Utrecht in the hope of
regaining at least Strasburg but there was a sad discrepancy
between its massive territorial demands and its miserable military
performance. It was felt that Britain and the Dutch had deserted the
Emperor when their own desires had been satisfied. It would have
been naive to have expected the Maritime Powers to fight on only to

---

[1] Hinsley, pp. 173–6. After periods of Spanish and French 'predominance',
no one power could claim hegemony after 1714: J. Chagniot, *Les temps
modernes de 1661 à 1789*, section 2 'La prépondérance partagée 1714–63'
(Paris, 1973). P. Dickson, *The Financial Revolution in England 1688–1756*
(London, 1967), p. 23: 'it is well to remember that the "prépondérance
anglaise" in this period was less evident . . . to contemporary observers
than it has seemed to posterity'.

obtain Alsace for the Empire but their off-hand rejection of German protests was a blow to collective German pride. Austria's gains, impressive on paper, in fact brought her expensive new commitments. It was quickly to become clear that the real losers of the war of the Spanish Succession were Austria and Spain.

Although many outstanding points were settled at Utrecht, there remained a live fear that war could easily break out again.[2] A residue of unresolved conflict remained in two areas and in both lay the seeds of a renewed continent-wide war: Austrian and Spanish ambitions crossed dangerously in Italy while in the Baltic the Northern Allies were busy dividing Sweden's empire among themselves. Not all the powers of Europe saw the settlement of 1713–14 as inaugurating an era of peace. Some, seeing the chance of gains in war and disturbance, were ready to play the part of trouble-makers; others needed a period of peace badly. The War of Spanish Succession had been long and wide-reaching: it had taken a heavy toll. Economic weapons had been used with effect: the economic blockade of the allies had helped to make the crisis of 1709–10 one of the most damaging in French history. The costs of war, rising sharply since the sixteenth century,[3] continued to rise and after 1714 states would have to consider carefully before investing heavily in war in the hope of making sufficient gains to show a profit. The idea of war feeding war, if it had ever been more than wishful thinking, stood clearly revealed as an illusion except perhaps in the colonial field. The possibility of substantial territorial gains within Europe looked remote after the tidying-up operation which partitioned the Spanish and Swedish empires. It seemed that any gain likely to upset a balance of power which had become more delicate after Utrecht would be frustrated by the enforced mediation of those powers anxious for their own reasons to preserve peace.

After 1714 three among the primary powers of Europe were concerned to keep the peace: Britain, France and the Emperor. In 1715 the ruling dynasties of France and Britain were insecure. George I sat uneasily on his throne and it was a major aim of his foreign policy to deprive the Stuarts of foreign friends. The precariousness of the Protestant Succession forced Britain into closer dependence on the Dutch, who had guaranteed to maintain it by armed force. As Britain would be unwilling to go to war if the Dutch were neutral and in a position to nibble at British trade the 'maritime powers' became virtually a unit in European diplomacy,

[2] B. Williams, *Stanhope: a study in eighteenth century war and diplomacy* (London, 1932), p. 273.

[3] G. Parker, *The Army of Flanders and the Spanish Road* (Cambridge, 1972), pp. 6 ff.

though relations between them were often strained. Dutch finances had suffered in the French wars and the peace party at The Hague had persuasive arguments on its side when it advocated a policy of non-involvement for the sickly republic. Britain was especially anxious to avoid war with Spain; the promotion and preservation of commerce, the other vital interest of Britain which George I's Whig government existed to serve, also dictated a peace policy.[4] The colonial trade may have had a fructifying effect on the economy but the most lucrative markets lay in Europe, especially in Spain. In December 1715 Britain achieved a very favourable commercial treaty with Spain which completed the exclusion of French competition. In May 1726 this was supplemented by a more favourable Asiento treaty giving profitable access to the Spanish overseas markets.[5]

In France Louis XIV's successor was a young child not expected to live long. In the event of his death without an heir a disputed succession seemed unavoidable, with the regent Orleans and Philip V of Spain as claimants. This might in turn reopen the whole question of the future of Spain. Although Philip had renounced his succession rights at Utrecht, it was held in France that this renunciation was questionable under French fundamental law.[6] The regent too was not popular. It was in his interest to maintain the Utrecht settlement and the division of the thrones of Spain and France. In addition France had suffered badly in the Spanish Succession war and needed time to recover.[7] There were sharp divisions within the French ruling group; in September 1715 the regent, with the support of the *parlement* of Paris, dismissed the regency council prescribed in Louis XIV's will and began to rule alone. Louis XIV's old ministers, representing anti-English and anti-Habsburg policies, remained influential in spite of their exclusion from power. They formed an opposition group with considerable support from French public opinion. All these factors contributed to a temporary weakness in French foreign policy

---

[4] Wilson, pp. 49 – 50.
[5] Williams, *Stanhope*, pp. 207 – 8, 434. The promise of the *Asiento* was not fulfilled. English traders in the Spanish American markets suffered chronic difficulties, largely because of the inability of the Spanish crown to control its own local agents: G. C. Gibbs, 'Parliament and the Treaty of Quadruple Alliance' in R. Hatton and J. S. Bromley (eds.), *William III and Louis XIV* (Liverpool, 1968), pp. 296 – 7, nn40,41.
[6] As the closest male relative of Louis XIV after the minor Louis XV, Philip was in French law heir presumptive.
[7] The financial weakness of the French crown also made necessary a less active and therefore less costly diplomacy: Chance, *Antecedents*, pp. 709 – 10.

symbolised by close cooperation with England.[8] French diplomatic freedom of action was curtailed, especially under the rule of the duke of Bourbon, who became premier of France on the death of the regent in 1723.[9] Even when France regained economic and political stability under Fleury and began to take the initiative again, a conscious peace policy was maintained.[10]

Of the 'peaceful' powers, the Emperor was the weakest and found it most difficult to maintain his position among the great powers. His involvement in two wars had brought him large gains in territory but little in extra resources to protect and exploit them. Charles VI was the last living male Habsburg and the future of his dynasty was insecure. The financial weakness of his state was worse than before, in spite of his efforts to deal with its basic causes.[11] Of the three, the Emperor was least satisfied with the Utrecht settlement but least able to do anything about this. His gains in the east were vulnerable in the face of a possible revival of Turkish power and discontent among the perennially insurrectionary Magyars. One of Charles's first actions on coming to power was to settle the eight-year-old Hungarian rebellion by the concessionary peace of Szatmar in 1711.[12] The areas gained under the peace of Passarowitz produced little in disposable revenue and needed large garrisons. The gains in Italy and the Netherlands were substantial on paper but, Austrian statesmen suspected, they had been deliberately chosen by the allies to bring the Emperor no advantage. The settlement seemed to have been designed to do the least possible damage to the interests of France and the 'maritime

---

[8]   Williams, *Stanhope*, p. 228. The French were frightened of isolation but Mecenseffy probably goes too far when she argues (p. 3) that under Walpole English diplomacy 'dominated' Europe and that French ministers were totally dependent on him or (*ibid.*, p. 5) that England was guardian of the European balance of power and held the Dutch and French firmly in tow.

[9]   Williams, *Stanhope*, p. 431. Wilson, pp. 18, 20, 114: 'The sacrifice of French freedom of action was the unenviable heritage which Fleury was forced to accept from his predecessor.'

[10] *Ibid.*, p. 54.

[11] Aretin, 'Kaiser Joseph I' pp. 697 – 8. In spite of subsidies from the maritime powers, the greater part of the financial outlay for the Turkish and Spanish Succession wars came from the Austrian lands, which were too poor to provide the resources to fight wars in many theatres simultaneously. Charles VI was deeply interested in commercial expansion and his reign saw concerted efforts to increase Austrian trade and to develop Fiume and Trieste. However, he contributed to his own troubles by his lavish court expenditure, especially on music and gifts: Mecenseffy, p. 83 n20.

[12] H. Hantsch, *Die Geschichte Österreichs* 3rd ed. (2 vols., Graz etc., 1962), vol. II, pp. 93 – 4.

powers' and was seen by the Emperor and others as a betrayal.[13] His territorial gains were scattered and far from the centre of Habsburg power. In Italy a revival of Spanish power could easily cut Naples off from Milan and defence was difficult, especially as Sicily went to Savoy in the Utrecht peace. Sardinia was useless to the Emperor.[14] The Austrian Netherlands were especially isolated and exposed.[15] The terms under which Charles VI took them over from the Anglo-Dutch interim government were most unfavourable. The privileges of the provinces were specifically retained and the Emperor found it most difficult to prise money out of the Estates to pay for troops sent from Austria. The annual deficit in the provinces' budget was about one million *Gulden*. The opportunities to increase indirect revenues by an expansion of trade were hamstrung by the Dutch closure of the Scheldt and an enforced commercial treaty with the 'maritime powers', which opened the Austrian Netherlands to exploitation by them. Charles tried to realize some of their potential by chartering the Ostend commercial company in December 1722.[16] In return for a share of the profits, Charles, as ruler of the Netherlands, gave the company a thirty-year monopoly of trade with India, Africa and the East and West Indies under the imperial flag. It was initially very successful, to the disgust of the sea powers, and the company became an important factor in the diplomatic manoeuvrings of the next ten years. It was ironical that the Austrian government received no direct benefit from the Ostend company as the yield of increased tolls went to the government in Brussels not to Vienna. The company did nothing to make the Netherlands less of a liability; if anything, because of Charles VI's passion for commercial enterprises, it made the Emperor more vulnerable to pressure. The initial success of the company was also due to unusual circumstances, especially the

---

13   Williams, *Stanhope*, pp. 157 – 8. It was a significant sign of the Emperor's bitterness that in the Baden peace with France he did not guarantee the Protestant Succession in Britain.

14   It was in Britain's Mediterranean commercial interests to have a non-maritime state, Savoy or Austria, in southern Italy. In addition the king of Savoy was a protégé of England. Under the terms of Utrecht he had reversionary rights to the Spanish throne and was a potential heir of the British throne.

15   In 1668 under an agreement with France to partition Spain's possessions, Leopold I gave up his claims to the Netherlands. Thereafter the Austrian Habsburgs were more interested in Spain itself and the Italian lands: Aretin, 'Kaiser Joseph I', *passim*.

16   H. Pirenne, *Histoire de Belgique*, vol. V (Brussels, 1926), pp. 174 – 8, 191 – 200. M. Huisman, *La Belgique commerciale sous l'Empereur Charles VI. La Compagnie d'Ostende* (Brussels/Paris, 1902). Naumann, p. 86.

very high price of tea, and it is unlikely that its high profit levels could have been sustained.[17]

The long-standing demand of the Dutch for a barrier of fortresses, garrisoned by their troops but paid for by the Austrian Netherlands, further burdened the Emperor's possession of the Belgian provinces. Without a powerful military establishment the country remained an open door for the French to enter north-west Germany and the United Provinces. The cost of maintaining this establishment was an added burden on stretched imperial resources.[18]

Alongside these three were a number of smaller powers, close to one another in resources, some on the way up in the world, enriched in many cases by the spoils of the Spanish and Swedish empires, such as Prussia and Savoy, and some, like Spain, Sweden and Denmark, in decline. A new feature in the picture was the emergence of Russia, firmly established as a factor in western European politics, even though tsar Peter I did not regard this area as of primary importance to his country. The division of the Spanish and Swedish empires had removed a source of easy gains for acquisitive powers and in the period after 1715 they had to play for much smaller gains. The next expected source of significant territories for disposal were the Habsburg hereditary lands and the belief that they would be dismembered on the death of Charles VI grew throughout his reign.

It was to meet this threat that Charles produced the enactment sometimes seen as the most important feature of his reign, the Pragmatic Sanction.[19] This had nothing to do with the Holy Roman Empire directly but began life as a purely internal dynastic arrangement of the Habsburg family. It originated in 1703 as a agreement between Leopold I and his two sons that female heirs might succeed to the whole Austrian Habsburg inheritance, first united under Leopold. In April 1713 Charles altered it to place his

---

[17] Wilson, p. 170 n4, K. Degryse, 'De Oostendse Chinahandel', *Revue Belge* (1974), pp. 306–47. Gibbs, G.C., 'Britain and the Alliance of Hanover', *EHR* (1958), pp. 404–30, advises against overestimating the seriousness of British opposition to the Ostend Company, though there were reports of Jacobite involvement in it.

[18] Mecenseffy, p. 7 describes the Netherlands as 'a leaden weight on the pinions of the imperial eagle'. As early as 1715 there were proposals in Vienna for an exchange of the Netherlands for Bavaria, a scheme often revived in the eighteenth century but usually seen as highly undesirable by other European states: Gehling, p. 120, Williams, *Stanhope*, p. 163.

[19] W. Michael, *Zur Entstehung der Pragmatischen Sanktion Karls VI* (Basle, 1939). Ziekursch, p. 84. Feller, pp. 198–9 quotes the prayers offered at the election of Charles VI containing a specific reference to the fact that he was last of his line.

own as yet unborn daughters before his two nieces, the two daughters of Joseph I, in the order of succession. More important, the Sanction contained the first statement of the indivisibility of the Habsburg lands, creating for the first time a Habsburg 'empire'. When Charles's nieces were married, Maria Josepha to the electoral prince of Saxony in August 1719 and Maria Amalia to the son of the elector of Bavaria in September 1722, both had to renounce all claims to the Habsburg lands. Charles had only one live son and he died in infancy in 1716. The Utrecht settlement guaranteed only the succession of male heirs. The sanction became politically significant in 1720 with the beginning of Charles's campaign to have it ratified by the Estates of the various provinces he held.[20] Although it only gradually acquired international importance, it was an additional factor predisposing Charles VI to a policy of peace.

In the period after Utrecht France, Britain and the Emperor tried to construct a system of collective security to preserve peace and contain trouble makers.[21] There was a scramble for alliances after 1715 as each power tried to come in from the cold of diplomatic isolation; all sought security in a comprehensive package of alliances to guard against all possible dangers. This system survived as long as Charles VI was alive though the signs of its breakdown were visible before 1740. At first the alliances were fluid and for some time an early 'diplomatic revolution' seemed possible with the division of Europe into two alliance systems on broadly religious lines, with France, the Emperor, Spain, Bavaria and Sweden against the sea powers, Denmark, Hanover and Branden-burg-Prussia. This potential Catholic alliance, based on a reconcilia-tion between the Emperor and France, was given a boost by the Emperor's difficulty with the Dutch over the Barrier in 1715. In November 1715 France was ready to make concessions to the Austrians in Italy but not to abandon any of Louis XIV's conquests from Germany.[22] The negotiations lasted without result until late 1716. Instead of this, a novel system aimed at keeping the peace came into being with the signing of three alliances, the Anglo-

20 Not only did this ratification give it extra weight but was also legally necessary as it altered in some cases the feudal terms under which a province was held and the established order of succession: A. Fournier, 'Zur Entstehungsgeschichte der pragmatischen Sanktion Kaiser Karls VI', HZ, vol. 38 (1877), pp. 16 – 47.

21 M. A. Thomson, 'The Safeguarding of the Protestant Succession' and 'Self-Determination and Collective Security as Factors in English and French Foreign Policy 1689 – 1718' in William III and Louis XIV, pp. 250, 271 – 86, sees the beginning of the system in 1698 with the First Partition Treaty.

22 M. Braubach, Versailles und Wien von Ludwig XIV bis Kaunitz. Vorstadien der diplomatischen Revolution im 18. Jahrhundert (Bonn, 1952), pp. 86 – 104.

imperial defensive Westminster treaty of June 1716, the Triple Alliance of France and Britain of November 1716, later joined by the Dutch, and the Quadruple Alliance of France, Britain and the Emperor of August 1718.[23] All three alliances were concerned mainly with the threatening situation in the Mediterranean.

From this point on Anglo-French cooperation was to remain a major factor in European diplomacy until the early 1730s.[24] Anglo-imperial collaboration in peace-keeping was to be short lived. There was little in common between them as was revealed in the negotiations leading to the Quadruple Alliance. Britain wanted peace and security, the Emperor a means of winning what he felt had been lost at Utrecht. Relations were not eased by British support of Dutch demands in the Barrier question and attempts to hustle the Emperor into settling with the Dutch to bring them into the alliance.[25] Britain was not prepared to promise aid in obtaining Spain and Sicily and in preventing any Bourbon prince obtaining territory in Italy, as Charles wanted. The Emperor needed an alliance to secure his rear while conducting the war against the Turks which had broken out in mid-1716 after Turkish attacks on Venetian possessions in the Adriatic. The Emperor was compelled to join an alliance on less than ideal terms as the security of his Italian possessions demanded the continued presence of a British squadron in the Mediterranean.[26] On the other hand, events in the north seemed to be moving in the Emperor's favour. Opinion in Britain was increasingly worried by the possibility of a reversal of alliances and cooperation between Russia and Sweden to monopolize Baltic trade and, more sinister, mount a Stuart restoration attempt.[27] The so-called Whig Split in England in April 1717 seemed

---

[23]   W. Michael, *Englische Geschichte*, vol. I, pp. 672 – 3. The Westminster treaty was a mutual guarantee of existing rights and possessions. Williams, *Stanhope*, ch. XI for the negotiations leading to the Quadruple Alliance, the key to the European security system. The Dutch were expected to join but failed to do so: *ibid.*, pp. 449 – 50. See Gibbs, 'Parliament and the Treaty of Quadruple Alliance', pp. 294 – 5 on Spain's vigorous propaganda campaign in the United Provinces to keep the Dutch out of the alliance.

[24]   Though some sections of opinion in Britain regarded it as unnatural: Gibbs, 'Parliament and the Treaty of Quadruple Alliance', p. 289.

[25]   W. Michael, *Englische Geschichte*, vol. II, pp. 637f. The Emperor was also irritated by the Anglo-Spanish commercial treaty of December 1715 and an Anglo-Dutch agreement of February 1716, under which Britain supported Dutch demands against the Emperor.

[26]   Williams, *Stanhope*, pp. 303 – 4.

[27]   J. J. Murray, *George I, the Baltic and the Whig Split* (London, 1969), pp. 203 – 4. Fears were increased by the danger of collaboration between Russia and Prussia after a meeting of the tsar and Frederick William I in November 1716: Williams, *Stanhope*, pp. 211 – 29.

to reinforce the influence there of the Hanoverian party and their Whig allies, who had tried to pursue a policy of using British resources in the service of George I as elector of Hanover. Hanover's ambitions towards Sweden's German possessions were likely to have a greater chance of success if the Emperor was sympathetic to them. The fact that the conduct of British foreign policy came into the hands of the flexible Stanhope was a small gain for the Emperor, as it gave him some slight leverage in London,[28] but all this was insufficient to offset his basic weakness.

The first part of Charles VI's reign, the period of the 'imperial reaction', can be seen in diplomatic terms as a prelude to the Spanish-imperial alliance of 1725, a deep change in the European system which has not received the attention given to the reversal of alliances of 1756, probably because it did not last. This sudden and unexpected end of long-standing hostility and the restoration of the Vienna-Madrid axis of the seventeenth century was in some ways a natural result of the frustration of two powers denied the opportunity to bustle at will in a Europe controlled by an arrangement between France and the sea powers.

The Emperor's acquisition of former Spanish possessions in Italy revived the dormant Italian element in imperial foreign policy just when that area was becoming a Spanish preoccupation.[29] Since the division of Charles V's empire it had been Spanish policy to weaken imperial rights in Italy. On the death of Charles II of Spain there grew in Vienna a determination to revive imperial power there; the wealth and strategic importance of Italy and memories of the exploits of medieval German emperors in the peninsula caused a revival of interest which has been regarded as part of the 'imperial reaction'.[30] In a dynastic agreement of 1703, which divided the Spanish and Austrian Habsburg lands between Leopold's two sons, Milan was expressly reserved for the now senior Austrian line. Imperial policy also aimed at the restoration of Habsburg power in Burgundy, in particular to create an imperial barrier against France, controlled from Vienna. This policy was sharply at variance with the plans of Austria's allies in the Spanish succession war, whose aim was to limit Austrian power. From the 1690s on imperial lawyers were busy defining imperial rights in Italy and imperial armies operating in the Italian theatre behaved as if the territories they occupied were imperial fiefs. This policy understandably roused the hostility of the pope and of Savoy. During the reign of Charles VI imperial and Spanish ambitions clashed over the

---

[28] *Ibid.*, pp. 236 ff., Murray, pp. 91–2.
[29] Mecenseffy, pp. 1–2.
[30] Aretin, 'Kaiser Joseph I', *passim*.

two central Italian states, Tuscany and Parma, suzereinty over which was disputed between the Emperor and the pope. In both states the native ruling houses were close to extinction; the last Medici duke of Tuscany had only a daughter, married to the elector palatine, and the Farnese family in Parma had only three members, the duke Francis, his brother Anthony and his daughter Elizabeth, queen of Spain. The acquisition of these territories would have considerably strengthened Austrian power in Italy by linking Milan and Naples; in Spanish hands they would represent a distinct threat to Austrian control.

After 1714 Spain quickly resumed a forward foreign policy aimed at recovering some of her lost lands. It has been argued that these ambitions diverted attention from the thorough internal reform which could perhaps have made her a substantial power again,[31] but this is questionable. The role of Philip V's second wife, Elizabeth Farnese, was important. She is said to have dominated her weak husband[32] manipulating Spanish foreign policy towards her own ambition to construct Italian states for herself or her sons. Philip bitterly resented the fact that he had been forced to abandon his claim to France in return for a Spain stripped of many of its possessions. Eager to reassert Spanish power, especially resenting the intrusion of British sea power in the Mediterranean, based on Gibraltar and Minorca, he even considered abdicating in order to make good his claims in France.[33] Under the influence of Elizabeth and his minister the Parmesan cardinal Alberoni, he embarked on an aggressive foreign policy, aimed in particular at smashing Austrian power in Italy, and supported by a naval building programme, internal financial reform and commercial concessions to the British and Dutch, by which Alberoni hoped to buy British acquiescence in his Mediterranean policy.[34]

Spain and the Emperor did not make peace in 1714 and neither abandoned claims on the other's territory and titles.[35] Charles still had hopes of gaining Mexico and Peru and rejected article VI of the

[31]   Lindsay, J. O. (ed.), *New Cambridge Modern History*, vol. VII (Cambridge, 1957), p. 275f.

[32]   S. de Madariaga, *Spain* (London, 1930), p. 75. Gibbs, 'Parliament and the Treaty of Quadruple Alliance', p. 288 n3 warns against overestimating the role of the queen as Philip V was by no means a cypher. Before their marriage Elizabeth had been described to Philip as docile and self-effacing.

[33]   G. Hills., *Rock of Contention* (London, 1974), pp. 238 – 9. Gehling, p. 159.

[34]   Williams, *Stanhope*, pp. 207 – 8, 282. Spain was still regarded, especially in Britain, as a potentially formidable naval power.

[35]   Gehling, p. 118 probably goes too far in claiming that the struggle for the whole Spanish inheritance remained Charles VI's main concern, in the light of which all political questions were judged and decided.

treaty of Utrecht which placed the house of Savoy before the Habsburgs in the Spanish order of succession if the Bourbon line failed.[36] It was clearly only a matter of time before the cold war turned into the real thing.

Spain began her offensive in May 1715 with the seizure of Majorca and Ibiza and in August 1717 attacked Sardinia. The Emperor was simultaneously involved in war against the Turks. One party in Vienna pressed strongly for an immediate truce with the Turks and an all-out effort against Spain but Charles VI was forced to recognise the reality of the situation: nothing would persuade Europe to allow him to have Spain and the Habsburg lands. British policy under Stanhope aimed at reconciling the two, as Britain's interests required friendly relations with both. The final settlement of the brief Mediterranean war, which ended with the destruction of a Spanish armada by the British fleet off Cape Passaro in August 1718 before war was officially declared, was largely based on a plan drawn up by Stanhope in December 1716.[37] This became the basis of the Quadruple alliance, under which Britain, France and, it was hoped, the Dutch would coerce Spain into accepting Habsburg possessions in Italy. In return for this help, which cemented the Emperor's hold in Italy, he had to agree to a number of unpalatable concessions.

By the treaty of London of 2 August 1718 the Emperor acceded to the Quadruple alliance and Britain mediated a settlement between an unwilling Savoy and the Emperor under which they exchanged Sicily and Sardinia. This consolidated imperial power in southern Italy but left Savoy, with unfulfilled desires on Lombardy, very aggrieved.[38] France and Britain recognized that Tuscany and Parma-Piacenza were imperial fiefs but forced Charles to agree to the eventual succession of Elizabeth Farnese's elder son, don Carlos, when the native dynasties died out, an essential bribe to Spain to restore peace to the Mediterranean. It became a major aim of imperial policy to wriggle out of this undertaking and to exclude Spain from Italy.[39] As early as November 1718 the Emperor was thinking in terms of installing the duke of Lorraine in Tuscany.[40]

---

[36] *Ibid.*, p. 125.
[37] Williams, *Stanhope*, pp. 276 ff. Gehling, pp. 132 – 4. After Passaro Spain recognized the Stuart pretender and seized all British property on its territory.
[38] Wilson, p. 12.
[39] Williams, *Stanhope*, p. 315 described these efforts as 'silly tricks' but the threat which a Spanish presence in central Italy represented was shown clearly in 1733 when the Spaniards attacked Naples from Parma and Tuscany.
[40] *Ibid.*, p. 318.

This settlement made the Emperor more dependent on British goodwill, which could only be bought by concessions elsewhere, especially in the Empire. Very unwelcome to the Emperor was a further provision of the Quadruple Alliance that a general European congress was to be held to deal with all outstanding points at issue and to restore tranquillity to Europe.

PART TWO

THE LITIGATION

5

The origins and early stages of the litigation

Mecklenburg

The key to Mecklenburg's troubles under Charles VI lay partly in the constitutional history of the duchies and partly in the character and behaviour of duke Charles Leopold (1713 – 28, died 1747). His policies were no different from those of his predecessors, his uncle Christian Louis I or his elder brother, Frederick William. He wished to make Mecklenburg count in a wider sphere and, like them, he believed the fulfilment of these policies required the total subordination of the Estates. He wished to cut a figure on the European stage and to break the ties of dependence which had long bound his country to Sweden, Vienna and the Circle 'capital' at Celle and Hanover.[1] He wished to form an army. The erection of a strong *Wehrverfassung* was an old dream of the dukes of Mecklenburg: they wished to construct fortresses and keep a standing army to escape a situation where they were the helpless plaything of their neighbours. Mecklenburg counted for nothing even in the limited Baltic sphere. The dukes sought security by increasing their power inside the country at the cost of the Estates and of Strelitz.[2] Perhaps they genuinely desired to strengthen themselves for the good of the Empire, to which they were usually loyal but from which they could hope for little real help and protection.[3] These plans needed money and, as the powers did not consider a strong Mecklenburg in anyone's interest, the dukes had no alternative but to finance their policies from their lands. This had been attempted by Charles

---

[1] Hofer, pp. 6, 22. After 1648 Mecklenburg had a reputation for great loyalty to the Empire and the Circle and provided money and troops regularly for both with the help of the Estates: *ibid.*, pp. 96 ff., 102. Feller, p. 152.

[2] Mediger, *Mecklenburg*, pp. 22, 36.

[3] Hofer, pp. 31 – 2, 36, 47.

Leopold's two predecessors and it had caused disputes with the Estates.

Charles Leopold's personality was a complicating factor. In certain respects his fate and character resemble those of Charles I of England; he inherited a difficult situation and rapidly made it worse by stupidity. He was in later life, if not earlier, certainly mad. His brutality and blind disregard of the realities of the political and diplomatic situation point either to monumental arrogance and stubbornness or to incipient madness.[4] His hero was Charles XII of Sweden and his model Peter the Great and there was much of both in him. He was one of the most colourful and unpleasant figures on a stage already well-peopled with remarkable men.

Tyrants had great influence on Charles Leopold and he tried to copy them. The king of Prussia's treatment of his Estates fascinated him[5] and later he tried to copy Peter the Great.[6] He is the subject of an historical novel, which portrays him as a far-sighted, if reckless, ruler, whose plans for his country's greatness were sabotaged by a pack of greedy and narrow-minded aristocrats, their vision bounded by the walls of their estates.[7] Some historians have found themselves in the awkward position of having to defend an irresponsible tyrant against a group of men who were, perhaps for base reasons, seeking to preserve their constitutional rights. Such writers often argue from the premise that absolutism was an essential stage in the social and political development of Germany.[8]

The Estates' first appeal to the Emperor was in 1664 and the case lasted until 1755. There was a well established tradition of imperial judicial activity in Mecklenburg dating back to the Thirty Years' War.[9] Trouble arose initially over attempts by the dukes to levy unconstitutional taxes, for the maintenance of fortresses, especially

---

4   An *Aufsatz* of count von Bothmer, Hanoverian prime minister, for the Wolfenbüttel councillor von Stein, described the duke as 'un prince d'un temperament vif, impatient et impetueux', who preferred the use of force to other means: Hanover, *Cal. Br.* 11 E.1 no. 278 fol. 1–4. According to Mediger, *Mecklenburg*, pp. 87 ff. he suffered persecution mania.

5   Schwerin, *Acta Diff.* II vol. 2/i no. 18.

6   *Ibid.*, Landst. Archiv E. III P.1.6.: a letter of 26 February 1718 of a certain von Fuchs described how the duke assaulted an elderly councillor who criticized his proposals to misquote imperial law.

7   F. Griese, *Der Herzog*, 2nd ed. (Munich, 1942), a work very much of its period.

8   For example, the works of Wick and von Ranke.

9   There is a full *Series Processsum* of the case between 1664 and 1707 in Vienna, RHR *Den. Rec.* K. 692(5) no. 1 *Beilage* P. See also Ballschmieter, *passim* and Hofer, pp. 48 ff., 65 ff., 88.

Dömitz on the Elbe.[10] Between 1673 and 1683 the Estates appealed frequently against the forced collection of excessive taxes by both dukes.[11] A verdict of 12 March 1683 confirmed the Estates' obligation to contribute to the maintenance of ducal fortresses under §180 of the 1654 imperial recess but ruled that sums taken improperly, to the amount of 90,000Rt., were to be restored.[12] A definite verdict of the council of 7 July 1698 confirmed the Estates' liabilities under imperial law 'notwithstanding objections based on the *Reversales* and *Assekurationes* of 1572 and 1621'.

The *spiritus litigandi* of the Estates remained strong and they immediately appealed against the verdict of 7 July 1698, stating their arguments at great length in an accompanying *Libellus Gravaminum*.[13] That the theoretical justifications they advanced were repeated with little change throughout their litigation, indicates how deeply these ideas were held.

They submitted that the verdict, which had come as a total surprise to them, had been issued by the council on the basis of only half the relevant information. It spelt out the ruin of the Mecklenburg Estates as it condemned them to pay the 'pretended costs' towards garrisons and fortresses *ad infinitum*. The council, they claimed, had rushed into a verdict so quickly that it could not possibly have considered the volumes of evidence presented by the Estates.

The duke's view of his rights is revealed in an undated essay, *Fundamenta aus welchen des zu Mecklenburg weiland Herrn Herzogs Hochf. Durchlaucht in Regalien-Sachen u. sonderlich quoad Collectus zur Landes-Defension die Jurisdiction des RHRs für incompetent erachten*.[14] Heavily larded with quotations from imperial law, this stated that the basis of the dukes' policy was the need in Mecklenburg for a strong 'defence system'. Conditions in the north had changed and the constitutional arrangements of the past would have to be reviewed. This idea was amplified at meetings of the ducal privy council on 26 April 1715 and 13 October 1716.[15] The prosperity of the nobility had increased and they could afford a greater share of

---

10 This little town on the Elbe was the object of the particular concern of the dukes of Mecklenburg, in whose eyes it grew from a toll collecting station into a fortress of all-German significance.
11 Hofer, p. 72.
12 *Ibid.*
13 Vienna, RHR *Den. Rec.* K. 693 (1) no. 1.
14 Göttingen, Aw 501 fasz. 2.
15 Schwerin, *Acta Diff.* III vol. xvi fasz. 1.

taxation. Agreements made earlier could not prejudice the sovereign rights of succeeding dukes and nothing could deprive the duke of his rights under imperial law.

The Estates' concept of the *jus territoriale* was quite different from that of the duke. The principle, implicit in the verdict of 1698, that every Estate of the Empire had the right to a fixed and uniform body of prerogatives regardless of the constitutional system in force in each province, was, the Estates claimed, totally false. In fact this *jus* varied greatly from state to state and could be measured only against provincial customs and traditions. The Estates seem here to have been asserting their own brand of particularism against the duke's claim to possess a defined set of rights by virtue of his being a prince of the Empire. Some Estates had lost their rights but those who had managed, like themselves, to preserve them enshrined in treaties and constitutional agreements could not be deprived of them:

> and that is the reason why so many have made the mistake of imagining a concept of *jus territoriale* according to their whim and of trying to base all decisions in all provinces on it, like a cobbler making all his shoes on one last . . . The agreements by which men submitted to the Emperor in a civil contract are not uniform but various.

The Empire was a *mixta et irregularis Republica* made up of states with extremely varied constitutional systems. The liberties of the German Estates were much older than the *jus territoriale*:

> the sovereignty of the princes was a thing quite unknown in the old Empire and is a new creation of our century.

This stated clearly the principles underlying the Estates' opposition to the dukes.

Neither protagonist in the Mecklenburg case had a monopoly of right on its side and both had many contemporary critics. The Mecklenburg Estates, with others, have been accused of clinging to outdated privileges and of opposing, in a spirit of unthinking obstructionism, the exciting state-building activities of their enlightened princes. This view is hard to maintain in the light of the above long and closely argued statement of principles. There is no evidence that, had the dukes of Mecklenburg succeeded in their plans, the duchies would have benefited one jot. To have allowed the princes absolute powers under the name of *jus territoriale* might

well have helped princes whose absolutism was genuinely enlightened and beneficent, but it could also have opened the door to petty
tyrants.[16] In addition, it was not the function of the aulic council to
reach decisions on questions of good and bad but on the basis of the
laws of the Empire.

Before the accession of Charles Leopold the aulic council seems to
have held that right was on the side of the duke but that he abused
his position by the use of force and other excesses.[17] In 1700 the
Emperor sent an obscure general, Geschwind von Peckstein, to
inspect Dömitz and to give his expert opinion on the amount
necessary for its maintenance. This step was taken on the advice of
the council in the *vota* of 5 June and 29 July 1700, as there was great
disputes as to whether Dömitz was, as the Estates claimed,[18] a
pitiful little fort offering no obstacle to a serious invader or, as the
duke would have it, a vital fortress of national significance. The
duke also claimed that the Estates were liable to contribute to the
costs of Mecklenburg's contingent to the imperial standing army
decreed by the Empire and approved by the Emperor in 1702 but
never established.[19]

The solution proposed by the council was, in view of its ignorance
of military matters, obvious and sensible. The main problem was
that neither side was prepared to accept the settlement mediated by
Geschwind, although both tried to bribe him.[20] The agreement of
1701 mediated by him, which established an annual *quantum* of
120,000*Rt.* for all permitted purposes[21] and confirmed the constitution, was attacked by nine members of the knighthood a few days
after the signing at Schwerin.[22] These were to form the core of the
party of so-called *Renitenten*, which grew in size until it embraced

---

[16] See the opposite view in Mediger, *Mecklenburg*, pp. 9, 119.

[17] Vienna, RHR *Vota* K. 34, *vota* of 5 June and 12 November 1700. In 1698 the
council had laid down a provisional *quantum* of 35,594*Rt.* for the
maintenance of the ducal fortresses.

[18] *Ibid.*, RHR *Den. Rec.* K. 693(1) no. 4, *Libellus Gravaminum* of the knights
1698.

[19] *Ibid.*, RHR *Den. Rec.* K. 696(5): ducal exhib. of 3 November 1714, 18 June
1715. On the decision of the *Reichstag* of 17 November 1702 on a standing
imperial army see: *ibid*, *Kleinere Reichsstände* K. 346, 'Mecklenburg, in pto.
interpretationis des Reichsgutachtens in pto. der beständigen Reichs-
Verfassung 1706'.

[20] Ballschmieter, p. 73.

[21] Vienna, *Kl. Reichsst.* K. 346, *Pro Memoria* of 26 June 1702. Additional sums
could be collected for the *Fräuleinsteuer*, a tax to provide dowries for
princesses of the ducal house. The anual *quantum* could rise to a maximum
of 170,000*Rt.* if imperial taxation rose above a certain level.

[22] Ballschmieter, p. 79.

almost the entire nobility. They argued that the Estates' representatives who had signed the agreement had exceeded their mandate and that Geschwind had been rushed into accepting this arrangement by the duke. As a majority of the Estates had accepted the recess, the Emperor confirmed it. There were distinct suspicions that all was not straightforward about the treaty but, until this was clearly demonstrated, the aulic council had to adhere to the recommendations of its commissioner on the spot.

By December 1703 the opposition to the agreement had won eighty-eight knights representing ten *Ämter*[23] and they had appointed two deputies to conduct the litigation on their behalf, Christian Siegfried von Plessen, a highly-placed minister in Denmark, and Andreas Gottlieb von Bernstorff, prime minister of the duchy of Celle and, after the death of the last duke of Celle in 1705, of the united duchies of Celle and Hanover. Bernstorff was one of the pioneers of agricultural reform in Mecklenburg and an early evictor of his peasants.[24] After the accession of George Louis to the English throne he exercised influence on English policy for a few years and thought himself first minister of England.[25] There has been some debate about the importance of the 'Hanoverian interest' in British policy-making in the early years of George I's reign[26] but there can be little doubt that George's German advisors played a major role for some time after his accession. It is argued that it was Bernstorff's position which eventually crowned the Estates' campaign with success.[27]

The idea that Bernstorff engineered the imperial execution against Mecklenburg and that it was no more than a part of Hanoverian foreign policy was current at the time. The duke himself complained that the execution would never have taken place had Bernstorff not used his influence on the king/elector in favour of his

[23] Vienna, RHR *Den. Rec.* K. 694(2) fol. 94 – 135.
[24] Steinmann, p. 46.
[25] R. Hatton, *Diplomatic Relations between Great Britain and the Dutch Republic 1714 – 21* (London, 1950), p. 56.
[26] G. C. Gibbs, 'Newspapers, Parliament and Foreign Policy in the Age of Stanhope and Walpole', in *Mélanges offerts à G. Jacquemyns* (Brussels, 1968), pp. 293 n2, 306; 'The accession of the Hanoverians, whose German electoral possessions brought inevitably a degree of permanent involvement in Europe and the risk of the subordination of British to electoral considerations.' McKay, *passim.* Williams, *Stanhope*, pp. 152 – 3, 156, 231 – 3. W. Mediger, *Moskaus Weg nach Europa* (Brunswick, 1952), p. 16. Borgmann, *passim.*
[27] Ballschmieter, p. 47 nn11 and 12. Göttingen, Aw 493, von Habichtstal to the duke, 3 June 1720.

fellow knights.[28] It seems rather far-fetched to suggest that one man was able to juggle European politics on behalf of the knights;[29] at most it could be said that he took advantage of a favourable situation. Had the Emperor not wished to put into effect the verdicts of the aulic council against Charles Leopold it is hard to see what Hanover could have done about it without breaking the law of the Empire and probably, in view of the close interest of other states, especially Prussia, in the future of Mecklenburg, unleashing another war in the North. Before 1714 relations between Hanover and the Emperor were close[30] and this mutual interdependence lasted for a short time after Hanover's acquisition of the English crown. As will be shown, a combination of circumstances, rather than the machinations of Bernstorff, enabled the execution to take place. Had the execution been contrary to English interests it is also difficult to see what Bernstorff could have done about it. Certainly his influence was greater when George I's ambitions moved in an exclusively German orbit.

This is not to deny the deep dependence of the Mecklenburg knights on the support and help of Hanover, which was freely given, no doubt partly because of the influence of Bernstorff. He seems to have acted as the leaven in the lump. The Hanoverian ambassador in Vienna, Daniel Erasmi, baron von Huldenberg, helped the knights from the early 1690's onwards, when he had been approached by their representative, von Maltzan. He solicited on their behalf and employed his influence and experience in their favour. All this he admitted in a letter to the Small Committee of the Estates on 1 July 1722, expressing his appreciation of their thanks. Already he was instructing his son, who was with him in Vienna, to continue in the knights' service.[31] He continued:

In the whole Holy Roman Empire no mediate nobility has been able to bring its liberty to such a level as the Mecklenburg

---

[28]   *Ibid.*, Aw 474 fasz. 1 no. 96, the duke to Eichholtz: 'It cannot be called the knights' case but Hanover's case or, better, Bernstorff's case.' The duke could not understand why imperial and royal courts should bend to the whim of an individual. J. M. Beattie, *The English Court in the Reign of George I* (Cambridge, 1967), pp. 219, 221–2. Mediger, *Mecklenburg*, p. 458.

[29]   Ballschmieter, p. 43.

[30]   *Ibid.*, p. 15.

[31]   Schwerin, Landst. Archiv, *Protocol* 1722 314b. Huldenberg was paid money by the knights: *ibid.*, *Protocol* 1719 I Accounts 1717–8. In December 1717 he received a payment of 1,000Fl. Several writers have made extensive use of Huldenberg's reports, e.g. Wick, Ballschmieter and Naumann. According to St Saphorin, Huldenberg was indiscreet and habitually exaggerated his own influence in Vienna: Gehling, p. 39.

knighthood. When I look at everything, it all depends on a few generous patriots, the Small Committee, the *Landräte* and deputies, and our prime minister baron Bernstorff. I count it great good fortune for the knights that one of their number is the greatest and most consummate statesmen in Europe with a position at such a powerful court

Although Bernstorff had by then lost much influence in London, his legend was in the making. Huldenberg stated that Bernstorff had been able to persuade the king of England to accept a commission which other princes would have refused out of community of interests with the duke, a gross oversimplification. He was correct in his assessment of the importance of a small group within the knighthood in organising the campaign. This was true of other states where a small and active minority organised opposition to the prince.[32]

The knights also received vital economic support from Hanover. The litigation was very costly but unlimited resources were made available 'All money is a mere bagatelle if used to conserve golden liberty'.[33] There is ample evidence of their financial dependence on Hanover in the Schwerin archive.[34] During their exile in Ratzenburg and elsewhere refugee knights were paid pensions by the king/elector.[35]

From 1713 to 1718 Bernstorff corresponded with the ducal government in the name of the knights[36] and the actual conduct of litigation was in the hands of the Hanoverian ministry under his direction. The Small Committee made suggestions and was kept informed of developments but it had abdicated control into the hands of Bernstorff. As well as Huldenberg, the knights also enjoyed the help and expertise of the Hanoverian judge of appeal *(Oberappellationsrat)* in Celle, Marquard, who drafted documents for presentation in the aulic council and conducted correspondence with Vienna, the Small Committee and the Hanoverian councillors eventually sent to Mecklenburg under the imperial Commission.[37] Money for the case was passed to Vienna through the Hanoverian

---

32   von Ranke, p. 115.
33   Schwerin, Landst. Archiv E. III P.1.6, Marquard to Behr, 7 November 1717. The litigation was also a serious financial burden on the dukes: Mediger, *Mecklenburg*, p. 13.
34   *Ibid.*, accounts for 1717 – 18.
35   *Ibid., Beilage* 31, fasz. 2 *Beilage* 36.
36   *Ibid., Acta Diff.* III vol. I, fasz. 1.
37   When the Emperor commissioned an Estate of the Empire to execute a verdict or investigate a matter it was customary to appoint subdelegates, who did the work and submitted reports.

Hofjude Michael David of Hamburg. Bernstorff's secretary in London, Hopmann, was a paid agent of the Small Committee.[38] Most of the knights' material was printed in Hanover.

From the beginning of the reign of Charles VI the number of cases in the aulic council involving the Estates and duke of Mecklenburg multiplied rapidly. As well as those inherited from the reigns of previous Emperors, each new appeal against the latest *attentatum* of the duke acquired a separate rubric in the records of the council; it is evidence of the council's sound organisation that it was able to preserve order among the ever-growing mountains of *acta* and *presentata*. The litigants' agents seem occasionally to have had difficulty in finding their way through the thickets of rubrics and in keeping pace with the various stages through which the case proceeded. In the records of the council each case had a rubric naming the litigating parties, the matter at issue and the stage which it had reached. When a verdict or *votum* dealt with more than one point in litigation, they were drawn up under the general rubrics *in diversis* or *diversorum gravaminum*. The stage the case had reached was indicated by such phrases as *Appelationis, nunc Commissionis* or *Executionis*.

It was through these phases that the litigation between the Estates and the duke quickly passed between the accession of Charles Leopold in 1713 and the execution of the imperial verdicts against him in 1719. A most important step was the issue by the council of a *Conservatorium* against him, which provided Hanover and Brunswick-Wolfenbüttel with imperial sanction for armed action. Once this had been put into effect, the aulic council took upon itself the indirect control and day-to-day supervision of the internal affairs of a substantial state of the Empire and from this point on the volume of *acta* in the council's records grew steadily.

In 1714 the aulic council recommended the issue of a *Conservatorium* in the Mecklenburg case. This was accepted in an imperial resolution in August 1715,[39] published in August 1717 and finally put into effect in March 1719. The delay was due to attempts to solve the dispute without the use of force and, when this proved impossible, to the diplomatic arrangements required before the main commissioner, Hanover, felt safe enough to commit himself in Mecklenburg.

The nature of the case changed sharply with the accession of Charles Leopold in 1713. It was his complete lack of moderation which lifted the case above an ordinary constitutional dispute. His predecessor, Frederick William, had operated within traditional

---

[38]   Schwerin, landst. Archiv. *Protocol* 1719 II no. 620.
[39]   *Merkw. RHR Conclusa* vol. II no. cii, verdict of 1 August 1715.

policies, applying violence moderately and knowing just how far he could, with safety, go. The new duke continued his brother's policies but with unprecedented vigour and violence. In 1714 he presented his first diet with a demand for extra taxes and, when this was refused, he collected the money by force. In particular he extended his campaign against the powerful city of Rostock, which formed an Estate of its own and had previously been a close ally of the knighthood. Charles Leopold wished to make the city a fortress and his principal residence.[40] In 1713 he placed a garrison in the city and took up residence there. He had a keen appreciation of the strategic importance of the city and wished to detach it from the knights, leaving them isolated as the only Estate opposed to him. The other towns had earlier been won over by duke Frederick William with a new taxation system which reduced the burden of taxes on them.[41] The steps taken by the duke look like a concerted and deliberate assault on the liberties of the Estates and have been dealt with as such in the latest work on the subject.[42]

He mounted a campaign of oppression against the city magistracy in order to force it to accept an agreement dictated by him. From the beginning the aulic council condemned the duke's actions: in a verdict of 28 March 1714 he was ordered to end all attacks on the city's rights, with the threat of a *Conservatorium* if he disobeyed.[43] By March 1715 the distinction between the various cases against the duke was becoming thin and the aulic council tended to deal with them together under the title *in diversis*. Through February and March 1715 reports had reached the council of more military executions against the knights accompanied by shocking excesses. In its opinion a *Conservatorium* on the convening princes of the Lower Saxon Circle was a matter of urgency 'for well-known weighty reasons'.[44] In his decision on this and a further *votum* of 24 December 1714 the Emperor resolved to postpone the issue of the recommended *Conservatorium*. The recommendation was repeated in a *votum* of 26 November 1715, after the Rostock magistrates had

---

[40] It has been a constant aim of duke Frederick William to revive Rostock and to secure the removal of the restrictive Swedish toll at Warnemünde: Mediger, *Mecklenburg*, p. 21.

[41] Vienna, RHR *Den. Rec.* K. 692(1) and 692(2). There is a copy of the *Konsumption- und Steuerordnung* of 19 March 1708 in *Beilage* 13 to the exhib. of 12 August 1710. This became the subject of separate litigation and the documentation is enormous.

[42] Wick, *Versuche*.

[43] *Merkwürdige RHR Conclusa*, vol. II, no. xcvii. On 20 December 1714 a further mandate was issued on pain of a fine of ten marks of gold in case of disobedience: *ibid.*, no. xcix.

[44] Vienna, RHR *Vota* K. 34.

given in to ducal pressure and signed an agreement abandoning most of the city's rights.[45]

The council again recommended the issue of a *Conservatorium* 'for highly urgent reasons and because no other means will put an end to the almost unheard of excesses of the duke against the city of Rostock complained of'. By now the council was specifying a *Conservatorium* on the two Brunswick states, Hanover and Wolfenbüttel, while earlier it had also included Brandenburg as a convening prince. It explained the reason:

> under the present circumstances, known throughout the Empire, and because both the duke, because of Prussian aggression against him in the Northern War,[46] and the Estates and Rostock, because of Prussia's claim to a right cf eventual succession in the country, would have a good reason to challenge the inclusion of the king in a commission; regarding the king of Sweden for the duchy of Bremen, he is involved in the troubles in the Lower Saxon Circle and the Estates suspect him of being an ally of the duke.

Each Circle had its own organisation to carry out its functions under imperial law and the directorate was usually shared between two of the stronger states. The Lower Saxon Circle was in several ways unusual. The directorate was shared between Brandenburg for the duchy of Magdeburg, Sweden for the duchy of Bremen and the house of Brunswick-Lüneburg. The active directorate in the latter house passed by rotation between the junior and senior branches of Hanover and Wolfenbüttel. After the Northern War, Sweden was practically excluded from the Circle and the ground was fought over by Hanover and Brandenburg-Prussia. In the council's view the two Brunswick houses were the only acceptable commissioners as the others were politically or judicially inadmissible. The council's insistence on the inclusion of Wolfenbüttel was interesting. The Emperor was in no way bound to appoint the Circle directors but in the Mecklenburg case additional factors made it necessary to

---

[45] *Ibid.*, K. 54. It was read and approved on 23 December 1715.
[46] Charles Leopold complained of Prussian violence against his country in letters of 17 November and 7 December 1715: Vienna, RHR *Prot. Rer. Res.* xviii 38. On 27 February 1716 he complained about the conduct of the Hanoverian troops besieging Wismar: *ibid.*, 39, verdict of 5 March 1716. On 20 March he complained against the Swedish vice-governor of Wismar on the grounds of forced levies: *ibid.*, 34.

appoint commissioners willing and strong enough to put the Emperor's verdicts into execution, by force if required.

This was made especially necessary by Charles Leopold's alliance with tsar Peter I in April 1716. To the duke this alliance, the first between the tsar and a German prince, was a sign of his arrival as a power worth allying with and an instrument to use against his knights. To Peter it meant a diplomatic, military and commercial window into the Empire, western Europe and possibly the North Sea and Atlantic. It also offered him a permanent base in north Germany after the destruction of Swedish power there and some guarantee against a separate peace with Sweden by the other Northern allies, which Peter always, with reason, feared. It reopened the possibility of a canal route from Wismar to the Elbe, which would have given Russia a route to the west avoiding the Danish-controlled Sound.[47] Part of the treaty allowed the Russians toll-free transport of goods from the Mecklenburg coast to Hamburg.[48]

The more immediate Russian motive for the alliance was to obtain the use of Mecklenburg as a base for attacks on Scania as part of the allied campaign against Sweden. Charles Leopold did not bring the Russians into his country; they came as members of the Northern League. The Mecklenburg case must be viewed against the background of the Northern War, which was for some time fought on Mecklenburg soil. The Emperor was anxious to see Swedish power in Germany destroyed but had no illusions: the allies were fighting for their own benefit, not that of the Empire. Imperial participation in the war was limited to futile attempts to neutralise the Empire and to preside over the division of the spoils. This was little help to the dukes of Mecklenburg, whose country seemed likely to be a theatre of war, against which threat they had long sought a firm alliance. The Russian connection was first mooted under Frederick William to escape the dangerous isolation faced after negotiations with Sweden had failed. Frederick William had allied with the Swedes in 1701 but the agreement did not last.[49] It is hard to see what advantage a Swedish alliance would have been as

---

[47] This was an old scheme and was still in the air in 1725: Vienna, RHR *Den. Rec.* K 705(5).

[48] Mediger, *Mecklenburg*, pp. 174–5.

[49] Vienna, *Kl. Reichsst.* K. 346, Frederick William to Leopold I, 24 August 1701. The Swedes had long been a source of greater concern to the Emperor than the Russians: *ibid.*, K. 347, fol. 84–7, 90–101. Frederick William had considered a Russian alliance in 1709 but had dropped the idea on Prussian advice as potentially too dangerous. In 1714 Charles Leopold was still thinking in terms of a Swedish alliance with the hope of obtaining Wismar and Warnemünde: Mediger, *Mecklenburg*, pp. 53 ff, 61 nn255, 105–6.

it would have only made more likely Mecklenburg's embroilment in a war, in which Sweden would have been unable to offer any real aid and protection.

At first Peter was not very keen on the alliance, fearing to alienate England and the Emperor. After the battle of Poltava he suggested a commerical treaty with Mecklenburg and after the Pruth treaty of 1711 he had greater freedom of action. As more Swedish provinces fell into Russian hands the commercial motive for an alliance with the duke grew in importance. In October 1715 the decision was taken in Schwerin to make a further approach to the tsar.[50] Developments in the north now made the proposal more attractive to Peter.[51] Before the return of Charles XII to Sweden in 1714 Russian troops had operated in the eastern theatre, entering the Empire only to besiege Stralsund. The king's return frightened Denmark into approaching the tsar to arrange a combined amphibious attack on Scania.[52] The tsar suspected that his allies were intending to make peace behind his back and to help the Swedes to win back the eastern provinces and saw the Danish offer as a chance to participate in the west to secure himself against betrayal.

On 19 April 1716 Charles Leopold married the tsar's niece, Catherine Ivanovna, in Danzig and on the same day an alliance was signed. The tsar undertook to help Charles Leopold against his internal and external enemies, by force if required, and to obtain Wismar and Warnemünde for Charles Leopold or to pay a dowry of 200,000 rubles.

This alliance was a mistake, as Peter very soon realised. The marriage was very questionable; Charles Leopold had already divorced one wife and had entered a morganatic marriage with one of the ladies of his court.[53] The aulic council considered the annulment of the first marriage void and there was a long dispute about the council's competence in a matrimonial case between Protestant parties.[54] A potential armed Russian protectorate over Mecklenburg was most unwelcome to the Emperor and the

---

[50] *Ibid.*, pp. 94 ff., 121.
[51] *Ibid.*, ch. 2 and 4 for the making of the alliance.
[52] J. J. Murray, 'Scania and the End of the Northern Alliance', *JMH* (1944) *passim* and the same author's *George I*.
[53] R. Wittram, *Peter I, Czar und Kaiser* (2 vols., Göttingen, 1964), vol. II, pp. 274–7.
[54] Vienna, RHR *Vota* K. 34, *vota* of 19 May 1716 and 24/30 January 1720, 'Meckl. v. Meckl. in pto. divortii'. In 1720 the tsar negotiated a settlement, under which the former duchess, Sophia Hedwig of Nassau-Dietz, accepted 30,000*Rt.* and 5,000*Rt.* a year in return for agreeing to the divorce. The aulic council refused to confirm this.

northern allies, especially Hanover.[55] The first symptom of growing mistrust of Russian intentions was the refusal of the western allies to admit Russian troops into Wismar after its fall in April 1716.[56] Hanover was afraid that the Baltic war could easily turn into a general war in north Germany, as Charles Leopold seemed ready to make his country available to any power prepared to support his internal political aims. England was not willing to see Russia displace Sweden as the dominant power in the Baltic and it was not in her commercial interest to allow the balance of power in the area to be destroyed. The growth of Russian sea-power could only be regarded as dangerous, as was the tsar's support for the duke of Holstein's attempts to recover Schleswig from Denmark.[57] Russia was to be kept at arm's length, not allowed to colonize a substantial north German state.

The close link between the Mecklenburg case and events in the north was recognised early by the aulic council. Its *votum* of 26 November 1715 and supplement of the same date.[58] stated that it was important for the Emperor to show clearly that he was motivated only by the principles of justice in his actions. This and earlier *vota* illustrate well the motives of the council. The duke's actions were, it claimed, illegal and an affront to the Emperor's jurisdiction and authority. It was therefore necessary to take the strongest action to stop them. In deciding what action was possible, the political circumstances had to be taken into account but, as the council had no competence in such matters, it could only make recommendations permitted under imperial law, leaving the decision on the political feasibility of the proposal to the political branches of the imperial government. The council claimed to have

---

[55]   Mediger, *Mecklenburg*, pp. 214 – 20, *Moskaus Weg*, pp. 28 – 30, 57 – 9: quotes a Hanoverian councillor, Joachim H. von Bülow, to the effect that the Russians were more dangerous than the Turks as they learned too well from the west. The only solution, in his view, was to seal Russia off hermetically and stop her westernization.

[56]   Wittram, vol. II, p. 278. At the time it was reported that the tsar allowed his troops to be employed against the knights in the belief that they had used their influence to secure the exclusion of Russian forces from Wismar by the Danes and Hanoverians after the fortress fell: *ibid.*, p. 295. Peter put this forward as his reason: Vienna, RHR *Den. Rec.* K. 697(1), exhib. of 12 March 1717, *Beilage* A, in which the tsar claimed that the whole knighthood was in conspiracy against him.

[57]   R. Lodge, *Great Britain and Prussia*, p. 16, Naumann, p. 19, Srbik, *Österreichische Staatsverträge*, vol. I, p. 407, Williams, *Stanhope*, pp. 234 – 5, 248. The duke of Holstein, Charles Frederick, married Peter's daughter Anna in 1725. As a nephew of Charles XII, he had a claim to the Swedish throne.

[58]   Vienna, RHR *Vota* K. 54.

demonstrated the manifest invalidity of the treaty of Schwerin. Now it was to be feared that the duke, to stamp out the latest sparks of resistance in Rostock, intended to proceed against it with even greater violence. This could lead to an endless process in the imperial court and a total destruction of the liberties of Rostock. The council was anxious to appear to be observing complete impartiality. The *vota* were not intended to come before the eyes of the public and this is clear from their content and style. They were usually short, precise and to the point, in complete contrast to the exhibits of the parties[59] and most of the rescripts despatched from the imperial chancery. The council gave its recommendations and the reasons behind the recommendations. It took care to present the arguments put forward by both sides in shortened form, though often whole phrases or sentences passed unchanged into the *vota* from the exhibits of the parties. There is no indication in the *vota* that the council suppressed facts or made recommendations at odds with the evidence. Its advice usually showed a firm inclination towards one side or the other especially when, as in the cases of Rostock and the Mecklenburg knights, right seemed firmly on one side. Even under these circumstances it was punctiliously careful to leave no loophole unfilled, that might later be quoted by a litigant as evidence of partiality.

The council repeated its recommendation for a *Conservatorium* in a supplementary *votum* of 12 March 1716.[60] The imperial resolution on the matter was reached at a meeting of the privy council on 18 May,[61] which decided to issue the recommended *Conservatorium* on the elector of Hanover and the duke of Brunswick-Wolfenbüttel. The secretary at the meeting noted that it was the best attended for a long time and the attendance list reveals that both 'imperial' and 'Austrian' interests were well represented. The *Conservatorium* was issued on 26 May 1716.[62]

This verdict was the first step in a process which was to end after three years with the entry of a Hanoverian-Wolfenbüttel army into Mecklenburg under a further *Conservatorium* protecting the knights. This was a period of intense diplomatic activity between the Emperor and the prospective executors, the former trying to press

---

59   *Ibid.*, RHR *Den. Rec.* K. 696(5). The knights' exhibit of 21 February 1715 is typical of this style.

60   *Ibid.*, 39, 10 and 12 March. The supplement is in RHR *Vota* K. 54.

61   A copy of the resolution is attached to the *Annectatur* of 12 March 1716: *ibid.*

62   *Merkw.* RHR *Concl.* vol. II, no. cxiii. This verdict contains a copy of the *Conservatorium* sent to the two princes. They were to protect Rostock against further violence and ensure that the city received the benefit of the Emperor's verdicts. There is a copy of the *Conservatorium* of 21 August 1716, *ibid.*, no. cxiv.

the elector and the duke[63] to carry out the imperial mandate and the latter to wring from the Emperor guarantees against any interference by the duke's allies, in particular Russia and Prussia. This explains the delay between the first *votum* of the aulic council and the final decision. The Emperor was not ready to expose himself to ridicule by dispensing *Conservatoria* without knowing if the recipient, as well as being highly honoured, would carry out the mandate. The Emperor's freedom of choice was further limited by the selection of states strong enough to carry out his wishes and legally unobjectionable. Further he could not choose conservators from the other ends of the Empire as this would have roused Circle jealousies and laid the foundations for complaints in the imperial diet that it was part of his campaign against the liberties of the Empire.

The aulic council had highlighted the problem in a supplementary *votum* of 23 December 1716,[64] in which it repeated its recommendation but with the following addition: 'However, whether and how far such provisions of the imperial rescript should be put into effect in the light of the present international circumstances *[Konjunkturen]* the obedient aulic council leaves to your Majesty's enlightened decision.' The political and diplomatic circumstances inside and outside the Empire were *Kabinettsachen*, the province of the imperial chancery and the two conferences. There is however no evidence that the conferences decided what verdicts the council was to arrive at but only how the verdict could, if at all, be best put into effect. Nowhere in the confidential protocols of the conferences is there anything to suggest that they dictated to the aulic council.

In September 1717 the wheels of imperial justice began to turn. They were difficult to start but, once in rotation, they turned until Charles Leopold's new born absolutist state was ground to nothing. The urgent need for intervention to protect the Mecklenburg knights was increasingly clear. One the tsar's orders, under pressure from England and the Emperor,[65] the main Russian army left Mecklenburg in June 1717 to take part in a proposed invasion of Sweden from Jutland. Charles Leopold took over 3,000 into his own service.[66] These were ostensibly to act as a body-guard for the duchess, the tsar's niece, but it soon became clear that their real function was to continue the duke's campaign of terror against the knights. Many knights fled into neighbouring provinces and the largest number, including the Small Committee, took up residence

---

63   Wolfenbüttel could not move without Hanover.
64   *Ibid.*, RHR *Prot. Rer. Res.* xviii 38, verdict of 23 December 1715.
65   Murray, 'Scania'.
66   Wick, pp. 100, 105 – 6, Witte, vol. II, p. 261.

on the Mecklenburg border in Ratzeburg in George I's duchy of Saxe-Lauenburg.[67] In their absence their lands were sequestered and placed under ducal administrators. Earlier in 1717 Charles Leopold had made it clear that his Russians would not leave until the knights agreed to a dictated settlement.[68] The departure of the main Russian army may well have brought the imperial government to resolve on action against the duke. The retention of Russian troops in ducal service raised the spectre of a perpetual Russian presence, an open door for the tsar to enter Germany.[69]

The knights predictably intensified their presence for a *Conservatorium*. On 13 September 1717 the aulic council began its *Relation*.[70] On 15 September Behr reported to Bernstorff that a member of the council, Berlepsch, had assured him that all but one of the councillors were hostile to the duke's cause and that the president, vice-president and councillors Steiningen, Bode and Langenbach had all promised their support to the Estates.[71] After four sessions the council decided on 2 October to send a *votum* to the Emperor.[72]

The new situation in Mecklenburg was outlined: with the addition of the Russians the duke's forces numbered some 4,900[73] and he was still recruiting. A permanent new system had been imposed on the knights to maintain this force, the system of *Portionen* and *Monatgelder*, under which each noble estate was assessed at a certain number of portions of food and rations of fodder in cash or kind.[74] This replaced the knights' share of the 1701 *quantum* of 120,000Rt. which the duke had abandoned unilaterally. The knights complained that this would enable Charles Leopold to maintain an army of 50,000, the whole country being farmed to this end.[75] The alternative before the knights was clear and terrible: they must either lose their lands and be reduced to penury or surrender their rights and submit to a ducal *Dominat*. The few knights who had submitted to the duke had been relieved of all burdens and he

---

67 Vienna, RHR *Den. Rec.* K. 698(1), exhib. of 12 and 27 August 1716.
68 Schwerin, E III P.1.5, Marquard to Behr, 4 April 1717.
69 *Ibid.*, Behr to Bernstorff, 14 April 1717, Behr to Rhaden, May 1717. Naumann, p. 19.
70 *Merkw. RHR Conclusa*, vol. 88, no. cxx.
71 Schwerin, E III P.1.5.
72 There are copies of this important *votum* in Vienna, RHR *Den. Rec.* K. 699(14) and RHR *Vota* K. 34.
73 Witte, vol. II, p. 261 gives the figure 12,000, which seems rather high. In 1719 the commissioners reported that Charles Leopold had 7,000 troops.
74 Accounts of the system and its workings are in Vienna, RHR *Den. Rec.* K. 474(2).
75 Schwerin, E III P.1.5., Small Committee to Behr, 11 August 1717, Marquard to Behr, 31 August 1717.

had unconstitutionally appointed new *Landräte* from among the loyalist nobles.

To date the knights had produced forty-four documented instances of ducal excesses. On 23 September the frontier had been closed to prevent further flights of the nobility and removal of their property. The knights' organisation in Ratzeburg and elsewhere was very efficient in collecting evidence and sworn statements and they maintained a regular correspondence with informants inside and outside Mecklenburg.[76] The duke, on the other hand, kept his representatives badly informed and his instructions were vague and inconsistent. Eichholtz had occasion to complain that the duke sent him unreliable information which brought the reproach that he was trying to pull the wool over the Emperor's eyes. He asked that he be sent only *realia, legalia und fundamentalia*, if possible supported by documentary proof.[77]

The aulic council listed the main points at issue. In its view the major issue was the fact that the duke had taken Russian troops into his service. Next was the matter of taxation. In both points, in the council's opinion, the duke had acted in direct contravention of the imperial constitution. It rejected his arguments based on his possession of a *jus armorum et foederum* under the imperial constitution:

> Under the imperial laws quoted there must be weighty reasons for the exercise of this prerogative, in particular the good of the subject, and the same prerogative is conditional upon certain circumstances laid down in the Emperor's capitulation of election . . . that it must be employed for the security and welfare of the Estates of the Empire and that it involves no danger to the Empire.

Article XV of the *Wahlkapitulation* laid down that subjects were liable to contribute to the maintenance of necessary fortresses but they retained the right of appeal to the imperial courts if burdened with unnecessary or excessive taxation. In case of such an appeal both sides were obliged to wait quietly for an imperial decision and were to take no action in the meantime.

---

[76] Schwerin, *Acta Diff.* III/1, fasz. 6 nos. 1, 2, 3: circular letters urging the knights to leave Mecklenburg and to abandon their property in order to increase the effectiveness of their appeal.

[77] Göttingen, Aw 474 I nos. 6 and 9,. Eichholtz to the duke, 8 and 12 April 1719. *Ibid.*, II no. 85, Eichholtz to Wolffradt, 13 December 1719.

The Russians were foreigners practising a religion illegal in the Empire and they were guilty of dreadful excesses. Under the imperial constitution their actions would justify the declaration of imperial war and, against the duke, the ban of the Empire *ex causa fractae pacis publicae*.

The recent history of Mecklenburg provided a precedent. In 1708 duke Frederick William had entered an alliance with the king of Prussia under which the king promised the duke armed aid against his Estates.[78] Shortly afterwards a thousand Prussian dragoons entered the country and were billeted on the knights' lands.[79] The duke justified this by claiming that the knights were plotting rebellion against him and that he needed the troops to protect himself.[80] The council had rejected these arguments and the Emperor had put a stop to Prussia's intervention by a mandate in June and a *Conservatorium* in December 1708, after which the Prussians withdrew.[81]

Since the accession of Charles Leopold a host of imperial verdicts and the Mecklenburg constitution had been thrown overboard and the rights of the Estates taken away by naked force. The duke had been threatened with a *Conservatorium* in five earlier verdicts without result. He had illegally taken large sums from the knights to finance an army which was clearly for internal use only, to intimidate the Estates. The council saw the only answer to the problem in a *Conservatorium* with real teeth.

In view of the dangerous possibilities for the authority of the Emperor, the welfare of the Empire and Mecklenburg and the 'public interests involved', the council considered it desirable to dispense with the 'rules, set procedures and solemnities of the judicial process', as it was entitled to do under its ordinance when the circumstances of the case were very special. The council therefore recommended a *Conservatorium* commissioning Hanover and Wolfenbüttel to enter Mecklenburg with sufficient troops to take Rostock and put into effect imperial verdicts in the case. As the basis for their action the commissioners should observe the Mecklenburg constitution, the recess of 1701 and all imperial verdicts. They were to drive out Charles Leopold's Russians, to put a stop to ducal recruiting and illegal taxation, to abolish the

---

[78] Ballschmieter, pp. 97–8. Vienna, *Kl. Reichsst.* K. 346, letter of duke Frederick William to the Emperor, 23 April 1708.
[79] Details in Vienna, RHR *Den. Rec.* K. 694(4).
[80] *Ibid.*, K. 692(5), exhib. of 11 May 1708.
[81] *Ibid.*, RHR *Prot. Rer. Res.* xviii 20A. The council argued that, in imperial law, a prince could only call in the help of a fellow-ruler against rebellious subjects. Disobedience was insufficient reason.

unconstitutional war-chest and restore the *Landkasten* to its former status and to ensure full security of persons and property for the knights. These tasks formed the so-called *liquida*, the matters already settled by imperial decision. The unsettled *illiquida*, claims for compensation for damage caused before and after the withdrawal of the main Russian army and for excess taxation and the overdue calling of a diet, were to be investigated by the commission and a report on them sent to the Emperor for an early decision. The knights and other interested parties should be invited to submit their claims to this investigating commission. The *Conservatorium* should be despatched without delay but should not officially be notified to Charles Leopold until the execution troops had entered the country. This last was an interesting recommendation and the reasoning behind it is not obvious. Perhaps the council was concerned in case premature publication of the verdict might give Charles Leopold a chance to mobilize anti-imperial feeling in the Empire, which might in turn create a climate in which it would be inadvisable for the Emperor to order armed execution against a prince or for Hanover to carry it out. Later the duke was to complain bitterly that he had not known of the impending execution until it had started but this was certainly untrue. On the eve of the execution he suddenly began to obey imperial orders which he had ignored for years. News of the *Conservatorium* spread rapidly in the Empire and caused considerable comment.

The council had more to say on the question of the secrecy of the commission. Under his capitulation of election the Emperor was obliged to inform the Electors and then the whole Empire of any decisions in important cases and was obliged to wait for their comments and advice. The circumstances of this case were special. In a patent dated 3 September 1717 Charles Leopold had employed very threatening language and openly stated his intention to seek the aid of his friends and to defend his *regalia* 'at whatever cost'.[82] He had already employed his foreign policy as a means of oppressing the knights and had steadily built up an army of Germans reinforced with Russians; the longer he was left unchecked, the greater became the danger that the whole business would get badly out of hand. If he were to resist the execution by force or to obtain active help from another power, the whole north might again go up in flames. For all these reasons and because the matter was urgent, the council argued that the Emperor should not reveal his intentions to the Empire but should seek the view of the

[82] Göttingen, Aw. 474 fasz. 1, Eichholtz to Wolffradt, 29 March 1719. This phrase, 'es koste, was es wolle', was to be quoted for years afterwards as evidence of Charles Leopold's violent and unreasonable character.

imperial diet on the case in general.[83] In the council's opinion this would move potential supporters of the duke to think again and strengthen the trust of the Empire in the Emperor's judicial office and fatherly concern for the welfare of all his subjects.

The *votum* was accompanied by a draft rescript to the duke stating that the Emperor could no longer tolerate flat disobedience but promising the duke imperial aid and protection if he should be threatened by a foreign oppressor. This last provision was probably intended for public consumption only: during the Northern War neutral Mecklenburg was ravaged by the armies of several states while imperial *Protectoria* rained down ineffectively.[84] Attempts to obtain compensation for Mecklenburg at the imperial congress of Brunswick were fruitless.[85] If anything had given Charles Leopold contempt for the effectiveness of imperial authority it was the total failure of the Emperor and the Empire to help Mecklenburg in this war when it could not help itself.

The *votum* was presented in the Privy Council on 22 October and approved in full. The recommended rescripts and *Conservatoria* were to be prepared at once but this was not to be announced in the public protocol of the council.[86] A copy of the *votum* was to be sent to the imperial Principal Commissioner in Regensburg, cardinal Saxe-Zeitz, for his private information and he was to consult other Habsburg representatives there on the drafting of a commission decree. This was to be drawn up in such a way as to avoid the impression that the Emperor was seeking to justify his actions and decisions as supreme judge. In fact the commission decree of November 1717 came to nothing as it was never introduced in the imperial diet, which was at the time paralysed by various minor disputes over precedence, to which it was always prone. As the Principal Commissioner informed Behr, who was in Regensburg in February 1718, the diet could do little to help the knights until the execution against Charles Leopold took place, as the Emperor would only seek the diet's advice if the duke resisted. The elector of Mainz was busy stopping attempts by the duke's agents to bring the case before the imperial diet as it was *causa justitiae*, over which

---

[83] A commission decree to the imperial diet to this effect was sent on 17 November 1717.

[84] Ballschmieter, p. 109. Between January 1713 and October 1716 six imperial decrees were issued to protect Mecklenburg from the belligerents. Ironically, the directors of the Circles whose function was to protect were among the states ravaging Mecklenburg: Vienna, *Kl. Reichsst.* K. 347 fol. 78 – 83, memo. of Eichholtz 21 May 1713.

[85] Williams, *Stanhope*, p. 355.

[86] The verdicts of the day intended for public announcement were posted outside the council's chambers in the *Anschlagsprotokoll*.

the diet had no competence.[87] The elector had imperial orders not to permit presentation of the duke's protests.[88]

The resolution was published in the council's public protocol on 25 October 1717 in a bare statement that the Emperor had approved the council's recommendations and had ordered the expedition of the recommended rescripts.[89] The *Conservatorium* listed Charles Leopold's manifold offences, which made it essential, for the security of the Circle and the Empire, that action be taken. The Emperor was anxious that the execution should begin as soon as possible. However, there was to be a delay of fourteen months, while the duke intensified his campaign against the knights. This delay was most unwelcome in Vienna, from where Huldenberg reported growing annoyance with Hanover, which, having pressed for an imperial sanction to help the knights, now refused to make use of it, thus exposing the Emperor to ridicule.[90] When it became clear that nothing was going to happen quickly, the anxiety of the knights, revealed in their correspondence with their various representatives, increased.[91] All decisions had to be taken in London and the government there was not ready to take any action without guarantees of security.[92] There was a great fear that circumstances would change in favour of the duke, who was slowly building up the size of his army. The Russians could, if they wished, put a force of 80,000 into the country from Poland. The duke's advisers realised clearly that the longer the execution was put off, the more difficult it would be.[93] The imperial government was not ready to court the possibility of war with Russia and Prussia

---

[87]   Schwerin, E III P.1.6, Behr to Bernstorff and Small Committee, 7 March 1718.

[88]   *Ibid.*, 17 March 1718. The same happened in 1728 when the elector of Mainz again hindered attempts by the duke to publicize his case in the imperial diet: Vienna, *Kl. Reichsst.* K. 348 fol. 22 – 39, the elector to Schönborn 24 July 1728. When the elector of Mainz was co-operative, imperial influence in the diet increased. As arch-chancellor of Germany, the elector controlled the introduction of material for debate (*Diktatur*) which gave documents the special status of *acta imperii*. Often documents were printed and distributed before *Diktatur* or if this was refused, an act regarded as an affront to the elector's office: Schwerin, *Acta Diff.* III vol. xx fasz. 1, elector of Mainz to Charles Leopold 21 May 1729.

[89]   A printed version of the full verdict with the rescript and *Conservatorium* was published later: *Merkw. RHR Conclusa*, vol. II, no. cxxii.

[90]   Ballschmieter, pp. 133 – 5.

[91]   Schwerin, E III P.1.6, *Landrat* Lehsten to Rhaden, 6 November 1717.

[92]   *Ibid.*, Rhaden to Small Committee, 6 November 1717.

[93]   *Ibid.*, Small Committee to Behr, 17 November 1717.

over Mecklenburg, especially as imperial forces were heavily committed in Italy and the Balkans.[94]

The news of the *Conservatorium* spread rapidly. In December 1717 the president of the aulic council, Windischgrätz, told Behr that Charles Leopold knew everything, probably because Eichholtz had secret sources in Vienna.[95] The tsar's displeasure was also made known to Vienna and dealt with at the privy conference on 19 December.[96] This did nothing to reassure the Hanoverian government. Clearly Bernstorff's enthusiasm for the knights' cause had misled the government in Vienna into the belief that Hanover was straining at the leash to smash Charles Leopold's little tyranny. The imperial government, the knights and, apparently, Bernstorff himself, probably overestimated the influence he was able to exercise on the king's councils in London.

The aulic council dealt further with the case in a *votum* of 5 August 1718.[97] Perhaps the most important part of the *votum* dealt with growing Prussian demands for inclusion in the Mecklenburg commission. Uncertainty about Prussia's attitude was one of the factors holding up the execution. The king of Prussia, though an ally of the duke, the 1708 alliance having been renewed in 1717, gave him no encouragement. In letters to Charles Leopold between October 1717 and October 1718[98] he urged the duke to pursue a course of moderation and warned him that he could expect no help from fellow princes if action were taken against him. On 4 October he stated that the duke had no right to treat his knights in the way he had in the mistaken belief that he was accountable to no one. The king made his attitude very plain:

I cannot and shall not assist Your Highness against the execution in the slightest way . . . I must declare once and for all that I

---

[94] The Emperor was also unwilling to become involved in the Northern War: Vienna, Staatskanzl. *Vortr.* K. 22 i-v fol. 129 – 43, *Vortrag* of 19 May 1717. There was fear of a Russian attack on Silesia and Bohemia from Poland. Relations between the Emperor and Russia deteriorated sharply in 1717 after the flight of the tsarevich to Vienna: Hantsch, *Schönborn*, pp. 234 – 5.

[95] Schwerin, E III P.1.6, Behr to Bernstorf, 25 December 1717.

[96] Vienna, Staatskanzlei *Vortr.* K. 22 ix-xii fol. 92.

[97] *Merkw. RHR Conclusa*, vol. II cxxiv. The *votum* is in Vienna, RHR *Den. Rec.* K. 699(14) and K. 701.

[98] Schwerin, *Acta Diff.* II vol. xxii fasz. 2, nos. 3, 5, 7, 23.

want nothing to do with the actions which Your Highness is taking against your nobility.[99]

At the same time, however, Prussian diplomats were working strenuously in Vienna either to prevent the execution or, if this failed, to ensure that Prussia was included. They were to assure the imperial government of the king's patriotism and ardent wish to assist the Emperor in carrying out the execution and to emphasize his efforts to bring Charles Leopold to reason. The king wrapped up his wishes in phrases which made it seem that he was eager to help the Emperor. In fact he was afraid of being left out in the cold while Hanover laid hands on Mecklenburg. He tried to keep a foot in both camps by approaches to the knights. In 1717 he offered them a loan of 200,000Rt. but the terms were too harsh and the knights eventually borrowed 100,000Rt. from Hanover.[100]

The council's opinion was that the inclusion of the king of Prussia was not required in imperial law. There were also weighty reasons, listed in an earlier *votum*, for excluding him: he was an ally, relative and possible successor of the duke. Furthermore the duke and the king were already in litigation over compensation for damages inflicted by Prussian troops in Mecklenburg in the Northern War. There were also fears that Prussia's inclusion would lead to a restriction *(Einschränkung)* of imperial jurisdiction. The council had harsh words for the king's attempts to dictate the Emperor's obligations under the imperial constitution: he was trying to set limits to the Emperor's authority and to restrict the freedom allowed him by the laws of the Empire in the exercise of his office.[101] In one exhibit the king offered his help against a prince who had overstepped his authority; in the next he demanded inclusion as a right. The council's distrust of Prussia shines through the measured language of its *votum*. Frederick William's desire to increase his possessions had led him to attempt to extend his rights over a number of small territories and towns, which had involved him in a

[99] 'Ich kann und werde Euer Durchlaucht dagegen nicht die geringste Assistenz leisten.'

[100] Frederick William wanted the knights to accept his right of eventual succession and to give him a mortgage on all their lands in return for aid: Vienna, RHR *Den. Rec.* K. 697(1), exhib. of 3 November 1717, *Beilage* 64. Schwerin, E III P.1.6, Behr to Bernstorff, 6 October 1717, *ibid.*, P.1.7, Marquand to Behr, 21 April 1718.

[101] Moser, *Justizverfassung*, vol. I, pp. 1231–9.

large number of cases in the council.[102] The king was still seeking inclusion in the Mecklenburg Commission ten years later and in a memorandum of September 1727[103] the aulic council quoted examples of how the king had exploited his rights as conservator, protector, creditor, eventual successor or heir to extend his possessions. Control of Mecklenburg would give Prussia the Elbe and most of the Baltic coastline of Germany. The council's dislike of the king was reciprocated and did nothing to improve relations between Prussia and the Emperor. On 15 February 1716 the Prussian envoy in Vienna reported:

The aulic council sticks its nose in all affairs of state and, as it knows how to mix these up with questions of justice, the Emperor can easily imagine that his conscience is under assault and that his judicial office has been insulted. Nothing can inflame the Emperor more than the belief that Your Majesty no longer wishes to obey his rescripts.[104]

In his political testament Frederick William warned his successor that the Emperor was very jealous of the power of Brandenburg-Prussia but, while she had a large army, there was nothing to fear from the Emperor's mandates.[105] But so harassing were the decisions of the council, culminating in 1725 in the decree of execution against him to be carried out by Sweden, Saxony, the elector Palatine and Worms,[106] that the king was moved to order that all communications from the imperial courts were to be referred to him for personal decision, whereas earlier they had been dealt

---

[102] The records of the aulic council between 1707 and 1733 contain details of disputes involving Prussian encroachments against Quedlinburg, Mansfeld, Limburg, Werden, Lübeck, Ansbach-Bayreuth, Kulmbach and Bentheim, among others. The king was also involved in a long-standing constitutional dispute with the knighthood of Magdeburg. In a *votum* of 16/ 27 June 1724 the council commented that it was becoming obvious that the king took no notice of imperial orders and that those who dared to appeal to the Emperor from his lands were punished: Vienna, RHR *Vota* K. 33, dealing with the Magdeburg case.

[103] Vienna, RHR *Antiqua* K. 343/344 I. It is likely that it is in this collection by mistake.

[104] Droysen, vol. 4/ii, pp. 151, 358 – 9, vol. 4/iv, pp. 297 ff. Naumann, p. 32. This and similar opinions of the role of the council have tended to colour the views of some historians.

[105] *Acta Borussica. Behördenorganisation*, vol. III, p. 464. Perels, pp. 47, 82.

[106] Koser, p. 220. The execution came to nothing.

with by the governments of the individual provinces.[107] Of all the council's *fulmina* against him, the king was most embittered by a case in the council, engineered by Schönborn, which foiled his attempts to secure the inheritance of Brandenburg-Kulmbach.[108]

However, it was to be feared that if the king's offer to help the execution was rejected, he might do all in his power to hinder it and to foil the whole purpose of the action, to bring speedy relief to the hard-pressed Mecklenburg nobility. Surprisingly, in the light of what had gone before, the council recommended the inclusion of the king of Prussia in the commission to execute and investigate provided there were no political reasons against this.

The *votum* bears a manuscript resolution of Charles VI, in which he rejected the council's recommendations. This was not surprising as, apart from the legal objections which the council had weighed against the possible dangers of Prussia's exclusion, there were important political reasons against it. The execution depended very much on the diplomatic situation. Certain powers, particularly Denmark and Spain, were only waiting for a good opportunity to fish in troubled waters in the north or the Empire. The question of Prussia's inclusion in the Mecklenburg commission was discussed at the imperial conference on 1 September 1718, which dealt with northern affairs in general.[109] The ministers present believed there was a plot of the tsar and the king of Prussia, close allies since November 1716,[110] and Charles Leopold against the Emperor and the Empire, preparations for which were being made inside and outside Germany. There were large numbers of Russian troops in Poland and Mecklenburg and Prussia was arming rapidly. A common understanding for the execution of an evil design (*gemeine Verständniss zu Ausführung eines üblen Vorhabens*) was to be feared. The dangers to the Empire and the hereditary lands was real, especially as there was a strong possibility of agreement between Sweden and Russia to win back the former's German possessions for her.[111] As first it had been reported that the imperial ministers were unwilling to agree to a *Conservatorium* until the Russians had left Mecklenburg as otherwise the repercussions might have been too dangerous.[112] A Russo-Swedish alliance would have been even

---

[107] Perels, pp. 69 – 71.
[108] Vienna, RHR *Vota* K. 7, *vota* of 14 February 1716, 14/18 June 1723. *Ibid.*, Reichskanzlei, *Berichte aus dem Reich*, fasz. 20 fol. 1 – 15.
[109] Vienna, Reichsk. *Vortr.* fasz. 6c fol. 89 – 96.
[110] Williams, *Stanhope*, p. 361.
[111] In the summer of 1718 Russian and Swedish representatives met in the Aland islands to negotiate terms for a separate peace and common action against the other northern allies: Wittram, vol. II, p. 406.
[112] Schwerin, E III P.1.5, Behr to Small Committee, 3 April 1717.

more dangerous and would have proved most unwelcome to England, with her strategic interests in the Baltic, and to Hanover, holding former Swedish lands. Earlier it had been believed that the tsar's ambitions were limited to Estonia, Karelia and Ingria. England had also encouraged an Austro-Russian alliance in the hope that the bulk of the Russian fleet would become involved against the Turks.[113] The prospect of a Russian occupation of Mecklenburg brought about a sharp change of course: in March 1718 St Saphorin was instructed to negotiate an alliance with the Emperor and Poland and the instruction was repeated with greater urgency on 2 September. On 23 August the imperial government resolved to break off diplomatic relations with Russia. The anti-Russian trend in England and Hanover was strengthened by the prospect of an overwhelming Russian victory in the Baltic and the possibility of alliances between Russia, Sweden and France. Peter I visited the French court in May 1717 and the report spread afterwards that the French had persuaded him to withdraw his main army from Mecklenburg. This immediately aroused the suspicion that France must have given something in return. In August 1717 France, Russia and Prussia entered an engagement at Amsterdam, which heightened fears that Russia was set fair to replace Sweden in the traditional French 'eastern system'. In fact the alliance was fruitless as the French still lacked sufficient confidence to enter an alliance with Russia without England, although the idea was very attractive.[114]

Prussia's offer of help in Mecklenburg was also the subject of discussion in the privy conference on 1 September 1718.[115] The conference voted unanimously that the Prussian offer, though laudable, could not be accepted. The imperial ministers seem to have been convinced that Prussia was a close ally of the Russians and planning to carry out 'evil designs' with them in Poland or the Austrian lands.[116] It was unlikely, therefore, that they wished to give Prussia an imperial mandate to march troops into Mecklenburg unless the king gave proof that he had abandoned his dangerous friendship. The peace of Passarowitz, which ended the Turkish war in July, and the death of Charles XII of Sweden in December 1718 altered the situation favourably. On 28 December France and England officially declared war on Spain, though hostilities had been under way for months. In January 1719 the Saxon field

---

[113] Mediger, *Moskaus Weg*, p. 33.
[114] Williams, *Stanhope*, pp. 228, 358. Wittram, vol. II, pp. 319–22. Wilson, pp. 18–19.
[115] Vienna, Staatskanzlei *Vortr.* K. 22 viii–xii fol. 27–8.
[116] Mediger, *Moskaus Weg*, p. 38: Poland was virtually a Russian colony.

marshal Fleming arrived in Vienna to negotiate a treaty of guarantee on behalf of the king of Poland, as required by England. The main function of the negotiations was to obtain satisfactory arrangements for the defence of Poland while the Mecklenburg execution was in progress. One condition was that George I should make available the English fleet in the Baltic to defend the Polish coast, especially Danzig and Elbing.[117] England wanted an imperial guarantee of payment of the costs of the execution and for compensation in case of loss. The English government apparently placed little faith in the provisions of the imperial ordinance of execution and Bernstorff, though in London, was able to do nothing to hasten the negotiations.[118]

If it were true that the execution was part of Habsburg foreign policy, permitted by the Emperor only because he wished to retain the English alliance vital to his interest elsewhere,[119] then this should become clear from the conference protocols. In fact they indicate the reverse. The conference concerned itself with finding the most efficacious method of putting the verdict of the aulic council into effect. Hanover was the only politically acceptable power in north Germany strong enough to carry out the execution and, with the added strength of England, likely to be able to proceed without interference from interested powers.

On 5 January 1719 a treaty was signed between the Emperor, England and Poland, containing a secret article on the execution against Mecklenburg providing the guarantee required by Hanover.[120] The basic aim of the treaty was to drive the Russians from Poland, by force if necessary.[121] Secret article I laid down that any attempt by another power to interfere with the Mecklenburg execution was to be a *casus foederis*. By secret declaration IV St Saphorin committed the English Baltic squadron. English ministers refused their counter-signatures.[122]

---

[117] St Saphorin agreed to this, having received assurances to this effect from Bernstorff and Robethon: Wittram, vol. II, p. 407. L. R. Lewitter, 'Poland, Russia and the Treaty of Vienna of 5th January 1719', *HJ* (1970), pp. 3 – 30.

[118] Schwerin, E. III P.1.6, Rhaden to Behr, 21 December 1717, P.1.8, Behr to Small Committee, 11 January 1719.

[119] Naumann, pp. 21 – 2, Ballschmieter, p. 135. Both represent this view.

[120] Naumann, p. 20. Hanover, *Cal. Br.* II El no. 179. Mediger, *Moskaus Weg*, p. 39 and McKay, pp. 375 – 6 state that Austria and not Hanover insisted on the inclusion of the Mecklenburg case in the treaty.

[121] In fact they had gone already. Peter I was outraged when he heard about the agreement.

[122] Wittram, vol. II, pp. 408 – 9.

On 28 February, while an English naval squadron cruised off the Mecklenburg coast,[123] a force of some 10,000 Hanoverian and Wolfenbüttel troops with artillery crossed the Elbe into Mecklenburg. After a brief skirmish with a detachment of ducal troops at Walsmühlen, in which, to the subsequent satisfaction of patriotic Mecklenburg historians,[124] the Hanoverians were badly mauled, they quickly occupied the country. The main Mecklenburg army fell back into Brandenburg while the duke, with a small force, entered Dömitz.[125]

On 13 March Charles Leopold's submission was presented in Vienna. Something of the seriousness of his position seems to have impressed itself on him in the weeks before the execution. In mid January he announced his intention of reducing the size of the army[126] and allowing the knights back but at the same time he continued his attacks on the commissioners in Vienna. On the eve of the execution he gave way on further points in a last attempt to stop an execution he had believed would never take place. He had been warned of its imminence by Eichholtz on 3 January: unless the dukes gave a pure and simple submission, the execution would take place without fail.[127] The ambassador prophesied accurately what eventually happened: once the execution troops were in the country, they would not leave until the duke paid hundreds of thousands of *Reichstaler* in costs, excess taxation, compensation for damages and any other claims likely to arise under the circumstances. Already the mother of the divorced duchess had appealed to the aulic council hoping to profit from the impending execution. All Eichholtz' attempts to mobilize support in Vienna had failed totally. The Emperor, it was well-known, was determined to put a stop to four years of violence and wanton illegality and he was tired of hearing the same old story from the duke.[128]

From the first the execution proved a profound disappointment to the aulic council. The duke had been stubborn before; now he became violently intractable. It very quickly became apparent that

---

[123] The fleet was designed to prevent Prussian attacks on Poland rather than Mecklenburg: Ballschmieter, p. 131.

[124] Witte, vol. II, p. 265. This skirmish was later to become very important. It was probably a mistake, as Charles Leopold had ordered his troops to fall back into Rostock and Schwerin, but later a frequently repeated charge against him was that he had opposed an imperial execution by force.

[125] This little fort, the object of the solicitude of three dukes and ultimately the cause of all the trouble, was never taken out of Charles Leopold's hands.

[126] Schwerin, E III P.1.8, Small Committee to Behr, 16 January 1719, Behr to Bernstorff, 4 February 1719.

[127] Göttingen, Aw. 478.

[128] *Ibid.*, Eichholtz to the duke, 14 and 18 January 1719.

the Mecklenburg question had simply entered a new and more difficult phase; it was further from solution than in 1701. Once the commission had secured control of the country and the duke had shut himself in Dömitz, all those with new or old grievances against Charles Leopold and his predecessors appealed to the aulic council, believing that the execution gave them a chance of redress. It gave Mecklenburg-Strelitz a chance to strike back at Schwerin, which had long trodden its rights underfoot.[129] The multiplying rubrics of the various appeals to the council read like a catalogue of the misdeeds of dukes of Mecklenburg for a generation or more. The Mecklenburg question proved to be a hydra: whenever one problem seemed near solution new ones grew up to replace it. The knights would never feel safe until the duke submitted to the Emperor and reconciled himself to the commission. Even then, it soon became clear, it would be difficult to hold the duke to his submission unless there were forces on the spot to coerce him. As it was, there was no sign that the duke had any intention of accepting what was happening. From the first he attacked the commission violently.

On 16 March the council resolved on a *votum* to deal with these points and on the twentieth a supplement was added.[130] Further developments were dealt with in another *votum* of 27 April.[131] The duke's complaints against the commissioners had continued to arrive. Large numbers of his servants and officials had been dismissed. A Hanoverian official, Werpup, had taken control of the country's finances, ordering all money normally paid to the duke to be paid from 1 March onwards into a new execution exchequer (*Exkutionskassa*).[132] His army had been driven out of the country.[133] The whole commission was patently biased against him: the

---

129   There was a rumour in 1717 that Strelitz was planning to reassert claims to the whole of the Güstrow inheritance: Schwerin, E III P.1.6, Behr to Jaxmund (a Strelitz councillor), 20 October 1717.

130   *Merkw. RHR Concl.*, vol. II, no. cxxxi, Vienna, RHR *Vota* K. 35.

131   *Ibid.*, RHR *Prot. Rer. Res.* xviii 40. This *votum* is in Vienna, RHR *Vota* K. 35, 'Conservatorii nunc Executionis, Mecklenburg-Strelitz, in pto. die russische Einquartierung betr'.

132   Witte, vol. II, p. 267. The ducal administrators of noble estates were arrested and ducal revenues confiscated: Vienna, *Kl. Reichsst.* K. 347 fol. 276 – 81, memo. of Eichholtz, 18 April 1719.

133   Crull, R. (ed.), *Mecklenburg: Werden und Sein eines Gaues* (Bielefeld and Leipzig, 1938), p. 84. By 1719 Charles Leopold had an army of some 8,500 infantry. Most left the country after the execution, some entering Swedish and Prussian service. The majority were embodied into the Russian army as a distinct unit.

commanders of the execution forces were members of the Mecklenburg knighthood and Werpup, the civilian head of the execution
administration, also held land in the country. The duke was being
executed against by his opponents, not by impartial agents of
imperial justice. He was being treated as an outcast, as if the
execution had deprived him of his rights as a prince.

The knights, in their exhibits to the council, were predictably
against any relaxation of the commission. The council shared this
view. In its opinion the duke had been given many opportunities to
obey imperial orders but, far from doing so, had challenged
imperial jurisdiction and bandied interpretations of the laws of the
Empire with the council. His offer of submission had been so
hedged about with conditions and reservations as to be unacceptable. During his life Charles Leopold was to present many
submissions but always with the condition that they could not
prejudice his 'regalia, territorial superiority and rights of sovereignty'.[134] In view of the fact that he interpreted these so liberally,
the council could only accept an unconditional surrender. In the
council's view there was nothing in Charles Leopold's behaviour to
suggest that he meant his submission sincerely. The duke's
Russians had indeed left, taking with them everything they could
carry, but the duke still had a substantial force of Germans in
Dömitz. It was essential to ensure not only that Charles Leopold no
longer wished to resist but that he lacked the means to do so.

The council's recommendations were approved and published as
a resolution on 28 March 1719.[135] The duke was ordered to submit
through the commissioners, into whose hands the investigation of
the case had passed. At the same time the commissioners were
ordered to reduce their forces in the country from 14,000 to 3,000,
because of the difficulties of maintaining such a large force in a poor
country.[136] Also the city of Schwerin, which had been bombarded
and seized, should be returned to the duke, who should be paid a
fixed annual Kompetenz from his revenues for his own maintenance.

If it were possible to draw a graph of the council's sympathy for
the duke it would reach its highest point at this time, immediately
after the execution. The council was obviously surprised and
disquieted by the extent to which Hanover had taken control of the
country. The occupation of Schwerin and the sequestration of the
duke's incomes had been undertaken without imperial instructions.
Charles Leopold's agents in Vienna and the king of Prussia urged

---

[134] For example, Schwerin, *Acta Diff.* III, vol. xx, *Parition* of 13 November 1726.
[135] *Merkw. RHR Concl.*, vol. II, no. cxxxii.
[136] Vienna, RHR *Den. Rec.* K. 696(6) no. 9: the country, poor at the best of
times, was still suffering the effects of the Northern War.

him to press this point.[137] In May Eichholtz reported a growing movement of opinion in the imperial government against Hanover and advised the duke against taking tempting short cuts. His optimism lasted into the autumn.[138] At the same time Windischgrätz advised Huldenberg to warn the knights not to give way to their desire for revenge and to emphasize that they were still bound to treat their prince with due respect.[139]

A further *votum* of 2/4 May,[140] dealing mainly with the skirmish at Walsmühlen, also revealed the council's unease at the speed and completeness with which Mecklenburg had been taken over. It suggested the despatch of another tactful rescript to the commissioners instructing them to take more care to observe their mandate. The council was also suspicious of the commissioners' recommendation that certain ducal incomes should be mortgaged to provide a loan of 600,000Rt. for the knights, who were in serious financial difficulty.

Before this and the previous *votum* were brought to resolution, the council voted a supplement dealing with a report from Charles Leopold that a Hanoverian force had tried to seize Dömitz by stealth on the night of 1 May.[141] This was a further indication that Hanover was trying to take possession of Mecklenburg. The council repeated its earlier advice that the commission troops in Mecklenburg be reduced to 3,000 and warned that any attempt to deprive the duke of Dömitz was likely to lead to trouble, especially from Prussia. It recommended a rescript to the commissioners ordering them to leave Dömitz alone.

The imperial resolution on these *vota* and supplements went further than the aulic council's recommendations. The number of troops was to be reduced to 1,200 and they were to be stationed only in Rostock and at the Elbe crossing points.[142] The resolution was published as a verdict on 31 May.[143] The commissioners were to be informed that the Emperor had no doubt that they would instruct their subdelegates in Mecklenburg to act in accordance with imperial orders, which was a polite way of saying that the Emperor

---

137 Schwerin, *Acta Diff.* III, vol. xxii fasz. 2, Frederick William I to Charles Leopold, 6 May 1719.
138 Göttingen, Aw. 471 I nos. 25, 27, 33, 88, 92, 95. II no. 5.
139 Schwerin, Landst. Archiv *Protokoll* 1719 II fasz. 3 no. 1: Marquard to Small Committee, 9 May 1719.
140 *Merkw. RHR Concl.*, vol. IV, no. dxcix. There are copies in Vienna, RHR *Vota* K. 35 and *Den. Rec.* K. 701.
141 Vienna, RHR *Vota* K. 35. The attack was easily beaten off.
142 There is no record of this matter having been dealt with at a meeting of the conference.
143 *Merkw. RHR Concl.*, vol. I, no. lxiii.

was worried by the liberal way in which the executors had interpreted their commission. It was impossible to avoid the impression that Hanover had virtually annexed Mecklenburg. It was to prove impossible to dislodge the commissioners, especially as they alone provided security against Charles Leopold. The duke rapidly lost patience and became increasingly violent in his threats against the knights and their foreign friends.[144] The execution had probably taken place too late. It coincided with and contributed to the steady deterioriation of relations between the Emperor and Hanover-England. In May 1719 Eichholtz reported to his master a rumour in Vienna that the Emperor and Schönborn, with most of the aulic councillors, were now in favour of ordering a total evacuation of the Lüneburg troops from Mecklenburg.[145] The Emperor found himself in a dilemma: the actions of his commissioners were involving him in increasing unpleasantness with Prussia and could produce an anti-imperial outcry in the Empire and they were strengthening Hanover in the north. But, if the troops left Mecklenburg, it was likely that the duke would wreak a terrible vengeance on the knighthood. On 31 May Eichholtz reported on an audience with the Emperor, whom he was unable to understand. Afterwards Schönborn explained that Charles had promised a favourable verdict, denied any evil intentions towards the duke and regretted that matters had gone so far.[146] The Mecklenburg case had entered a new phase.

East Frisia

The constitutional disputes in East Frisia under Charles VI were, as in Mecklenburg, an encounter between old and new.[147] Against a long-established tradition of 'Frisian liberty'[148] prince George Albert was moved to pursue the doctrines of absolute monarchy more

---

[144] Göttingen, Aw. 474 II no. 6.
[145] *Ibid.*, nos. 36, 42.
[146] *Ibid.*, no. 54.
[147] Great interest was shown in the outcome of the case by the Mecklenburg Estates: Schwerin, Landst. Archiv, *Protocol* 1721, protocol of the Small Committee, 17 March 1721. Instructions were given to the *syndicus* to buy a copy of the *Ostfriesische Historie*, lately published, as it might prove useful in the Mecklenburg litigation.
[148] There is an outline history of the case in an undated *Relation* in Vienna, *Kl. Reichsst.* fasz. 406, which attributed all the troubles to 'ingenio Nationis libertatis tenacissimo novarumque rerum cupidissimo' and the fact that the East Frisians had entered a kind of *pacta subjectionis*, reserving their liberties, when the territory had become part of the Empire.

seriously than his predecessors. The constitutional troubles of the country in the sixteenth and seventeenth centuries had been increased by four long regencies under women and a serious attempt to curb the power of the Estates under the last of these regents, Christine Charlotte, who ruled for her minor son from 1665 to 1690, brought the problems to a head. As in Mecklenburg the basic question at issue, whether the rights and privileges of the Estates could limit the prince's *regalia* and *Territorialsuperiorität*, was linked with important side issues: whether the prince possessed power before he received the Estates' allegiance,[149] the rights of the prince over diets, the use of the Estates' special seal and the claim of the Estates to an exclusive control over taxation without the participation of the prince.

The roots of the troubles under Charles VI were both personal and economic. Returning prosperity in the early eighteenth century brought a period of peace between the prince and his subjects but this was disturbed by the introduction of a new factor into the long-standing litigation, the East Frisian chancellor, Enno Rudolph von Brenneysen, a historian and theologian.

Like many of his forebears,[150] prince George Albert fell easily under the influence of a strong personality. Brenneysen's influence on him was established early: while George Albert, as crown prince, attended the university of Leyden, Brenneysen corresponded with him, establishing a link which lasted for life.[151] He rose rapidly in the prince's service and came to exercise virtual personal government.[152] In 1697 he became *advocatus fisci* and took charge of all the prince's litigation.[153] He began to reorganise the princely archive at Aurich, a task earlier neglected, at the same time adding to it by purchase. His discoveries among the documents convinced him that the wide-ranging privileges claimed by the Estates had no legal justification.[154] His own background predisposed him to monarchical absolutism: he grew up in Esens in Harlingerland, a

---

[149] Christine Charlotte's son received no allegiance for five years after his accession and only received it in 1695 in return for an express confirmation of the constitution, including wider rights for the Estates: Klopp, vol. II, p. 464.

[150] Although Christian Eberhard's majority was declared in 1690, when he was twenty-five, he remained firmly under his mother's influence until her death in 1699.

[151] For Brenneysen's career and importance see I. Joester, *Enno Rudolph von Brenneysen (1669–1743) und die ostfriesische Territorialgeschichtsschreibung* (Diss. Münster, 1963).

[152] *Ibid.*, pp. 57–8.

[153] *Ibid.*, p. 32.

[154] *Ibid.*, pp. 44–9.

part of the prince's territories without Estates or constitution.[155] More important was his legalistic conviction that he was right and the Estates wrong. He believed that the Estates could be deprived of their arrogated rights by due process of law and from the beginning he organized the prince's litigation in the aulic council. Brenneysen enjoyed a considerable reputation among his fellow jurists in the council and saw it as a means of revolutionizing East Frisian politics. But, his refusal to compromise and his rigid adherence to what he regarded as legally correct, however far removed from the realities of the East Frisian situation, have been blamed by subsequent historians for the miseries which afflicted the country.[156]

Brenneysen was an ardent publicist and desired to inform the world of true conditions in East Frisia which, he maintained, were no different from those in any other state in Germany. He did not attack the *Akkorden* but sought to reinterpret them, maintaining that some were invalid, having been forced on counts Edzard II and Enno III by the Dutch.[157] The view that East Frisia was constitutionally unique, first set out in detail in the sixteenth century in an extremely one-sided history of Frisia by Ubbo Emmius, had been repeated so often that it had become the accepted credo not only of the Estates[158] but also of constitutional commentators.[159] Thus, the desire to assault the edifice of East Frisian liberty had long been present in the princely court; the opportunity to mount the attack was conveniently provided by nature in 1717.

After thirteen years of untroubled peace and prosperity between 1702 and 1715, the country was visited by a series of natural disasters:[160] in 1715 a cattle epidemic and floods;[161] in the spring of 1716 the destruction of the crops by a plague of caterpillars; in 1717 a plague of mice; on Christmas Eve 1717 the whole coast was ravaged by severe storms and large areas were swept by salt floods. This made necessary a large-scale repair of the damaged dykes and

---

[155] *Ibid.*, p. 4, König, p. 310.

[156] Reimers, p. 255, Joester, pp. 506 – 7, Kappelhoff, pp. 71 – 6.

[157] Klopp, vol. II p. 500.

[158] They never abandoned this view: e.g. the exhib. of 18 March 1721 in Vienna, RHR *Den. Rec.* K. 884(2) no. 9 fol. 387 – 8.

[159] In one exhibit the prince quoted Gottfried Lange's *Einleitung zur teutschen Histoire in Jure Publico* to the effect that the East Frisian Estates could hold diets at will, that the prince had no say in the country's finances and had to submit to the verdicts of the *Hofgericht*, which belonged to the Estates: Vienna, RHR *Den. Rec.* K. 885 fasz. 2 no. vi *Beilage* 229.

[160] Klopp, vol. II, pp. 485 ff.

[161] East Frisia was, like the Netherlands, heavily dyked. Its sea defences appear to have been long neglected by the early eighteenth century: Reimers, p. 250.

gave Brenneysen the opportunity to begin his attack on the Estates. It began a serious constitutional crisis which culminated in civil war. The ground was carefully prepared in Vienna before the case was opened there. Through von Brawe, the East Frisian envoy in Vienna,[162] Brenneysen built up a network of friends and influence among the Emperor's ministers and the aulic councillors.[163] There can be little doubt that the council was already well-disposed towards the prince's cause before the litigation began.[164] Brawe's reports of 1720 and 1721 contain many assurances of support from people of influence in Vienna, including the president of the council, though in a letter of 5 November 1721[165] Brawe reported that he believed Windischgrätz nursed a special hatred of the prince and his house. He would be given a chance to damage the prince if news of attempted bribery leaked out and the president had a pretext to dismiss the old, well-informed and, by implication, favourable *Referenten*. He advised the use of small bribes and big promises and listed those members available for money. In June 1720 the prince announced his intention of giving Schönborn a pair of coach horses 'to hasten the *votum* and to retain his good will'.[166] In July Brawe sent in a list of advisable bribes to persuade the prince to find the necessary funds. The *Referent*, Stein, was especially important, as was the imperial vice-chancellor. Without bribes, he argued, the prince could not hope for rapid help from the council.[167] Payments to councillors continued, large sums again being paid to named members, but by 1729 Brawe admitted that Stein, although heavily bribed, had achieved nothing and suggested that he had also been bribed by the opposition. This supports the view that bribery achieved little in important cases.[168]

Before the main case began, the prince received considerable encouragement from verdicts issued in minor cases. In May 1717 the aulic council issued a favourable decision in a case concerning

---

162 There were two Brawes; the father, Joachim, was East Frisian envoy in the imperial diet and the son, Georg Joachim, in Vienna.

163 Reimers, pp. 251–2 states that the prince's success was due to Brenneysen's influence in Vienna and to the fact that the prince was related to the Öttingen family and the Empress.

164 The correspondence between Brawe and Brenneysen is in Aurich, *Rep.* 4 A xvii no. 415 and A IV c 244 ff.

165 *Ibid.*, A IV c 246.

166 *Ibid.*, A IV c 245.

167 *Ibid.*

168 Aurich, A IV c no. 252, report of 19 October 1727. *Ibid.*, no. 254, report of 10 December 1729. It is significant that most of those described as bribable were on the bench of jurists. Perels, p. 89 also states that councillor Stein was known to take bribes from litigants.

the jurisdiction of the East Frisian high court (*Hofgericht*) which was under the control of the Estates. The prince consistently portrayed it as deliberately encouraging and fomenting disobedience among his subjects and lending a favourable ear to complaints against his officials. The Estates often paid the legal costs of appeals to it and it was easy to obtain *Remissoriales* removing a case from the prince's chancery to the court.[169] In a letter of 1 October 1717 Brenneysen announced to Brawe his intention to concentrate his campaign against the most important privilege of the Estates, their control and administration of the country's public finances to the total exclusion of the prince, who administered only his private domains and his share of secularized Church lands.

To finance the urgent repair of the dykes, the Estates' College of Administrators proposed to raise loans in Holland and Hanover. Although money was available, there was no agreement on the conduct of the work. In Harlingerland a princely official had taken charge of the repairs and they were speedily finished.[170] Elsewhere the half-finished repairs of the Estates' administrators were repeatedly washed away and the Estates' only solution to the problem was to raise further loans and levy heavy taxes to repay them.[171] The prince refused to authorise this, which caused great bitterness as the work was clearly urgent. The records of the College from this time give an impression of mounting debt and meagre resources. For example, the entries of 20 May and 20 June 1720 revealed that there was no money to pay the Prussian troops and, when the commander came in person to protest, the administrators could only propose further borrowing. The entry for 18 May 1722 admitted the country's deep poverty and the Estates' inability to pay their debts.[172]

Brenneysen's researches in the Aurich archive were consummated in his East Frisian *Historie*, finally published in 1720 at the

---

[169] *Ibid.*, K. 884(2) exhib. of the prince 30 January 1721, K. 921(2), exhib. of the prince 26 June 1722. The Estates claimed the court as the 'asylum of our liberties': K. 921(2), exhib. of the Estates 4 October 1717. In an exhib. of 17 April 1719 the prince described it as 'asylum petulantiae et inobedientiae'. This exhibit catalogues the prince's objections to the operation of the *Hofgericht* with lavish documentation.

[170] Klopp, vol. II, pp. 495 – 500.

[171] The East Frisian taxation, the *Schatzungen*, were a combination of a poll-tax and a land-tax, the *Kapital- und Personalschatzung*, supplemented by an excise on consumption, the *Pacht*, farmed to the highest bidder. The system was outdated and corruptly administered: König, pp. 343, 351 – 3. Klopp, vol. II, pp. 465 – 7 estimates the annual tax income at 400,000Fl. Loans amounting to several years' income were raised.

[172] Aurich, *Dep. I* nos. 705, 706.

prince's expense. The chancellor had initially been commissioned by Christian Eberhard to write an account of the constitution.[173] The two-volume work eventually produced consisted of a documentary collection which was and remains very valuable,[174] but the comments were as biased in favour of the prince as was Ubbo Emmius' work, against which it was a self-confessed counterblast, towards the Estates. Equipped with this work, copies of which were distributed among the aulic councillors,[175] Brenneysen set in motion the wheels of imperial justice which, he believed, would prove inexorable.

The main East Frisian case began with an appeal of the prince presented in the aulic council on 14 May 1720.[176] This was before the long and detailed exhibits on the Estates' financial mismanagement were ready but Brenneysen's timing was thrown awry by a report that the Estates were planning to have one of their number[177] appointed commander of the imperial Salva Guardia on the imminently expected death of the ailing commander, von de Ley. The dominant party in the Estates already controlled the only regular native troops in the country, the *Landschaftstruppen*, and the Prussian marines and Dutch garrisons were sympathetic to them. They were also negotiating for the renewal of the old *Conservatorium* on Münster. Had they been able to lay hands on the imperial force and engineer the despatch of Münster troops into the country at any imagined threat to their liberty, the dominant element in the Estates would have been able to lord it over the country and the prince at will.

This point was dealt with in a *votum* of 27/28 May 1720.[178] The council believed that the presence of many bodies of troops was a heavy burden on a small poor country, supporting Brenneysen's view that the root of the country's troubles lay in the presence of foreign troops under substitution agreements arranged by the Estates. The total annual cost of the Salva Guardia, the Prussian troops and the subsidy to Münster was about 24,000Fl. The foreign troops, the Emden garrison and other extraordinary expenses cost

---

[173] Joester, p. 50.
[174] It was widely quoted by the Estates themselves in their exhibits to the council: e.g. Vienna, RHR *Den. Rec.* K. 885 fasz. 3 no. 48 §31.
[175] Joester, pp. 76 – 7, n69: the case was not supposed to begin until the *Historie* was ready.
[176] Vienna, *Den. Rec.* K. 884(2), fasz. 1, fol. 1 – 25.
[177] The younger count Fridag was spoken of in this connexion. After his death in January 1722 Brawe reported that he had documentary proof that Fridag had been given an *Expektanz* on the post: Aurich, AIVc no. 247, reports of 21 January and 4 February 1722.
[178] Vienna, RHR *Vota*, K.44.

well over 3,000,000Fl in twenty years. The Estates also had to
service their debts and pay the running costs of the *Hofgericht* and
the College and subsidies to the prince.[179]

Apart from the financial cost, the council also regarded the
continued presence of the Prussians as an affront to imperial
authority and advised the Emperor to repeat the resolution of 1695
ordering their evacuation. It found the reports that the Estates were
seeking to revive their connexion with Münster and to secure
control of the Salva Guardia very disturbing, though unconfirmed
and requiring closer examination. It was vital to establish the
principle that the prince and the Estates were to seek the aid and
protection of no one but the Emperor. It would be dangerous to the
authority of princes if subjects were permitted to choose mediators
at will. The council was convinced of the prince's moderation but
feared that, if he received no help, he in turn would seek a violent
solution. The first draft of this *votum*, filed with the final version,
stated that it would be easy for the prince to find powerful friends to
intervene on his behalf, which would only introduce further
complications into an already delicate situation. This referred most
probably to Denmark or possibly Hanover and the remarks were
not included in the final version sent to the Emperor.

The main litigation, under the rubric *diversorum gravaminum*,[180]
began with a letter of the prince to the Emperor presented in the
council on 29 August 1720.[181] It was clear that Brenneysen planned
to settle everything at one blow and, by the summer of 1721, the
prince had filed appeals covering all the points at issue, the
Hofgericht, the foreign troops, the Estates' conventions with foreign
powers, the position of the city of Emden, the special rights of
Harlingerland and the Dutch garrisons, as well as the points in
dispute with the Estates. The exhibits set out in detail the main
theme of the prince's case, that the root of East Frisia's troubles lay
in the fact that the granting, collection, administration and
spending of all taxation lay in the hands of a small group within the

---

179 Klopp, vol. II, pp. 464 – 7. According to Klopp this was within the capacity
of the country, which produced over 400,000Fl a year in taxation revenue.
At the end of the seventeenth century the Estates had debts amounting to
700,000Rt. The additional burden of the natural disasters finally brought
the system down.
180 As in the Mecklenburg case, several distinct cases quickly merged and were
treated under general headings, though minor cases also retained their
separate rubrics. These were dealt with only in so far as they impinged on
the main litigation.
181 Vienna, *Den. Rec.* K. 884(2), fol. 29 – 60. The whole course of the case from
May 1720 to September 1736 can be seen in outline in a *Designatio Actorum
ibid.*, which lists all exhibits, verdicts, *vota*, rescripts and decrees.

Estates led by the town of Emden. Already the prince was seeking to widen divisions in the Estates revealed during discussions in the diets of 1719 and 1720 on the grant of extra taxation for dyke repairs. The administrators proposed borrowing 600,000 Dutch *Gulden* in the Netherlands but the prince refused to countenance this until the Prussian troops left and his supervision of the economy was accepted. He was supported by some members of the Estates.

In great detail the author of the letter, certainly Brenneysen or someone composing to his dictation, revealed how the administration of the revenues had grown corrupt and inefficient, how, although the prince contributed heavily to taxation from his own lands, his commissioner had no part in the perfunctory annual account and how the rest of the Estates were afraid to question the dispositions of the College out of fear that this might be interpreted as a betrayal of 'Frisian liberty'. Emden and its party, who paid nothing,[182] were holding the whole country in servitude, based on a false and so-far unchallenged interpretation of the East Frisian constitution. In clear and concise arguments, the style remarkable for its economy and lack of verbosity, the author demonstrated how money had been squandered on improper projects, on gifts to unnamed 'patriots'[183] or 'certain distinguished gentlemen', to finance litigation against the duke, to maintain foreign troops in the country and to keep alive conventions with foreign powers. Huge sums were spent on stationery and books and the servants of the Estates enjoyed high salaries and *Diäten*. The prince wanted 424,240*Rt.* back, his share of taxation used for 'improper purposes' since 1693. Later, when an imperial commission investigated these charges of maladministration, it found them justified.[184] The prince's main attack was levelled against the city of Emden, which had been recognized in earlier imperial pronouncements as insolent, unbridled and turbulent. This first comprehensive catalogue of the abuses of the College ended with seventeen specific requests to the Emperor, designed to correct the abuses, and was supported by a mass of documentary evidence. It was rapidly printed and distributed as part of the 'paper war' which always accompanied major litigation in the Empire.

---

[182] After 1683 the city of Emden agreed to pay 1,000*Rt.* a year and to maintain its own garrison. In fact the city paid only irregularly: Vienna, *Den. Rec.* I 925(4) exhibit of Emden 4 October 1723.

[183] The prince claimed that payments were made unconstitutionally to members of the *Hofgericht* but no documentary evidence was produced: Vienna, *Den. Rec.* K. 885, fasz. 2, no. xi, fol. 305–310.

[184] Vienna, *Den. Rec.* K. 907, fol. 40, *votum* of 2 March/16 August 1725, *Relatio* VI.

A separate appeal was lodged by the prince against the unauthorised establishment of a commercial company in Emden.[185] He claimed that the city had no right to do this without his consent. By three verdicts of 24 March, and 4 and 7 April 1721 the council decided to send *vota* to the Emperor on the three main points: the presence of foreign troops in East Frisia; the Emden commercial company; and the prince's complaints against the College of Administrators.[186]

These last were dealt with in the *votum* of 24 March. The council stated that it could not come to any decision on the rectitude or legality of the East Frisian constitution until the Estates had been given an opportunity to state their case. However, after examination of the prince's submissions, it believed that the conditions reported amounted to a perversion or abuse of the constitution and found the prince's complaints justified. The Estates had for years exercised complete control over the country's finances to the exclusion of the prince, a long-standing source of friction. The court accepted the prince's unsupported statement that the towns of Aurich and Norden and the Third Estate would welcome a reform of this system, which had opened the door to a régime of corruption and tax evasion. More important, the exclusion of the prince was illegal under imperial law and a breach of the prince's rights as an estate of the Empire. It was in the Emperor's interests to ensure that each province of the Empire adhered to the constitutional norm established by the act of investiture, the imperial law, imperial resolutions and the established order between ruler and ruled. Only within this framework could each province enjoy its own particular constitutional systems. The council placed great emphasis on the importance of an undisturbed order between ruler and ruled (*ordo parentium et imperantium*). Certain actions of the Estates, such as the calling of meetings without the prince's consent, were contrary to the Emperor's *Wahlkapitulation*. There was no reason why East Frisia should exempt itself from constitutional rules binding on the whole Empire and it was inexcusable that the Estates should challenge their prince's exercise of his territorial right to the disadvantage of the common good. The court did not question the

---

[185] This was established in 1720 as a joint-stock company to engage in wholesale trade, marine insurance and the Greenland whale fisheries in an effort to restore the failing economy of the city. A large amount of Dutch capital was invested in it: Klopp, vol. II, p. 508, Vienna *Den. Rec.* K. 916(11). There was also trouble over Emden's claimed right to extend its protection to Jews, which the prince held to be his sole prerogative: Vienna *Den. Rec.* K. 722(3).

[186] These *vota*, all read and approved on 9 May, are in Vienna, RHR *Vota* K. 44.

fact that the East Frisian Estates enjoyed greater privileges than others but stated that these could not be extended to the total exclusion of the prince from all affairs of state. Their liberties were bounded by the rights of the *Landesobrigkeit*, the public good and the jurisdiction and sovereignty of the Empire. This is very similar to the court's view of the constitutional rights and wrongs of the Mecklenburg case and showed the same strict adherence to the law. In the court's view, East Frisian liberty had degenerated into license; it believed that the only factor which had so far prevented a minority of the Estates securing a complete *Dominat* in East Frisia was their failure to secure control of the imperial Salva Guardia, though they were now trying to achieve this. In addition the Estates were bound by imperial law to help their ruler financially.

The court presented the Emperor with a draft resolution for his approval and this was published as a verdict on 18 August 1721.[187] It accepted the validity of the East Frisian constitutional agreements, the *Akkorden*, in so far as they were not prejudicial 'to the sovereignty, rights and jurisdiction of the Emperor and the Empire and to a reasonable good order between the prince and his subjects'. It was almost totally favourable to the prince. The Estates were to refrain from all intercourse with foreign powers, were to enter no negotiations with foreign powers without the prince's consent and were to stop the payment of all substitution money. Emden was to pay its due, one sixth of the annual taxes and its deputies were to leave diets when the city's affairs came under discussion. The prince's commissioner was to be allowed to question any item in the annual accounts and the whole accounting system was to be reformed. All improper expenditure was to cease, the yield of taxes was not to be employed to finance litigation against the prince, to pay for the Emden garrison or to maintain foreign troops in the country, and all subsidies and payments to foreign states were to cease. In a separate *votum* of 7 April/9 May 1721[188] the council stated that it was convinced of the truth of the prince's claims about the foreign troops. It believed that the cause of the country's troubles lay in the absence of an effective government: the prince was virtually excluded from all important business. The Estates were ready to pay thousands to Münster and

---

[187] *Merkw. RHR Concl.* Vol. II, no. ccclvii.

[188] Vienna, RHR *Vota* K. 44, 'das Conservatorium und die darin liegenden Völker betr'. The prince's side realized that the Prussians were a major problem, as most German rulers would think twice before starting a war against a state with an army of 60,000. Brawe senior reported on 22 October 1721 that he did not believe there was any hope of help against Prussia from anything less than the whole Empire: Aurich, AIVc, no. 246.

Brandenburg, the former for nothing and the latter for troops brought in without the Emperor's consent under a *Conservatorium* long since abolished. Millions had been poured into the Prussian war chest under an illegal arrangement and the Estates maintained a permanent correspondence with Prussia. The prince was 'mild and pious' and was suffering from the Estates' lust for power. The presence of foreign troops constituted 'a tearing away of East Frisia, a substantial imperial fief, from the Emperor's supreme feudal power'. The verdict of 18 August also ordered a re-examination of all accounts since 1693 if the prince so wished, and a proportion of the taxes from his lands employed for improper purposes since that date was to be refunded. An annual subsidy was to be paid to him. In case of future dispute no appeals were to be made to anyone but the Emperor. The Emden Commercial Company was also abolished by a further decree, as recommended in a *votum* of 4 April/9 May 1721.[189] If the city or the Estates had any complaint against these decisions they were to bring them before the Emperor 'as supreme head of the Holy Roman Empire and the fountain-head of all rights and liberties of subjects, including those incontestably held by Emden'. The verdict gave the Estates and Emden two months in which to report their obedience.

Some subsequent historians have uncritically accepted the view, almost immediately advanced by the Estates themselves, that the aulic council acted improperly in issuing these decrees before the Estates and Emden had been given an opportunity to put forward their case.[190] They were certainly very favourable to the prince and were welcomed ecstatically in Aurich. On 12 September 1721 Brenneysen wrote to Brawe, instructing him to thank the Emperor and the Empress personally for the fine princely crown which the imperial decrees had placed on the prince's head.[191] The prince himself was less optimistic and believed that force would be necessary.[192]

The view that the council acted improperly does not take into account the fact that the aulic council was not a court in the strict sense but an advisory body, dealing with cases of petition and possession and coming to verdicts on the basis of the information put before it. If the prince's arguments were true then the East Frisian constitution was being perverted; the commands given to the Estates were, in the council's view, so unquestionably right under existing German and East Frisian law that there was no need

---

[189] Vienna, RHR *Vota* K. 44.
[190] For example Reimers, p. 252.
[191] Joester, p. 79 n4.
[192] Aurich, CIIIa, no. 128, the prince to Brawe senior, 10 October 1721.

for any comment from the Estates, only for obedience. If the situation portrayed by the prince did not exist in the country and the Estates were already doing what the Emperor ordered, they had merely to report this fact; if not, there was no effective argument they could bring forward to justify their disobedience. Those who have condemned the aulic council for its failure to hear the Estates have failed to appreciate its workings. The council saw itself as restoring the balance to a constitution disturbed by one party. The legality of the situation which the council hoped to introduce in East Frisia by its decrees was open to no doubt and could not become the subject of dispute.

These views were repeated in a *votum* of 7 April dealing with the foreign troops in the country. The council was of the opinion that the king of Prussia might well have been planning to make East Frisia a satellite and to depose the Emperor as supreme sovereign over a considerable fief of the Empire.[193]

The Estates at once complained to the council that the verdict of 18 August 1721 had been issued before consideration of their case. During the autumn and winter of 1721 Gräve, agent for the Administrators, and Heunisch for Emden appealed repeatedly for the communication of the prince's exhibits.[194] They were supported in their appeal by Prussia; on 21 July 1721 the king reported that he believed the prince was taking advantage of calamitous times to bring about a complete destruction of the East Frisian consititution.[195] According to Gräve's exhibit of 15 December 1721 the prince's party had been quick to take advantage of the imperial verdicts: the decrees had at once been printed and distributed and the prince's officials had begun to collect submissions to them, mainly among the Third Estate. On 13 November the prince announced his intention of introducing a new inspector into the College, the councillor Bluhm. This was, the Estates maintained, an unconstitutional act. The burden of the Estates' complaint was that they had received no copies of the prince's exhibits and did not know what arguments had been used to bring this disfavour on their undeserving heads. They were prepared to give a provisional submission to the two rulings that they were not to undertake any

---

[193] The king of Prussia claimed that the troops were there for the benefit of the Estates. On 27 October 1722 the king wrote to the College to complain about the non-payment of his troops: 'Now you know very well that these troops are stationed in the country not so much for our benefit as yours and to maintain your liberty, privileges and old constitution.' If the troops were to leave, he claimed, all would be overthrown and the country placed at the arbitrary disposition of the prince: Aurich, *Dep.* I, no. 706.

[194] Vienna, *Den. Rec.* K. 884(2), nos. 21, 22, 23 and 25.

[195] *Ibid.*, no. 14, fol. 393 – 6.

violent action or to seek foreign protection but emphasized their determination to preserve their old and dearly bought liberties.

The resolution did not satisfy the prince's party and on 7 May 1722 nine letters of George Albert to the Emperor, under the title *Further Notice and Presentation*, were presented in the council.[196] These letters, amounting to 914 folio pages, were a massive indictment of the Estates and the city of Emden. The prince's aim was to put a stop to the 'old song', that the Estates had a right to control the finances of the state, gained when the Dutch controlled East Frisia.[197] The theme of the prince's argument was that a small group in the Estates, following the principles of Althusius,[198] were planning to set up a despotic oligarchy by controlling the College and the *Hofgericht* and making every act of the prince dependent on their consent. All respect for the prince had been lost and he was treated as a subordinate. At a diet called to announce the Emperor's resolutions, the Estates, stirred up by Emden and the nobility, had refused to submit. In a letter to him they stated openly that it was their function to decide, his to carry out the decisions.

The rest of the letters were taken up in a more detailed rehearsal of the earlier complaints, again with massive documentation. The prince emphasized that the blame lay not with the whole Estates, but with a small group. There was always friction below the surface of the Estates but in the past attacks by the prince had usually caused them to close ranks. The city of Aurich, the seat of the court, was usually attached to the prince. The court cost 20,000*Rt.* a year, almost all spent in Aurich, and in 1735, out of 297 houses in the city, seventy-one were occupied by persons attached to the court.[199] There was also general resentment among the other Estates against the supremacy of Emden, the ravages of its garrison and its refusal to contribute to taxation. A clear division in the Estates first appeared at the 1722 diet when the nobility and Emden republished Ubbo Emmius's *Historia Nostri Temporis* as a counterblast to Brenneysen's *Historie*. This was opposed by the rest.[200]

In one of the letters of 7 May the prince detailed his grievances against Emden.[201] He described the steps by which the city, with foreign help and in pursuit of totally false principles, had made itself virtually independent. His main complaints related to the

196   Vienna, *Den. Rec.* K. 885, fasz. 1.
197   Aurich, CIIIa, no. 128, letter of Brenneysen 19 February 1723.
198   Vienna, *Den. Rec.* K. 921(2) exhib. of 17 April, no. 4: 'In Althusii politica findet man den Ursprung alles Übels.'
199   W. Conring, *Aurich unter den Cirksena* (Aurich, 1966), pp. 59, 72.
200   Klopp, vol. II, p. 511.
201   Vienna, *Den. Rec.* K. 885, fasz. 1, no. III.

city's contribution to taxes, the use of its garrison, its pretensions to a right to keep Jews, its abuse of a printing press, denial of the prince's jurisdiction and right to a share of fines, a refusal to post the prince's ordinances, the exclusion of Lutheran worship, a refusal to submit the city accounts to the prince, the issue of ordinances without consulting the prince and an abuse of the right to make all shipping on the Ems call at Emden, which gave the city a virtual monopoly of East Frisian trade. The prince argued that the city was becoming ever more unbridled, seeking new powers over his officials.

The prince asked the Emperor to assert his rights over the Estates in the matter of diets. The Estates denied his right to call diets at will, to share in the examination of the credentials of the deputies and to determine in advance the matters to be debated there. He also wished action taken against the great disrespect shown directly or through attacks on his servants. The prince wanted an imperial resolution that the Estates were not his *Mitregenten* and that their decisions were no more than recommendations submitted for his approval. The Estates had developed the practice of not replying directly to the prince's *Proposition* but of sending in anonymous extracts of the protocols of their meetings containing offensive statements. Also they frequently ended diets before the prince's *Abschied* had arrived.

The third letter dealt specifically with complaints against the city of Emden, which had again appealed for Dutch support. The Dutch seemed at first most unwilling to become involved in trouble with the Emperor. The prince continued his complaints about the College's correspondence with them.[202] In two resolutions of 6 April 1723[203] the States-General refused to mediate in East Frisia unless requested to do so by both sides and repeated that they were not happy about interfering in a case pending in the aulic council, possibly affronting the Emperor's jurisdiction. At most they were prepared to make representations to the Emperor on the Estates' behalf.

The fourth letter reported contraventions of the Emperor's resolutions of 1721; the sixth dealt with the whole history of the Estates' illegal conventions with foreign states and the College's misuse of the Estates' seal without their or the prince's knowledge. There was obviously still great resentment on the part of the prince

---

[202] See his exhibit of 18 November 1723: Vienna, *Den. Rec.* K. 925(4).
[203] *Ibid.*, *Beilage*

against the Emperor's grant of a seal to the Estates in 1678.[204] The seal was, said the prince, an emotional relic of a long-passed age and should be abolished.

The prince's requests for compensation were rapidly expanding and his claims amounted to over 500,000Rt. He also claimed to need protection against his own subjects, who had made threats of violence against him and his servants.[205] The Estates were intending to tax the prince's ministers and servants, by tradition exempt, and had stated that, if necessary, they would use force to collect these taxes. The eighth letter reported the approach of Prussian troops to Aurich to carry out the collection; in the event the citizens had manned the walls and the Prussians had withdrawn.

The ninth letter reported the readiness of many of the Third Estate to submit in full to the imperial resolution of 18 August 1721. One deputy, Folkert ter Borg, who had proposed submission to the Emperor's verdicts, had been castigated by the representatives of the nobility and Emden as a traitor and expelled from the diet.[206] He had appealed to the prince's chancery against this but, when this body called witnesses, the College complained to the *Hofgericht* on the grounds that before, during and after diets they were not subject to the prince's jurisdiction and could say what they liked.

A further batch of four letters from the prince was presented in the council on 22 June 1722[207] giving further information on the growing division within the Estates and the increasing recalcitrance of the Emden party. For their part, the Estates continued to complain that they had received no communication of the prince's exhibits[208] but in August the prince's agent presented evidence that this had taken place.[209] On the following day the council reissued the decrees of a year earlier with a further warning to the Estates to submit to them within two months.[210]

---

204 This seal, showing the East Frisian *Upstallboom*, an armed man under a tree, was by tradition the emblem of the old free Frisian nation. In granting the right to use it for 10,000Fl, Leopold I was probably ignorant of the great psychological importance of the seal to the Estates. The diploma granting the seal referred specifically to it as an ancient emblem as described by Ubbo Emmius: Klopp, vol. II, pp. 397–8.

205 Vienna, *Den. Rec.* K. 884(2), no. VI, *Beilage* 234.

206 *Ibid.*, *Beilagen* 255–62 are submissions from certain *Ämter* of the Third Estate.

207 *Ibid.*, K. 885, fasz. 2, nos. x, xi, xii and xiii. These listed the members of the Estates whom the prince regarded as ringleaders of opposition. These included eight noblemen, many of them members of the *Hofgericht* and the College, and Hessling, the *syndicus* of Emden.

208 Vienna, *Den. Rec.* K. 885, fasz. 2, no. 40, exhibit of 26 June 1722.

209 *Ibid.*, no. 42.

210 *Merkw. RHR Concl.* vol. II, no. ccclviii.

Only now did the Estates' real counterattack begin with four exhibits of 3, 9, 13 and 18 November 1722.[211] In these they produced a startlingly advanced constitutional theory amounting to a denial of the Emperor's jurisdiction over the internal affairs of East Frisia. The Estates drew a clear distinction between *status publicus Imperii* and the internal situation in East Frisia. Under imperial law the Emperor had in theory unlimited jurisdiction over the whole Empire but, against this, the Estates stated the theory of a voluntary *pacta submissionis* to the Empire by the old free Frisians, in which all their age-old rights had been retained.[212] They disputed the prince's interpretation of the constitutional situation. They agreed that the *Akkorden* could not stand against the imperial constitution, as far as it touched relations between the state of East Frisia and the Empire, but, as far as the internal government of the territory was concerned, imperial law only applied in so far as it was compatible with the country's constitution. The *Beilagen* of this letter contain many quotations from learned studies to illustrate this principle, that pacts and agreements made between subjects and rulers could not lose their validity even if they were contrary to the law of the Empire. In the past counts and princes had sworn at their coronations to observe the *Akkorden* and the prince could not now appeal to imperial law to free him from this oath. The prince's claim that the *Akkorden* had to be interpreted in the light of the imperial constitution was false: they were perfectly clear in themselves and required no interpretation. The exhibit includes a copy of the printed *Vorstellung, den Grund der ostfriesischen Regierung und den Gebrauch der Landesaccorden betreffend,*[213] containing the statement: 'and in particular the *status publicus imperii* has no connexion with the *status publicus Ostfrisiae* and arguments cannot be transferred from the one to the other'. The other three exhibits dealt with specific points in the prince's appeals, which, they claimed, were no more than pretexts to justify his unconstitutional claims to supervise the economy. They denied absolutely that there had been any misuse of taxation, dealing with each of the prince's complaints in turn. The principle that the Estates administered the revenues *privative* had long been established in East Frisia. They also enjoyed the right to raise loans at will without reference to the prince if they considered it necessary. The prince was being led astray by his ministers into an attempt to destroy the constitution.

---

[211] Vienna, *Den. Rec.*, K. 885, fasz. 2, nos. 45 – 8.
[212] *Ibid.*, no. 45, §§5 and 6.
[213] *Ibid.*, fol. 450 – 88.

In the fourth exhibit[214] the Estates stated humbly but firmly that they were unable to obey the Emperor's orders as this would involve the loss of their liberties and privileges. They gave a detailed account of the development of the system of administrators, a system confirmed and recognized by past counts and princes and confirmed by the Dutch and the Emperor. They also repeated their contention that the *pacta provincialia* took precedence over imperial law when the internal government of East Frisia was in question.

On 22 February 1723, after reconsideration of the whole case, the aulic council decided to send a *votum* to the Emperor,[215] read and approved with a supplement on 4 May.[216] The copy preserved among the records of the council is in various parts: the actual *votum*, a draft verdict, a draft decree to the College, draft patents and draft instructions to a proposed imperial Commission. In the first the council reminded the Emperor that the two decrees of 1721 and 1722 had so far not been obeyed. In §14 of the draft decree it proposed a ban on the intimidation and persecution of those Estates who wished to submit. The prince had reported that many were ready to obey but were afraid of the Emden party. The council accepted this, although it was based on the prince's unsupported submissions. The council repeated its view that the Estates' exclusive control of finances was illegal and dangerous. The council believed part of the Estates had dangerous intentions in claiming that the Frisians were a free people not ready to tolerate any government over them, an attitude it roundly condemned. It was not a question of the Estates' control of the taxation system under the consitution but whether the administrators were liable to have their stewardship checked and their accounts audited. Each prince of the Empire was duty bound to ensure that taxes raised by the sweat of his subjects were used honestly, carefully and properly. This could be achieved within the East Frisian constitution if the prince's commissioner had the right to question the College's accounts, as ordered by the verdict of 1721. The administrators had to be responsible to someone for their husbandry. Therefore, in spite of the 'trivial objections' of the Estates, the council recommended that the resolution of 1721 be repeated in full. It was unlikely that they would obey willingly because the Emden party was winning support by claiming that the prince was planning to set up a despotism.

---

214 Vienna, *Den. Rec.*, K. 885, fasz. 3, no. 48, fol. 521–95.
215 Vienna, RHR *Prot. Rer. Res.*, xviii, 56.
216 This long and very important *votum* is in Vienna, RHR *Vota*, K. 44 under the rubric '*diversorum gravaminum*'.

Significantly the council warned the Emperor of the danger of Prussian interference:

The removal of the disorders weighing down on the country, a considerable fief of the Empire, and its salvation from the imminent decay and miserable decline consequent upon the long delay in repairing the dykes, the restoration of peace and unity between the prince and his subjects and the prevention of interference by the king of Prussia in disputes between them, to the detraction of the highest imperial jurisdiction, are all of great importance to H.M.

The best remedy was a commission of investigation, which could attempt to bring about a compromise between the parties. As commissioners the council recommended the king of Poland, as Elector of Saxony, and the duke of Brunswick-Wolfenbüttel.

The reasoning behind this choice of commissioners seems clear: the convening princes of the Circle, Prussia, Cologne and the elector palatine, were not seen as impartial. The elector of Hanover and the king of Denmark, as ruler of Oldenburg, both convenient as regards size and proximity, were also in some way involved in East Frisia and relations between the Emperor and Hanover were very strained. It was politically advisable that the commissioners chosen by the Emperor should be Protestants like the parties. Saxony was a large state with no interest in East Frisia, while Wolfenbüttel had a reputation for loyalty to the Emperor. The appointment of Wolfenbüttel without Hanover would be an unmistakeable sign of imperial disfavour. The council believed this would prove an effective means of preventing Prussian interference, though it was not envisaged that the commissioners would have to despatch troops to East Frisia. To save money, each was to send only one subdelegate. They were to deal with the *liquida*, that is to put into effect the imperial resolutions of 1721 and 1722, undertake the repair of the dykes, observing the customs of the country, and supervise the appointment and introduction of the prince's commissioner in the College. They were also to investigate and report on certain *illiquida*, the proposed Dutch loan, agreements made by the Estates with foreign powers involving the payment of subsidies and means of relieving the country of its burden of debt. As its guide it was to keep in mind the constitution of the country, as far as was compatible with imperial law. The main aim of the commission was to bring about a settlement acceptable to both sides.

It is interesting that in this *votum*[217] the council was already distinguishing between the so-called 'obedient Estates' and the Emden party, which was assumed to be the cause of all the trouble. Again the council's main object seems to have been the restoration of the balance between the different forces in the East Frisian constitution. This verdict was a definite assertion of dualism and firmly protected the *Akkorden*.

In 1723 divisions deepened in East Frisia with rival diets of the two parties in the Estates. The Emden party increased its appeals for help to its foreign protectors, Prussia and Münster.[218] There were several skirmishes between Prussian and Emden troops and villagers loyal to the prince and on one occasion Prussian troops threatened the town of Aurich, causing the ailing princess to go into a fatal relapse.[219] From June to September 1723 the case was in suspension as the Emperor was in Prague for his Bohemian coronation but after this the Estates and the prince continued their appeals throughout the autumn.[220] The main issue was becoming clear: the Estates resolved to vote large taxes to meet the many demands on them but the prince refused to permit their collection[221] and actively encouraged his supporters not to pay. This was a serious mistake as it led to more occasions of confrontation and threatened to lead to serious disorder. In East Frisia *Obrigkeit* was, in reality, shared between the prince and the College of administrators[222] and, by encouraging challenges to the authority of the latter, the prince placed his own and all authority in great danger.

Relations between the two sides became increasingly bitter. In the *Proposition* to the diet which opened on 19 April 1723, the prince openly blamed the administrators for the death of his wife. He refused to accept the Estates' proposed stamp duty, by which they

---

[217] The supplementary *votum* of 4 May, also in Vienna, RHR *Vota* K. 44.

[218] *Ibid.*

[219] This was Louise of Nassau Idstein. After a decent interval George Albert married Sophie Caroline of Brandenburg-Kulmbach, which made him a relative by marriage to the king of Denmark. The touching death-bed scene between the prince and Louise, quickly printed and distributed, won the prince much sympathy: Reimers, p. 253.

[220] These are all in Vienna, *Den. Rec.*, K. 925(4).

[221] They complained of this in several exhibits, especially that of 24 September 1723, 1 October 1723 and 7 January 1724: *ibid.*, no. 84. The prince refused to consent to taxation voted in December 1723, approved by all the Estates except Norden, whose deputies were absent. The prince seized on this as a pretext. The Estates argued that a majority decision was binding on all. The exhibit of 7 January made further attacks on the prince, claiming that tax revenues belonged to the East Frisian *Volk*, not to the prince.

[222] Klopp, vol. II, p. 398: in certain spheres, notably in finance, the Estates possessed sovereign power in the state.

intended to raise a grant for the prince on his remarriage. The growing acerbity of the relations was shown in the sharp communications exchanged and the prince's refusal to meet the Estates in person.[223]

By this time the aulic council seems to have been anxious to wash its hands of the whole affair. The verdict of 26 January 1724 referred the Estates to the commission with their complaints and warned them not to bother the Emperor with 'unnecessary and vain documents' before the commission had completed its work and sent its report to the Emperor.[224] This was repeated in a verdict of 20 October 1724.[225] Having completed its judicial dispositions, the council clearly no longer felt it had any important function in an area which was becoming politically tender. In further verdicts of 14 February and 6 March the council again referred the prince and the Estates to the commission.

The progress of the case was noted in a *votum* of 29 May/10 July 1724, which dealt with developments since the issue of the commission. Civil war had broken out after attempts by the Emden garrison to collect taxes by force led to a fight with the prince's supporters in the town of Norden. The division within the Estates was now clear. A diet held on 19 June 1724 was attended by the 'obedient' Estates, who declared openly that a minority of the Estates was perverting the constitution to consolidate their domination of the country: the administrators had boasted openly of the promises of protection they had received from the king of Prussia. If imperial authority was to be vindicated, it was essential to secure the removal of the Prussian troops, whose commander, Fridag, sat in the diet and allowed himself to be used as a tool of the College.

The council recommended that Prussia be given a serious warning not to allow her troops in the country to interfere with the imperial Salva Guardia, but left the decision on this essentially political question to the Emperor. The council also suggested that it might be best to repeat earlier orders for the removal of the troops, at the same time communicating the orders to the king *extrajudicialiter*, that is by diplomatic rather than judicial channels. This might convince him of the likely unpleasant consequences of his continuing opposition to the Emperor's supreme judicial authority:

---

[223] Vienna, *Den. Rec.*, K. 925(4), exhibit of Gräve, 31 January 1724, *Beilage*, no. 126. After her death the prince refused to receive the delegation of the Estates and excluded the knights from the funeral procession. According to the Estates, he allowed no chance of attacking or insulting them to pass unused.

[224] Vienna, RHR *Prot. Rer. Res.*, xviii, 58, fol. 47.

[225] *Ibid.*, xviii, 60.

'bearing in mind that a serious extrajudicial representation and declaration usually carried far more weight than a judicial decision'.[226] This is an interesting comment on the court's idea of its own importance.

Between May and August 1724 Brawe was ill and the prince's litigation was suspended.[227] On 22 May 1724 Gräve, for the king of Prussia, presented an appeal arguing that, as heir presumptive to East Frisia, the king had a duty to ensure that no foreign powers became too strong there. The king, very annoyed at his exclusion, also wanted an annulment of the commission, as yet inactive, and the issue of a new commission to the directors of the Westphalian Circle, including himself. The whole question of the choice of commissioners under imperial verdicts, whether or not they ought to be restricted to Circle directors, roused some controversy during Charles VI's reign but the aulic council consistently maintained that the Emperor had total freedom of choice in civil cases. Only in criminal cases, involving the execution of the ban of the Empire, was his choice restricted under the *Walkapitulation*.[228] Acceptance of the principle advanced by the Circle directors would mean a considerable loss of imperial authority. The increased power of the convening princes would also be most unwelcome to the other princes of the Circle, as it would mean that the directors would themselves be immune from commissions and executions. If the composition of a commission was determined in advance, the door would be open to all kinds of abuses and the larger states would never execute verdicts against one another.

The council totally rejected the king's arguments. The *Expektanz* on East Frisia was a poor excuse for his actions; the heir was supposed to show proper respect and devotion to the Emperor as the feudal overlord. If the king sought to use his *Expektanz* to the Emperor's prejudice, then the Emperor had a right to cancel it and to give the vacant fief to another.

The council recommended that new instructions be given to the commission. It was to receive and investigate the complaints of the prince, to draw up a report on this and submit it to the Emperor. It was also to arrest and interrogate the ringleaders of the recalcitrants and to put into effect the punishments laid down in the Emperor's decrees.

---

[226] 'anerwogen, dass die ernstliche extrajudiciale Vorhaltung und Erklärung weit mehreren Nachdruck als die judiciale Verfügung mit sich zu führen gepflegt'.

[227] Aurich, AIVc, no. 249.

[228] Vienna, *Den. Rec.* K 907 fol. 58 – 9, *votum* of 2 March/16 August 1725.

This *votum* bears a note of Schönborn, dated 10 August 1724, to the effect that the Emperor approved it. The resulting verdict of 17 August[229] promised that there was to be an end to attempts to hold up the work of the commission by 'frivolous appeals and improper and presumptuous legal expedients'. In fact the work of the commission was being held up by a civil war.

The East Frisian civil war (the 'Appelle-Krieg'), if three years of skirmishing between diminutive armies deserve the name, lasted from 1724 until 1727 and ended in complete victory for the prince's supporters and a small mercenary army financed by heavy borrowing. The small professional armies on both sides were reinforced by bands of armed peasants.[230] It was surprising that war had not broken out earlier. There had been several occasions in the previous half century when armed conflict had seemed imminent: there were too many bodies of troops in the country, all under different control,[231] though, in the event, foreign troops took little part in the hostilities.[232] The emergence of peasant committees, the so-called *Communen*, which rejected control by both sides and spread a violent jacquerie through the countryside, was a most significant aspect of the war. The people, impoverished by the burden of taxation and confused by the political manoeuvrings of their two rulers, the prince and the new and old Colleges, mutinied.[233] Nominally supporting 'Frisian Liberty' and the Estates, they attacked both sides. The *Communen* signed their decrees with 'L for *Libertas*', collected taxes, raised armed bands and terrorized loyalists. Their violence lost the Estates much support.[234]

The war was fought between a minority of the Estates, Emden and its surrounding *Ämter*[235] and most of the nobility, called the

---

229   *Merkw. RHR Concl.* vol. I, no. cccci.
230   Emden recruited between three and four thousand peasants in Reiderland: Aurich CIIIa, no. 128, the prince to Brawe, 15 April 1726. The Emden sailors and ships' boys also reinforced the city garrison and artillery, which formed the core of the Estates' army. For a detailed account of the war see Kappelhoff, pp. 251 ff.
231   Klopp, vol. II, p. 408.
232   *Merkw. RHR Concl.* vol. I, no. ccc. Early in 1725 the Prussians again began to collect taxes by force for their own maintenance: Aurich, CIIIa, no. 128, the prince to Brawe sen., 16 January 1725.
233   Klopp, vol. II, pp. 532, 535.
234   *Ibid.*, pp. 537–40, Vienna, Kl. Reichsst., K. 404, memorandum of the prince 2 October 1726.
235   Religious and economic divisions played an important role. The predominantly Calvinist and more prosperous areas were most consistently *renitent*: Vienna *Den. Rec.* K. 924(1) no. 1.

Renitenten, and the prince supported by the 'Obedient Estates', Aurich, Norden, five *Ämter* and a few noblemen.[236] In East Frisia the war is called Von dem Appelle's War after the leader of the *Renitenten* and it was fought more with pen and ink than powder and shot.

The course of the war has been dealt with in general histories of the country and is not relevant to this study. More important is the fact that the aulic council could do nothing to stop it and attempts to reach a compromise failed completely. During the course of the war the council issued several *vota* but these were little more than commentaries on the deteriorating situation in the country. The prince's victory alone enabled him to put the Emperor's verdicts into operation. This had several results. The 'obedient' Estates, who had supported the prince during the war, became less co-operative when they saw their liberties in danger. More important, the foreign friends of the Estates, who had earlier stood by, began to show alarm.

The commissioners' subdelegates Ritter and Röber arrived in Aurich in spring 1724 but they were able to achieve little. Dependent on the prince's hospitality and exposed to Brenneysen's high-powered arguments, they acted and reported consistently in favour of the prince. Attempts to achieve a compromise were torpedoed by the chancellor. They called a diet to Aurich but the administrators in Emden ordered the Estates to stay away. Eventually in August 1724 most of the Third Estate and the towns of Aurich and Norden sent their deputies to Aurich. The council had instructed the subdelegates to arrange the election of a new College from the obedient Estates and this was done. The rest had until October 1724 to submit. On 9 October Gräve reported that the Estates had been quite ready to find *güttliche accomodements* on all matters at issue but that this offer had been rejected out of hand by Brenneysen, who declared that everything had to be settled according to the Emperor's decisions.[237] By the verdict of 27 October[238] the council referred the Estates to the commission and warned that no more exhibits in the *Kommissionssache* would be accepted. Again the council washed its hands of everything.

In the meantime the subdelegates forbade the Emden College to collect taxes. Like Mecklenburg, East Frisia now had in effect two governments, with the new College in Aurich and the old in Emden. Each government controlled part of the country and each

---

[236] At an extraordinary diet called by the prince on 23 November 1724 only one member of the nobility attended: Vienna, *ibid.*,

[237] Verdict of 20 October 1724: Vienna RHR *Prot. Rer. Res.* xviii 60.

[238] *Merkw. RHR Concl.*, vol. VII, no. cxxvi.

had its own apparatus of government.[239] The *Renitenten* organized their efforts through the Privy Commission in Emden. The prince and the Aurich College controlled three of the six zones into which the country was divided for tax purposes,[240] Aurich, Norden and Friedeburg, while the Emden College controlled the Emden and Oldersum *Comptoires*. The Leer *Comptoire* was between the two and was a target for both sides. It was also the seat of the imperial Salva Guardia. Both sides sent troops and tax farmers to the town and the first major 'battle' of the war took place there in February 1725. Thereafter the town was the scene of constant trouble.[241] More ominous, five Dutch companies arrived to reinforce the garrison in Emden and a further three hundred Prussians arrived from Minden.[242] Victories for the prince in summer of 1725 caused a flood of submissions to the Commission but a hard core of resistance remained alive around Appelle, men afraid to make any concessions in the knowledge that constitutions even older than theirs had been destroyed and seeing their only salvation in foreign help.

A *votum* of 18/22 October 1725 dealt with further reports of the subdelegates,[243] the main content of which was the deteriorating condition of public order: 'in East Frisia now every one does what he likes'. The *Renitenten* continued their appeals to foreigners, there was widespread refusal to pay taxes and many acts of violence were recorded against tax collectors and the Salva Guardia.[244]

The subdelegates were frank in admitting that they had so far been able to carry out very little of their commission. Their attempts to investigate the various points at issue had been flouted by the disobedience of the *Renitenten*, who refused to attend hearings called by them. In spite of this, in the council's view, the commissioners had undertaken their task willingly. It was not surprising that the Dutch and Prussia accused them of partiality as they had faithfully reported all the activities of the *Renitenten* and the foreign troops against those who had submitted. The subdelegates were extremely depressed and the Saxon, Ritter, was known to be anxious to leave. This was, the council felt, a pity as the work was almost complete.

---

[239] From early 1725 the 'obedient Estates' employed their own aulic agent in Vienna, Fabricius.

[240] This was for the excise on milling, drink, meat etc., which was farmed out to the highest bidder: Vienna, *Den. Rec.*, K. 923(3), *Beilage A*, a letter of von der Ley, 3 August 1725.

[241] Klopp, vol. II, pp. 527 – 9.

[242] Vienna, *Den. Rec.* K. 924(1) nos. 8 and 9.

[243] Vienna, *Den. Rec.* K. 907.

[244] *Ibid.*, K. 924(1): the reports of the commander, Ley, give useful material on the war.

If the aulic council really believed this it was deluding itself. It recommended the Emperor to urge the commissioners to persist with their work.

The council's attitude was stated even more uncompromisingly in a second *votum* of 18/23 October dealing with Dutch protests against the commission.[245] The States-General and Prussia cooperated in protest. The Dutch claimed a protectorate over the county and had an immense financial interest there. The Dutch ambassador in Vienna, Hamel Bruininx, reported to his masters in 1725 that the Emperor's ministers were furious at what they saw as an attack on imperial authority.[246] Emden kept up a barrage of appeals to the Dutch for help. In a resolution of 3 August 1726 the States-General referred the matter to their committee on East Frisian affairs.[247] A further resolution of 19 August revealed that the Dutch thought it better not to become involved in the troubles, although much had been done in contravention of the *Akkorden*, of which they were guarantors. Königsegg, the imperial ambassador in The Hague, reported on 20 August 1726 that the Dutch were afraid that the prince would come to an agreement with the king of Prussia on the succession question and that the two would then drive out the Dutch garrisons, or that Münster would send in troops if given Emden as security for the costs. In his opinion the Dutch were more worried about East Frisia than the Ostend Company and openly stated that they had English and French support in the matter.[248]

In its *votum* the council rejected Dutch claims to a traditional right of mediation and arbitration. It put forward the view that the *Renitenten* were planning to hand over 'sovereignty, honour position and supremacy' in East Frisia to the Dutch in return for military aid against the prince.[249] It is difficult to judge whether the council seriously believed this. It continued to express the opinion that the situation in East Frisia would not be so difficult had the Dutch not put troops into the country, an act amounting to a hostile invasion of the Empire. The Dutch presence had stiffened the *Renitenten* in their opposition, convinced them that the Emperor lacked the means to put his decisions into force and encouraged the king of Prussia to keep troops there. In appealing to the Dutch, the

---

245   *Ibid.*, K. 907.
246   Aurich, CIIIa, no. 113, fasz. 3, report to the prince from The Hague, 20 January 1725.
247   Vienna, *Kl. Reichsst.*, K. 404, printed *Kurze Facti Species*, nos. 86 – 8, 91 and 93. Appeals of Emden to the Dutch, 2, 6, 9, 13, 16, 18, 19, 20 and 27 August 1726.
248   *Ibid.*
249   *Ibid.*, fol. 10 – 18.

Estates were breaking established imperial law. The council denied any intention of destroying properly founded privileges or of bringing in unjust innovations: it aimed only at correcting abuses. It was the Emperor's duty to look to the welfare of the East Frisian subjects and a majority of the Estates had accepted his dispositions. The *Renitenten* had therefore no right to call themselves Estates and the Dutch had no right to appeal on their behalf as the Estates of East Frisia. The true Estates and the prince had already come to an agreement, so there was no longer any need for a compromise with the rest. The *Renitenten* had persistently refused to obey the commission's summonses to meetings called to discuss the points still at issue.

The council opposed any concessions to the Dutch, as these would only encourage the rebels: 'Behind the sweet words and offers of a compromise is hidden a plan to drag out the negotiations for so long as to give the rebels and the Prussians a permanent reason for their presence.' The argument that the *Renitenten* had not been heard was an old trick of those with a bad case. Their aim was to have the case started again in the hope of benefiting from Dutch protection.

The council advised the Emperor to reject all Dutch claims. If they continued to interfere in German affairs he would be justified in calling on the help of the Empire to exclude them by all the means necessary.

This *votum* bears a long manuscript resolution in Schönborn's hand, dated 18 June 1726.[250] The Emperor found the *votum* 'well and properly drawn up', but for certain weighty reasons it was considered necessary that only certain aspects of the matter should appear in the public protocols of the council. The Dutch ambassador was to be informed of the Emperor's intention to deal with the case of East Frisia, which was subject only to his and the Empire's jurisdiction, in accordance with German law. He did not doubt that the Dutch would accept this and would refer any East Frisian subject appealing to them to the imperial commission.[251]

The actual course of the rebellion and war was dealt with in two *vota* of 2 March/16 August 1725 and 17 April/2 May 1726.[252] The case had by this time become politically very delicate and the council's recommendations were tempered by political considerations: the

---

[250] Vienna, *Kl. Reichsst.*, K. 404, fol. 52 – 3.

[251] There is no record of any verdict based on this in the protocol of resolutions of the council for 1726.

[252] Both in Vienna, *Den. Rec.*, K. 907. They deal in the main with reports sent in by the commissioners. Both were very large, respectively 196 and 115 folio pages.

most significant decisions no longer appeared in the public protocols. The resolution on the *votum* of 16 August 1725 gave specific instructions that nothing concerning the commission, the punishment of the rebels, the question of the Dutch and Prussian troops or political matters was to be made public. By the time of the first *votum* all the Estates except Emden, part of three *Ämter* of the Third Estate and five noblemen had submitted to the Emperor's verdicts. The new College had been chosen in January 1726 and, through their agent, the obedient Estates expressed their humble obedience and complete satisfaction with the Emperor's verdicts. Five deputies of the *Renitenten* had appeared before the commission but they were only ready to submit if negotiation on points already settled was allowed and were only ready to accept the Emperor's verdicts in so far as they were compatible with the *Akkorden*. The subdelegates had rejected this out of hand. The five deputies also refused to give up the title of 'Estates'. The Emden party had tried to mobilize the king of England on their behalf, claiming that the prince's actions were holding up the repayment of loans raised in Hanover.[253] This had received a sharp reply from George I, who had also written to the king of Prussia rebuking him for allowing his troops to support rebels. More Prussian troops had entered Emden and had been taken into the sworn service of the city, which was also trying to persuade the Dutch to order their troops to take part in tax collections.

The council recommended strong action to deal with what had developed into a *Generalaufstand*. The *Renitenten* should be declared rebels, the names of ringleaders published and the citizens of Emden encouraged to disobey the city magistracy. The city's garrison right should be abolished and the whole Empire mobilized to help capture the ringleaders and put a stop to the activities of the old College.

To deal with Prussia the council could only recommend an absolutely final mandate on pain of a fine of 2,000 marks of gold, the punishment laid down for breaches of the peace of the Empire. An *Auxilatorium* on Sweden should be confirmed and extended to the elector-Palatine, Cologne and Hanover. Denmark, Hanover and Münster should be asked to prevent the march of Prussian troops through their territories. The council admitted that these were the most extreme measures it was competent to advise and stated baldly that it doubted whether they would have the slightest effect. The actions of the king of Prussia were such that only a small step

---

253 Aurich, Dep. I, no. 3140. George I wrote to the prince from St James's on 2 January 1725, assuring him that the Estates would receive no support from Hanover.

separated them from war against the Emperor and the council could only leave it to the Emperor to decide what was required to defend his authority. If anything was to be done about the case, the use of military force was essential. This had long been clear to the prince.[254] There was great difficulty in finding someone willing to undertake an execution and the main trouble lay, as always, in the *Konjunkturen*. The king of Prussia would not oblige unless the Emperor added him to the commission and the council was firm in its opinion that this would affront the principles laid down in earlier verdicts.

Both commissioners were already equipped with a *Conservatorium* to protect the prince and the obedient Estates and could employ troops under this but their troops would have to cross Brandenburg territory to enter East Frisia. Distance and other factors made it unlikely that any help was to be looked for from Sweden. Already part of the council were of the view that the only likely source of help was Oldenburg and urged that its ruler, the king of Denmark, be commissioned. This would frighten the rebels and might move Cologne and the Palatinate to act. Other councillors saw serious objections to this, as in the past Denmark had failed to obey the Emperor.[255]

The council had a clear programme ready when troops eventually entered the country. They were to be billeted on the rebels, that is all those who had not paid taxes to Aurich, especially on the rebel leaders and the Emden lands. The rebels were also to be liable to compensate those who had suffered in the war or had paid forced taxation.

[254] On 24 April 1726 Brawe reported 'gloomy stirrings' in Vienna. Everyone realized the need for the use of force but no one was in a hurry to start. The *vota* of 20 October 1724, 2 March and 18 October 1725 had all made the same recommendations but there had been no decision on them. Brawe had appealed to the Emperor, the Empress and Schönborn without result: Aurich, CIIIa no. 113, fasz. 1. It is significant that Brawe was well informed of the details of the aulic council's recommendations in its supposedly secret *vota*. He reported that he had assurances of support from the *Referent* in the case, Braillard, but the latter's hands were tied: external circumstances made it difficult to order matters strictly according to imperial law. The council could only base its decisions on what the commission or the appellant party said; otherwise it would be accused of taking decisions without evidence: *ibid.*, report of 27 April 1726.

[255] The memory of Denmark's annexation of Holstein-Gottorp during the Northern War remained strong in Vienna. The Danes had an interest in East Frisia as good neighbours and in their unwillingness to see the Dutch established there, in addition to the king's relationship to the prince by marriage: *ibid.*, AIVc, no. 243b, report of 25 May 1723, no. 254, report of 24 September 1729.

These proposals were accepted by the Emperor in the resolutions on the *vota* of 2 May and 16 August, but with important reservations clearly born of political considerations. At a conference on 9 June 1726 the decision was taken to dispatch the *Auxiliatoria* to Hanover, Cologne and the elector palatine as recommended and the execution was to commence at once. Brawe reported on 12 June 1726[256] that the vice-president of the council, Wurmbrand, was ill and unable to attend. Schönborn told him that he had forced through the *Auxiliatorium* on Hanover but could not move the Emperor to give one to Denmark. The prince still had the opportunity to consult the commission and invite in the Danes as good neighbours, as he was permitted to do under imperial law. The Emperor's decisions were embodied in the verdict of 19 June.[257] *Auxiliatoria* were sent to Hanover, Cologne and the elector-palatine. The verdict also contained a note on the duty of neighbouring princes to help their fellow prince against rebellious subjects. Attached to the copy of the verdict sent to the council was a *Referat* of the imperial chancery,[258] with the information that, although the conference of 9 June had decided 'for important reasons' not to despatch an *Auxiliatorium* to Denmark, the subdelegates were to be informed that, if the prince requested it, they could ask for Danish help without delay. It was considered important that a joint request should be sent.

Peace and order were eventually restored to East Frisia by the prince's own small army and the Salva Guardia. On the invitation of the commission the king of Denmark offered armed help after other leading princes of the Circle, to whom *Auxiliatoria* had been sent, refused it.[259] Danish troops moved to the Oldenburg-East Frisian border in April 1726 and a Danish agent visited Emden to put pressure on the *Renitenten*, without success. Danish troops actually entered the country in the following April.[260] More active Danish help was held up by a number of factors. On 29 October 1726 Königsegg reported from The Hague that the Prussian government had informed the Dutch that no mediation, by the Danes or anyone else, would be permitted without Prussian participation.[261] The Dutch were also said to be putting pressure on the German princes to prevent armed aid reaching the prince of

---

[256]   *Ibid.*, CIIIa, no. 113, fasz. 1.
[257]   *Merkw. RHR Concl.*, Vol. VII, no. cxxvii.
[258]   Vienna, *Den. Rec.*, K. 907.
[259]   *Ibid.*, *votum* of 17 May 1734, fol. 49. Kappelhoff, p. 290.
[260]   Aurich, CIIIa no. 113 fasz. 3: declaration of the Danish agent Witzleben to Emden, 1 May 1726.
[261]   Vienna, *Kl. Reichsst.* K. 404.

East Frisia. The archbishop of Cologne, as bishop of Münster, refused to take any action because the Dutch had warned that they would not view with pleasure the despatch of any foreign troops.[262] The English and French ambassadors in The Hague had informed the Cologne ambassador there that any attempt to send troops into East Frisia would be regarded as *casus foederis* under the Herrenhausen treaty. Eventually it became clear that it was not in the interests of Prussia or the Dutch to go to war with the Emperor or Denmark over East Frisia and Danish intervention proceeded. The real test for the aulic council and imperial authority came when, as a result, the situation in East Frisia was favourable to an execution of the Emperor's orders.

The difficulties began to exercise the council's mind in the *votum* of 17 October/20 November 1726.[263] This *votum* is especially interesting as among the records of the council is a record of the opinions expressed by named individual councillors.[264] A comparison of the names and the list of councillors present for that day reveals that the writer was Burckhard. He was at the time twenty-eight and a new member of the council. It is likely that this is a personal record, as it is the only such record found and may well have been filed in the imperial chancery among his papers on his death. The *votum* stated that imperial patience had been severely abused. The imperial decrees of 1721 and 1722 had threatened Emden and the rebels with severe punishment in case of disobedience but no submission had been received by 10 August 1724. On 18 January 1726 a further two months' grace had been granted but without result. Many submissions had been received but many had subsequently been revoked when the possibility of foreign protection for the rebels began to appear. The obedient Estates were also clamouring for some action to make a reality of the Emperor's protection and to put his orders into effect. Many reports of the aulic war council told of the sorry state of the Salva Guardia.[265] The

---

262   The prince sent his minister Münnich to Bonn to appeal to the archbishop for help. Cologne was a member of the Vienna alliance while the Dutch were in the rival Hanover grouping and the archbishop feared involvement in war against the United Provinces, Prussia and Britain: Aurich, CIIIa, no. 113, fasz. 3, extracts from Münnich's diary.

263   *Ibid., Den. Rec.*, K. 907.

264   *Ibid.*, RHR *Relationes*, K. 134, fol. 562–576. The *Relation* is printed in H. Wiemann and M. Hughes, 'Ein Sitzungsprotokoll des kaiserlichen Hofrats über Ostfriesland aus dem Jahre 1726', *Jahrbuch der Gesellschaft für bildende Kunst und vaterländische Altertümer zu Emden*, vol. 54 (1974), pp. 47–58.

265   Vienna, *Den. Rec.* K. 924 contains the reports of Ley's successor as commander of the Salva Guardia, Höfflinger.

general opinion was that a larger imperial force was necessary in case of further risings: the spark was still glowing in the ashes.[266]

The council was unable to come to a unanimous decision on action to recommend. Dankelmann stated the main difficulty: the case was a *Kabinettsache* and, he believed, could only be settled by a compromise.[267] Other councillors advised that the Emperor do nothing without consulting the Empire under Article II of the *Wahlkapitulation* because of the dangers involved in armed action in East Frisia. It was likely that this would be resisted and, under the dangerous circumstances of the time, it could unleash a general European war. This danger attended all the expedients so far suggested. Others were of the opinion that it was too early to consult the Empire *in corpore*. The Emperor had not reached the ultimate straits in which this was necessary and many in the Empire were already keen to diminish the Emperor's judicial power and to interfere with his authority. The Emperor had already approached the two Saxon and the Westphalian Circles but no one had been willing to restore order in East Frisia. Under the ordinance of execution the Emperor could requisition five Circles to execute his orders and, if necessary, the whole Empire. Only when these devices had failed was he required to ask the Electors for their advice. These councillors advised the Emperor to extend the requisition to the Upper Rhenish Circle. The whole Empire would be held up to ridicule if a handful of rebels was ably to defy the Emperor with impunity. It was shocking that the Herrenhausen allies should regard the execution of just and proper imperial orders as a *casus foederis*. East Frisia showed all signs of being lost to the Empire if the Empire did nothing to retain it. Princes called upon to carry out imperial orders had no right to refuse and the council recommended that the four Circles should be ordered to take armed action against the rebels.

A similar division arose among the councillors on the question of an imperial ban against Emden, which would require the consent of the Empire. Some considered it inadvisable in view of the close links between Emden and the sea powers. The whole question could anyway be postponed until after the verdicts were put into effect.

It had also been suggested that the Emperor should carry out the execution with his own troops and increase the Salva Guardia to

---

[266] *Ibid.*, no. 15, report of 5 July 1727.
[267] Vienna, RHR *Relationes*, K. 134, fol. 567.

four hundred men. In the present circumstances the council did not believe it advisable for the Emperor to take on the role of Circle director and use Burgundian Circle troops.[268] The council was not in favour of an increase in the size of the Salva Guardia, which at the time numbered about forty, as it was quite unable to support itself.

Some of the councillors favoured referring the question of Prussia's actions to the Empire; others recommended no action until the execution was complete. All were of the opinion that a further mandate to Prussia was pointless as the king had already ignored two.

The *votum* gave a united opinion that only force could achieve anything, though Burckhard's protocol shows that this view was not unanimous. It dismissed Dutch claims that their only interest in East Frisia was the restoration of peace. This could only mean that the prince and the Emperor would have to give way. Without Dutch support and encouragement matters would not have reached the extremes they had. In two resolutions the States-General, while deploring the violence of the rebels, had stated plainly that they could not be indifferent to what happened on their borders and would do all possible to bring about a compromise settlement. They could not do so if there was a threat that the constitution was to be destroyed and the letter of the imperial verdicts executed in their full rigour, as the prince wanted.[269] Despite this, a majority of the councillors was in favour of employing all the weapons of imperial law to enforce imperial verdicts against the rebels and only a minority advocated an attempt to reach a compromise under imperial auspices in order to avoid further bloodshed and because of the serious diplomatic ramifications of the case.

On 23 April 1727 the privy conference resolved to suspend decisions on most of the questions raised in the *votum*, whether to bring the matter to the Empire, whether to declare the ban against Emden and the rebels, whether the Emperor should employ his own troops, whether a further patent against the rebels and a

---

[268] In letters to Windischgrätz, prince Eugene and Schönborn on 23 August 1726 the prince suggested that the Emperor might send his own troops, as other princes refused to help and the rebels were threatening Aurich itself. He repeated this in a letter to the president of the council on 24 October, quoting the Rheinfels case, where imperial troops had been used, and suggesting that forces could enter East Frisia from the Austrian Netherlands: Aurich, CIIIa, no. 110.

[269] *Ibid.*, CIIIc no. 140 fol. 2 – 6.

further mandate to Prussia[270] had any purpose and whether the subdelegates were to be kept informed of all imperial decisions. Schönborn explained the Emperor's difficulties to Brawe. He wished to bring real help to the prince but feared that no state would do anything because of mutual jealousy and because of the uncertainty of the times. Despite assurances, it was unlikely that Prussia would stand by while foreign troops entered East Frisia. The Emperor did not intend to accept Prussia's offer of mediation.[271]

The conference decided[272] to send *Auxiliatoria* to the convening princes of the Westphalian Circle and to instruct the imperial envoy in The Hague to make strong remonstrations to the Dutch. The prince was to be informed that the times were not favourable for an increase in the size of the Salva Guardia. Nothing of this was to appear in the public protocols.

In the meantime the prince had helped himself. In spite of a series of victories won by the Emden party in the spring and summer of 1726, the hire of more mercenaries enabled the prince to win a complete victory by the spring of 1727. By May of that year all East Frisia except Emden was in his hands. A diet called on 17 June began by voting money for the prince.[273] Although not in the manner intended, the situation desired by the aulic council had come about, except for the continued immunity of Emden. It was now in a position to have its verdicts put into effect. Given the diplomatic situation in Europe, this was to prove very difficult.

---

[270] On 13 May 1727 the imperial resident in Berlin, Demerath, reported that Prussia intended to send more troops into East Frisia. He commented that it was easier to get Prussians in that out, as Vienna already knew too well. He also reported that the Prussians were intending to award themselves membership of the imperial commission by sending a subdelegate to join it from Cleves. At the same time the archbishop-elector of Cologne seemed to have found his courage; on 16 May 1727 he wrote to the Emperor announcing that his troops were ready to enter East Frisia: Vienna, *Kl. Reichsst.*, K. 404.

[271] Aurich, CIIIa, no. 113, fasz. 1, report of 19 March 1727. In the background imperial ministers were working to obtain real help for the prince. In December 1726 Schönborn told Brawe that an agreement had been reached with the elector of Cologne for this purpose: *ibid.*, no. 128, report of 17 January 1727.

[272] The resolution is attached to the supplement of 20 November in Vienna, *Den. Rec.*, K. 907.

[273] On the final stages of the war see Klopp, vol. II, pp. 536–42 and the reports of Höfflinger of 13 May and 5 July 1727: Vienna, *Kl. Reichsst.*, K. 404. Three companies of Danes entered the country in April 1727. On 28 April Brawe reported that the king of Denmark had written to London justifying his intervention on the grounds that the rebellion constituted a danger to neighbouring lands: *ibid.*

6

The Mecklenburg Commission
and European diplomacy

1719 – 1724

It soon became clear that the successful execution had brought an end to the Mecklenburg case no nearer. If anything, it had become more intractable. Three major difficulties faced the aulic council: the attitude of Charles Leopold; the mushrooming financial difficulties of the duchy; and the problems of controlling the commissioners. None offered an easy solution, especially as the whole affair became more deeply involved in the diplomatic manoeuvrings between the European great powers.

In the months after the execution Charles Leopold was in a stronger position than for years. He had powerful friends, notably Russia and Prussia. He had numerous potential allies among the German princes, seriously worried at the aulic council's assaults on the rights of a fellow ruler. Deteriorating relations between the Emperor and George I made the imperial government eager to find reasons to bring the Mecklenburg commission to a speedy end. If Charles Leopold had been prepared to make a gesture of submission, a token to save the face of the aulic council and the Emperor and allow them to withdraw from the affair with their integrity undamaged, his troubles would have been eased. This he was not ready to do. He gave up the unequal struggle in the aulic council early and abandoned the roads of diplomacy and legal procedures in the belief that he could obtain his aims by the use of 'secret channels' of communication and pressure on the Emperor. The growing frustration which this produced among agents of his, such as Eichholtz, can be read between the lines of their private correspondence with other members of the ducal government.[1]

---

[1]   Göttingen, Aw. 492, letter of Eichholtz 26 March 1721. Aw. 474 II no. 13 Wolffradt to Eichholtz, 3 September 1719, no. 21b Eichholtz to the duke, 23 August 1719.

Increasingly Charles Leopold sought out 'short cuts' (*Nebenwege*) to extricate himself. As a result he succeeded only in putting swords in the hands of his enemies. Then he mounted a vigorous and well-organised campaign to mobilize support among the German princes. In addition to direct approaches by his agents in Regensburg and elsewhere, large numbers of circular letters were prepared and sent to various rulers asking their support in defence of his rights as a prince of the Empire.[2] He saw himself as a full member of the 'league' of absolutist and would-be absolutist princes of the Empire and tried to reactivate the unions of the seventeenth century against the rights of Estates. In 1719 he hawked round a draft treaty, dated 1 February, which proposed common princely action against imperial attempts to infringe princely rights, the establishment of a common army of 20,000 available to all to coerce Estates, an arrangement for the arrest of ring-leaders of troublesome subjects on one another's territory and a common intelligence system to discover plots among subjects. This miniature Holy Alliance came to nothing.[3] He also placed great hope in mobilizing the opinion of German princes against the Emperor's verdicts. Although he received some sympathetic replies from his correspondents, most repeated the advice Eichholtz was passing on from Vienna: the duke must submit to the Emperor's verdicts.

The *Nebenwege* trodden by the duke during the case throw interesting light on his character and go a long way towards explaining his total lack of success. He became increasingly divorced from the reality of his situation and moved in a world of wild schemes. From June to December 1720 he was in Vienna. There was a rumour that he had come to be converted to Catholicism. He obtained an audience with the Emperor who was sympathetic but promised nothing. Schönborn and Sinzendorff left Vienna to avoid meeting him and no imperial minister called on him during his stay.[4] Schönborn treated him to a written homily on the imperial constitution: the Empire was a true state consisting of head and members, the latter bound to the former by a double bond, the feudal nexus and the *nexus subjectionis*. The special jewels of the Emperor's power were his supreme judicial authority and his rights as feudal overlord. The rights of princes had to be considered in the light of their due obedience to the Emperor.[5]

---

2   Drafts of these and the replies received are in Schwerin, *Acta Diff.* III vol. xviii fasz. 4, vols. xx and xxi.
3   *Ibid.*, vol. xviii, no. 2, report Kassel 30 February 1719.
4   Witte, vol. II, pp. 268 – 9. Göttingen, Aw. 493 no. 14/1.
5   Schwerin, *Acta Diff.* III vol. xx fasz. 7m, Schönborn to the duke, 6 March 1733.

The duke's two favourite 'short cuts' were an offer of conversion to Catholicism and an alliance with Austria.[6] Attached to the report of an interview with aulic councillor Wurmbrand in May 1720[7] is a draft treaty between the duke and the Emperor which shows the way Charles Leopold's thoughts were turning. It proposed an offensive and defensive alliance, under which the duke would recover his army and the Emperor would help him to obtain compensation for his losses in the Northern War. No further appeals from Mecklenburg subjects were to be entertained in the imperial courts. The Emperor would also pay the duke subsidies and help him to obtain Wismar. This treaty existed only in the imagination of Charles Leopold though there was a rumour in Vienna that, as early as 1716, the Russians had offered the Emperor a force of 10,000 Russian and Mecklenburg troops, with all expenses paid, in return for concessions for Charles Leopold[8]. Improving relations between the tsar and the Emperor, marked by a visit to Vienna of the Tsar's favourite Yaguzhinsky in 1720, caused fears than an alliance between the two was in the offing.[9] This prospect was very disturbing indeed to England. In fact, Peter I seems only to have been going through the motions in his diplomatic efforts on behalf of the duke; as early as the autumn of 1717 Peter's western ambitions appeared to be waning and he seems to have come to the conclusion that his alliance with Mecklenburg had been a terrible mistake.[10]

The duke was probably led astray by misinformed or deliberately deceptive councillors. The solid core of good advice remained; to submit. But Charles Leopold seems to have lived in a world of wonderful schemes and intrigues which would provide a complete solution overnight. His representatives found quickly that they could achieve nothing and that their advice was falling on stony ground. Many quickly gave up and moved to greener pastures. The Göttingen archive contains reports from many persons who were in the duke's service for a short time only. His early representatives, men like Eichholtz and Seger, were well-informed and were able to keep in touch with opinion in Vienna. But Charles Leopold ignored their advice. Eichholtz complained: 'I have been clearly informed that all the side-paths tried by the duke so far can only bring him

---

6   Göttingen, AW. 505 fasz. 4. Borgmann, p. 37.
7   Göttingen, Aw. 505 no. 7083.
8   Schwerin, *Acta Diff.* III/1 fasz. 6: von Lehsten to an unnamed *Kammerjunker*, 1 June 1716.
9   Naumann, pp. 37–45, 47.
10   Wittram, vol. II, p. 410.

nearer the precipice.'[11] In addition the duke did not pay his agents: Eichholtz complained often that his case was being paralysed by lack of means.[12] Charles Leopold insisted on conducting the case personally, with the result that the papers fell into terrible disorder.[13] His aulic agents suffered from his total lack of reason. Klerff did his best in the face of crazy orders. In January 1719 he abandoned the case, because the duke had issued patents insulting the Emperor,[14] after conducting it virtually alone for years.[15] Charles Leopold made life very difficult for his agents by persistently attacking the aulic council and the Emperor's jurisdiction. In 1719 Eichholtz warned him that the Emperor was very sensitive about his office and the council and urged the duke not to insult them in any statements.[16] On 18 December 1720 Eichholtz asked to be allowed to resign.[17]

After the passing of Eichholtz and the legation secretary, Seger, the conduct of the duke's affairs fell into the hands of a succession of dubious characters who appear to have won his trust by claims that they had the ear of the great and famous. These men quickly realized the futility of trying to persuade the duke and turned to vague assurances, which he seems to have swallowed without question. The comforting news given by these people bore no relation to the reality of the situation. The duke fell into the hands of charlatans in his search for the by-paths, which he believed would solve everything. He saw hopes in a connexion with Tonnemann, the Emperor's confessor, and corresponded directly with him in 1726.[18] Protestants habitually exaggerated the influence of the confessors of Catholic rulers.[19]

Charles Leopold also tried to revive the old connexion between his state and France. In May 1726 he sent an agent to Stockholm with a proposal for an alliance of France, Sweden and Mecklenburg aimed against Hanover and the Emperor.[20] He also approached the

---

[11]   Göttingen, Aw. 474 nos. 17, 22, Aw. 474 II no. 56. The only way out was for the duke to follow 'sane, moderate and practical counsels'.
[12]   In May 1722 Eichholtz appealed to the aulic council for an order to the duke to pay arrears of salary amounting to 10,500Rt.: Vienna, RHR *Prot. Rer. Res.* xviii 53, verdict of 9 June 1722.
[13]   Mediger, *Mecklenburg*, p. 110.
[14]   Göttingen, Aw. 460, Klerff to the duke, 15 January 1719. His son took over the case on Klerff's death in April 1719 and abandoned it in 1740.
[15]   *Ibid.*, Charles Leopold to Klerff, 28 February 1728.
[16]   Ibid., Aw. 474 no. 5, Eichholtz to the duke, 5 April 1719.
[17]   *Ibid.*, no. 110.
[18]   *Ibid.*, Aw. 505 fasz. 1.
[19]   Borgmann, p. 37.
[20]   Ballschmieter, p. 108. Schwerin, *Acta Diff.* III vol. xxii fasz. 4.

king of France as guarantor of the Westphalian peace.[21] These efforts to moblize foreign help lost him considerable support.

The duke's inanity reached its height in the years 1737 and 1738. In a set of instructions, dated at Wismar October 1737, the duke ordered Simon Abraham to go to Vienna, to take up contact with Michael Simon, a Jewish financier with close contacts with the imperial government, and to offer him, if the duke were restored, 400,000Rt. for the Emperor and 30,000 for himself. Abraham left Vienna in April 1738, this project to bribe the Emperor having come to nothing.[22]

During the Summer of 1720 the aulic council began to concern itself with the financial situation in Mecklenburg, which was to be a cause to growing worry over the years. The costs of the commission for one year amounted to over 800,000Rt., an enormous sum, partly accounted for by the slowness of the commissioners to carry out the Emperor's often repeated order to reduce the number of their troops in Mecklenburg.[23]

It was clearly impossible to pay the whole sum due in commission costs at once. Until it was paid or adequate security provided, the commissioners were to have the right to keep troops at Rostock and Boitzenburg. The council admitted that it had no idea what the annual income of the duke was; this was obvious from the gay abandon with which it proposed to pay off commitments amounting to millions of *Taler* from ducal revenues. The council did not yet appreciate the deep poverty of the country and declined to give any final decisions until accounts of ducal incomes were provided. It was clear that the council did not envisage that the commission's services would be required for much longer as it was already thinking of paying it off. In fact, the commission was to remain in Mecklenburg for a further twelve years, although not in its original form, and the costs were not finally paid off for fifty years.

The hope for a speedy solution of the rapidly ramifying Mecklenburg case was becoming increasingly remote. The knights

---

21   *Ibid.*, vol. xx fasz. 1.
22   Göttingen, Aw. 506 fasz. 7.
23   Vienna, RHR *Prot. Rer. Res.* xviii 49, 18, 23 and 24 July 1720. RHR *Vota* K. 35. Detailed accounts of the operating costs of the subdelegate commission and of the execution exchequer are in Vienna, RHR *Den. Rec.* K. 700 (8) no. 7 and K. 701 no. 27. The Estates claimed *c.* 822,000Rt. in excess taxation. In a good year the ducal revenues could produce a surplus of some 40,000Rt. The annual revenue was usually *c.* 350,000 but in the year 1719–20 there was a deficit of 11,000. After 1721 the economy again went into surplus, due to the sound administration of the commission, among other factors.

continued to complain of the contumacy of the duke,[24] while he, in a typical *punctirte Vorstellung* presented on 26 September 1721, asked the Emperor to put a stop to the oppressions against him and to restore the totality of government to him.[25] On 12 August the Prussian ambassador Kanngiesser again presented a request that the king of Prussia be joined to the commission or at least be allowed to send a representative to the forthcoming Mecklenburg diet, which the commission was to call. The time for such an appeal was not well-chosen. Relations between the Emperor and Prussia reached a low point in the summer of 1721 when there was a virtual breach of diplomatic relations.[26]

The Mecklenburg case also contributed to growing friction between the Emperor and England/Hanover. George I was reputedly furious at the council's decision of May 1719 placing restrictions on the number and location of the commission troops. He sent a rescript to Huldenberg threatening to give up the whole business. Copies of this circulated freely in Vienna and one was presented in the council by Seger, an agent of the duke.[27] The council's growing disenchantment with the commission was expressed more explicitly in a number of *vota* in the months after the execution.[28]

In his resolution on the *votum* of 12/15 June the Emperor approved the despatch of a rescript to Charles Leopold urging him to submit to the commission. The aulic council was to be instructed secretly that:

> for many important political reasons and weighty causes it is necessary in this crisis to restore peace as quickly as possible. The aulic council should therefore devote itself with its usual energy to bringing the case to a conclusion, saving the law.

A major difficulty concerned the future of former Swedish provinces in Germany acquired by Hanover and Prussia in the

---

24   *Annectatur* to the *votum* of 28 February/18 March 1721: Vienna, RHR *Vota* K. 35, 'den Landkasten betr'. On 15 July 1721 the council issued warnings to the duke and penal mandates against those who continued to obey his orders against the commission: Vienna, RHR *Prot. Rer. Res.* xviii 52.
25   *Ibid.*, verdicts of 17 and 21 October 1721, 'Commissionis in specie den Landtag and Landkasten betr'.
26   Naumann, pp. 70 – 2.
27   Göttingen, Aw. 474 no. 95
28   *Votum* of 12/15 June 1719: Vienna, RHR Vota K. 35, for example.

Northern War. The Emperor was reluctant to see the whole power structure in north Germany transformed without his participation and the Protestant 'theatre kings'[29] strengthened considerably. Although he had taken no part in the war, Charles VI tried hard to formulate the peace settlement. He called the victorious allies and the Swedes to a congress at Brunswick and hoped in this way to exert some influence on the final outcome and to bring about a settlement in the north acceptable to the claims of imperial authority in the area. The congress sat for years but achieved nothing.[30] The imperial government was quite happy to have the Swedes out of Germany but not about the resulting distribution of the spoils. The privy conference[31] considered the proposed division between Denmark, Prussia and Hanover, with an unspecified 'satisfaction' for Poland, unacceptable as it left too many unanswered questions:

and the most objectionable feature is that the consent of your Majesty and the Empire to these unilateral divisions and dispositions of such considerable provinces of the Empire has been postponed until the signing of an alliance between the two kings.

It was also highly questionable whether the Emperor could give his consent to the division. The conference recommended that he should reject the project and refer the whole matter to the Brunswick congress. It was probably only rivalry between the beneficiaries of Sweden's defeat which prevented them from ignoring the congress and dividing the Swedish provinces at will. Only the smaller states, as was usual with imperial projects, saw any value in the congress.

Since 1717, when imperial foreign policy had been based, for the want of any alternative, on the old alliance with England, relations between the two had deteriorated and the causes of the friction could be found in both the northern and southern theatres of European politics. After two years of frustrating delay, Hanover had carried out imperial verdicts against Mecklenburg but had gone far beyond what the Emperor had intended. At the same time

29 Droysen, vol. IV/1, p. 324.
30 Hantsch, *Schönborn*, pp. 212 ff. O. Haintz, *König Karl XII von Schweden* (3 vols., Berlin/Stockholm, 1951 – 8), vol. II, chapter XI *passim*.
31 A meeting of the privy conference of 27 May 1719 drew up a *Referet* on the new plan for a Northern peace proposed in London: Vienna, Staatsk. *Vortr.* K. 23. fol. 47 – 9.

Prussia and Hanover had begun to move closer together: English foreign policy increasingly required Prussia to help contain the Russian 'threat' in the western Baltic.[32] Hanover and Sweden entered a treaty of peace in November 1719. The settlement of international differences outstanding after the peace of 1714 was again making the European alliance system fluid. Under the influence of Alberoni and Elizabeth Farnese, Spain went over to a vigorous offensive. A new fleet was created and attacks on English commerce began. Alberoni also tried to moblize the Swedes, Russia and the Jacobites against the Quadruple Allies. In March 1719 a Jacobite fleet left Cadiz to invade England. It was dispersed by rough weather but not before it had frightened the English government into bringing in Dutch troops to defend the Protestant Succession.[33] Under the terms of the Quadruple Alliance France and Britain proceeded to use force against Spain. A French army invaded Spain while the main Spanish forces were locked in Sicily by an English blockade.

By February 1720 Philip V had dismissed Alberoni and Spain had joined the Quadruple Alliance.[34] The immediate result was that France and England began to move away from the Emperor and closer to Spain, a more natural ally for both under the circumstances of the time. Simultaneously the link between France and England was weakening. French policy was to obtain from Spain the same commercial concessions as those possessed by England. To persuade the Spaniards of her good intentions, she made it her business to urge England to restore Gibraltar to Spain. The regent seems to have been listening more to Louis XIV's former ministers than to the more pacific Dubois. France was finding her feet again and the Law System seemed to offer a means of solving the country's financial troubles.[35] Law had links with the growing number of Jacobites tolerated in France, in the eyes of English ministers a calculated act of hostility, and a number of other minor irritations damaged relations between the two allies.

In July 1720 it was resolved to open the great congress to remove all remaining sources of international tension at Cambrai in October that year. But the chances of a comprehensive European settlement, which had seemed possible in 1719, quickly slipped away. The congress was not convened until January 1724 and it was not until

---

[32] Mediger, *Moskaus Weg*, p. 43, Beattie, p. 236.
[33] Williams, *Stanhope*, pp. 318 ff.
[34] *Ibid.*, pp. 345 ff.
[35] *Ibid.*, pp. 341 – 3, 365. The Royal Bank founded in 1718 was united in 1720 with the great monopoly Mississippi Company, which also ran the state tobacco monopoly and the Mint.

1731 that the system of peace-keeping envisaged in the Quadruple Alliance came into being. In the meantime Europe was to go through an even more serious crisis. Britain and France's firm position was weakened further in the autumn of 1720 by the South Sea Bubble and the collapse of the Law System, which produced a crisis of confidence at all levels and shook the finances of both states.[36] The death of Stanhope in February 1721 and a reconciliation between George I and his son healed the Whig split, finally destroyed the influence of the Hanoverian party in English diplomacy, restored Walpole and Townshend, the first victim of the Split, to power and confirmed the trend to a more specifically British foreign policy.[37] It would be an exaggeration to describe Townshend's policy as 'isolationism' but it lacked Stanhope's European commitment. He was also more abrasive and adventurous than his predecessors. Even before the death of Stanhope, the Quadruple Alliance, the basis of the earlier security system, had been breaking up on the rocks of Anglo-French colonial rivalry, the Emperor's unwillingness to join as anti-Russian alliance, Anglo-Dutch annoyance over the Ostend Company and a number of German issues including the Mecklenburg case, George I's investiture with Bremen and Verden, the possession of Hadeln and the question of Hanover's *Erbschatzmeisteramt*.[38] None was in itself vital but, taken together, they fed the bitterness growing up between the former allies.

The Emperor was left least satisfied with the outcome of the Quadruple Alliance. Although he gained Sicily, his allies proposed to establish a large Spanish Boubon state in the centre of Italy. Relations between the Emperor and his allies deteriorated sharply as mutual suspicion grew.[39] The Emperor's supposed connivance at

[36] P. Dickson, pp. 159–62.

[37] Hatton, pp. 210–11, Beattie, p. 239, Mediger, *Moskaus Weg*, pp. 45–7. In October 1719 the king forbad the Germans to give him advice on British affairs. In the summer of 1720 Bernstorff went to Hanover and did not return. According to McKay, pp. 382–3, English policies were triumphant as early as July 1719.

[38] Hanover, like all the electors, wanted an arch-office, which involved a function in the ceremonial of the imperial coronations. The other electors wanted him to have the newly created *Erbstallmeisteramt* but he wanted the *Erbschatzmeisteramt*: see Naumann, p. 26. Investiture with Bremen and Verden was important. Although the territories were in Hanoverian possession, the attached votes in the imperial diet continued to be exercised by Sweden.

[39] Williams, *Stanhope*, has a marked anti-Austrian bias characterised by statements such as : 'The Emperor, though one of the main beneficiaries from the Alliance, was always giving trouble' (p. 337), and 'But Vienna was rarely grateful for services rendered' (p. 356).

the romantic events surrounding the abduction of the Pretender's bride, Clementine Sobieska, from imperial territory was taken as further evidence of his untrustworthiness. The Emperor found himself in isolation, the weakest member of an alliance which did not really need him. Only the question of Gibraltar, not itself a major issue to the English government,[40] stood in the way of an agreement between Spain, France and Britain, as a new peace-keeping alliance, prepared if necessary to use force. Too late George I realised that the destruction of Swedish power in the Baltic would upset the balance there and shift the tender point of Europe from the West to the North by strengthening Denmark and Russia. At the same time the excessive regard of the Hanoverians for the Emperor, earlier dictated by their desire for investiture with Bremen and Verden and the Mecklenburg commission, quickly evaporated as the potential dangers of imperial expansion in Italy became more appreciated. Before 1719 English policy in Europe and Germany had been based on a mutually advantageous co-operation between the Emperor and England.[41] Just at the time when the Emperor was free to devote himself to the Empire and to increasing his influence in the imperial diet, Hanover and England found it in their respective interests to oppose imperial policies in Germany.

They were given an opportunity to do so by the outbreak in 1719 of a serious religious dispute in the Empire, which considerably weakened the Emperor in Germany and Europe.[42] The actual crisis, which could have produced a religious war in Germany, was over within two years but its echoes embittered German politics into the 1730s. Some writers[43] argue that much of the blame for the troubles must rest on Schönborn, whose policies were supposed to have been motivated above all else by his Catholicism, which led him to actions which alienated many small Protestant states and drove them to look to their powerful coreligionists for protection against a proselytizing Catholic Emperor. Schönborn is also accused of

---

[40] G.C. Gibbs, 'Laying treaties before Parliament in the 18th century' in R. Hatton and M. S. Anderson (eds.), *Studies in the Diplomatic History of Europe in memory of D. B. Horne* (London, 1970), pp. 125 – 9.

[41] Mediger, *Moskaus Weg*, p. 27.

[42] On the religious crisis see Borgmann, *passim.*, and Naumann, pp. 24 ff. Wilson, p. 109, quoting a report of St Saphorin, argues that the crisis strengthened the Emperor's position. He did not 'exploit religious differences for political purposes and centralization', though it was convenient for France and Britain to accuse him of this.

[43] Typically, Naumann, p. 18.

reviving religious antagonism which might otherwise have died away. Both propositions are questionable. Religion was certainly declining in significance after 1648 in both European and German politics but it was still important.[44]

The roots of the crisis lay in the so-called Ryswick clause, article four of the peace treaty of Ryswick.[45] During the French occupation of the Palatinate from 1688 to 1697 many Catholic churches were rebuilt or reopened and a Catholic *Simultaneum* was introduced into Protestant churches.[46] Catholic churches were also built in areas seized under Louis XIV's *réunions* policy.[47] Under clause four of Ryswick, these provisions were to remain in force. In the Palatinate this added another strand to the long-standing bitterness between the majority Calvinists and the small minority of Lutherans over rights, incomes and property, which gave doctrinal differences a sharper edge. The Ryswick clause added Catholic rights to the already confused picture.

The Palatinate was the scene of the incidents which sparked off the crisis but religious hostility had been building up for a long time in many parts of Germany. The religious settlement of 1648 had left too many points unsettled and many potential sources of friction remained. The *Simultanea*, the continued existence of states with religious minorities[48] and religious divisions within princely houses produced a persistent undercurrent of mistrust. There was always a built-in possibility of religious dispute in the German political system. Since 1648 Protestantism had been under growing pressure. In 1679 the elector of Saxony had become a convert to Catholicism to make himself more acceptable to the Poles as king. At first this was a purely personal conversion but in 1717 the crown

---

[44]   Epstein, pp. 174 – 5 sees religion as a German hobby in the eighteenth century. M. Schlenke, *England und das friderizianische Preussen 1740 – 63* (Freiburg/Munich, 1963), pp. 163 – 6 on the long survival of religion as an element in states' 'abiding interests'. Religion was frequently mentioned as a favourable predisposing factor in negotiations for a Franco-imperial alliance: Braubach, *Versailles* p. 55.

[45]   Borgmann, pp. 26 – 7.

[46]   Under the *Simultaneum* one building was used by two religious groups. Sometimes a building was physically divided and used simultaneously; in other cases it was used at different times.

[47]   Dureng, p. 12.

[48]   This state of affairs often increased with territorial changes: e.g. Prussia acquired a substantial Catholic minority in the secularized sees of Magdeburg and Halberstadt.

prince also converted.[49] In 1685 the electoral Palatinate was inherited by the Catholic Neuburg line. These changes gave the Catholics a majority of six to three in the electoral college of the imperial diet in addition to their large majority in the college of princes. Only in the weak college of the free imperial cities was there a Protestant majority. Under Article 52 of the peace of Münster all religious questions in the Empire were only to be settled in the imperial diet by an amicable composition negotiated after the diet divided into two nominally equal parts (*itio in partes*), not by a simple majority. In spite of this, the numerical weakness of the Protestants increased their feelings of insecurity and they looked increasingly to the large Protestant states of Europe and the Empire.

The years immediately before 1719 saw increasing religious tension. The death of Louis XIV and the end of the threat of French invasion reopened religious and constitutional troubles which had been in suspense during the French and Turkish wars. In March and April 1719 the imperial diet was paralysed by the revival of a dispute over the elector of Hanover's arch-office.[50] Under the pretext of the Ryswick clause a number of Catholic rulers in the Rhineland, including Mainz, Trier and Speyer, whose bishop was the brother of the imperial vice-chancellor, and the elector palatine began to persecute their Protestant subjects. This encouraged many of the small counts and knights in the area, which was politically fragmented and very mixed in religion, to do the same. There was growing conviction among the Protestants that the Catholics were again mounting a campaign to wipe out heresy with the support of the pope, the Emperor and the Jesuits.[51] A leader of the movement was the elector palatine. In 1698 the elector John William issued an ordinance introducing the *Simultaneum* in all churches, making them available to Lutherans and Catholics as well as Calvinists. This calculated blow against the Calvinists moved them to appeal to their powerful coreligionist, the elector of Brandenburg, who replied by taking reprisals against his Catholic subjects in Cleves and Mark. Prussian pressure produced a negotiated settlement in 1705 but the Ryswick clause revived the troubles. The Protestants exerted considerable pressure to have it annulled in the negotiations leading

49 Williams, *Stanhope*, p. 389. It was an anomaly typical of the Holy Roman Empire that the elector, in spite of his personal conversion, was still legally head of a Protestant state and director of the *Corpus Evangelicorum*, established in 1653. Naumann, p. 25 states that Saxony lost the directorate in 1718; in fact, though challenged by Prussia and Hanover, the elector retained the position.
50 Naumann, pp. 23–4.
51 Borgmann, pp. 38–9, Gehling, p. 147.

to the peace of Baden but the French refused and there was a distinct suspicion that the imperial negotiators were not encouraged to press the point very ardently.[52]

John William's successor, Charles Philip, continued divisive policies and a propaganda war of mounting bitterness between the two major faiths in the Palatinate broke out. On 18 July 1715 Charles VI issued an edict banning any public attack by one faith on another in an effort to take the heat out of growing religious disputes in several parts of the Empire.[53]

In some ways the affair was artificially inflated. Men like Wrisberg, a Hanoverian agent in the imperial diet and a fanatical anti-Catholic, did much to stir up passions; he saw evil in every Catholic proposition and the hand of the Jesuits behind all their actions. He was encouraged by his government, which saw the religious issue as a valuable aid in the arch-office dispute and the question of investiture with Bremen and Verden. These and other political considerations combined to turn the religious crisis into a first class constitutional dispute, which foreign powers were quick to join.

The German Protestants as a whole were involved by an appeal from the Palatinate Protestants to the *Corpus Evangelicorum*. The Protestants front was never completely united: Hanover backed the Lutherans and Prussia the Calvinists and there was rivalry between the two for the leadership of the *Corpus*. There is some evidence that, at least among the smaller states, there was a real fear that the fate of the Huguenots was threatening them and a genuine belief in an international Catholic conspiracy.[54] The *Corpus* at first took a moderate line, resolving to appeal to the Emperor to put pressure on the persecutors, Mainz and the elector palatine. To add weight, the leading states, especially Hanover and Prussia, began to persecute their Catholic subjects as a reprisal. This was also started in Protestant states outside Germany, such as the Netherlands.[55] This caused a hardening of attitude on both sides, as many Protestant states were using the issue as a weapon against the Emperor. Hanover's reprisals were mild, amounting to little more than a gesture; Catholic worship was suspended in Celle. The English government regarded the whole affair as a useful way of

---

[52] Wilson, pp. 111–12, Williams, *Stanhope*, pp. 158, n1, 356, 391 to the effect that the Emperor connived at the persecution of the German Protestants.
[53] Borgmann, p. 30.
[54] Naumann, p. 30.
[55] Borgmann, p. 47. McKay, p. 385 n130 quotes a treaty signed between England and Prussia in March 1720 for joint action in the religious crisis.

forcing the Emperor into concessions in political matters and tried to restrain the king of Prussia.

The response from Vienna to the religious crisis was quick and careful. The matter was referred to the aulic council which, on 16 October 1719, ordered the elector of Mainz to release certain Protestant citizens of Worms illegally arrested and on 8 November asked Mainz and the elector palatine for their account of the matter. The Emperor and the aulic council were already ill-disposed towards the elector palatine because of his actions against the Estates of Jülich and Berg.[56] An imperial rescript was drafted in December ordering the elector to restore everything to the condition it had been before the crisis began.[57] This was delayed in the imperial chancery and Schönborn was able to persuade the Emperor to drop it as on 28 December the *Corpus Evangelicorum* sent a sharply worded memorandum to the Emperor containing attacks on the imperial courts of justice. Charles VI was especially hurt by criticism of his exercise of his judicial office.

Prussia's extremism made Schönborn's position stronger. In the conference he favoured strong action, while other ministers urged a more diplomatic and unspectacular response. Schönborn won. The first imperial reply, sent on 23 February, was drawn up in the aulic council. Prussia's accusations were firmly rejected and the king soundly condemned for his unheard of presumption. A second even stronger letter was drafted on 24 February. This rehearsed all Prussia's crimes against her neighbours, her own subjects and the peace of the Empire.[58] The rolling phrases of majesty of the letter had not been heard for many years and it caused amazement in the Empire. Vienna seems to have interpreted Frederick William I's actions as another blow in his anti-imperial campaign, though it is more likely that he had overreacted and blundered into excessive reprisals. Other Protestant states received milder orders from the aulic council. On 8 March imperial letters were sent to the main Catholic offenders leaving no doubt of the Emperor's intention to settle the affair justly.[59] All these communications were published in the imperial diet on 12 April, together with an imperial decree to the principal commissioner dated 31 March replying to complaints of the *Corpus Evangelicorum*. This was also sharp in tone, chiding the Protestants for their illegal reprisals, appeals to foreign powers and their attacks on the imperial office and jurisdiction. The Emperor

---

[56] Carsten, pp. 288 ff.
[57] Naumann, pp. 35–8. Borgmann, p. 74.
[58] *Ibid.*, pp. 80–3, Vienna, Reichskanzl. *Vortr.* fasz. 6c fol. 143–70.
[59] Naumann, p. 40, Pachner von Eggenstorff, vol. IV, pp. 105–17, commission decree of 12 April 1720.

threatened to cancel the privileges of their universities if they continued to spread ideas undermining the imperial constitution. Even the Catholics did not receive this uncompromising statement of intention to exercise imperial jurisdiction with joy and the Protestants were horrified. Saxe-Zeitz was instructed on 19 April to accept no more insolent answers to imperial orders from Protestant states: 'an imperial diet which exists only to denigrate imperial authority is superfluous'. To settle the dispute the Emperor suggested the revival of the imperial deputation, which had last met in 1704, consisting of one state of each religion from each of the three colleges of the imperial diet.

In the meantime Hanover was playing a clever game in Vienna. St Saphorin took a line of sweet reasonableness while simultaneously the Hanoverian and Prussian agents in Regensburg were stirring up the Protestants to more vigorous action in an effort to make the Emperor more ready to grant political concessions to their principals.

At this point English policy became more conciliatory. In April 1720 lord Cadogan arrived in Vienna as a representative of George I. His aim was to mend relations between the two and obtain his master's investiture with Bremen and Verden and Prussia's with Stettin.[60] The future of Bremen seems to have been his prime concern and the religious question was only a side issue to be exploited to the best advantage. There was a serious division here between Hanoverian and English ministers, the former wanting the religious issue kept on the boil as a useful means of increasing Hanoverian influences in the north and among the smaller Protestant states. The negotiations moved quickly as extremists on both sides were kept out,[61] to the disgust of Wrisberg. George I's position was ambiguous: as elector of Hanover he seems to have become emotionally involved in the religious dispute. He sent letters to St Saphorin in May instructing him to separate religious from political questions in his negotiations for the king was not ready to abandon the German Protestants for the Bremen investiture. At the same time it was becoming increasingly important to England to keep the Emperor out of a Russian alliance. In May 1720 Russian amphibious operations were launched against the Swedish coast and England began recruiting troops for Sweden in Hesse and other parts of the Empire. Russia also continued diplomatic efforts

---

[60] He passed through Berlin on his way to Vienna. Frederick William I gave him 50,000*Rt.* to promote the Stettin investiture as the Prussian minister in Vienna, Kanngiesser, was suffering the effects of Prussia's actions in the religious crisis: Naumann, p. 45.

[61] Borgmann, p. 102 argues that Schönborn was deliberately excluded.

on behalf of the duke of Mecklenburg and the duke of Holstein, who was in Vienna in the early summer of 1720 to seek support in his efforts to regain the duchy of Schleswig, taken by Denmark in the Northern War. The duke was a possible heir to the Swedish throne and for this and other reasons it seemed in England's interests that Schleswig should stay in Danish hands. By this time the usefulness of the religious issue for political purposes was waning and in June proposals for the settlement of the religious issue were exchanged. In August the Emperor instructed the principal commissioner that the whole matter was to be settled within a year. By now much passion had gone out of the affair. Since March the elector palatine had begun to reverse his policies, though Schönborn was still setting his face against compromise and dreaming of a grander Catholic league which might win a replay of the Thirty Years' War.[62] At a conference on 1 July he continued to press for a hard line while the Austrian ministers favoured a quick compromise settlement[63] and there is a distinct suspicion that he used deliberate forgery to further his policies.[64] On 26 July Eugene, Sinzendorff and Saxe-Zeitz discovered that Schönborn had given the Emperor an inaccurate version of the conference resolution to sign and that Charles had not bothered to read it. The whole affair created a mild sensation and Schönborn had to disappear for a while. The conduct of the whole business was taken over by the Austrian chancery and new regulations were issued to prevent a recurrence. Surprisingly this affair did little to weaken Schönborn's power but was seen as further proof of his slyness, which made him even more feared.

The religious crisis gradually died away as both sides made concessions and the extremists became isolated.[65] Saxe-Zeitz worked assiduously among the smaller Protestant states and the unity of the Corpus Evangelicorum, never strong, began to weaken. On 19 October 1720 the Corpus voted to end all reprisals and on 14 November imperial mandates were sent to the Catholic persecutors, ordering them to stop their actions. Schönborn was outraged, seeing this as a sacrifice of the Reich for Austrian interests in Italy. Hanover and Prussia continued to use the religious issue as an

---

[62] Hantsch, Schönborn, p. 262, Naumann, p. 61.
[63] Ibid., p. 40.
[64] The account of this episode given by Borgmann, pp. 116–18 differs from that in Hantsch's biography of Schönborn, pp. 247 ff.
[65] In an aulic decree of 31 May 1721 the Emperor informed the aulic council of his intention to dispense justice on the basis of extreme impartiality and imperial law without regard to religion: Vienna, RHR Verfassungsakten fasz. 8/44.

171

instrument to put pressure on the Emperor and it simmered on in the *Reichstag*. The Emperor continued to pursue a moderate policy and more important matters began to occupy the diet and the Emperor's councils in Vienna.

From 1720, by which time it was clear that the case was not going to be settled quickly, until the death of George I in 1727, the work of the Mecklenburg commission continued along lines already laid down. From the point of view of the aulic council, this period was significant in two respects. The council had constantly to be on its guard to ensure that the commission did not act without reference to Vienna. At the same time it acquired an important directive and supervisory control of the politics and administration of a sizeable state of the Empire. The number of *vota* increased, as did references to the case among the records of the conferences and it is from these that a picture of the progress of the case can be built up. Only where the litigation in the aulic council encroached on larger political and diplomatic considerations did the conference show any interest. This was clearly expressed in the protocol of a meeting of the conference held on 8 August 1720.[66] Charles Leopold, then in Vienna, had asked for a meeting of imperial ministers and ambassadors of foreign powers and Estates of the Empire, to present his point of view. The conference decided:

The duke's cases are pending before the aulic council and the Emperor is not permitted under his capitulation of election to refer a pending case to the conference. The duke must appear before the appointed imperial commission to deal with the liquidation of the knighthood's debts. It would be scandalous to dissolve the existing commission as the duke has opposed the imperial execution by force. His complaints can, however, be heard but he should present his grievances in writing to discover whether he has any complaints against the aulic council or the commission.

The Emperor wanted the Mecklenburg commission brought to a close as soon as possible. The knights on the other hand wanted it extended to all points at issue between them and the duke, as otherwise there could be no hope of peace in the country.[67]

---

[66] Vienna, Staatsk. *Vortr.* K. 23 vii – xii fol. 93. The conference was attended by both 'Austrian' and 'imperial' ministers.
[67] Schwerin, Landst. Archiv *Protokoll* 1720 II no. 783.

Already an unpleasant reality of the situation in Mecklenburg was beginning to appear. There were two governments in the country, each with its officials, forces and supporters. The duke's influence spread far beyond the walls of the two towns he controlled, Schwerin and Dömitz.[68] One government would have nothing to do with the imperial commission and did everything in its power to sabotage the efforts of the commissioners to bring about a settlement. The aulic council was compelled to support its own government, the commission, to the hilt and to enlarge its powers and functions far beyond those originally intended in the *Conservatorium* of 1717. Although instructions to the commission were despatched in the name of the Emperor they were based almost entirely on the findings of the aulic council, as expressed in its *vota*. The council now did all possible to help the commission, which was in theory its own instrument. The work which the commission's subdelegates did during this period under most difficult circumstances has not been fully appreciated. It was clear that the moment the commission troops left the country, the duke had means to take control of it readily available. The possession of Dömitz and Schwerin enabled him to keep his administration and part of his army intact and the resources from the surrounding areas provided him with the means to finance what amounted to a government in exile inside the country. The duke lived much of the time in Danzig but his orders could be in Schwerin in a few days.

Although he could do nothing to help them and regarded them only as a source of money and recruits, Charles Leopold kept the loyalty of the Mecklenburg peasantry. The appeals of peasants against eviction by improving landlords were sent to Dömitz and commissions were established to investigate their complaints. In spite of this, his title of the 'peasant's friend' was totally undeserved.[69]

A long *votum* of 3 November/30 December 1722 dealt with the latest development in the country.[70] The duke's policy on non-cooperation with the commission had lately been further translated into action. He had ordered the removal of the two supreme courts of Schwerin and Güstrow, the justice chanceries, and the provincial court, (*Land- und Hofgericht*), from their seats at Güstrow and

---

68 The duke was able, for example, to arrest his opponents. In August 1724 a certain captain Bassewitz of Petershof was arrested and taken to Schwerin, where a fiscal prosecution had been started against him: Vienna, RHR *Prot. Rer. Res.* xviii 60, verdict of 11 September 1724.

69 Steinmann, pp. 53 ff., 64–6, 85. Mager, pp. 241 ff. G. Schneidewind, *Herr und Knecht* (Berlin, 1960), p. xvi.

70 Vienna, RHR *Vota* K. 34.

Rostock to Dömitz and Schwerin.[71] This was a clever move as it meant that both Mecklenburg courts of appeal and cassation were locked up inside fortresses controlled by ducal troops, which gave the duke ultimate control of all litigation. At best he could cause great inconvenience to any litigant he did not like; at worst a withdrawal of favour could mean a complete denial of justice.[72]

The duke also renewed the urban excise system of taxation in Dömitz and Schwerin. The Mecklenburg towns, except Rostock, suffered considerably under the commission as, from the first, they were treated as allies of the duke. With the ducal domains they bore the burden of the commission troops[73] and the urban excise (Licent) system, which favoured them at the expense of the knights, was suspended with the approval of the aulic council. Early in 1722 they revived their old litigation against the knights over the modus contribuendi and the noble claim to exemption from taxation.[74] The Licent agreement of 1708 set out to confine all trade and crafts to towns where they could more easily be taxed, which the knights resented as a form of double taxation on them.[75] The victory for the knights' interest, which the commission represented, forced the towns to make common cause with the duke. The Licent agreement was suspended at the first commission diet in 1721. The towns did not send representatives on orders from the duke and remained recalcitrant. They were joined by a small group of loyalist noblemen, who refused to attend the commission diet.[76] The towns continued to object to the tax system based on the Landbeede, which, they claimed, took no account of the great decline they had suffered since the early seventeenth century. In the council's view there was sufficient evidence to justify a prosecution of ducal tax commissioners and collectors in Schwerin and Dömitz who had disobeyed the imperial commission. The core of the trouble lay in the presence of ducal troops in two towns. The council rejected a

---

71 Ibid., Den. Rec. K. 704(6), exhib. of the commission 11 September 1722.
72 The courts granted lavish moratoria on debts to the duke's supporters and decreed executions against his opponents: ibid., exhib. of the knights 9 January 1725.
73 Ibid., K. 699(9), exhib. of the towns, 12 December 1719.
74 Ibid., RHR Prot. Rer. Res. xviii 53, verdict of 17 March 1722. The records of the litigation are in ibid., Den. Rec. K. 705(1).
75 The knights also resented the ducal monopolies, which covered salt, copper, scythes, chimney cleaners, pig-butchering, tobacco, milling and soap: Schwerin, Landst. Archiv Protokoll 1721, no. 2421.
76 Before the imperial execution Charles Leopold had been able to convene complaisant diets from their number. They were mainly officers and courtiers and a few who believed that the duke was to be obeyed without question.

plan of the commissioners to mount military raids to kidnap the ducal agents; the council's aim was to avoid a 'bloody collision'. However, it did not object to secret instructions being given to the commissioners to make discreet arrangements to capture ducal tax officials if they could be caught without escort outside the vicinity of the two ducal fortresses. But all collisions with ducal troops were to be avoided. The council was afraid of giving Hanover a pretext to strengthen her military presence in the duchy, which might bring in the Prussians, adding another strand to what was already a case of frightening complexity.

The aulic council clearly still clung to the hope that a settlement of the Mecklenburg affair was attainable; the alternatives would without exception have been deeply embarrassing to the Emperor. He could wash his hands of the affair and order the commission to withdraw, throwing the country back on to the mercy of the duke and opening it to Swedish and Russian influence, both unacceptable to Hanover. Or he must accept a permanent foreign military presence in Mecklenburg to restrain the duke. It was unlikely that Hanover would give up this role during the lifetime of the duke and Charles Leopold was a robust man. The Emperor was not prepared to go to war with Hanover over Mecklenburg;[77] and it would be very difficult to dislodge the Hanoverians while they could, with reason, argue that their presence alone was saving the nobility from a bloodbath. Even if the Hanoverians could have been persuaded to leave Mecklenburg, which was unlikely in view of the increasingly strained relations between the Emperor and George I, the natural interest of Hanover in the duchies and the fact that an important commission was a prestigious asset for any ruler, the question of an alternative peace-keeper would have been most difficult, as the council was later to discover.

There are indications that Vienna was already thinking of ending the commission as early as August 1719. The last thing the Emperor wanted was a permanent Hanoverian occupation of the country. He wanted a restoration of the *status quo*. The conference appreciated the serious danger that the Emperor could find himself isolated in north Germany and in Europe, even more likely if Prussia and Hanover should come to an agreement over Mecklenburg. Had Charles Leopold been prepared to make a gesture of submission at this point he might well have obtained a verdict ending the commission and ordering the evacuation of the execution troops. He squandered the opportunity.

---

[77] Göttingen Aw. 474 II no. 39 Eichholtz to Scharff, 20 September 1719.

On several occasions Charles Leopold seemed ready to give way. He had repeated his offer of submission to everything which the Emperor should be pleased to order in a letter presented on 21 October 1719 and passed into the council on the 22nd. He was still asking for the removal of the Lüneburg troops and was anxious that the Emperor should take the decision on this matter personally without reference to the aulic council, which he regarded as biased against him, and, until this decision was reached, there should be a 'general armistice' in the case.[78] But his submission was so hedged about with conditions as to be unacceptable. The council concluded in a *votum* of 3 November/30 December 1722 that a sudden change of heart on the part of the duke was not to be looked for:

> Under these circumstances and as no improvement on the part of the duke can be hoped for, it is no longer possible to ignore the fact that Your Imperial Majesty can no longer avoid employing the other measures permitted under the imperial constitution without notable damage to the supreme imperial authority, further disturbance of the whole Empire and especially almost unavoidable delays, disruption and denigration of the imperial commission.

The council was clearly already thinking in terms of depriving Charles Leopold of his powers. The fact that he had opposed an imperial execution by force of arms made him liable to the ban of the Empire. As this would be a *bannum delicti* not a *bannum contumaciae*, it was not subject to restrictions under the *Wahlkapitulation*. The distinction was between the ban for a crime or crimes under imperial law and the ban because of disobedience to imperial orders, the offence of contumacy. The Emperor could initiate a ban process in the aulic council or the cameral court and was obliged only to refer the verdict and *acta* of the case to the imperial diet for ratification. The Emperor had already agreed to a prosecution of Charles Leopold on 31 May 1719, because the skirmish at Walsmühlen represented armed opposition to the execution of an imperial verdict but this had been suspended in the hope that there would be an improvement in the duke's behaviour.

By 1722 the duke had accumulated a great *concursus criminum*. He was guilty of contempt of imperial orders and of high treason, perjury and sedition against the Empire in civil and canon law. In

---

78   Vienna, RHR *Prot. Rer. Res.* xviii 49.

spite of this awesome catalogue of crime, the aulic council, realizing perhaps the difficulties likely to arise if the Emperor should propose to the German princes to depose a reigning prince from one of the oldest ruling houses, recommended yet another rescript to the duke, because of the importance of the matter and as it concerned not only the Emperor but the whole Empire. The Emperor would also be well advised to obtain the support of the Empire in case any arrangement he decided on should require protection against foreign interference. The rescript should warn Charles Leopold against further abuse of the Emperor's patience combined with the often repeated lecture on the baselessness of the duke's claims, the error of his principles and the duties of the imperial judicial office. The duke should be given once last chance to obey or the Emperor would be obliged to make a reality of the frequent threats against him. He should have three months to show his submission by his actions; otherwise the Emperor would order the commission to take Dömitz and Schwerin.

In a manuscript resolution dated 13 May, Schönborn expressed the Emperor's approval but the chosen course was milder than that advocated by the council. A strong and secret *Dehortatorium* was to be sent to the duke giving him a further chance to show the dutiful obedience proper to a prince of the Empire. The growing embarrassment of the Emperor was further shown in two *vota* dealing with the Hanoverian and Wolfenbüttel claims for payment of their substantial execution costs.[79] The council left the decision on this matter to the Emperor 'and finds that this sort of question, which is of political significance, cannot be decided on the basis of law, but must be dealt with according to the circumstances'.

Although the case was taking up a large part of the council's time it was becoming clear that progress was slowing up. The Emperor's decisions on *vota* were becoming very slow. Huldenberg reported on 19 May 1723 that these delays were holding up important work.[80] He had intimate knowledge of the progress of the case. On 22 May he reported that the vice-president of the council had informed him that strict orders had been given by the president that *vota* were to be submitted in all Mecklenburg cases, a sure sign of the political tenderness of the affair.[81] The imperial resolution on the *votum* of 31 May included the following:

---

[79] Those of 17/24 December 1722, 18 February/22 March and 21/31 May 1723 in Vienna, RHR *Vota* K. 35.
[80] Hanover, *Cal. Br.*, Des. 24 Mecklenburg no. 84 fol. 1 – 2.
[81] *Ibid.*, fol. 41 – 2.

H.M. reminds the aulic council confidentially that the highest necessity in this whole Mecklenburg case is to proceed with the business with the greatest possible caution and the most assiduous discretion. In future nothing but the essentials must be committed to the public protocols. H.M. is passing on certain important facts and suggestions about the commission itself and on the economic situation, as the president of the council is due to leave Vienna shortly. He wishes the council to act on these facts with all caution and to do all that is possible to bring the matter to a quiet conclusion.

The Emperor's resolution is an illustration of the extent to which the case was becoming linked with many other considerations. The duke's propaganda activities among the states of the Empire continued undiminished and he was finding increasing sympathy. The case was considered at a conference held on 22 July in Prague, where the Emperor and his leading ministers were for the Bohemian coronation.[82] The ministers dealt with relations between the Emperor and Hanover and advised the Emperor not to abandon the position taken up earlier. The conduct of the Hanoverians in the religious crisis had been most reprehensible and the conference could not recommend any concessions to George I. Otherwise the Emperor would be compelled to bow to all the wishes of his vassal, the elector, and the princes who made common cause with him. In the past the policies of the elector and his friends, in word and deed, had aimed at a diminution of the high sovereignty of the Roman Emperor and a limitation of his supreme judicial authority. Acceptance of his wishes would mean accepting him as a co-ruler and dictator at the Emperor's side and would endanger the future election of a Catholic king of the Romans. The Hanoverian ministers, by their combinations and intrigues inside and outside the Empire, their continuous pressure, threats, importunity and contempt for the Emperor and his high judicial office, would not reach their aim but would have to abandon all hope of achieving anything except what was right and just. The voice of Schönborn can be heard speaking clearly here through the protocol of the conference.

In view of these opinions it was not surprising that the Emperor should be anxious to end his unhappy collaboration with Hanover in Mecklenburg as quickly as possible. At the same time, relations between the Emperor and Prussia began to improve as the religious

---

[82]   Vienna, Reichsk. *Vortr.* fasz. 6c fol. 186 – 97.

crisis came off the boil. For these reasons, if the exercise of the imperial jurisdiction in Mecklenburg was not be undermined by the knowledge that the more important of the two commissioners and his principal were at odds, it was essential to maintain secrecy and bring the commission to an end as quickly as possible.

Threats against the duke made no impression and the view that he was insane appears to have gained currency in Vienna.[83] He had grown more violent in his proclamations and his manifestos and there was fear that he could be positively dangerous. There were strong rumours in 1722 that he was recruiting an army and there was uncertainly as to where he was at any given time.[84] His reputation suffered a severe blow as a result of the so-called Dömitz 'blood trials' dealt with in a *votum* of 26 November 1723. The duke claimed to have discovered a conspiracy among his ministers and troops in Dömitz to hand over the fort to the Hanoverians. The whole affair was very obscure. It made a deep impression on contemporary opinion though it has apparently never been fully investigated. Confessions had been extorted from the duke's secretary, Scharff, by torture and, after his resulting death in prison, his body had been hanged, drawn and quartered. The chancellor Wolffradt was also executed and his widow, Charles Leopold's mistress,[85] went to the duke in Danzig. A number of soldiers were executed[86], others escaped by flight.

Despite this and other examples of the duke's excesses, the aulic council recommended yet another rescript on 21 March 1724 giving him another final warning to submit fully and unconditionally. The Emperor approved the recommendations; a final period of grace was to be allowed to the duke 'out of special imperial clemency'.

But the Dömitz trials had revealed exactly what those who had incurred the duke's displeasure could expect if he were allowed uncontrolled freedom of action, and it may be that it had finally tipped the scales against Charles Leopold. For on 14 February 1724,

---

[83] Wick, p. 158.

[84] Göttingen, Aw. 459 no. 10, Seger to Wolffradt, 1 July 1722.

[85] The Russian duchess Catherine returned to Russia with her daughter soon after the execution but she continued to send the duke money: Witte, vol. II, p. 273.

[86] The reports are strangely contradictory on the numbers punished and their identity. Different versions are given in Witte, vol. II, pp. 270 – 1 and Vienna, *Kl. Reichsst.* K. 347 fol. 405 – 7, 459 – 64. Charles Leopold denied everything in a letter of 15 September 1728: Schwerin, *Acta Diff.* III vol. xx. His version of the affair is in Vienna, RHR *Den. Rec.* K. 693(1) no. 2 lit. A, B, C and D in the letter of 1 December 1722. The *votum* is *ibid.*, K. 701 and *Vota* K. 35. Mediger, *Mecklenburg*, pp. 461 – 2 sees the trial as evidence of the duke's growing persecution mania.

even before the rescript had been despatched, the Emperor sent an aulic decree to the president of the council and Schönborn instructing them to set up a *Deputation*, including prominent members of the aulic council, to take action if Charles Leopold refused to submit. For the first time recorded, this decree openly mentioned the possibility of depriving the duke of his powers as ruler of Mecklenburg. Two possibilities were mentioned, a prosecution of the duke leading to the imperial ban or the temporary investment of the duke's brother and heir presumptive, Christian Louis, with the government of the country, with or without the existing commission.[87] The decree did not order the council to take a definite course of action but made clear what the Emperor wanted.

The deputation, which consisted of Windischgrätz, the vice-president Wurmbrand, Schönborn, Berger and Hartig, sent a completed report to the Emperor on 30 March 1724. A protocol of the meeting of the deputation of this date shows the opinions expressed by various members.[88]

Berger believed a ban process was grounded in law but that the times and circumstances made a provisional administration (*Provisorium*) more advisable. Surprisingly, the word was used without comment; it was a bold solution. He thought it advisable to consult the existing commission, with a view to their leaving troops in Mecklenburg, and possibly the Estates. Hartig agreed with this. Schönborn also agreed and believed that the commission should retain troops in the country until the case had been brought to a more settled condition and security established. Wurmbrand considered that the many crimes of the duke had more than earned him the ban of the Empire but believed that circumstances made this an unrealizable proposition.

The *votum* of the deputation as a whole[89] stated the common view that there was no hope of obtaining a satisfactory *Parition* from the duke. Under §161 of the last imperial recess, anyone opposing an execution by force made himself liable to the ban of the Empire. Charles Leopold was incorrigible and guilty of a multitude of offences against the Emperor, the imperial aulic council and his own subjects and under Article 17, §7 of the treaty of Osnabrück was liable to a fiscal prosecution and the ban of the Empire. Article XX of the Emperor's *Wahlkapitulation* had not abolished but only

---

[87] There is a copy of the aulic decree in Vienna, RHR *Vota* K. 35 no. 14 and *Den. Rec.* K. 698(2).

[88] This is in Vienna, RHR *Vota* K. 35 under the incorrect title Conferenz-Protokoll 30 March 1724.

[89] *Ibid., Den. Rec.* K. 715(1), Votum Deputationis, die herzogl. Mecklenb. Parition betr.

moderated this and imposed new conditions on its exercise by the Emperor.

The deputation considered the best solution would be for the Emperor to exercise his right to issue orders for the provisional administration of this province of his Empire. The emphasis was on the word 'provisional'. The solution would deprive the duke of the exercise of his government, without the troublesome formalities of the ban process, for a limited but undefined period, until a required set of circumstances arose, in this case until the duke should show himself ready to submit absolutely to the Emperor's orders. An imperial *Provisorium* would enable the Emperor to exercise his judicial office, without the need to consult the princes, and in this way to confirm confidence in his authority. A similar device had been used occasionally in cases of disputed succession to imperial fiefs and in the matter of the reform of the calendar, a matter which involved religious considerations and remained in dispute in the *Reichstag* into the eighteenth century. There was a recent case of a decree of a provisional administration by the aulic council in the deprivation of an admittedly much less powerful prince, William Hyacinth of Nassau-Siegen.[90]

The deputation also suggested the means for putting the proposed Mecklenburg *Provisorium* into effect. Until further imperial orders, but decidedly not in perpetuity, Charles Leopold should be deprived of the exercise of his government, which should be vested in his brother Christian Louis, to whom the Mecklenburg subjects should pledge their obedience. Possibly the new ruler could be assisted by a subdelegate well experienced in Mecklenburg affairs 'together with a fellow Estate well-versed in the affairs of the country'. The administrator, as he was to be called, should issue a set of *Reversales* promising to rule according to the Mecklenburg constitution and all imperial decisions based on this. The Emperor had instructed the deputation to suggest methods of restoring the

---

[90] As supreme judge, the Emperor had a suspending power; any enactment of any Estate of the Empire was appellable to him and was therefore subject to the *jus provisorium*: Vienna, RHR *Vota* K. 35, *votum* of 28/30 June 1719. On the Nassau-Siegen case see J. Brennert, 'Reichsexekution im alten Reich', *Zeitschrift für Politik*, vol. 22 (1933), p. 818 and C. Spielmann, *Geschichte von Nassau* (Wiesbaden, 1912), vol. I, pp. 213 – 20. This was the first time this procedure had been employed against an Estate of the Empire. The process of the case is detailed in a number of *vota* from the period 1707 to 1740 in Vienna, RHR *Vota* K. 40 under the rubric 'Nassau-Siegen'. The principality of Nassau-Siegen was a single territory shared between two princes, one Calvinist and one Catholic, William Hyacinth. The case was a constitutional dispute arising from the refusal of subjects to pay taxes. The prince was suspended from his government from 1707 to 1740.

battered economy of the country. Without going into detail, the members stated that the administrator should be given exact instructions on the conduct of the economy and should be required to submit annual accounts. Schwerin should be taken with the help of commission troops and a garrison, perhaps of the same troops, should occupy it. Dömitz should however be left in the hands of the duke to avoid an unwelcome sensation in the Empire and elsewhere, though measures should be taken to prevent its use as a base for attacks on the administrator. The deputation showed trusting faith if it really believed that the retention of Dömitz by the duke would prevent an 'unwelcome sensation' among the princes of the Empire while the deprivation of a reigning prince and the release of his subjects from their oath, solely by a peremptory imperial decision (*Machtspruch*), would pass without comment.

Finally the deputation recommended that the Emperor reserve all decisions in vital matters to himself and that the administrator should be bound to obey all imperial orders. He should be paid an annual salary of 20,000*Rt.* from the ducal revenues, in addition to his incomes as a prince of the house of Mecklenburg. From this he was to finance his administration. Charles Leopold was to receive an annual *Kompetenz* of 40,000*Rt.* On the key question of the commission troops, the deputation recommended that a decision on this be postponed until peace and security had been restored.

It is impossible to say which of the imperial advisers suggested the *Provisorium* but it is likely to have been a lawyer, a member of the aulic council, in conjunction with the vice-chancellor Schönborn. It had been in someone's mind before 1722 when the *Deputation* officially suggested it. On 23 September 1722 Seger reported a conversation with Schönborn on a remark of Fabrice, a Hanoverian administrator in Mecklenburg, who had ordered the ducal foresters to respect Christian Louis 'as he would be ruling duke before Charles Leopold'.[91] Schönborn had replied that Fabrice could well be right if the duke continued on the same path as before. Either the Emperor as judge or the duke as litigant would have to give way. The commission could not stay in the country for ever and, if Mecklenburg were to escape ruin, the Emperor would have to think of an alternative administration. Windischgrätz did not however approve of Fabrice's statement. In the Schwerin archive is a report of the Russian ambassador, Lanczinski, of 30 September 1722.[92] The envoy had protested to Schönborn about Fabrice's statement and the vice-chancellor had retorted that only the tsar's support had kept the duke safe for so long.

91 Göttingen, Aw. 459 no. 18.
92 Schwerin, *Acta Diff.* III, vol. xvi fasz. 4.

The solution proposed was bold in the extreme, even taking into account that Windischgrätz, Wurmbrand and Schönborn were imperially minded. The proposed deprivation of Charles Leopold was a far step from that of William Hyacinth, who had only some eight hundred subjects and half a tiny territory. The Mecklenburg *Provisorium*, eventually established by a decree of 11 May 1728, may perhaps marked the pinnacle of the 'imperial reaction'. By the time the aulic deputation made its startling recommendations, the Emperor's ability to pursue an active policy in Germany was already being undermined by his international vulnerability.

1724 – 1727

The congress of Cambrai opened officially on 26 January 1724. The various delegations had been waiting there since mid-October 1722 and all the serious business had already been settled in the capitals of Europe. The Emperor's diplomatic position was seriously weakened and he found himself being dictated to by what looked like a concerted front of France, Britain and Spain,[93] though in fact there were growing differences between Britain and France as the latter and Spain moved closer together.[94] In September the Franco-Spanish connexion was cemented by a triple betrothal involving Louis XV and the four-year-old Infanta Maria Anna, prince Luis of Spain and the duchess of Orleans and don Carlos and madamoiselle de Beaujolais. This last union was especially disturbing to the Emperor, who now faced the prospect of a Spanish state in central Italy backed by France. It was clear that Britain was not the selfless mediator at Cambrai portrayed by St Saphorin and George I's frequent assurances that he wanted to maintain the old policy of a common front against the Bourbons were not very convincing. At the same time both France and Britain were becoming increasingly irritated by what they saw as the Emperor's obstructiveness.[95]

The main cause of trouble remained the future of Parma, Piacenza and Tuscany. Charles VI was determined, if possible, to evade his engagement under the Quadruple Alliance to accept a Spanish prince as heir to the central Italian duchies but the chances of this would be slim if he agreed to the presence of Spanish troops in the area, as Spain wanted. This was to be avoided at all costs, as was an

---

[93] Mecenseffy, p. 11.
[94] Gehling, p. 168; Wilson, p. 14.
[95] Gehling, pp. 169 – 72, 184.

alternative scheme for neutral garrisons, which might also give the Spaniards a chance to take control. At a conference on 20 March 1720 it was decided that a useful delaying tactic would be to refer the matter to the imperial diet; as imperial fiefs, Parma and Tuscany could only be disposed of with the consent of the Empire. On 9 September 1720 the question was introduced in the *Reichstag* by imperial representatives, who also suggested that the Empire should send representatives to Cambrai. The Empire and Spain had been at war since 1702 and no formal peace treaty had been agreed.[96] The diet accepted don Carlos's right of eventual succession in the duchies on 9 July and it became imperial law on 10 December 1722. Schönborn was able to engineer a further delay while the relevant documents were drafted in the imperial chancery but the process was completed on 3 January 1723. The Emperor had reluctantly fulfilled the essential condition laid down by Britain and France for the opening of the congress and he now had, in the imperial constitution, another argument against the stationing of Spanish troops in imperial fiefs.[97]

The first business session of the congress of Cambrai was held on 28 April.[98] Representatives of Spain and the Emperor sat in separate rooms while French and British mediators moved between them. The Austrians would have preferred face-to-face negotiations, as they hoped that Spanish policy might change after the abdication of Philip V.[99] From the beginning the Emperor found himself expected to give way on all points at issue and his lack of male heirs was already being used by Britain and France to put pressure on him. The points in dispute between Spain and the Emperor were many but the main issue was Italy. The Emperor also wanted a Spanish guarantee of the Pragmatic Sanction, claiming that Britain and France had already guaranteed it in the Quadruple Alliance. It came as a shock when both powers denied this, arguing that they had only guaranteed his possessions but not the order of succession. Townshend was not ready to give the guarantee of the Sanction.

The Emperor's isolation, especially his worsening relations with his main ally, Britain, had many of its origins in imperial politics. A major grievance of George I's was the Emperor's flat refusal to

---

96   Naumann, p. 58; Mecenseffy, pp. 12–3.
97   Gehling, pp. 183–4.
98   Michael, vol. III, p. 235 f.
99   Gehling, p. 187. In one of his periodic fits of depression Philip V did what he had often threatened and abdicated in favour of his son Luis. The Austrians only discovered this in January after they had handed over documents agreeing to don Carlos's eventual succession. They were very irritated.

invest him unconditionally with Bremen and Verden. By the summer of 1720 negotiations had reached the stage where the Emperor was ready to give the investiture in the male line only and with strong safeguards for the free city of Bremen. The free cities were of importance in imperial politics as centres of imperial loyalty. The Hanseatic towns were also to play an important part in imperial plans for the commercial development of Germany.

With the hardening of lines in the summer of 1721 Schönborn proposed even tougher conditions: a restoration of the Lower Saxon Circle institutions with regular Circle diets and an alternating Circle Directory to deprive Prussia and Hanover of their overwhelming predominance after the decline of Denmark and Sweden, the restoration of religious conditions as in 1624 and a full guarantee of the constitutional rights of subjects. The commerce of the Hanseatic cities on the Oder, Weser and Elbe was to be unrestricted.[100] If accepted, Schönborn's scheme would have meant a great increase in imperial authority in north Germany. The king of Prussia was disgusted by the equally severe terms for his investiture with Stettin and this contributed to the virtual breach of relations between the Emperor and Prussia in August 1721. This strengthened Schönborn's position but annoyed Sinzendorff, who saw it as a sacrifice of Austrian interests for the trivia of a dying Empire. After delays the new imperial ambassador, Starhemberg, reached London in September and by then the Emperor was ready to moderate his terms, insisting only on the preservation of Bremen's rights and the restoration of Catholic foundations. The brief dream of a revival of imperial power in the north seemed to have died and now religion and commerce were dominant motives. In September 1723 Starhemberg and Townshend met in Hanover and worked out a list of nine points at issue between the Emperor and George I, including the religious dispute, Wrisberg's behaviour in Regensburg and the implied challenge to imperial authority, don Carlos's future, the investitures and the Emperor's relations with the rest of Europe.[101] Starhemberg was an agent of the Austrian aulic chancery and had strict instructions not to allow the imperial representative, Metsch, into the negotiations.

In 1723 relations between the Emperor and Prussia seemed on the point of improvement. While Charles VI was in Prague for the

---

[100] Naumann, p. 69–70, 75. There were rumours that the Emperor also intended to reserve imperial trading rights in Hadeln, especially when reports spread that Hanover was planning to use it as a base for British trade into Germany.

[101] Ibid., pp. 92–3.

Bohemian coronation, the elector of Saxony mediated a reconciliation between the Emperor and the king. Frederick William seems to
have believed that this would mean an end to the barrage of aulic
council edicts against him but this hope did not materialize.
Frederick William then swung back into the Hanoverian orbit and
religious trouble was again stirred up in the *Reichstag*.

By May 1724 the Emperor's dissatisfaction with negotiations in
Vienna and London was becoming serious. English public opinion
had reacted with hostility to the suggestion that Gibraltar might be
returned to Spain, which made British negotiators more anxious to
obtain compensation for Spain in Italy.[102]

In July 1724 it was decided to leave only the Italian question for
settlement at Cambrai.[103] By then the Austrian representatives were
beginning to press for their recall, arguing that nothing of value
could be achieved and pointing out that the Emperor faced the
danger of being forced into yet more dangerous concessions as his
position was dangerously weak. At a conference on 9 January 1724
the Emperor's advisers stated baldly that he could not hope to
survive another European war without serious loss.[104] Although the
congress dragged on until May 1725, its work was over by the
previous August, by which time the most important delegates had
left. In the same month king Luis of Spain died and Philip V
resumed the throne, bringing back his wife's dominance and
policies. She was dissatisfied with the paper promise Spain had
received. She was ready to go to war with Austria again but France
and Britain refused to support this or to give an undertaking to
place don Carlos on the Tuscan throne by force, should this be
necessary. Increasingly Spain and the Emperor were being thrown
together by mutual disgust over their supposed allies. It was
ironical that the basic purpose of the congress of Cambrai was to
settle differences between the Emperor and Spain; by failing to do
this, it threw them together.[105]

The midwife of the alliance was a Dutchman of Spanish
extraction, Ripperda. A clever but unstable man, he converted to
Catholicism and entered Spanish service in 1718. Gaining the ear of
the queen, he proposed a revolutionary solution for Spain's
problems, a double marriage alliance between the Habsburgs and

---

[102] Wilson, p. 14 n20; Michael, vol. III, p. 207; Gehling, p. 169; Hills, pp. 237,
       249 – 50; G. C. Gibbs, 'Laying Treaties before Parliament', pp. 125 f.
[103] Gehling, pp. 190 ff.
[104] Mecenseffy, pp. 16 – 17.
[105] Gehling, p. 196: rumours that the two were negotiating were current in
       Cambrai early in 1725. Chance, 'Treaty of Hanover', p. 619 describes 1725
       as 'a revolution in European politics'.

Spanish Bourbons, don Carlos to the archduchess Maria Theresa and don Felipe to her sister.[106] Don Carlos could then be elected king of the Romans and his brother could have Parma, Tuscany and the Emperor's Italian lands as a separate state. Spain might also get back the Netherlands. The scheme was not original. The dream of an alliance with Spain, cemented by marriages, had long been present among Spanish exiles in Vienna.[107] However strong public hostility between Spain and the Emperor, the indirect links between the two had never disappeared. There was always a pro-Austrian party in the Spanish court, though it remained weak until autumn 1724, when its members won power in alliance with the queen's Italian party. It was significant that Elizabeth wanted the marriages for her own sons, not her step-son, the epileptic Ferdinand.

At first it appeared unlikely that Charles VI would accept Ripperda's lavish plans as the intention was, above all, to preserve his possessions intact. This, more than anything, led to an immediate weakening of his position in the *Reich*. However, the Spanish connection seemed to offer a refuge from diplomatic isolation, money, military and naval aid and commercial concessions and it could have become a vehicle for a revival of imperial as well as Austrian power. The prospect was very tempting.[108]

At the end of November 1724 Ripperda was sent on a confidential mission to Vienna. His instructions, dated 22 November, contained an odd mixture of proposals reflecting the various schemes of the parties in Vienna but Elizabeth Farnese's marriage alliance scheme was central to the whole thing. In return Ripperda was to offer commercial, military and subsidy alliances.[109] Spain still wanted central Italy, with the possibility of exchanging the area for the Netherlands or Lorraine; she was already considering rebuilding at least part of her European empire.

Ripperda's proposals were debated at a conference on 9 February 1725.[110] The Emperor's advisers were in favour of the alliance, with reservations about the proposed marriages. Charles's daughters were potentially his strongest trump card and were not to be given away lightly. Since summer 1723 the prince of Lorraine, Francis

---

[106] Charles VI had three daughters who survived early infancy: Maria Theresa born in 1717; Maria Anna in 1718; and Maria Amalia in 1724. The youngest died in the autumn of 1725.

[107] Gehling, pp. 198 – 200 for details.

[108] Mecenseffy, pp. 21 – 2.

[109] Gehling, p. 197.

[110] *Ibid.*, p. 203. The importance of the business was shown by the fact that the meeting was held in Carnival.

Stephen, had been living in Vienna and he was widely regarded as the future husband of Maria Theresa. By 1725 it was considered unlikely that the Empress would produce more children so the Pragmatic Sanction was growing in importance. The conference raised an important question, whether Spain would be prepared on Charles's death, to maintain his possessions intact or whether Austria would be forced to cede large areas to buy off the hostility of Europe which the alliance would inevitably arouse. Sinzendorff, perhaps persuaded by cash as well as arguments, was from the first an enthusiastic advocate of the alliance. Starhemberg and prince Eugene feared that Austria might become little more than a province of Spain; if the marriages took place and Philip V's eldest son died, the empire of Charles V would be recreated. Both men were supporters of the traditional anti-French alliance with the sea powers but they were deprived of credible arguments by England's clear and undeniable unfriendliness to the Emperor. In 1725 relations between the two reached their lowest point. The conference resolved to pursue negotiations with Spain.

On 12 February serious negotiations began between Ripperda and Sinzendorff in deep secrecy.[111] Maria Thereas's youth was put forward as an excuse for postponing discussions of the marriage alliance. It was believed that Spain would break off the whole thing without a firm undertaking on this but, amazingly, this was not so. The Emperor insisted that Parma and Tuscany should remain imperial fiefs but was ready to accept don Carlos as heir to them. Negotiations on the great number of minor points at issue proceeded with great speed and the Emperor accepted a number of compromises, insisting only on an amnesty for his former supporters in Spain. He refused to give anything but vague assurances of support for Spain in winning back Minorca and Gibraltar but agreed to proposals for a common army and a Spanish fleet for use if one party to the alliance were attacked.

On the surface Spain seemed to be making little tangible gain from the proposed alliance; in fact it seemed a very bad bargain, but her appetite was whetted by the gratuitous insult offered by the French prime minister, the duke of Bourbon, in sending Louis XV's betrothed, the Infanta Anna Maria, back to her parents in March 1725. This was precipitated by the king's illness in February. The Infanta was still too young to marry and the need for a royal heir

---

[111] St Saphorin, in spite of his close co-operation with the French and Savoyard agents, had great difficulty in finding any reliable information: Gehling, pp. 203–5. Chance, 'Antecedents', p. 700 states that the first reports of Ripperda's activities appeared in February but they were not believed.

was seen as urgent by Bourbon, who feared the succession of the duke of Orleans.[112] The incident caused a complete breach between France and Spain and was a severe blow to England's 'southern system' based on Franco-Spanish friendship. It also increased France's dependence on Britain.[113] On 2 April Ripperda was ordered to sign an alliance even without promises from the Emperor on the question of the marriages. Sinzendorff gave a declaration that the Emperor would allow the marriage of one of his daughters to a Spanish prince when she was old enough and this satisfied Ripperda.

Three treaties of Vienna were signed on 30 April and 1 May, a formal peace between Spain and the Empire, ratified by the imperial diet on 7 June,[114] a treaty of alliance and a commercial treaty. Great pleasure in government circles in Vienna was reported. For the first time a foreign power ratified the Pragmatic Sanction and, in return, Charles agreed to the investment of don Carlos with Parma and Tuscany when they became vacant. Spain undertook to put no troops into the area until then. Imperial subjects obtained the same trading rights in Spain and her possessions as were enjoyed by the Dutch and the British. This fitted in with the Emperor's plans to increase his prosperity by forming a powerful economic system including Spain, the Hanse towns and the Ostend company to challenge Anglo-Dutch supremacy. St Saphorin was given notice of the peace treaty on 3 May[115] and news of the commerical treaty leaked out in June. The published agreement was bad enough; England and the Dutch were alarmed at the prospect of the Ostend company's gaining a share of Spanish-American trade, making Belgium a centre for smuggling into Britain and a potential naval and privateering base.[116] More, there was a strong suspicion that the most important parts of the agreement had been concealed. On the surface Spain had gained little more than she had from the Quadruple Alliance and it was considered highly unlikely that she would have given so much without something very big in return. The only concession held to be important enough were Gibraltar and a marriage alliance, which was exactly what Spain imagined the alliance did involve and

---

[112] Wilson, pp. 29–31.
[113] After rumours of a marriage between Louis XV and George I's grand-daughter Anne, the king's betrothal to Maria Lesczinska was announced in late May. This was a blow to Saxon hopes of securing a permanent hold on Poland and worrying to Austria as evidence of a greater French interest in Polish affairs: Gehling, p. 208.
[114] Mecenseffy, p. 29n; Naumann, pp. 101 ff.
[115] Gehling, p. 211.
[116] Wilson, pp. 124–5.

exactly what the Emperor was determined it did not. There was a firm conviction in England that the initiative for the whole arrangement had come from the Emperor, who intended to use his new strength to take the offensive in Europe and Germany. The continued simmering of the religious dispute added a sinister dimension: perhaps the agreement was the first step in a new crusade against heresy.[117] In May and June St Saphorin reported rumours that Charles intended to revive Catholic absolutist policies in the Empire,[118] to support the Stuarts and to strip France of Louis XIV's conquests. The Pragmatic Sanction was seen as the symbol of these ambitions. For Britain the possibility of war in the North, the Mediterranean and Germany seemed a great deal closer. The Emperor seemed to have found new confidence and began to take the diplomatic initiative. He offered to call a congress at Brussels to restore tranquility to Europe and to mediate between France, Britain and Spain.[119]

Fear of this led Britain and France into a closer defensive alliance, the treaty of Hanover signed on 3 July, which was left open for other powers to join.[120] The Emperor was forced either to surrender to France and Britain or commit himself more deeply to Spain. In June 1725 Ripperda began to press for a firm undertaking on the marriages. A conference on 10 July rejected this and another on 20 July debated deeply the future of the Austrian lands and Habsburg foreign policy. Sinzendorff, in favour of closer links with Spain, argued against the pro-English Eugene and Starhemberg that England had proved such a useless ally that the Emperor had no choice but to seek other friends to secure himself. On this occasion Eugene refused to offer any advice on the grounds that he was a foreigner.[121] The Emperor backed Sinzendorff; whereas previously he had been ready to give only general assurances on the future of his daughters, he now agreed to the marriage of any two of them, when they became nubile, to don Carlos and don Felipe. Maria Theresa was to marry don Carlos if the Emperor died before she attained marriageable age. However, Charles was most unwilling to be dragged into war for Spain before a firm alliance system was constructed. The Emperor was also very anxious to keep the marriage plans from the Empire, where anti-Spanish feeling was

---

[117] Chance, 'The Treaty of Hanover', pp. 657–8.
[118] Ibid., p. 667 quoting St Saphorin's report in June 1725 on the threat of 'imperial despotism' in Germany.
[119] Gehling, pp. 212–14.
[120] Chance, 'The Treaty of Hanover', pp. 669–71.
[121] Mecenseffy, p. 34.

strong. Most princes favoured the marriage of Maria Theresa with a German prince.[122]

The Emperor was pushed into a closer dependence on Spain by the growing hostility of England and France in spite of the Emperor's wish expressed at the conference, to keep relations with England as good as possible. Vienna was evidently ill-informed about the objects of English foreign policy.[123] Simultaneously there was a battle in the French court between Fleury, bishop of Fréjus and the king's tutor, and the count Morville in charge of foreign policy. Fleury favoured a policy of peace while Morville's aim was to complete the alienation of Britain from Austria, to sabotage the Sanction, rebuild a French anti-Habsburg party in Germany and eventually to secure the election of an anti-Habsburg Emperor. English policy had more limited objects, aiming mainly at settling the North, and building Hanover into a powerful independent force in the *Reich* while keeping approval of the Sanction as a bargaining counter to win gains from the Emperor to this end. An effort was made to win over as many German princes as possible. It was believed that, if nothing came of the marriages, Spain would soon desert the Emperor, who would then face total isolation as the Anglo-imperial alliance of 1721 seemed finally to have broken down. The northern situation was also resolving itself and here too the two emerging alliance systems looked for new members. Russia, with interests in seeing Poland kept weak and in opposing the Turks, was in some ways a natural ally of the Emperor. A major obstacle was the Holstein restoration question. England and France had both guaranteed Denmark's possession of the duchy[124] while the tsar, as father-in-law of the dispossessed duke Charles Frederick, made some accommodation for him an essential condition of any agreement. Increasingly the imperial government had moved to support a restoration or at least compensation for Charles Frederick, who was also a candidate for the Swedish throne with the backing of the pro-Russian party in Sweden.

The position of Prussia was also important. Since the Charlottenburg treaty of 1723 Frederick William I and George I had been allies. Common hostility to the Emperor over the religious dispute and the vigorous operation of the aulic council were enough to override traditional Prussian-Hanoverian rivalry, at least temporarily. The two states were further united by common hostility to Saxony after

---

[122] Gehling, pp. 246 – 7.
[123] *Ibid.*, p. 224.
[124] This was one of the conditions for Hanover's possession of Bremen and Verden, which Denmark had also coveted.

the Thorn 'blood trials' of November 1724.[125] The Polish Protestants had been under pressure for a long time as Catholicism and Polish national sentiment were closely identified. King Augustus claimed he could do nothing about it and that it was an affair of the Polish diet.[126]

In July 1725 Frederick William agreed to join the negotiations for an Anglo-French alliance then under way in Hanover.[127] In return for the lure of a guarantee of his succession rights to Jülich and Berg he agreed to join the alliance without consulting his advisers[128], and subsequently, after consulting his ministers, he obtained a declaration restricting the use of his troops under the alliance to Europe, excluding Spain and Italy. He was unable to obtain official English and French backing for his complaints against the imperial aulic council.[129] On 3 September the wider alliance of Hanover or Herrenhausen was signed.

Although on paper defensive, the alliance served the forward policy being initiated by France in Germany and England/Hanover's offensive against the Ostend company and in the Empire. Technically it constituted treason against the Empire; Hanover and Prussia agreed that they would remain neutral in any imperial war against France arising from the alliance, a clause insisted on by the French. In a war for other reasons they would supply their imperial contingents but no more aid to the Emperor. This provision soon became known in Vienna. The Emperor also took the view that the mutual guarantee of possessions and rights as princes of the Empire in the alliance was illegal as only the Emperor, as supreme judge, could decide who owned what.

Fear of this new hostile alliance pushed the Emperor into a closer alliance with Spain, cemented in a further secret agreement signed

---

[125] Mecenseffy, p. 40n. and Chance, 'Antecedents', p. 697 for details of the incident. Rioting in the largely Protestant Polish town of Thorn (Toruń) involved an attack on a Jesuit school. It was followed by the speedy condemnation and execution of a number of magistrates and citizens by a royal commission. Predictably the affair became fuel for the religious troubles: N. Davies, God's Playground. A History of Poland, vol. 1 (Oxford, 1981), pp. 179 ff.

[126] Williams, Stanhope, p. 389; Wilson, pp. 145–6.

[127] Chance, 'The Treaty of Hanover', deals mainly with the wooing of Prussia by France and Britain. In his 'Antecedents', pp. 691–2, 703–4 he argues that Prussia was originally not seen as a major member of an anti-imperial alliance. The northern powers and Russia were regarded as much more desirable.

[128] Gehling, p. 219. Chance, 'The Treaty of Hanover', p. 685 argues that Frederick William was pushed into the alliance when he heard that the Emperor had guaranteed Jülich and Berg to the Sulzbach claimants.

[129] Chance, 'Antecedents', p. 694 n12.

on 5 November 1725.[130] In fifteen articles this confirmed that Spain, and Austria, and Spain and France were to remain separate. No Habsburg princess was to marry a French prince. In the event of a successful war against France the outcome of the Thirty Years War was to be reversed: the Emperor was to regain lost land in the Netherlands, Alsace, Metz, Toul and Verdun; and Spain was to regain Navarre and Roussillon. Lorraine was to be restored to the condition it had been in before the reign of Louis XIV and don Felipe was to receive a re-established free county of Burgundy. The imperial army was to be placed on a war footing with Spanish financial help, though no definite decision on the amount of Spanish subsidies to Austria was recorded. The two states agreed on a policy of close co-operation and the commercial privileges enjoyed by the Emperor's subjects in Spanish possessions were widened.

At the end of 1725 Europe seemed very close to war.[131] The continent had divided into two hostile leagues, each seeing agression in the other's acts and each seeking to increase itself by attracting new members. Even the German princes, weak in themselves, were eagerly wooed as additional allies. Vienna revived its tough policy towards Hanover with Schönborn in the van of the movement. The Emperor's alliance with Spain led to a revival of the religious dispute in the imperial diet with Wrisberg given his head and the Dutch, until now slow in reacting, urging on the Protestants. There was an attempt in the diet to prevent an imperial ratification of the Spanish alliance.[132] There were rumours in Vienna that a religious war was imminent, while the Emperor pursued his policy of trying to dampen the conflict by channelling it through the aulic council.

The Emperor was in a difficult position. The imperial idea was an uncertain tie at the best of times and most princes were only ready to commit themselves to providing troops or facilities for the Emperor in return for cash or advantages. There was a common fear among them of being exploited for Habsburg ends under the guise of imperial loyalty. Of the major princes, only Frederick William I of Prussia, surprisingly, seems consistently to have held loyalty to the Empire to be an important factor in his policy-making. He was emotionally *reichspatriotisch* but believed the Emperor's ear had been captured by evil anti-Prussian councillors who made it their

---

[130] Details of this remained secret until 1843: Wilson, p. 39; Hills, p. 261 n36 questions the validity of Ripperda's later revelations on the November treaty, of which there was no record in the Spanish archives.

[131] Gehling, p. 229 writes of 'cold-war' conditions in Europe.

[132] Naumann, pp. 103 – 6; Chance, 'The Treaty of Hanover', pp. 680 – 1.

business to malign him and who engineered the harsh treatment he received from the aulic council.[133] He was most afraid of being dragged into a war over the Ostend company, which he believed was of advantage only to the Emperor and made imperial 'despotism' all the more feasible. This was the propaganda line which the Emperor's opponents chose to use in Germany and in many cases it found a ready reception.[134]

It was Charles VI's aim to extend his alliance system by attracting into it Mainz, Trier, Cologne, Bavaria, the elector palatine, Portugal, Sardinia, Sweden and Russia. As far as the German rulers were concerned, the success of this plan depended on whether the Emperor received enough money from Spain to buy friends. His position was clearly stated in the instructions issued to the new imperial ambassador in Spain, Josef L. Königsegg.[135] The Emperor was not ready to give Spain any promises of help in recovering Gibraltar and Minorca nor to enter any undertaking regarding the marriages or the future of central Italy, all the points closest to Spain's heart. His main concerns were the commercial treaty and the provision of lavish Spanish subsidies. He was frightened of an attack by the sea powers and France and wanted Spanish money to increase the Austrian army, a million florins for the fortification of Ostend and money to subsidize the German princes. In all he asked three millions and this was agreed.[136] The first payment was made in December 1726.

By now Ripperda, his prestige enhanced by the successful conclusion of the alliance, had taken complete charge of foreign policy in Spain and had also brought finance and military affairs under his control.[137] He had grandiose plans for the thorough reform of Spain and saw himself as the Olivares of the eighteenth century. Time and Spain's financial weakness were against him: his

---

133   *Ibid.*, p. 660: 'Frederick William I had in his life one single aim, to organize his state and make it strong enough to assert its position as a European power . . . Before all things he was a German prince, loyal to the emperor as distinguished from the head of the vast dominions of Austria.'
134   Mecenseffy, p. 42 suggests that there was no national feeling among the electors. This is oversimple, as she recognizes in a footnote on the same page. The odd psychology of the German princes allowed them to see nothing anomalous in professing loyalty to the ideal of a strong Empire as guardian of order and peace and a bulwark against foreign encroachments while at the same time vigorously opposing the head of the Empire: W. Mediger, 'Great Britain, Hanover and the Rise of Prussia' in Hatton and Anderson, p. 199 – 202.
135   Mecenseffy, pp. 43 – 4.
136   *Ibid.*, p. 99 n71 states that, by April 1729, the Emperor had received 2,172,283Fl. Wilson, p. 173 n10 gives the total as over 2.9 millionFl.
137   Mecenseffy, p. 45.

reforms and the alliance both needed increased revenue but the only source of disposable money was, as before, Spanish American bullion. For these reasons Charles VI's requests for more money were not well received. Spain refused absolutely to pay subsidies directly to the German princes in peace time, as the Emperor wished.

England at once struck at the alliance through the Ostend company, in collaboration with the Dutch, who wanted its total abolition, though Holland had great difficulty persuading the other provinces to agree to Dutch accession to the Hanover alliance.[138] Among the Dutch provinces bordering the Empire there was considerable fear of Prussia and the enlargement of Prussian territory on the Lower Rhine through the acquisition of Jülich and Berg, which the alliance undertook to promote. There was also nervousness about possible Spanish reprisals against Dutch trade and the possibility of becoming involved in a land war in Germany. The United Provinces eventually acceded to the alliance on 9 August 1726.

The basic strategy of the Hanover allies was to detach Spain from the Emperor, arguing that their only quarrel was with Charles VI. They were clearly convinced that Spain was the junior partner in the Vienna alliance. Ripperda refused all advances, arguing, by what mandate is not clear, that the Emperor would rather die than give up the Ostend company. Ripperda took an aggressive line from the beginning, presenting England with a list of demands including the cession of Gibraltar. It is not difficult to see why the sea powers became convinced that the iron in the alliance came from the Emperor and why they devoted their main efforts to detaching Spain from it.

The threat of real war frightened the Emperor,[139] whose policy was now to separate France from England and reconcile her with Spain.[140] Tensions relaxed slightly in May 1726 when Ripperda fell from power, having become too powerful and aroused jealousies. Power passed to the marquis de la Paz but there was no change in Spanish foreign policy. Under his control, the imperial alliance became even firmer; in the second half of 1726 imperial influence

---

[138] Wilson, p. 152.

[139] At a conference on 24 September 1726 Sinzendorff stated baldly that the Emperor's lands were too poor to sustain a war: Mecenseffy, p. 82.

[140] Negotiations for an alliance between France and the Emperor had never been abandoned since the last years of Louis XIV's reign though for long periods they were very subterranean: Braubach, *Versailles und Wien*, ch. I – III. Mecenseffy, pp. 135 – 6 is of the opinion that Austria's alliance with Spain would only have been of lasting benefit to Austria if it had led to an alliance with France.

in Madrid reached its height. Königsegg was able to keep Spain loyal to the alliance even after queen Elizabeth began to lose interest in it.[141] By August Spain had sent almost two million florins in subsidies to Vienna. By then the Emperor was desperate for funds to finance arrangements with certain German princes: the main burden of extending the alliance fell on him and money was vital.[142]

Schönborn had high hopes of winning over Saxony, the Thuringian states, Bavaria, Cologne, Sweden and Hesse-Cassel.[143] At the same time he began a vigorous propaganda campaign against England and Hanover in Germany. Most of the ecclesiastical princes were imperialists, with the notable exception of the prince-bishop of Würzburg.[144] Negotiations with Saxony came to nothing. The elector Augustus had very great demands and believed he could gain more by mediating a settlement than by commiting himself to one side. Both Saxony and Bavaria, militarily important states with influence in the Empire, had claims on Habsburg lands if Charles VI were to die without heirs and Bavaria had ambitions on the imperial crown. The Emperor's main effort was devoted to winning the ecclesiastical electors. Mainz proved the easiest to win over and signed a treaty readily on 12 September 1726. Trier, the poorest and most exposed of the ecclesiastical electors, was also loyal and signed in August. In return for imperial subsidies of 150,000Fl over two years to finance recruiting and the repair of fortresses, he agreed to support the Emperor in the imperial diet and to supply his imperial contingent in the event of war. So loose had the bonds of the Empire become that even normal obligations could become the subject of special arrangements.[145] Other Rhineland princes presented greater difficulty, being motivated above all by fear of France.

Bavaria and Cologne were also very troublesome. The elector of Bavaria was anxious to renew the alliance with France which had lapsed in 1723 but was not ready simply to subscribe to the Herrenhausen alliance. In November 1725 St Saphorin went to Munich to woo him but, against his advice, England would not meet the main Bavarian demands, the payment of subsidies in peacetime and a commitment to vote for Bavaria in a future imperial

---

[141] Gehling, p. 238.
[142] Mecenseffy, p. 59 n17 lists subsidies paid by the Emperor to Cologne, Bavaria, Mainz, Trier and Brunswick-Wolfenbüttel. Up to June 1728 they totalled almost 3.2 million Fl.
[143] Britain was equally optimistic about at least the last four: Gehling, p. 231.
[144] The imperial vice-chancellor stood for election to the see in 1724 but was unsuccessful in spite of imperial backing: Naumann, p. 107.
[145] Mecenseffy, p. 56.

election.[146] France was also making a determined play for Bavaria. The elector Max Emmanuel died on 26 February 1726 and the Emperor began negotiating with his successor, Charles Albert, and the elector of Cologne in May.[147] The elector wanted lavish bribes: 300,000Fl a year in subsidies, a galaxy of ecclesiastical posts for his relatives, wide commercial concessions and more. Eventually Bavaria came to terms with the Emperor, a blow to French policy but, as the elector explained to Fleury, Bavaria was impoverished and defenceless.

The elector palatine, Charles Philip, was even more demanding. His main ambition was to ensure that Jülich and Berg remained in Wittelsbach hands.[148] By 1726 the Palatinate-Neuburg house was much depleted, consisting only of the elector of Trier, the bishop of Augsburg and the elector-palatine, who had one daughter. England and France had been approached but had refused to give the elector the assurances which would have driven Prussia into the opposing camp. Negotiations with the Emperor began in November 1725. In addition to the provision of Jülich and Berg, the elector wanted guarantees of imperial protection against France and imperial aid in making good claims to lands held by a satellite of France, in particular the territory of Veldenz on the Moselle, seized by the house of Palatinate-Birkenfeld with French help in 1694. A treaty was signed on 16 August 1726. Its most important provisions were an imperial undertaking to pay 600,000Fl in subsidies and a promise to promote Sulzbach claims to Jülich and Berg. This was a blunder: at the same time the Emperor was trying to lure Prussia into an alliance and the future of these provinces was the issue closest to Frederick William's heart.

The long negotiations in Berlin were conducted for the Emperor by the Protestant imperial general, Frederick von Seckendorff, a member of prince Eugene's circle of diplomatic agents. Seckendorff fitted in well with the military atmosphere in the Berlin court, enjoyed a considerable reputation there and extended his influence by bribes to high and low.[149] Eugene was a firm advocate of the

---

[146] *Ibid.*, p. 57 n11. George I refused the latter demand on the grounds that it was unlawful. A free hand in such matters was very valuable. Naumann, p. 108 states that St Saphorin promised England's support for Bavaria in obtaining the imperial crown. If so, he had apparently no authority to do so.

[147] At the same time Austrian military manoeuvres were held near the Bavarian border as a reminder of what had happened to Bavaria during the Spanish Succession War: Gehling,p. 247.

[148] Mecenseffy, p. 61 n20. Under the Vienna treaty Spain and the Emperor had entered a mutual engagement to help to ensure this.

[149] Pretsch, pp. 17 – 18.

Prussian alliance, in spite of the religious dispute and the multitude of cases against Prussia in the imperial aulic council. He was opposed in this by Sinzendorff and the 'Catholic party', which preferred an alliance with France and Spain. Frederick William had joined the Herrenhausen alliance, seeing it as a better hope of obtaining Jülich and Berg, but his heart was never in it. When the Dutch acceded to the alliance in August 1726 they specifically refused to accept the clause supporting Prussia's claims to the territories.[150] He feared a war with Russia and his policy towards Poland had much in common with that of Russia and the Emperor in desiring to limit Saxon ambitions there. The death of the tsar Peter I in February 1725 had for a time caused considerable doubt about the future direction of Russian foreign policy. The prospect of an isolationist policy caused mixed feelings in Vienna, partly relief at the removal of a potential threat to Poland and partly regret at the loss of a potential ally against England.[151] In the event, the succession of Catherine I marked a victory for the 'Petrine' party and Peter's minister, Menshikov, remained influential. As late as April 1725 there was still hope in England that Russia might withdraw altogether from European diplomacy[152] and there was fear of a combined Russian-Prussian attack on Poland or Denmark, perhaps to restore the duke of Holstein-Gottorp. Hanover was keen to have Prussia in the Herrenhausen alliance to keep Frederick William out of more dangerous temptations. The king was basically frightened of the prospect of war and his nervous and vacillating policies reflected this. In November 1725 reports reached Berlin that an alliance between the Emperor and Russia was imminent and this increased the king's nervousness. The offensive implications of the Herrenhausen alliance were a source of serious worry. He realised that he was in no position to dictate terms to the Emperor and was mollified by a promise that cases in the aulic council would be dealt with according to justice and law.[153] He was anxious to have a seat on the Mecklenburg commission and to be invested by the Emperor with Stettin but his main desire was a promise of eventual succession to Jülich and Berg, since March 1725 under an imperial *Protectorium* with the bishop of Münster, the elector of Cologne, as protector.[154] The Emperor refused to compromise his judicial office or to grant the unlimited *jus de non appellando* for all his possessions, which the king wanted. He offered to mediate a compromise

---

150 Mecenseffy, p. 48.
151 Chance, 'Antecedents', p. 699.
152 *Ibid.*, p. 712.
153 Mecenseffy, p. 65.
154 Gehling, pp. 249 f.

solution with the elector palatine over Jülich and Berg and gave vague promises of compensation if the king did not gain Jülich and Berg. Bremen and Verden were mentioned during Seckendorff's negotiations as possible compensation. Imperial ministers were anyway convinced that the Dutch would never tolerate Prussian possession of Jülich and Berg.

Although the terms were not satisfactory, Prussia was given the final push into alliance with the Emperor by the signing of alliances between Russia and the Emperor and Russia and Prussia in August 1726. It was significant that Prussia did not join the Vienna alliance but came to a separate arrangement signed at Wusterhausen on 12 October. Frederick William guaranteed the Sanction, a mutual guarantee of possessions was exchanged, it was agreed to set up a common army, which was to be used only in the Empire or the Netherlands, and a common policy towards Poland was formulated. The Emperor undertook to move the elector palatine to agree to Prussia's acquisition of at least Berg. If he failed to achieve this within six months the whole alliance would lapse. By accepting this, the Emperor placed a weapon in the hands of the Hanover allies, who quickly learned the details of the treaty.[155]

The Prussian and Russian alliances completed the main outlines of the imperial system but both weakened rather than strengthened Charles VI's position. In the alliance with Russia of 6 August 1726 the Emperor again committed himself foolishly. Russia joined the Vienna alliance and the Emperor guaranteed Russia's European possessions. He also agreed to aid Russia in any European warfare against the Turks. This alliance was a trap:[156] the Emperor had bound himself to enter a war started at Russia's initiative or run the risk of losing an ally. If Russia defeated the Turks alone, Austria would be faced with a dangerous rival in the Balkans.

The Emperor's hopes of detaching France from the hostile alliance came to nothing. In summer 1726 the prospects for a Franco-imperial alliance seemed good. In June the duke of Bourbon fell from power and his place was taken by Hercule de Fleury, the bishop of Fréjus.[157] There was a strong belief in Vienna that he would bring France into the Austrian alliance system and initially he did not reject Austria's advances.[158] However, he refused to abandon France's allies unless the Ostend company was abolished,

---

[155] *Ibid.*, p. 251. The efforts of the imperial agent, Stefan Kinsky, to persuade the elector-palatine to give up Berg failed completely.

[156] K. A. Roider, *The Reluctant Ally: Austria's Policy in the Russo-Turkish War 1737–9* (Baton Rouge, 1972).

[157] Wilson, *passim.*

[158] *Ibid.*, p. 91.

as this was making it difficult for France to drive a wedge into the
union of the sea powers and to strengthen the traditionally pro-
French peace party in the Netherlands,[159] and he also refused to
guarantee the Sanction[160].

By November 1726 Paris and Vienna seemed superficially to be
moving closer together; in that month the Emperor informed the
French that he was ready to make concessions on the Ostend
company.[161] In reality Fleury was trying to break out of France's
diplomatic subordination to Britain and was simultaneously trying
to revive friendly relations with Spain; even when relations
between the two powers were at their most hostile, links had been
kept alive through Philip V's confessor and the papal nuncios.[162]

France was also active among the princes of the Empire. In
September 1726 new English and French agents took up their posts
in Regensburg, Issac Le Heup and Theorore de Chavigny.[163]
Chavigny's mission was a considerable success story. Under very
unfavourable circumstances he was able to rebuild a formidable
French influence among the German princes. His instructions
warned him against an overactive policy at first. France had not
been represented in Regensburg for ten years and there was a large
legacy of mistrust among Germans after Louis XIV's aggressive and
contemptuous policies towards the Empire.[164] Since 1714 considerable obstacles had been put in the way of French representatives at
the imperial diet and there were typical difficulties over ceremonial
because the French refused to accord the electors the honours they
demanded. Chavigny was very skilled in the traditional French
policy of depriving the Emperor of the resources of his Empire.
Although based in Regensburg, he had a commission covering the
whole Empire and was very mobile. If anything, his excessive
independence worried his principals and he had an exaggerated
view of his own importance, flattering himself that the imperial
court regarded him as the most dangerous man in Germany.[165]

In 1726 occurred a revival of the long-standing dispute between
the princes and the electors, which further disrupted the business
of the diet at a time when the Emperor was anxious to increase his
influence there. Only two months after his alliance with the

---

[159] Carter, p. 60 warns against exaggerating the influence of such groups.
[160] Wilson, p. 105.
[161] Gehling, p. 262.
[162] Wilson, pp. 159–61.
[163] On Chavigny see Dureng's work. Chavigny had no official character.
[164] Wilson, pp. 111–12, 147. Dureng, pp. 11, 14–15, 20. On p. 11 he describes
Germany as a field abandoned for thirty years, which had to be drained
and cleared before it could bear fruit for France.
[165] Ibid., p. 94.

Emperor, the elector of Bavaria was clearly wavering and began to move towards France. France and England were putting increasing pressure on the German rulers to remain neutral in any war growing out of the alliance system of 1725. However, Fleury consistently refused to provide subsidies for offensive alliances with German princes, which England wanted. In January 1727 Fürstenberg reported that the rulers of Liège, Würzburg and Württemberg were negotiating with Chavigny for pacts of neutrality. As so often in the past, the German princes seemed forced to look to foreigners for protection against their own Emperor. Suspicion was increased when it was revealed that the Emperor had 'promised' Jülich and Berg to both Prussia and the elector palatine. The prospect of war terrified most of the princes and many listened with willing ears to French claims that the Emperor was planning to unleash a European war for his own dynastic ends.

War seemed imminent because of British naval action against Spain and the Spanish decision to begin a blockade of Gibraltar.[166] The imperial garrisons in Freiburg and Alt-Breisach were brought up to strength but the Emperor was extremely unhappy about Spain's actions, wishing the members of the hostile alliance to take upon themselves the onus for starting the war. Imperial finances were even worse than usual because of lavish subsidy payments to German princes and mounting costs. There were deep divisions within the financial administration, centered on the rivalry between the head of the exchequer, Starhemberg, and count Kollowrat, president of the *Bankalität*, into which the Spanish subsidies were paid.[167] Demands for money came from imperial commanders on all sides for the maintenance of an army of 70,000, costing eight million Fl a year.

Early in 1727 a new Spanish ambassador, the duke of Bournonville, arrived in Vienna with secret instructions which revealed that the main aim of Spanish policy continued to be the marriages. Spain also wanted don Carlos to be elected king of the Romans and imperial help against Gibraltar.[168] Only then, it was made clear, would the dribble of Spanish subsidies swell into a broad river. The Emperor was in the difficult position of having to finance his German policy with his own resources in the absence of Spanish money. The whole imperial alliance system was beginning to look very shaky. News that Prussia had asked in London in February whether George I would maintain the neutrality of the Empire in case of war caused a great stir in Vienna: it was obvious that

---

[166] Mecenseffy, p. 85.
[167] Stoye, p. 68f.
[168] Mecenseffy, p. 87.

Frederick William I was looking for a chance to wriggle out of his obligations though, in this case, George refused to give such an undertaking.[169] The Emperor was only ready to go to war if France attacked the Empire and, even then, would need at least ten million *Fl* in subsidies from Spain. His army was still quite unprepared for a war on several fronts.[170] Spain seemed eager for war and there was growing anger against the Emperor in Madrid because of his alleged coolness and the revelation that he was in negotiation with the French. When the Spanish treasure fleet arrived in March 1727 nothing was paid to Vienna.

The Emperor's weakness in Germany crippled his initiative. At the end of 1726 the whole Empire, except Hanover and Hesse-Cassel, was linked to the Emperor as ruler of Austria and co-leader of a powerful alliance. On paper he was as strong as in 1719 but this strength was illusory and it had been bought at the cost of imperial authority. The German princes were not ready to commit themselves totally to either side as their main aim was the preservation of peace in Germany. England and France did their utmost to convince them that the issues at stake were of vital concern to Germany; typical was Chavigny's memorandum of 27 February 1727, drafted by Fleury.[171] This claimed that the Herrenhausen alliance was purely defensive and that the Emperor was the only power in Europe desiring war. This was answered at once by a sharply worded commission decree and counter declaration, dated 7 March 1727, accusing France of trying to divide the Empire from its ruler. The French document several times referred to the Empire belittlingly as *le Corps Germanique*, which was seen as a calculated

---

[169] *Ibid.*, p. 94. In June 1726 France had offered to send Prussia an auxiliary army of 60,000 if she were attacked by a Russo-imperial army. The Hanover allies hoped to persuade Frederick William to attack Silesia in case of war but he demanded 300,000*Rt.* and a free hand in Mecklenburg, East Frisia and Jülich-Berg, totally unacceptable to Hanover and the Dutch.

[170] Mecenseffy, p. 88 n35 estimates the total armed forces at 170,000, though the Emperor could not field anything like this number in 1726. Gehling, pp. 268–9 quotes reports of St Saphorin from the spring of 1727 with estimates of the Emperor's financial and military resources. At that time he had about 160,000 men and his potential strength from the hereditary lands was some 200,000. With his German and other allies the Emperor might field forces of 387,000, though large garrisons in Hungary and Italy had to be deducted. Against this the Hanover allies could oppose some 315,000 with 60,000 militiamen in France. B. Williams, 'The Foreign Policy of England under Wapole', *EHR*, vol. 15 (1900), p. 697 estimates that the Emperor had 212,210 troops available for war in Germany. In fact, because of financial weakness, it was extremely unlikely that anything like these figures was available.

[171] Dureng, p. 33 n1.

insult.[172] The formal acceptance of Chavigny's memorandum was also held up until an imperial counterblast was ready, though its contents were well known. Chavigny seized on this as further evidence of the monstrous dictatorship exercised over the diet by imperial agents. The main imperial wrath was aimed against the elector of Hanover, a subject of the Emperor.[173]

The hostility was answered in kind. George I opened Parliament on 28 January 1727 with a speech from the throne extremely hostile to the Emperor. Initially the treaty of Hanover had been attacked in Parliament as a breach of the Act of Settlement, an engagement to defend Hanover. It was the aim of the government to convince critics that commercial interests, Gibraltar and the Protestant Succession were under threat. It was able to achieve majorities for the treaty in both houses.[174] Townshend, who made no secret of his belief that Charles VI was as dangerous to Europe as Louis XIV, had drafted an even more strongly worded speech but Walpole moved him to moderate it.[175] Among other things, the king accused Spain and the Emperor of plotting to bring back the Stuarts and Roman Catholicism to England by force. Parliament replied by voting a large land tax for fitting of the fleet and, in spite of the Act of Settlement, stated the principle that the king's German possessions could not be left defenceless by England. The construction of the fleet was carried out rapidly.[176]

The Emperor replied by having Palm, his agent in London, print and distribute a rebuttal of the charges. His approaches to the Opposition had already made Palm most unpopular with the government and he was expelled. On 8 April St Saphorin and Huldenberg, after months of isolation and coolness, were expelled from Vienna. In an unusual show of solidarity with the Emperor, the imperial diet ordered the expulsion of Le Heup from the Empire a week later.[177] Diplomatic relations between Spain and Britain had ended early in February when the Spanish bombardment of Gibraltar began. England increasingly concentrated her efforts on weakening the Emperor while the French, the only state in the hostile alliance with which the Emperor still had diplomatic relations, mediated. The role of France was decisive: had the French

---

[172] Vienna, Reichsk. *Weisungen an die Prinzipalkommission* Fasz. 5c. Dureng, p. 35 n2.

[173] When Le Heup presented a declaration similar to Chavigny's he was expelled from Regensburg: Naumann, p. 128.

[174] Chance, 'The Treaty of Hanover', pp. 687–8. Hills, p. 278.

[175] Michael, vol. III, pp. 443–7. It was reported that the two men came close to blows over the conduct of foreign policy at this time.

[176] *Ibid.*, p. 449.

[177] Gehling, pp. 236–7, Mecenseffy, p. 90.

supported England in an armed action against Spain, a European war would have resulted in which France would have been fighting a related dynasty for the benefit of Britain. By taking the opportunity of exploiting the rivalries of others, France could now gain the arbiter's role. Fleury insisted that the Emperor agree to terms acceptable to England and the Dutch, especially the suspension of the Ostend company for a substantial period. Fleury also refused to accept the Spanish attack on Gibraltar as a *casus foederis* and French armies were not mobilized. By the end of March 1727 serious negotiations between France and the Emperor were in train and Charles VI began to give way.[178]

The Emperor's carefully built alliance system crumbled. The Prussian alliance of October 1726 ran out after six months because the elector palatine refused to negotiate on the future of Jülich and Berg, arguing that it was not in the Emperor's interests to strengthen Prussia on the Rhine. Attempts by the Imperial ambassador, Stefan Kinsky, to bring the elector to terms with Prussia failed; attempts to find a substitute for Berg acceptable to Frederick William came to nothing. The Hanoverian party in Berlin and the anti-Prussian party in Vienna were both active, arguing that the Prussian-imperial alliance was unnatural anyway.[179]

Among the German princes there was a growing fear that Charles intended to nominate a foreign prince as his successor.[180] Early in 1727 the Emperor mounted a campaign to revive the useful institution of the Circle Association. Agents, including Wurmbrand, the president of the *Reichshofrat*, were sent out into the Empire in the autumn and winter of 1726 to bring this about but everywhere their efforts were countered by Bavarian agents and Chavigny.[181] It was obvious that the princes were playing one side off against the other to win the greatest benefit for themselves. Nevertheless the imperial agents had some success. Württemberg, the major state of the Swabian Circle, was at first difficult to win because of fears of the Herrenhausen powers, especially French pressure on Montbéliard,[182] but eventually joined the imperial party in May 1727. Five Circle diets were convened in April in the traditionally loyal areas of the Rhine and south west. They were favourable to the Emperor and a congress of all five was called at Frankfurt on 31 May.[183] The

---

[178] Wilson, pp. 158–9.
[179] Naumann, p. 123 n14.
[180] Mecenseffy, p. 93.
[181] Naumann, p. 125; Dureng, pp. 27 ff.
[182] *Ibid.*, p. 41. English efforts to persuade the French to settle this matter to win over Württemberg came to nothing: Wilson, p. 157.
[183] Aretin, pp. 100 ff.

Association was renewed at once but major reservations, traceable to Chavigny's influence, were included in the act of association. It would have proved a feeble instrument of imperial policy, as its army was specifically reserved for defensive purposes. On the same day as this minor victory was won, peace preliminaries between Spain and England were signed and the Emperor's European position collapsed.

7

The Emperor's search for allies

Mecklenburg

The impact of the European diplomatic situation on the activities of the aulic council was immediate. In 1724 the aulic deputation on the Mecklenburg case recommended the establishment of a provisional administration under duke Christian Louis to replace the commission. In his resolution on a *Referat* of the aulic deputation, dated 8 December 1726,[1] the Emperor accepted the necessity of removing Charles Leopold and of investing his brother with the administration of the country and this was issued as a verdict on 11 May 1728. Many years were to pass before the verdict was put into effect.[2] The years between the initial recommendation and the verdict had been taken up in diplomatic activity aimed at creating a favourable climate for such far-reaching changes. By 1728 change was obviously necessary. The finances of Mecklenburg were sinking into chaos, helped by the aulic council, which granted away the same money twice without concern.[3] The Mecklenburg case could not be handled in isolation from the diplomatic situation in Europe; several more years of intense activity were needed before obstacles in the way of the abolition of the Mecklenburg commission and the creation of the administration, the last important exercise of the supreme judicial office in peace time, could be removed.

The difficulties were legion. Among the great powers, England, Prussia and Russia were immediately interested and each had to be won over to accept the proposed change. The Empire, disquieted by recent examples of a vigorous imperial policy in the religious

---

[1] Vienna, Reichskanzl. *Vortr.* fasz. 6c fol. 290 – 307.
[2] Wilson, p. 195 n10 is mistaken in his statement that the verdict resulted from the Emperor's resentment against George II, though Wilson is generally confused about the role of the aulic council in the case.
[3] *Votum* of 23 July 1726: Vienna, RHR *Vota* K. 36.

dispute and a number of cases in the imperial courts, had to be convinced of the need for an administration if it was to have a chance. The future of the existing commission with its large financial claims and the question of Prussian participation in the affair also exercised the minds of imperial ministers. Prussia had received comparatively mild imperial dispositions in Mecklenburg very fretfully and the new administration was likely to succeed only if king Frederick William agreed. In addition the Emperor was anxious to have Prussia as an ally and the Mecklenburg question was one of the points which could make or break this ambition.

The council was given the occasion to make a change by the death of George I and the automatic lapse of the old commission in April 1727. The administration was formally established by the verdict of 11 May 1728.[4] By virtue of his supreme judicial authority 'for reasons well known throughout the Empire', Charles VI deprived Charles Leopold of the government of his lands and vested it in his brother, as heir presumptive, until further notice. Christian Louis was to administer Mecklenburg-Schwerin in the name of the Emperor for as long as it should please the Emperor to allow him to do so. All Mecklenburg subjects were released from their oath of obedience to Charles Leopold and were to swear allegiance to the imperial administrator. He was to rule according to the constitution and customs and would confirm the *Reversales*. He was to keep strict accounts, to be submitted annually to the Emperor, and to administer justice. By implication, the commission's *Exekutionskassa* was to be abolished. The aulic council apparently also envisaged that the security of the country would be taken out of the hands of the commission, as the verdict stated that Christian Louis was to recruit his own troops. Although he was equipped with all the attributes of a reigning prince, including, it seemed at first, the Mecklenburg votes in the imperial diet,[5] his every act was subject to the ultimate approval of the Emperor. The leading strings for Christian Louis were already being woven in this verdict.

The *Conservatorium* of 1717 was renewed, with the significant addition of the king of Prussia as duke of Magdeburg, to protect the country and the administrator. Only the *Conservatorium* was renewed and extended; the commission to execute, investigate and administer was thereby abolished and it was exactly this which

---

4   *Merkw. RHR Concl.*, vol. VI nos. dci and dcii.
5   On the advice of the elector of Mainz it was eventually decided to allow Charles Leopold to keep his votes: the deprivation of the votes was seen as tantamount to the loss of the lands which went with them: Vienna, *Kl. Reichsst.* K. 347 fol. 456–7.

Prussia had long wished to share. The concession was in reality far less than the king had wanted.

By these verdicts the Emperor, with little apparent preparation, placed an accomplished fact before Europe and the Empire; the many difficulties had not been removed and the Mecklenburg case was, as quickly became apparent, no nearer solution.

Similar difficulties were experienced by the Emperor in the East Frisian case. The prince's victory in the civil war and its consequences proved profoundly disturbing to the Dutch[6] and other foreign friends of the Estates. The prince's victory was followed by a minor 'white terror', when the princely party took revenge on the *Renitenten*. The persons and property of the Emden party were subjected to a campaign of victimization at the hands of the Salva Guardia, the Danes and the prince's army.[7] Troops were billeted on the *Renitenten* and contributions taken from them by force, all with the consent of the subdelegates.[8] The Aurich College was all-powerful and diets were purged to admit only 'reliable' elements. It was significant that even the 'obedient' Estates clung fast to the *Akkorden*, resisting any attempt to dispense with the constitution where imperial law seemed to override it.[9] The *Hofgericht*, even under the control of the 'obedient' Estates, resisted all attempts by the prince to restrict its jurisdiction.[10]

The Dutch, it was believed in Vienna, were above all else afraid that Prussia would acquire East Frisia and that they would, in consequence, lose Emden. They might therefore attempt to annex the city or to persuade their allies, Britain and France, to put diplomatic pressure on the Emperor in favour of the Emden party.[11] Klopp's analysis of subsequent events[12] is that, under pressure from the Dutch and their allies, the Emperor abandoned the original position he had taken up and, by accepting the Emden submission so often rejected, undid all the work of the aulic council. In fact the genesis of two important documents, the imperial verdict of 12

---

6   This had long been clear to the imperial government: ibid., Staatsk. *Vortr.* K. 27 viii fol. 47 – 50, *Vortrag* of 7 August 1728.
7   Ibid., *Kl. Reichsst.* K. 404, report of Königsegg 5 March 1728.
8   Klopp, vol. II, p. 551.
9   Ibid., p. 547.
10 Vienna, RHR *Den. Rec.* K. 923(8), exhib. of *Hofgericht*, 23 August 1730.
11 Reports of Königsegg 1 June, 20 July, 6 and 10 August 1728: Vienna, *Kl. Reichsst.* K. 404.
12 Klopp, vol. II, pp. 552 – 4.

September 1729, which accepted the Emden submission, and the 'Declaration touching E. Frisia', which the Emperor issued as part of the agreement eventually reached with the sea powers after long negotiation, was far more complicated than this suggests.

Neither the Mecklenburg nor the East Frisian case could be settled as a purely imperial matter as major powers were deeply interested in the fate of both countries. Both cases were items of international diplomatic negotiation and the diplomatic weakness of the Emperor at this time influenced the outcome.

By 1729 a new system of alliances was emerging in Europe. Spain's attack on Gibraltar in February 1727 showed up the basic weakness of the Emperor's position: he could not afford to go to war in support of Spain but, if he failed to do so, he ran the risk of driving Spain into the waiting arms of Britain and France, who would reward her with lands in Italy at his cost. He had no reliable ally. The dangerous isolation of the Emperor and the pressing need to obtain further guarantees of the Pragmatic Sanction began to bring imperial ministers, especially prince Eugene and Starhemberg, back to the view, never completely abandoned, that the traditional alliance for Austria, with the sea powers, should be revived.[13] The Spanish alliance system, which Sinzendorff had made his own special policy, began to collapse and simultaneously his influence began to weaken.[14] The Spanish alliance proved to be a disastrous trap for the Emperor, making his position in Europe much worse without bringing him any advantage. In a weak bargaining position and with his diplomatic freedom of action severely diminished, the Emperor was forced to buy allies.

Peace preliminaries were signed in Paris in 31 May by imperial, French, Dutch and British plenipotentiaries. The Emperor agreed to the suspension of the Ostend company for seven years and to the calling of a congress of the powers, originally to be held at Aachen, within four months to restore tranquillity to Europe. The preliminaries also confirmed the treaties of Utrecht and Baden, the Quadruple Alliance and commercial treaties entered before 1725.[15] The suspension rather than outright abolition of the company was a device to save the Emperor's face; its loss was a severe blow to his prestige but it was not a vital Austrian interest. By August 1727 France and Spain were clearly moving closer together. Further change was heralded by the deaths of the tsarina and king George I,

---

13 Mecenseffy, p. 132.
14 Braubach, M., 'Friedrich Karl von Schönborn und Prinz Eugen', in *Österreich und Europea: Festgabe für Hugo Hantsch*, p. 120 on the revival of Eugene's influence between 1727 and 1731.
15 Naumann, pp. 131 – 2.

though there was no immediate change in the foreign policy of either state.[16] The political situation in Britain was more stable than earlier: the Hanoverians sat more firmly on the throne, there was no real danger from Jacobitism, financially stability had been restored after the South Sea Bubble and Walpole managed the Commons with skill.[17] The Russians were most annoyed that the Emperor had been ready to come to terms without consulting them, his allies, and that he had done nothing for the duke of Holstein. In September Menshikov fell from power and, under the control of the reactionary Dolgorukii family, Russia for a time withdrew from her involvement in western affairs, symbolized by the transfer of the imperial court back to Moscow. The Emperor was deprived of another potential source of help.

The Hanover allies continued their attacks on imperial policies in Germany as a means of further weakening the Emperor's position in preparation for the forthcoming congress, where they hoped to extort more concessions from him.[18] The Emperor was anxious for the congress to start and finish quickly, as he was faced with a huge expenditure on defence in the meantime, but it was frustratingly held up. Spain refused to ratify the preliminaries and haggled over details.

Especially unwelcome to the Emperor was the allies' proposal to refer to the congress 'affairs of the Empire', including the religious dispute and a number of important cases pending in the imperial courts. Chavigny devoted great effort to persuading the German princes to seek representation at the congress, though Fleury did not welcome the prospect of hordes of princelings holding up important business with their petty squabbles and turning the congress into an imperial diet. Only Bavaria and the elector-palatine sent ministers to the meeting, eventually convened at Soissons, to represent their interest in the Jülich-Berg question and in the matter of the imperial succession.[19] The States-General announced their

---

16 Mecenseffy, p. 99. On the tsarina's death in May 1727 there was increased fear in Vienna that Russian policy would change direction and that no help would come from there. English statesmen, especially Townshend, were apprehensive about Russo-imperial ambitions.

17 J. B. Owen, 'The Survival of Country Attitudes in the 18th century House of Commons' in J. S. Bromley and E. H. Kossman (eds.), *Britain and the Netherlands*, vol. IV (The Hague, 1971), p. 51.

18 Dureng, p. 56. In October 1727 the Hanoverian representative in Regensburg received orders directly from London to consult Chavigny in stirring up the German princes against the Emperor: the exchange of letters between England and Hanover in Hanover, *Cal. Br.* II E.1 274m fol. 42, 45, 46–7.

19 Dureng, pp. 58–60.

intention of bringing up the East Frisian case, in collaboration with France and Britain, in a resolution of 9 July 1728.[20] In December Sinzendorff, the chief imperial representative at the congress, was instructed to agree only to discussion of the Holstein case.[21] The Emperor regarded the allies' proposal as an affront, involving as it did the reference of matters under his sole jurisdiction to an assembly of foreigners and the submission of his imperial authority to the scrutiny of an international tribunal.

The position regarding the Mecklenburg and East Frisian cases was considered at length in a conference *Vortrag* of 15 June 1728[22] and a *Memoire pour servir à l'éclaircissement sur les affaires d'Ostfrise et de Mecklenbourg*, apparently produced at the end of December 1728 for the information of imperial diplomats.[23] In the Mecklenburg case, two main objectives were recommended: the maintenance of imperial authority and the avoidance of any action which might alienate the king of Prussia, whom the Emperor hoped to win for a lasting alliance. This hope had been strengthened by signs of a growing breach between Prussia and Hanover early in 1728.[24] At the same time Frederick William seemed to be moving closer to the elector of Saxony, whom the Emperor was also wooing. It was Augustus's ambition to play the role of mediator and lead a 'middle party' in German and European politics, though he lacked the essential ingredient, power. Saxony was impoverished by his lavish court expenditure and his Polish ambitions and could maintain an army of only 18,000. In reality the elector was out for the best bargain he could get and, had the cash been available, the Emperor might have been able to buy him. Augustus would also have liked to form a block with Prussia to dominate the north and hopes of this rose in January 1728 when the two kings signed an agreement to preserve the neutrality of the Saxon Circles in case of war.[25] In March the two rulers formed an exclusive drinking circle, the *société des antisobres*, joined by the imperial ambassador Seckendorff and leading Saxon and Prussian ministers. This cordiality was not very welcome in Vienna but it seems to have been superficial. The basic mistrust between the two rulers persisted.[26] In May 1728 control of Saxon foreign policy passed to Ernst Christoph von Manteuffel. As

20 Aurich, C III c no. 140 fol. 34 – 41.
21 Mecenseffy, p. 105.
22 Vienna, Staatskanzl. *Vortr.* K. 29 v – vi fol. 99 – 114.
23 *Ibid.*, xii fol. 41 – 6.
24 Hanover, Cal. Br. II E.1 no. 274m fol. 105 – 7.
25 Naumann, p. 139.
26 Pretsch, pp. 25 – 30, 51. M. Braubach, ' "Le Diable". Ein Mentor Friedrichs des Grossen als Agent des Prinzen Eugen' in *Diplomatie und geistiges Leben in 17. und 18. Jahrhundert*, pp. 437 – 63.

a close friend of prince Eugene, he tried to take Saxony into the imperial camp but was unable to convince the elector, who dreamed of uniting Poland and Saxony and acquiring the imperial crown. He also had ambitions on Silesia and Bohemia as a land-bridge between Poland and his electorate, the so-called *via regia*. His impossibly high demands ruined negotiations for an alliance with the Emperor in the spring of 1728.[27]

A new alliance between the Emperor and Prussia was eventually signed on 23 December 1728. After acting as Hanover's catspaw in the religious crisis, which brought imperial displeasure on his head, and fluctuating between the two alliance systems in Europe without gaining what he wanted, Frederick William had now found his feet.[28] He remained strongly *reichspatriotisch* but nursed a sense of grievance against the aulic council.[29] He wanted protection against unfavourable decisions there and support in the Jülich-Berg succession case, still an obsessively important consideration in his foreign policy.[30] The Emperor was ready to offer a selection of alternatives to Jülich and Berg, including Bremen and Verden, Swedish Pomerania or land in the Austrian Netherlands, an indication of the value placed on the Prussian alliance.[31]

Serious negotiations were pursued by Seckendorff from summer 1727. It was clear from his reports and contributions to conferences that the king could be won only by real concessions in the Jülich-Berg case. The question was discussed at conferences on 13 January and 30 June 1728,[32] which held that the alliance was highly desirable but not at the cost of the supreme judicial office, the total shipwreck of the Emperor's relations with the Wittelsbachs and a dangerous enlargement of Prussia. An aulic commission under the president of the aulic council to look into the whole Jülich case was recommended. The Emperor was ready to instruct it to do all possible to reach a verdict favourable to Prussia and would abandon any personal claims to Berg[33] but would not give Frederick William what he wanted, a mandate to send in troops if it became vacant or if the elector palatine took measures to seize it. On 30 June the ministers rehearsed in detail the excellent reasons for not allowing Prussia to

27   Pretsch, pp. 18 ff, 28 ff.
28   Naumann, pp. 100 – 1.
29   Koser, p. 217.
30   Mediger, *Moskaus Weg*, pp. 351 – 2.
31   Mecenseffy, pp. 117 ff., Droysen, vol. IV/2, pp. 416 f. for details of Seckendorff's negotiations.
32   Vienna, Staatskanzl. *Vortr.* K. 27 i – vii fol. 1 – 15, 100 – 10.
33   Mecenseffy, p. 121 n12. The dowager empress renounced her rights in 1676 though this fact was later ignored when Prussia and the Emperor came to an agreement: *ibid.*, p. 123 n14.

have the two territories: it would be against the Catholic and imperial interest, it would upset the Dutch and would strengthen a greedy and violent state, whose neighbours, Catholic and Protestant, lived in fear of her. But the Emperor needed allies and Prussia was available in exchange for Berg. An exchange of drafts followed, leading to final agreement in November. The Emperor offered to declare his own claims to the two provinces when the last Neuburg ruler died and to divide the inheritance, giving Berg to Prussia. This was to be an interim settlement until an imperial commission arranged a definitive division. The Emperor, anxious not to drive Saxony and the elector palatine into the arms of France and to preserve his judicial authority, wanted the provisions on Jülich and Berg kept secret but Prussia refused.[34] The king did however agree to do nothing until the extinction of the Neuberg line even if, as he feared, the elector palatine took steps to seize the territories in advance of this. Secret articles committed Prussia to vote for Maria Theresa's husband in a future imperial election and the two powers were to concert action in the *Reich*. The final treaty on these lines was signed on 23 December 1728.

The Prussian alliance altered the Mecklenburg situation. The conference *Vortrag* of 15 June 1729,[35] drawing heavily on the aulic council's analysis of the nature of the Mecklenburg provisional administration, stated the belief that both Prussia and Hanover had territorial ambitions in Mecklenburg and were doing their best to disguise this. It was vital to the Emperor's interests to prevent a dismemberment of the province and the strengthening of two already powerful Protestant states. The right of the Emperor to change or abolish commissions at will was open to no doubt and it was too easy to claim that, in setting up a provisional administration, the Emperor was seeking to gain control of Mecklenburg. Charles Leopold was being suspended, not deprived.

The Emperor approved and ordered that Schönborn should be informed of the conference's views. He was still imperial vice-chancellor even though his elevation to the sees of Bamberg and Würzburg, the last in March 1729, meant that he spent long periods away from Vienna.[36] According to Brawe, all *Reichssachen* were

---

[34] Pretsch, pp. 47, 59: the Saxons already suspected what was going on as they, like the Prussians, had bought a copy of the aulic council's *votum* on the matter.

[35] Vienna, Staatskanzl. *Vortr.* K. 29 v – vi fol. 79 – 114.

[36] There was some compensation in the fact that his bishoprics provided the Emperor with a reliable strong-point in Franconia.

reported to him, which accounted for delays in dealing with them.[37] The status of the imperial chancery and conference declined as the Emperor's international position deteriorated. A vigorous expansion of imperial authority was only possible when the Emperor was diplomatically strong. Under pressure Charles VI fell back on the real basis of his power, the Habsburg lands and their security. By 1728 the Emperor had begun to abandon the weaker outworks and to strengthen the central fortress.

Hanoverian opposition to imperial decisions in Mecklenburg and East Frisia was considered at a conference on 14 July 1728.[38] The ministers concluded that Britain and the United Provinces had taken advantage of verdicts in these cases to make violent and groundless attacks on the emperor's authority, attacks which had not been answered with sufficient emphasis. A conference report of 5 September again urged the Emperor to defend himself with vigour against the accusations of the Herrenhausen powers.[39] The two conferences of 29 July and 30 August 1729 considered the growing alienation of Hanover and Prussia, in which the Mecklenburg case had played an important part. In Summer 1729 it looked as if war would break out between the two over a number of apparently trivial issues.[40] Had this happened it could have involved the whole of Europe and the crisis shattered the front against the Emperor. Some ministers, including prince Eugene, welcomed the friction in the belief that it gave the Emperor a chance to take decisive action and perhaps recover the initiative in

---

[37] Aurich, A IV c no. 254, report of 6 April 1729. In a report of 8 September 1728 Brawe bewailed the growing influence of the Austrian ministers in Vienna, in particular of Sinzendorff, who, he said, put the interests of the moment before the Emperor's *Hoheit* and was encouraged in this by the absence of Schönborn and Wurmbrand. Rumour was also rife in Vienna that the Emperor intended to make wide concessions to the king of Prussia in all the cases at issue, including Mecklenburg and East Frisia: *ibid.*, no. 253, Naumann, pp. 139–40.

[38] Vienna, Staatsk. *Vortr.* K. 27 i – vii fol. 108–10.

[39] *Ibid.*, K. 28 x.

[40] *Ibid.*, K. 29 vii fol. 101–7, viii – x fol. 40–53. The king of Prussia had indulged in a crude double game during his negotiations with Vienna, agreeing to co-operate with Hanover and at the same time revealing everything to the Emperor. Hanover was well aware of this but ignored it out of fear of losing Prussia as a result of the Emperor's policy of divide and rule. See also: Arneth, vol. III, p. 261; Naumann, pp. 154–5; Dureng, p. 86 for details of the dispute, which grew out of grievances over the encroachments of Prussian recruiters and disagreement over the hay harvest in some border fields. The Hanoverian government arrested some Prussian troops on leave in Hanover and Frederick William mobilized his army. In September he unexpectedly gave way and the crisis passed.

Germany. It is interesting that while, at the beginning of Charles VI's reign, largely under the influence of Schönborn, Prussia had been regarded in Vienna as the most dangerous rival to imperial influence in the north, now, perhaps as a sign of the extent to which imperial consideration had declined in importance, the imperial ministers had no doubt which side the Emperor should support in case of a war. The imperial ministers emphasized that it was in the Emperor's interest to stop the two largest Protestant states in Germany acting in concert against him but that it would be equally dangerous if they became irreconcilably hostile as imperial policy required that both should be won over as allies. Earlier it had seemed that Hanover would be drawn fully into the French system in Germany but there were still serious points of difference between them: France was not ready to give a guarantee of support for Hanoverian ambitions in Mecklenburg while Britain had reservations about offering wholesale support to France's clients, the Wittelsbachs.[41]

The ministers concluded that the Emperor had to view the issue from two distinct positions: 'namely as Roman Emperor and supreme judge in the Empire and, on the other hand, as lord and ruler of the hereditary lands and an ally of Prussia'. In the latter capacity it was the Emperor's duty to try to bring various matters to a conclusion favourable to Prussia. 'The first quality, however, prevents the Emperor from offering formal mediation to the Hanoverian court, especially in view of the existing circumstances.' The ministers considered particularly important the fact that Hanover was guilty of great arrogance and presumption and had been organising a campaign against the Emperor in the imperial diet for years.

The conference advised the Emperor to accommodate Prussia as far as possible but also to avoid the impression that he had failed to do all that was necessary to prevent dangerous developments in the Empire. Eugene believed a settlement between Hanover and Prussia would make one between London and Vienna easier. By September 1729 it was clear that war would not break out and in April 1730 a new English minister, Charles Hotham, arrived in Berlin with orders to encourage the pro-English party around the queen of Prussia and to arrange a double marriage alliance between the two houses. By summer 1730 Seckendorff was becoming seriously worried at the king's weakening loyalty to the Emperor.[42]

The chances of trouble elsewhere in the Empire were again increasing. The French were actively reviving their traditional and

---

[41] Dureng, pp. 87–8.
[42] Pretsch, pp. 76 ff. Seckendorff was apparently mistaken.

worrying policy of building up a party among the stronger German princes. Chavigny's influence in Regensburg grew with the Emperor's surrender to the Hanover allies. At first his activity was restrained by Fleury, still considering the possibility of a rapprochement with the Emperor. Chavigny, convinced that this was impossible, sometimes exceeded his instructions in his ambition to build up a French party. He had lavish plans for the formation of a union under French auspices to exclude Habsburg authority from Germany.[43] He concentrated his efforts among the Wittelsbach electors who, convinced now of the Emperor's weakness, began an offensive against him in the imperial diet. France's main agent was the elector of Bavaria, who had good reason to oppose the Pragmatic Sanction as he, like the elector of Saxony, had claims to part of the Habsburg lands.[44] Bavaria was firmly committed to the French connexion. A secret alliance was concluded on 12 November 1727, to come into force publicly when Bavaria's alliance with the Emperor expired in 1730. Under this treaty Bavarian claims to the imperial crown were recognised and she undertook to act as an agent for France in building an alliance system among the princes. Bavaria was also active in stirring up anti-Habsburg sentiment among the Italian states.[45] In October 1728, also at Fontainebleau, France and the elector-palatine came to a secret neutrality agreement, under which the elector promised to provide only his imperial contingent in any imperial war against France and France guaranteed his house the possession of Jülich and Berg.[46] Relations between the elector and the Emperor had been deteriorating for some time before this, although Vienna continued to pay subsidies. The Emperor's double-dealing over Jülich and the convoluted intricacies of the Zwingenberg affair led to a total breach.[47] Zwingenberg was a small county on the Neckar, the succession to which was disputed between the elector and the minor Protestant counts, Göler von Ravensburg. In 1725 the aulic council found in favour of the Göler but the Emperor allowed the imperial diet to consider the case, an unusual step, as he was normally extremely jealous of his judicial authority. In the imperial diet the case became a religious question; the Protestants saw referral of the case to the

---

[43] Dureng, pp. 49 ff. Lodge, R., 'The Treaty of Seville (1729)', *TRHS* (1933), p. 31. L. Auer, 'Das Reich und der Vertrag von Sevilla 1729 – 31', *MIÖG*, vol. 22 (1969), pp. 64 – 93.

[44] Naumann, p. 137.

[45] Pretsch, pp. 106 – 8.

[46] Naumann, p. 137.

[47] For details of the background to the Zwingenberg case see Dureng, pp. 65ff. and Naumann, p. 134.

diet as another Catholic machination to cheat the course of justice and they boycotted the diet every time the matter was mentioned. In September 1727 the Palatinate representative moved a debate on the case but in the college of princes all but three of the Protestants voted against and all the Catholics in favour of this. The Emperor wanted a quick settlement and suggested that the elector keep Zwingenberg, pay all the legal costs and give the Göler a suitable alternative but the Göler refused this solution. The aulic council ordered the rulers of Würtemberg and Konstanz to execute imperial verdicts against the elector but they did nothing. The whole affair provided Chavigny with valuable ammunition for his campaign against the Emperor and threatened to revive religious troubles, especially when reports spread that the elector palatine was persecuting the Zwingenberg Protestants. The Protestant princes refused to consider the matter except by the proces of *eundi in partes*, by amicable composition. Eventually in November 1728 the elector gave way in the face of a clear verdict of the aulic council against him and the Göler took possession of Zwingenberg. By then relations betwen the Emperor and the elector were in ruins.[48]

With French backing the Wittelsbachs began a concerted attack on the Emperor. The elector palatine raked up the old *Erzamt* affair and a number of other inflammatory matters. A new attack was mounted on the Emperor's handling of the religious dispute. In the background Chavigny was working steadily towards an alliance of the larger German rulers, centred on the Wittelsbachs and Württemberg, possibly with George II as nominal head.[49] A beginning was made on 16 April 1728, when Bavaria, Cologne and the Palatinate signed the Wittelsbach Union,[50] which was specifically anti-Habsburg. The wording of the treaty was innocuous: the electors pledged themselves to preserve the peace of the Empire on the basis of the settlement of 1648 and to act in concert in imperial matters, in particular the election of a king of the Romans, the Jülich, Zwingenberg and arch-office cases, and outside Germany. They also stated that they had no objection to the reference of imperial cases to a European congress. France had nothing to fear from an enlarged Bavaria and the Union was an ideal vehicle for French influence and trouble making in the Empire. It could be developed into an instrument to sweep Habsburg power from Germany.[51]

---

48 *Ibid.*, p. 144.
49 Dureng, pp. 61–4.
50 A further secret pact of neutrality was signed at Marly on 15 February 1729 with the addition of the elector of Trier.
51 Naumann, p. 138. Dureng, pp. 75 ff.

Indeed, the whole future of the Austrian state was now coming into question. Among the Mecklenburg documents in Göttingen[52] is an undated *Plan de Partage* envisaging a partition of the Habsburg lands on the death of Charles between Bavaria, Saxony, France, Spain and Savoy, which would have left a truncated monarchy of Hungary, Styria, Carniola, Carinthia and part of the Netherlands. As a result, Habsburg power in Germany and Europe would disappear. The Emperor's need for friends was manifest and his position was only slightly improved by increasing British worries about the revival of French influence in Germany and the proposed redrawing of the map of Europe. After Fleury came to power France's diplomatic dependence on Britain, caused by the duke of Bourbon's foolish alienation of Spain and the lack of another ally, quickly evaporated. There were signs in May 1728 of growing suspicion in London about French aims, in particular the ambitions of the *garde des sceaux* Chauvelin. The report that the French were encouraging the duke of Holstein to seek an equivalent in Germany for his lost lands increased this mistrust: it was not in Britain's interests to reopen the whole Northern question.[53] The British were unhappy about French attempts to perusade them to finance a French alliance system in the Empire and at the prospect of becoming the junior partner in such a system.[54] In both London and Vienna opinion was moving in favour of reconciliation.

Formal diplomatic relations were restored between England and the Emperor in April 1728. To save money the Emperor sent the wealthy but inexperienced twenty-four-year-old count Philip Kinsky as his ambassador in London. Although there were signs of a thaw, there remained a certain coldness between the two powers over certain issues, including deep differences on a number of cases in the imperial aulic council. Imperial action in Mecklenburg was deeply resented by George II, who warned Sweden and Denmark that if the Emperor and Prussia gained control of the area, the north would not be safe from their ambitions.[55] The Mecklenburg Administration was portrayed as an assault on the rights of the 'old princely houses', some of which had in July 1727 come together in a

52 Göttingen, Aw. 404.
53 Dureng, p. 61.
54 Dureng, pp. 40, 83, Naumann, p. 146, 156–7, 160.
55 Hanover, *Cal. Br.* II E.1 no. 274m fol. 147–9. Reck, the Hanoverian agent at the Soissons congress, was instructed to spread a report that the Emperor planned to put imperial troops into Mecklenburg. The Emperor had no such intention: Naumann, pp. 141–2.

new league to maintain their rights against the electors.[56] In a report of 6 July 1728 to Chauvelin, Chavigny warned of the dangerous implications of the latest verdict in the Mecklenburg case for the liberties of the German princes.[57] He berated the usurpations of the aulic council and its attempts to introduce a 'new jurisdiction'. Chavigny was given even greater scope for troublemaking when the Emperor asked the diet's approval of his *Provisorium* in Mecklenburg in a commission decree of 11 June 1729. In spite of imperial opposition, the Hanover allies resolved to bring the case up at the forthcoming congress.[58]

Hanover was still determined to take every advantage of the weakness of the Emperor's international position. The Hanoverian government argued strongly that the Emperor should not be allowed to speak at the congress in the name of the whole Empire and that it should be George's II's policy to persuade the Empire to send a deputation from the imperial diet or to place its interests in the hands of 'foreign friends'.[59] The grievances of the German princes were many and weighty. The house of Austria had taken too many states into subjection, robbed them of their rights and abused its majority in the imperial diet to increase its powers while paring away the rights of the Estates of the Empire.[60] When the European congress eventually met, it was Hanover's plan to turn it into a forum for the airing of general and specific grievances against imperial policy, the religious dispute and 'many and various other political presumptions and despotic actions of the imperial court contrary to the imperial constitution'.[61] The aulic council came in for special attack as the main instrument with which the Emperor had assaulted the sovereignty of the princes. In the eyes of the Hanoverian government it was Charles VI's aim to make himself master of the Empire, a serious threat to the rest of Europe. It is

---

[56]   Auer, p. 76. The initiative for the league came from Wolfenbüttel and Württemberg and it was eventually joined by Saxe-Gotha, Hesse-Cassel, Denmark and Sweden. Originally the formation of the league had been encouraged by the imperial roving ambassador Wurmbrand. After his alliance with Wolfenbüttel it was George II's ambition to take the league over and make it the core of a new Protestant group: Naumann, p. 142.

[57]   Dureng, pp. 71–4.

[58]   Droysen, vol. 4/3, p. 47.

[59]   The proposals of the Hanoverian government were stated in reports to the king d.d. 5 August and 12 September 1727: Hanover, *Cal. Br.* II E.1 no. 274m fol. 1–6, 13–7, 105–7.

[60]   Naumann, p. 144.

[61]   Wilson tends to accept these anti-imperial views uncritically: *e.g.* on p. 193 he writes of the Emperor's 'encroachments on the rights and privileges' of the German princes.

unlikely that the British government shared this imaginative view of German politics but the legend made a useful weapon against the Emperor at the congress.

The long-awaited congress opened at Soissons on 14 June 1728 after Spain, under considerable French pressure, had ratified the peace preliminaries by the convention of Pardo. The real business of the congress[62] was conducted behind the scenes at Paris and Versailles under the influence of Chauvelin and Fleury, itself an indication of the extent to which France was recovering diplomatic primacy in Europe.[63] The Emperor's position, which had seemed very weak on the eve of the congress, was directly strengthened by the growing divergence of policy between Britain and France. By summer 1728 it had become British policy to keep the meeting brief and, if possible, to restrict its business to a straightforward confirmation of the peace preliminaries. Britain no longer wanted a general discussion of European problems and was particularly afraid that the Schleswig question would be raised as this would reopen the whole northern settlement.[64] It continued to be the main aim of French policy to bring Spain into the Hanover alliance and to complete the Emperor's isolation but there was always the danger of driving the Emperor and the sea powers together if this ambition was pursued too hastily. Unlike the other powers involved, France had no major grievance and the natural role of a mediator fell to her[65] Fleury's position was strong: the official reconciliation between France and Spain had taken place in July 1727 and a French ambassador reached Madrid in September. Fleury could afford to be patient and wait and he was not under pressure from a parsimonious parliament anxious for a quick return on its investment.

By late autumn 1728, after Britain's refusal to cede Gibraltar, it was clear that the Soissons congress could achieve nothing useful. Although negotiations continued until 1730, the real business was transferred to the European capitals. At the beginning of 1729 the British government was still taking a bellicose stance but was anxious for a rapid resolution of the European crisis, even at the cost of war.[66] Spain was again building a fleet, which made war more likely. It was also clear that the Spanish-imperial alliance was

---

[62]   For detailed accounts of the Soissons congress see Wilson, ch. VI and Mecenseffy, ch. VII.
[63]   Mecenseffy, p. 107.
[64]   Wilson, p. 192.
[65]   Ibid., pp. 196 – 9.
[66]   See George II's speech in Parliament on 21 January 1729: Journal of the House of Commons (London, 1803), vol. 21, pp. 184 – 5.

crumbling away and Spanish ambitions were turning more firmly to Italy.[67] The Emperor stubbornly refused to give way on the question of the Spanish garrisons and was not ready to accept the Hanover allies' offer of a mere guarantee of his Italian possessions.[68] Spain was moving steadily towards the Hanover allies and a guarantee of don Carlos' succession in central Italy would have been enough to win her over. In June 1729 Königsegg reported from Madrid that queen Elizabeth was totally inflexible on the question of the garrisons. The Emperor had informed Spain in March that Maria Theresa would not marry a Spanish prince; her engagement to Francis Stephen of Lorraine was announced in August 1729.[69] Since the Soissons congress had begun, Spain and France had been moving closer together and Fleury demanded only the settlement of minor trade grievances before coming to terms.[70] There were also clear signs that Britain and the Emperor were moving together and serious negotiations for an alliance began in London in spring 1729.

Various pressures were predisposing the European states to settle their differences quickly. Changes in the personnel of the British government in May 1730 gave Walpole a cabinet more docile and more favourable towards a rapproachment with the Emperor in pursuit of more specifically British aims.[71] Neither Britain nor France wanted war, believing that more concessions could be extracted from the Emperor by the possibility of it alone. Walpole was ready to offer a guarantee of the Sanction if Charles would suppress the Ostend company and permit Spanish garrisons to enter central Italy. In spite of its warlike noises, the British government was afraid of parliamentary criticism if heavy expenditure on war preparations and subsidies to allies continued.[72] Walpole risked losing the French without gaining the imperial alliance unless a firm decision was made. The realization that England was wavering saw the beginning of the end of the Anglo-French alliance and the movement of France towards a closer and perhaps more natural

---

[67] Naumann, p. 159.

[68] Auer, p. 73 n45, Wilson, p. 217.

[69] The formal betrothal of Maria Theresa and Francis Stephen was not announced until August 1729 but Francis was regarded as her future husband after his brother's death in 1723: Mecenseffy, p. 134 n14.

[70] Wilson, p. 206.

[71] *Ibid.*, p. 220 n19: Townshend had been strongly anti-imperial and a zealous exponent of the Hanoverian 'interest'. He was replaced as secretary of state by William Stanhope, the former ambassador in Spain, now lord Harrington.

[72] *Ibid.*, p. 222.

alliance with Spain.[73] With the revival of French trade under Fleury there were also the beginnings of the commercial rivalry which was to play an important part in the relations of the two powers later in the century. There was growing unrest in England over the refortification of Dunkirk and French recruiting in Ireland was banned.[74]

However, on 9 November, before these trends produced lasting changes in the alliance system, the alliance of Seville was signed between France, Britain and Spain.[75] The most important clause, article IX, recognized Spain's right to put garrisons in Tuscany, Parma and Piacenza. The Emperor was given until May 1730 to accept the terms, after which they would be enforced. Elizabeth Farnese also wanted allied support to end imperial suzereinty over Parma and Tuscany but this was refused.[76]

Britain's refusal to implement the Seville treaty and to put Spanish troops into Italy by force finally drove Spain into the arms of France, which could no longer prevent the Emperor and the sea powers moving together. Anglo-French co-operation in Germany was also ending. In October 1729 Townshend formally rejected French plans for an extended Union of Electors in the Empire, envisaged as a vehicle for allied influence.[77]

With a return to the threatening situation of the late seventeenth century, the growth of a constellation of French client states all over Europe and renewed fears that France had ambitions against Luxembourg and Flanders,[78] the European alliance system began to take on the appearance of the anti-French coalitions of that period. But the reality was different. The new alliance of the Emperor and the sea powers was not aimed at preventing Bourbon expansionism

---

73 This was to culminate in the first Bourbon Family Compact of November 1733.

74 Wilson, pp. 59, 226.

75 The Dutch joined on 21 November. There is dispute as to where the initiative for the alliance came from: Mecenseffy, p. 114 concludes that it was from the Hanover allies but Wilson, p. 207 claims that it came from Spain.

76 Dureng, p. 98 n1 argues that Fleury realized that this would lose France considerable popularity in Germany.

77 Ibid., p. 95. As early as October 1724 St Saphorin had warned Townshend that the French were quite happy to allow England and the Emperor to fall out while France remained quietly in the background. He also reminded Townshend that England's foreign policy needed a viable Austria.

78 It was significant that in the later war of Polish Succession France, in order to avoid frightening the sea powers into a coalition with the Emperor, deliberately abstained from offensives in sensitive areas such as these. There were rumours that the French were trying to stir up trouble for the Emperor in Poland, Hungary and the Balkans: Pretsch, p. 110.

and the Netherlands and England were no more ready than in the Spanish succession war to support Austrian ambitions in Italy. Growing French influence in the Netherlands was worrying to Britain. The French supported the Dutch in the East Frisian case and, as in the past, threw their influence behind the republican 'party' and against William of Nassau, head of the house of Orange. The prospect of war was becoming unpopular in Britain and leadership of the anti-imperial campaign in Germany had clearly passed to France by 1730. France wanted a neutral Germany refusing to support imperial ambitions in Italy, where, from December 1729, the Emperor was concentrating his forces to meet what seemed the imminent threat of war after the Seville alliance.[79]

As the Seville deadline of 9 May drew closer, rumours of imminent war increased. Bavaria and the elector palatine were very hostile to the Emperor, whom French strategy sought to portray as totally unreasonable: he was only being asked to accept the Seville terms, with adequate guarantees of his possessions, but his stubbornness was threatening the whole *Reich* with war. There was some truth in this: Charles' pride prevented his acceding to a treaty he had had no hand in making.

An imperial conference on 28 December 1729 debated at length the growing prospect of an alliance with the sea powers.[80] The ministers openly admitted the Emperor's vulnerability. The internal weakness and poverty of the hereditary lands were well-known and, so far, it had proved impossible to maintain the troops already in service. A war would be disastrous. The Emperor's influence was not paramount in the Empire and the evil designs of Saxony and Bavaria were winning support. As the only solution they recommended reconciliation with the sea powers. They continued:

> On the other hand, the obedient conference cannot and will not advise that H.M. should give way to the wishes of the Sea Powers in those matters which would involve injustice to his other allies, an infringement of the rights of a third party or a breach of the imperial supreme judicial authority, or which would be contrary to his sworn capitulation of election and the laws of the Empire.[81]

---

[79] Naumann, p. 165.
[80] Vienna, Staatsk. *Vortr.* K. 30 fol. 3 – 34. The resulting *Vortrag* was dated 4 January 1730.
[81] *Ibid.*, fol. 5.

Negotiations for an alliance between the Emperor and the sea powers were to be pursued until a successful conclusion in 1732. Before any settlement was possible a number of points in dispute between the prospective allies had to be resolved. The Emperor had to accommodate Hanover in several imperial cases, including the future of Mecklenburg, and the States-General in the East Frisian case. In spite of the weakness of his international position, in neither case did the Emperor abandon his imperial judicial authority. The Emperor was clearly desperate for allies and the circumstances were most unfavourable for an impartial exercise of the imperial supreme judicial office. Yet this remained a factor which the conference had to take into account in reaching decisions on imperial and Austrian foreign policy. The Austrian *Hausinteresse* remained the main consideration in reaching such decisions but the maintenance of imperial influence in Germany was an important factor in this. The Emperor was more likely to be able to reassert imperial power with a strong *Hausmacht* behind him. Otherwise he was unutterably weak. The Empire was Austria's back door and remained so even when Austria's eyes were turned to the south and east. A hostile Empire, in clientage to foreign powers, would have been a constant source of danger. If the Emperor wished to strengthen his power in Germany as the head of the Empire, Austria would have to give way elsewhere in Europe so that all efforts could be devoted to this end without outside interference. Otherwise the Emperor would have to seek allies among the princes of the Empire as their equal and in competition with other European powers, in which case he could not really pose as an impartial supreme judge over them. In reality the choice was an artificial one. The abandonment of pretensions to imperial authority would have been impossible for the Habsburgs.[82] During these years the Emperor tried to pursue both policies at once against a background of conflict betwen the 'Austrian' and 'imperial' parties in the Vienna government, culminating in the inevitable victory of the former. The demands of the Pragmatic Sanction made this victory more certain.[83]

The conference of 17 January 1730, in which the Emperor took part, proposed the issue of a commission decree asking the Empire for political and military support in the rebuilding of an alliance system. The ministers also advised a direct approach to certain well-disposed princes. This recommendation led to the despatch of

[82] Auer, p. 70 recognizes this. Imperial policy relied on the Empire for some military aid, at least north of the Alps.

[83] Naumann, pp. 131 – 2.

baron von Kuefstein and general Seckendorff into Germany on a diplomatic tour of capitals to whip up support and to win over some or all of the pro-French electors, Bavaria, Cologne, Mainz and the Palatinate.[84]

Kuefstein set out in March 1730.[85] His main aim was to improve the Emperor's position in Germany and, indirectly, in Europe. The imperial ministers clearly regarded the Emperor's Italian possessions as the object of the most dangerous threat. When news of the Seville alliance spread in Germany in December 1729 it was seized on by the imperial government as good anti-Hanoverian propaganda; the proposed admission of Spanish troops to central Italy was portrayed as a breach of imperial law by the elector as king of England.[86] The imperial principal commissioner was informed of this in March 1730 but he was also warned to avoid the impression that the Emperor was mindful only of Habsburg interests; it was still his intention to protect imperial rights and the small princes.[87] He wanted the Empire's support but he did not want to be told to give way in Italy in order to remove the risk of war from Germany. Kuefstein was also to canvas support for a revival of the Circle Association of the early years of the century. Other important matters, including the Jülich-Berg, Mecklenburg and East Frisian cases and the imminent vacancy in the electorate of Mainz, were also included in his briefing. He was to concentrate on the elector of Cologne who, although a member of the Wittelsbach alliance system, was pro-imperial and terrified of the prospect of a war spilling over into his vulnerable possessions. He was ordered to

---

[84] Wilson, p. 208. To command a majority in the college of nine electors, the Emperor or France needed to control the allegiance of respectively four or five.

[85] There is an extract from his instructions as imperial envoy extraordinary among the records of the East Frisian Estates in Aurich, Dep. II no. 3140 and in the conference Vortrag of 19 January 1730 in Vienna, Staatskanz. Vortr. K. 30 1730 i fol. 229 – 43. His itinerary was carefully planned: he was to visit Mainz, Trier, Eichstätt, Bamberg, Würzburg, Ansbach, Gotha, Hesse-Darmstadt, Fulda, Ludwigsburg, Constance, Augsburg and Speyer. The predominance of ecclesiastical states in the list is significant. From August his efforts were reinforced by a roving embassy consisting of Frederick William I and Seckendorff among the Franconian and south German Protestant states, as had been proposed, without much hope, in a Vortrag of 20 December 1729: ibid., K. 30 1729 xi – xii fol. 44 – 78. In fact it enjoyed some success.

[86] Auer, pp. 66 – 7, 87 – 8.

[87] Vienna, Reichsk. Weisungen an die Prinzipalkommission fasz. 5c fol. 111 – 8.

take copies of the *vota* of the aulic council in the Mecklenburg and East Frisian cases to illustrate the purity of the Emperor's motives and the still inviolate imperial supreme judicial office. He was to argue that certain over-mighty states of the Empire were aiming to destroy imperial authority to enable them to lord it over the weaker states unchecked.

The Emperor's manuscript resolution on this conference recommendation is an interesting illustration of the 'split personality' of the head of the house of Habsburg: he was not sure whether he was to issue instructions to Kuefstein as Emperor or as archduke of Austria. Kuefstein was eventually provided with two sets of credentials and he submitted reports to both the aulic and the imperial chancery, those to the former usually much fuller. If he was able to bring any prince to the point of entering a formal alliance, this was to be signed with Austria but representations on specifically imperial topics were to be made in the name of the Emperor as sovereign of the Empire. His efforts were supported by the issue of an imperial commission decree to the diet on 18 March 1730 appealing for support. Carefully drawn up in general terms, it rehearsed the Vienna version of recent diplomatic history and made a moving appeal to German patriotism.[88]

Kuefstein's mission was not very successful. Cologne was won over to support the Emperor and the elector palatine agreed to the Rhenish-Westphalian Circle's joining the proposed Circle Association and stated his readiness to discuss the Jülich-Berg question with Prussia. Neither was prepared to compromise his neutrality; few princes were ready to commit themselves while Chavigny continued to issue assurances that France would respect the neutrality of the *Reich*. Kuefstein's greatest achievement was to engineer a revival of the Circle Association.[89] Meetings of the Circle assemblies were held in March and April. Franconia and Swabia favoured a policy of neutrality; Württemberg, the leading state in the Swabian Circle, was playing a double game in an effort to preserve neutrality.[90] In spite of this on 17 July a convention of five Circles at Frankfurt agreed to form an association based on a purely defensive policy. Fervent assurances of this were at once sent to France. Chavigny could be pleased with his achievement. On 1 August he reported his success: although he could not deny

---

[88] Auer, pp. 68–9.
[89] For which see Aretin, *passim*.
[90] Dureng, p. 112, Auer, pp. 80–1.

Charles VI a voice in the Empire, as a result of his work the Emperor could not rely on it or take its support for granted.[91]

Even with the eclipse of the north as a major theatre of European diplomacy, Mecklenburg remained a most delicate area and its future could not be regarded with indifference by any power with interests in the Baltic or northern Germany. Contemporaries believed that Hanover, which regarded it as a shield against attacks from the Baltic, had territorial ambitions against Mecklenburg,[92] a claim consistently denied in pamphlets.[93] It was unlikely, as the outright annexation of the country or part of it would have exposed Hanover to attack from jealous neighbours, in particular Denmark and Prussia, already resentful of Hanover's growth. There is little question that, during the primacy of Bernstorff, the Hanoverian government regarded it as vital to the security of the electorate to maintain a protectorate over the duchies through the possession of Rostock, the presence of troops and the entrenched supremacy of the knights to keep Mecklenburg weak and a natural satellite of Hanover. Hanover's huge financial claims were an added device for keeping the country in firm subjection without risking an attempt to incorporate it among the electoral possessions. There is some evidence that under George II the Hanoverian government seriously considered annexing at least that part of Mecklenburg leased to Hanover in settlement of claims arising from the commission.[94]

Immediate trouble seemed likely from the former commissioners, bitter at the cavalier fashion in which the Emperor had dispensed

---

[91] Dureng, pp. 114–15. A *Vortrag* of the imperial chancery of 27 February 1730, putting forward the conclusions of an imperial conference, drew the Emperor's attention to the sad fact that the *aequilibrium* in the Empire had so changed that he was no longer able to control the larger states. The small states were afraid of their strong neighbours but had lost almost all hope of real protection from the Emperor: Vienna, Reichsk. *Vortr.* fasz. 6c fol. 424–55.

[92] Mediger, *Mecklenburg*, pp. 435, 438: the Hanoverian councillor Alvensleben compared Mecklenburg to a nerve ganglion, where varied interests crossed in complicated confusion. Naumann, p. 152 writes of Hanoverian *Eroberungspläne* in the territory. The Emperor, with conscious memories of the Donauwörth case, certainly believed this: Vienna, Staatsk. *Vortr.* K. 27 viii instructions to Wratislaw, 30 July 1728 fol. 51–6.

[93] Naumann, pp. 152–3. Mediger, *Mecklenburg*, pp. 440 ff. produces evidence against this view, at least for the reign of George I.

[94] Göttingen University Library, manuscript collection, *Mecklenburgensia des 18. Jahrhunderts*, fol. 13–4, an undated *Gutachten* for the Hanoverian government. There were also attempts to gain permanent control of the Mecklenburg post office: Vienna, *Den. Rec.* K. 693(1) no. 2.

with their services in the verdict of 11 May 1728.[95] By stubbornly refusing to accept the Emperor's dispositions they were able to prevent the administration becoming a reality and only eventually agreed to changes when their requirements had been satisfied. They also began to organise opposition to the administration in the imperial diet. On 11 June 1729 the Emperor approached the diet for its advice on the matter but, so great was the uproar stirred up by Hanover and the Wittelsbachs with claims that Charles Leopold's deprivation was illegal, that the imperial representatives hurriedly withdrew the whole business from discussion.[96]

English opposition to imperial verdicts in the Mecklenburg and East Frisian cases was dealt with in a conference of 14 July 1729,[97] at which Britain and the Dutch were condemned for taking advantage of the verdicts to launch violent but groundless attacks on the Emperor. In a letter presented on 16 May 1729 George II announced that he would not remove his troops from Mecklenburg nor hand over the execution exchequer until his financial claims had been satisfied.[98]

Attempts were also made to put pressure on Christian Louis. In February 1729 a Hanoverian deputation visited him at Bützow to warn him not to be in a hurry to assume his duties, as the legality of the administration was very dubious.[99] They commented that the administration was no less than the ban in disguise and pointed out that the administrator had no money and no troops, did not control the revenues of the country, lacked the means to put his wishes into effect, the officials and Estates were, if not actively hostile, frightened and uncertain, and the clergy, two fortified towns and the law courts were all in the hands of his implacably recalcitrant brother. At the same time the Hanoverian government was trying to inveigle Christian Louis into a secret agreement. In April 1729 a Hanoverian councillor, Ludolf Hugo, was sent to Rostock to negotiate this.[100] He was to offer Christian Louis money to persuade him to refuse the administration and to resist all offers of help from

---

[95]   This was shown in the protocol of a Brunswick *Hauskonferenz* of 25 November 1730. The Hanoverians were afraid above all of Prussian ambitions in the area and refused to accept the legality of the verdict of 11 May: Hanover, *Cal. Br. Des.* 24 no. 87 fol. 45–50.

[96]   Vienna, RHR *Vota* K. 47: copy of the elector of Mainz' *Ohnmassgebliches Project Voti* in reply to the imperial commission decree of 11 June 1729, dd. Regensburg 31 October 1729.

[97]   *Ibid.*, Staatsk. *Vortr.* K. 27 i – vii fol. 108 – 10.

[98]   *Ibid.*, RHR *Den. Rec.* K. 708(4).

[99]   *Votum* of 8/22 March, *ibid.*, RHR *Vota* K. 36 and *Den. Rec.* K. 701 no. 4.

[100] Hanover, *Cal. Br. Des.* 24 Meck. no. 87 fol. 2 – 3 contains Hugo's credentials,

Prussia. He was to devote all his efforts to winning the full government of Mecklenburg, by means approved under the imperial constitution, but was to refuse it while his brother was still alive or had not been deprived by a formal ban process.

On 25 February 1729 Klein, the knights' agent, informed Verpoorten, Christian Louis' representative in Vienna, that there was news from Soissons that the Hanoverian allies would never permit Prussia to put troops into Mecklenburg and would not allow the administration to be put into effect.[101] Enclosed was a letter from the king of Sweden to Christian Louis' wife, to be passed discreetly to her husband with a request that he give up the administration, which was opposed by many grands seigneurs. The whole thing, it continued, was open to serious objection and it must be clear to Christian Louis that, if he accepted it, it would place the fate of all princes at the whim of the Emperor and the aulic council. The duke would soon realize what a dangerous friend he had in Prussia if he called upon the king to carry out his duties under the new Conservatorium.

Simultaneously Hanover mounted a campaign against the administration in the imperial diet.[102] On 12 June 1730 Verpoorten reported a discussion with Schönborn, who believed that the Konjunkturen would soon change and would permit the administration to be put into effect. Why he believed this was not reported.[103] In letters presented on 4 July 1730 the former commissioners expressed impatience at the slowness in settling their claims. They wanted the old arrangements to continue, as this would allow them control of ducal revenues. They alone, they claimed, were competent to deal with the accumulation of grievances and they would also be able to handle the necessary negotiations in the imperial diet before Charles Leopold could be legally banned. Hanover seemed anxious to see the duke banned, presumably in the belief that Christian Louis would be more amenable to Hanoverian control and to obtain a further lever against the Emperor by shepherding the ban process through the imperial diet.[104] The Emperor was forced to tread very carefully, as shown in

---

[101]   Göttingen, Aw. 491.
[102]   Ibid., draft letter of Klein to Verpoorten, 1 June 1729.
[103]   Ibid., Aw. 497 fasz. 2. See also the correspondence between Klein and Bassewitz, the knights' agents in Vienna, ibid., Aw. 506 fasz. 6, in particular a letter of Bassewitz to Klein of 17 November 1731. The case, he wrote, was in a most miserable state, being virtually in suspense. The Emperor did not dare to bring the matter before the imperial diet and could not find a system which would satisfy both Hanover and Prussia. He advised Christian Louis to keep very quiet.
[104]   Vienna, RHR Vota K. 36, votum of 27 May/20 June 1729.

an aulic council verdict of 30 August 1729,[105] which made no comment on the refusal of Hanover and Wolfenbüttel to abandon their hold on Mecklenburg. This was certainly influenced by a report from Regensburg and a letter of the principal commissioner Fürstenberg of 21 July and 19 August.[106] The first dealt with the attitude of the Protestant princes to the Emperor's actions. They were reportedly very unhappy about the dispossession of Charles Leopold and the establishment of the administration but would be prepared to consider a full ban process against him. 'In addition the Protestants object in general to this and other examples of the aulic council's violent and uncontrolled actions and believe that in future it should be better controlled.' They were also considering renewing their often repeated general complaints against the council 'in particular of renewing recourse to the imperial diet, possible under imperial law and observance, against the many abuses appearing recently in the imperial courts'.

As Schönborn reportedly told Verpoorten, the *Konjunkturen* were changing slowly with the rapprochement between Britain and the Emperor. In June 1730 new Hanoverian and British ambassadors, Diede and Thomas Robinson, arrived in Vienna to undertake negotiations for an alliance. At a series of meetings with imperial ministers, the various points at issue, including the Mecklenburg case, were debated in the search for an acceptable settlement.[107] Major decisions were therefore taken at a diplomatic rather than judicial level and the aulic council's share in the matter declined. Robinson wished to combine Hanoverian and British demands against the Emperor in comprehensive negotiations but this was to prove impossible. The Hanoverians took advantage of the Emperor's weakness to press a whole catalogue of accumulated grievances and demands. George II wanted enfeoffment with Bremen and Verden, including the city of Bremen, which was to lose its free status; imperial ministers insisted on firm guarantees of the city's rights.[108] The Emperor was ready to end the sequester of Hadeln, provided the rights of the Estates were guaranteed. He would also recognize Hanoverian sovereignty over Hildesheim until a judicial decision. Various minor grievances and disputes, in themselves trivial, including the grant of an acceptable arch-office for George II, were settled to Hanover's satisfaction without difficulty. They had

---

[105]   *Ibid.*, RHR *Prot. Rer. Res.* xviii 73.
[106]   The first is in Vienna, RHR *Den. Rec.* K. 700(8) no. 6, the second in *ibid.*, K. 701, 'in pto. consultationis in comitiis'.
[107]   Naumann, p. 167.
[108]   This had long been a concern of the Emperor: Hanover, *Cal. Br.* 24 Österreich I no. 131 fol. 19–20.

only become grievances because of the deterioration of relations between Hanover and the Emperor. The imperial ministers refused to write into any agreement a guarantee of the *jura in politicis et ecclesiasticis* of German princes, considering this an affront to imperial dignity.[109] The Emperor flatly refused to give an undertaking that he would exercise his imperial office justly. He was prepared to give no more than verbal promises to recognize Hanover's right to inherit East Frisia and refused to abolish Prussia's *Expektanz* there.

England's demands were less complicated and were settled first. The Emperor had no choice but to give away and abandon plans to acquire central Italy and control the whole peninsula. The last native duke of Parma died on 20 January 1731 and imperial troops immediately occupied the country, ostensibly to protect it for don Carlos against the threat of papal encroachment. This finally broke the Seville alliance. On 28 January the Spanish ambassador in France announced that Spain had renounced the treaty, as she had gained nothing from it.[110] Britain was afraid that Spain, cheated of the gains promised at Seville, would throw herself into the arms of France. Britain's need to secure the imperial alliance as an escape from threatening isolation was pressing. On 3 February Robinson was ordered to come to terms quickly, leaving Hanoverian issues to be dealt with later. It was unlikely that the Emperor would offer much resistance as he needed Hanoverian support to obtain a guarantee of the Sanction from the *Reich* against the opposition of France and her clients.

On 16 March 1731 the second Vienna treaty, between the Emperor and George II as king of England, was signed. The contracting powers swore eternal friendship, Britain guaranteed the Pragmatic Sanction and the Emperor agreed to the suppression of the Ostend company and to admit 6,000 Spanish troops to Parma and Tuscany. Charles VI also gave an undertaking that he would not marry his daughters to princes of the Bourbon or Hohenzollern houses.[111] Although he subsequently tried to demonstrate his continuing freedom of action by a few feeble gestures in summer

---

[109] Naumann, pp. 167 – 9.
[110] Gibbs, 'Newspapers, Parliament and Foreign Policy', pp. 311 – 13. The British government had tried to keep the negotiations with the Emperor discreet but they soon leaked out: Wilson, p. 223.
[111] Pretsch, p. 116 n152: it was reported in Vienna that many were of the opinion that the Emperor was crazy to give away so many real advantages for the Sanction.

1731,[112] the Emperor's position was patently hopeless. The alliance with the sea powers had one overwhelming advantage as far as Charles VI was concerned: Britain was ready to give a straight guarantee of the Sanction.[113] In July, when Spain joined the Anglo-imperial alliance, he recognized don Carlos' rights to Parma in the absence of a male heir. Spanish troops eventually arrived in October, after the duke's widow had held matters up by declaring herself pregnant.[114] On 11 May the Emperor sought the *Reich's* consent to the admission of foreign troops into imperial fiefs. France now tried to move the Empire to reject this when earlier she had urged the princes to put pressure on the Emperor to agree.[115] In fact the Empire agreed without fuss, with even Bavaria and Saxony raising no objection. The dominant emotion seems to have been relief at the removal of a potential cause of war. The Emperor was unable to obtain the Empire's permission to negotiate with Britain in its name but on 22 July the Empire acceded to the Vienna treaty.[116]

Agreement with Hanover on Mecklenburg was to prove more difficult. In June 1730 Charles Leopold returned unexpectedly to his duchy. At once waves of panic began to spread. To maintain security, the Emperor had no alternative but to order Hanover and Wolfenbüttel to increase their forces in the country. Neither Christian Louis nor the king of Prussia was informed.[117]

Hanover was keen to have the *Conservatorium* on Prussia abolished and an assurance that no Prussian troops would be permitted to enter Mecklenburg under any circumstances. This the imperial negotiators flatly refused but they were ready to give an undertaking that the Emperor would not instruct Prussia to send

---

112 When, in July, duke Gian Gastone of Tuscany nominated don Carlos as his heir and agreed to admit Spanish troops, the Emperor protested and announced his intention to sequester this imperial fief when it became vacant. Contacts with Spain and France were continued during the negotiations with Britain and the Spanish marriage project was mentioned again. France was prepared to give only vague reassurances about the Sanction and demanded in return Luxembourg and territory in Lorraine. The negotiations were not serious: Pretsch, p. 118; Braubach, *Versailles*, pp. 175 – 9.

113 Wilson, pp. 224 – 5 sees this alliance as an amazing departure in British foreign policy, in which the Hanoverian 'interest' had been an important element since 1717. The French, he argues, were taken by surprise, especially by the fact that Britain was prepared to give away her main bargaining counter, confirmation of the Sanction, for so little.

114 *Ibid.*, p. 229 n43.

115 Dureng, p. 118, Auer, p. 91.

116 Naumann, p. 175.

117 *Ibid.*, pp. 167 ff.

troops into Mecklenburg. On 20 March 1731 the Hanoverian government wrote to Hugo in Mecklenburg[118] that the 'heart of the matter' was to convince Vienna and, if necessary, Prussia that no new dispositions were needed in the country. All attempts by Prussia to elbow her way into the affair were to be resisted, though this was likely to prove difficult. A letter of the Prussian to the Hanoverian government of 24 March offered co-operation but also contained a thinly veiled statement of an intention to put troops into Mecklenburg.[119]

The conference again considered the Mecklenburg case on 29 October 1730 and 7 January 1731.[120] The Emperor's main aim, according to the ministers, should be to preserve the duchies from dismemberment and relieve them of the huge burden of the commission. Hanover's two major objections were that the administration was illegal and prejudicial to the rights of the princes and that large amounts of money, the arrears of the commission costs, were still owing. According to the head of the Austrian exchequer, Gundacker von Starhemberg, the question of costs was the most difficult. It would certainly not be in the Emperor's interests to allow Prussia to pay them, as she was reportedly willing to do. The Emperor must avoid giving offence to Frederick William I but he must also be denied any opportunity to increase his influence in Mecklenburg. Having given way to Prussian requests for participation in the Mecklenburg case to prevent Hanover from obtaining unchallenged control there, the imperial government was now anxious to prevent Prussia from interfering further in the case.[121] It was convenient to allow the threat of Prussian intervention to deter Hanover from decisive action in Mecklenburg but not to let either power win hegemony over the duchies. The conference arrived at the 'established principle' that the Emperor should make concessions to Hanover only as far as his supreme judicial authority, the laws of the Empire and the rights of third parties allowed.

The conference rejected the suggestion that the administration should be replaced by direct imperial rule as:

unheard of and the worst solution of all. The Administration is heartily disliked in the Empire and it is easy to see that it is giving

---

118 Hanover, *Cal. Br. Des.* 24 Mecklenburg no. 87 fol. 63 – 7.
119 *Ibid.*, fol. 68 – 71.
120 Vienna, Staatsk.. *Vortr.* K. 31 ix – xii fol. 97 – 128, K. 32 i – ii fol. 1.
121 This was stated baldly in a further *Vortrag* of 11 January 1731: *ibid.*, K. 32 i – ii fol. 3, 7 – 11.

the king [George II] an opportunity to pose as a guardian of the liberties of the Estates of the Empire. It will therefore require great care to turn aside animosity from this court and to cheat the intentions of the king of England.

The ministers urged that the Emperor should refuse to enter a formal treaty with Hanover on imperial matters but should be ready to issue a decree of declaration and assurance (*Erklärungs- und Versicherungsdecretum*) including an unequivocal reservation of imperial jurisdiction and rights of third parties.

A draft decree was sketched at a conference on 24 April 1731, which produced a *Vortrag* dated 26 April.[122] The future of Bremen-Verden and Hadeln was agreed but decisions on the Mecklenburg case were postponed.[123] The conference was not happy about Diede's proposed declaration: George II wanted a statement that his troops were in Mecklenberg to keep the peace on imperial orders and were to remain there at the duke's expense. The imperial negotiators wanted to add 'until further instructions' (*bis auf weitere Verordnung*), fearing that the Hanoverian version would offend Prussia while the Emperor did not want to give Hanover a licence to put as many troops as he wished into Mecklenburg. The conference suggested an unobjectionable formula: 'H.I.M. declares that the Hanoverian and Wolfenbüttel troops at present in Mecklenburg and remaining there on H.M. orders for the maintenance of peace there are to be maintained at the cost of the contumacious party [*i.e..* the duke].'

At this point the Emperor wrote in the margin of the *Vortrag* that this was as far as he was prepared to go. The declaration did not say that the troops were in the country on imperial orders, as Hanover wanted, but that they were to remain there on imperial orders to maintain peace and security and could therefore be removed when this task was complete. Diede was to be informed flatly that the Emperor would not exclude Prussia from the *Conservatorium* nor alter it to Prussia's disadvantage. The Mecklenburg case made it especially necessary to keep the king of Prussia closely bound to the Emperor.[124] Great care was needed to reconcile Diede's statements

---

122 *Ibid.*, K. 32 iii – iv fol. 155 – 61. Naumann, pp. 172 – 3 states that the meeting on 24 April produced the final settlement. He seems to have mistaken a draft for the final version, though the differences were small.
123 Hantsch, *Schönborn*, pp. 331 – 2.
124 See the *Vortrag* of 12 October 1731, Vienna, Staatsk. *Vortr.* K. 34 ix – x fol. 114 – 19.

with Frederick William I's firm resolve, reported by Seckendorff, to exercise the *Conservatorium* in fact as well as in name: 'It is right to worry that, unless a solution is found acceptable to both sides, Your Majesty will not be able to retain the friendship of both kings for long.'

The conference was quite right. The Anglo-imperial reconciliation marked the beginning of the end of co-operation between the Emperor and Prussia. The Emperor had to carry out a very delicate juggling operation to avoid giving Frederick William the impression that he had been abandoned and at the same time prevent Hanover and Prussia coming together. England was still using the queen of Prussia as an agent to promote plans for a double marriage. Seckendorff was periodically absent from Berlin in 1731 and imperial influence in Prussia was very dependent on his presence. Frederic William's policies remained as clumsy and unpredictable as ever.[125]

In the last months of 1731 the case was moving to a critical stage. Although major decisions were reserved for the conference,[126] the aulic council was not ignored. The special *Deputation* of council members continued to operate, meeting on 23 August on the recommendation of the conference to discuss the latest Hanoverian demands.[127] On 11 July Diede had proposed that the case should be referred to the whole Empire, which should be asked for an opinion on two questions: what further action was to be taken against the duke and, if it should be necessary to set up an interim government, what form should this take? It was obvious that the administration existed in name only.[128] On the first point the councillors were of the opinion that the Emperor had a right to institute a ban process against the duke in the aulic council without any prior reference to the imperial diet. He was only required to submit the fiscal *acta* of the case to the diet for its approval after completion. They did not recommend this course of action: 'In view of the difficult, indeed

---

[125] Pretsch, p. 100. The delicate balancing operation was made doubly difficult by the systematic campaign of forced recruiting which the Prussians were mounting in Mecklenburg: *Vortrag* of 3 November 1731 in Vienna, Staatsk. *Vortr.* K. 34 xi – xii fol. 3 – 9.

[126] A conference of 22 November 1731 advised a complete suspension of the case until the Empire guaranteed the Pragmatic Sanction and the Emperor's diplomatic situation improved: *ibid.*, fol. 31 – 2.

[127] The conference of 26 July 1731: *ibid.*, K. 33 vii – viii fol. 99 – 100. A record of the meeting of 23 August is in Vienna, RHR *Den. Rec.* K. 700(8) no. 28. The deputation now consisted of Wurmbrand, Hartig, Berger and Metsch, the last as a representative of the imperial vice-chancellor.

[128] *Ibid.*, a letter of Berger to the RHR president of 23 August spoke of 'the suspended Provisional Administration'.

disturbing circumstances inside and outside the Empire as Charles Leopold would almost certainly not answer the charges but would allow everything to proceed against him in *contumaciam*.' It would also be difficult to execute the ban against him and the whole process would be long and involved.

Behind the second point lay Hanover's intention to bring about a *Konkurrenz* (participation) of the Empire in the affairs of Mecklenburg. This was unnecessary and would bring about a surrender of the imperial *jus provisorium*. Even though the administration did not exist, the maintenance of the legend that it did was useful. The *Deputation* did not consider any change in the existing arrangements necessary, except that the king of Prussia might also send a subdelegate to Rostock; the rivalry between Hanover and Prussia would guarantee the Emperor's continuing influence.

This fell in with the wishes of the king of Prussia as discussed at a conference of 19 January 1732.[129] The king wanted a Prussian subdelegate, orders to the other conservators to keep him fully informed and rapid repayment of the commission costs to deprive Hanover of a pretext for keeping a finger in what was possibly a future part of the king's possessions. The conference condemned the actions of Hanover as illegal: the commission was void, as conservator Hanover enjoyed only the same rights as Prussia and, as Circle director, the rights of Wolfenbüttel and Prussia took precedence. The Emperor had consistently rejected many of Diede's original *Desideria*, the exclusion of Prussia and a formal ban against Charles Leopold, and Hanover continued to make difficulties in the case to embarrass the Emperor. Hanover's attitude alone made the king of Prussia anxious to put troops into Mecklenburg as he feared Hanoverian annexation plans. No solution could be found acceptable to both sides; only a middle way would succeed. The ministers suggested that the administration continue in name and that a Prussian member be added to the subdelegation within a set period, although legally there was no subdelegation.

On the question of commission costs, the conference commented that the aulic council had found much to object to in the accounts[130] but had recommended acceptance. It was obvious that, if the Emperor rejected the claims, it would only make the situation

---

[129]   *Ibid.*, Staatsk. *Vortr.* K. 34 i – ii fol. 21 – 48.

[130]   See the *votum* of 5 July 1731, of which there is a draft in Vienna, RHR *Den. Rec.* K. 701. The council objected in particular to the costs of the subdelegates' mourning for dowager empress Eleonora, large gifts to Huldenberg and fines paid for the subdelegate Alvensleben for the offence of non-residence in Magdeburg.

worse, especially as the council's recommendations were probably well-known to George II.

It was felt that Hanover would be less inclined to make problems for the Emperor if faced with the threat of Prussian participation in Mecklenburg. As well as paying off the commission costs, it was urgently necessary to raise a security force for Christian Ludwig to deprive Hanover of the pretext for keeping troops in the country. The Emperor approved the recommendations and a further series of discussions with George II's representatives followed, the outcome of which were discussed at an imperial conference held on 1 February 1732 and a privy conference on 4th.[131] There were two alternative solutions to the Mecklenburg problem, the administration or continued rule by the conservators with the addition of Prussia; the choice lay with George II. At first Diede accepted the second option on condition that no Prussian troops entered Mecklenburg and Seckendorff had, with great difficulty, persuaded the Prussians to agree. Diede then changed his mind and supported the administration, provided means could be found of instituting it which did not infringe the rights of the German princes. In reality, it seemed, Hanover was ready to accept it only if it was no more than the old commission under a new name, that is, that Hanover and Wolfenbüttel would keep military and financial control. Hanover objected to the administration as it sought to release subjects from their oath of allegience, required them to swear a new oath and was subject to the control of the aulic council. In fact, as ministers pointed out, the administration depended solely on the Emperor's supreme judicial office, which Hanover should be the first to respect as she had administered Mecklenburg by virtue of it for a long time. The administration could, however, be given to Christian Louis in a manner unobjectionable to the Emperor and the king. Diede had no objection in principle, provided a simple edict of notification was given to the imperial diet informing it of the decision and an imperial verdict was issued accepting the claims for commission costs. Wurmbrand strongly opposed bringing the matter before the imperial diet in any way but the other ministers had no objection, as the method proposed would not initiate any debate there. The Emperor approved the recommendations, again commenting that this was as far as he would go.

The attitude of the king of England softened somewhat over the following months, as was shown in a set of instructions given to Diede on 30 June 1732.[132] The king had accepted the need for the

---

[131]   *Ibid.*, Staatsk. *Vortr.* K. 34 i – ii fol. 68 – 73, 97 – 102, *Vorträge* of 29 January and 5 February.
[132]   Hanover, *Cal. Br.* II E.1 no. 342 fol. 4 – 10.

administration as the best means of settling the country's troubles.[133] He had been satisfied with the Emperor's letter of 10 June 1732 from Prague, which had given assurances that the claims of the former commissioners would be met. The Emperor had also stated his intention of giving Christian Louis the unobjectionable title of imperial commissioner, which would still the opposition raised in the Empire against the 'revolutionary' adminstration. Relations between the king and the Emperor seemed to be approaching the cordiality of 1717. Christian Louis was to issue new *Reversales*, in which there was to be no mention of a *Provisorium* or 'Administration'. Hanover and Wolfenbüttel should be allowed to keep control of the execution exchequer and its adjuncts until all liquidated costs had been paid off and adequate means to preserve security had been found. Britain favoured the proposal to hire troops from a neighbouring German state to protect the new commission.

The proposals referred to by the king seem to have been Wurmbrand's draft proposals for February 1732, presented to the Emperor in Prague. A conference *Referat* of 22 June 1732[134] informed the Emperor that, at last, a way out of the Mecklenburg case seemed near without trouble from either Hanover or Prussia. The ministers advised the Emperor to send a *Billet* to Wurmbrand instructing him to make the necessary arrangements in the aulic council and issue the required *expeditiones* without delay. The Emperor agreed. Another conference of 6 July[135] repeated the hope that the case had been settled without damage to the *suprema jura judicialia*. Nothing was needed except to instruct the aulic council and imperial ambassadors in the Empire. The idea of bringing the matter before the imperial diet was rejected as likely to delay rather than further the affair.[136]

During August 1732 the conduct of the case passed back to the aulic council. Once the decision on policy had been taken in the conference, the work on drawing up the various rescripts and patents and of finally settling the key question of the amount of the

---

133   Vienna, *Kl. Reichsst.* K. 348 fol. 175 – 8, letter of George II, Hampton Court 2 November 1731. The king described the administration as 'this constitutionally correct and innocent expedient' and stated that he would be satisfied with a *Spezialhypothek* and the continuing presence of his troops in Mecklenburg until Christian Louis was firmly established in power.

134   *Ibid.*, Reichsk. *Vortr.* fasz. 6c fol. 555 – 7.

135   *Ibid.*, fol. 561 – 6.

136   Charles Leopold was still trying to bring the diet to discuss his affairs: *Fabri Europäische Staats-Canzley*, vol. LX (1732), ch. 12, p. 597, letter of Charles Leopold 19 April 1732, vol. LXII (1733), ch. 11, p. 595, letter of 24 October 1732.

commission costs was left to the council. On 25 August the Emperor sent an aulic decree from Linz and this was read in the session of 1 September.[137] The Emperor had made representations in London and Berlin 'with the result that the matter has prospered in such a way that it can be settled in the manner described in the accompanying papers[138] and it is believed that the whole thing can be done without difficulty'. The aulic council was to undertake the necessary work without delay. Speed was essential and the council was to aim at a total settlement of the grievances, which had for so long disturbed the internal unity of the Mecklenburg Estates.

The administration was formally ended and Christian Louis created imperial commissioner by the verdict of 30 October 1732.[139] He was to exercise the commission on the same terms as the previous commissioners. His first task was to call a diet. He was to observe the utmost economy, to enable him to pay off the commission costs, and to recruit a force to maintain security. The council recommended the hire of troops from a disinterested neighbouring state rather than native Mecklenburgers. Until this had been arranged at a diet, the Hanoverian and Wolfenbüttel troops were to remain in Mecklenburg to protect the new commission. Some three or four hundred would then remain as security for the arrears of commission costs, an agreed figure of 1,058,611Rt.

The administration was not destroyed, as it never came into operation, nor, despite the opinion in Hanover, did the verdict of 30 October merely change the name while preserving the substance of the administration, a fig-leaf to cover its nakedness.[140] The Emperor avoided declaring Charles Leopold permanently unfit to govern so there was always the possibility he might be restored. The verdict was another far-reaching decision which appeared to settle the Mecklenburg case to the satisfaction of all interested parties, except Charles Leopold. It involved no great sacrifice of imperial interests, the right of the Emperor to decree a *Provisorium* was not given up, the possibility of an eventual end of Hanoverian control in Mecklenburg was in view, the new ruler of the country was firmly bound to follow imperial instructions and the Emperor's international position seemed stronger as a consequence of the alliances

---

[137] Vienna, RHR *Den. Rec.* K. 700(8).
[138] These are unfortunately not attached but refer presumably to the various *Referate* of the conferences which had dealt with the matter.
[139] *Fabri Europäische Staats-Canzley*, vol. LXII (1735), ch. 11, pp. 602 – 11.
[140] Göttingen, University Library manuscript collection, Histor. 508, fol. 3 – 19.

with Prussia and Hanover-England. Diede and Moll, the Wolfen-büttel ambassador in Vienna, reported the formal end of the old commission on 10 July 1733.[141] As so often in the past, in 1701, 1719, and 1728, this verdict proved to be a beginning rather than an end.

East Frisia

While diplomatic negotiations continued between the Emperor and England-Hanover for a 'settlement' in Mecklenburg, so the Dutch had to be accommodated on East Frisia before they would join the Anglo-imperial alliance. The Dutch position was stated in a series of reports from the imperial ambassador in The Hague, Karl Wenzel von Sinzendorff, in July 1729, considered in a council *votum* on 9 August.[142] At a number of conferences with the envoy early in July the Dutch had stated repeatedly that they could not stand by and see the East Frisians deprived of the benefits of the imperial amnesty at the instance of a partial commission. The States-General were of the opinion that the Emden party had submitted on the understanding that the *Renitenten* would receive all the benefits of the amnesty and they saw it as their duty to guarantee this.[143] Sinzendorff was afraid there would be a civil war with active Dutch participation and advised the Emperor to make wide concessions, though apparently his advice was far from impartial. According to certain letters of Appelle to correspondents in Emden, reputedly intercepted by agents of the prince and passed on to the Emperor,[144] he was in close correspondence with the leader of the *Renitenten*. According to Appelle a 'comte de S.', from the context almost certainly Sinzendorff, had assured him of support in obtaining a pardon. Appelle had had several meetings with 'count S.' in The Hague. If the letters were genuine and Appelle was telling the truth, the imperial ambassador was most sympathetic to the cause of the Emden party. 'Count S.' agreed with Appelle that the Emperor lacked the means to reduce Emden by force and his threats were therefore empty. Sinzendorff wrote in similar terms to the

---

141 Vienna, RHR *Vota* K. 36, *votum* of 11 August 1733.
142 *Ibid.*, RHR *Den. Rec.* K. 907.
143 Aurich, C III a no. 113/3, report of Steuermann 4 June 1728, quoting a resolution of the States-General of 25 May 1728.
144 They arrived in July 1731: *ibid.*, *Kl. Reichsst.* K. 405. The interception of these letters from the Netherlands caused trouble with the Dutch: Aurich, C III b no. 89, report of 10 August 1731.

subdelegates. In July 1728 he instructed them to avoid any action and eschew all violence as the Emperor intended to make new dispositions in the case.[145] Sinzendorff admitted that he had no imperial mandate but warned that otherwise the Dutch might resort to force.[146] The subdelegates obeyed him and suspended all actions, stating that, although they had no imperial orders: 'H.M.'s intentions in this matter are not unknown to us.'[147]

In a *votum* of 5 May/16 July 1728[148] the aulic council dealt coldly with Sinzendorff's reports and advised the Emperor to reject Emden's submission. As Wurmbrand and Stein assured Brawe,[149] the council had no sympathy with Emden and the rebels, who had tried to set up an oligarchical tyranny over their fellows and would have succeeded but for the Emperor's intervention. On the grounds of the constant intercessions of the States-General and Prussia and the fact that the Emperor was more inclined to mercy, the council recommended that a final chance for submission be given to the rebels.

The recommendations were accepted after debate in the conference on 24 August 1728.[150] The ministers agreed that the rebels deserved the full severity of the law, but, because the affair was growing very complex, agreed that an act of clemency would show the world, especially the Dutch, that the Emperor's main interest was in justice. The subdelegates were to be instructed to take no action likely to inflame the situation. The ministers finally recommended that copies of the council's *votum* and details of its reasoning should be sent to the imperial representative at Berlin, The Hague and Soissons, where the Dutch minister, Goslinga, was making a great fuss about East Frisia.

The Emperor approved this and the resolution was put into effect by the verdict of 13 September 1728.[151] This announced that the Emperor, as a sign of patience and grace, gave the rebels a further chance to submit.

The aulic council's view on the case did not change. In a *votum* of 19 July 1729[152] it again advised the rejection of Emden's latest submission of 24 March, believing it to be a matter of words not

---

145   *Ibid.*, C III c no. 140 fol. 30.
146   *Ibid.*, fol. 150.
147   *Ibid.*, fol. 156–8.
148   Vienna, RH. *Den. Rec.* K. 907. This *votum* of 131 folio pages was the product of a *Relation* which took eighteen days to read between January and April: *ibid.*, RHR *Prot. Rer. Res.* xviii 69.
149   Aurich, A IV c no. 252, report of 6 December 1727.
150   The *Referat* produced by this conference is in Vienna, RHR *Den. Rec.* K. 907.
151   *Ibid.*, RHR *Prot. Rer. Res.* xviii 70.
152   Vienna, RHR *Den. Rec.* K. 907 fol. 203 ff.

deeds, a joke and a means of winning more time to intrigue against imperial decisions. In the council's opinion, if given the chance, Emden would again unleash on East Frisia a regime of terror, murder, rape and plunder.

In several *vota* the council advised against the removal of the Danish troops as they were an important restraining influence on the city.[153] In case of further violence they were a useful reinforcement for the Salva Guardia.

The council saw nothing behind the interest shown by the Dutch in the case except a desire to save rebels from the consequences of their rebellion. It warned that, if the Dutch appeals were accepted, the rebels would take this as a tacit annulment of the ban on recourse to foreigners and an opportunity to resume their old principle of exempting themselves from the jurisdiction of the Emperor.

In the resolutions of the States-General and the many memoranda presented in Vienna by Hamel Bruininx, the Dutch claimed that their interest was based on a desire to be good neighbours and the fact that they could not with equanimity accept deep changes in a province on their borders. They believed that a conspiracy between the prince, the subdelegates and the Danes was planning to overthrow the ancient East Frisian constitution and establish an absolute government.

A conference held on 3 May 1729 did not accept the aulic council's recommendations.[154] Although the president, Wurmbrand, strongly opposed acceptance of the submission, the general conclusion was in favour of acceptance, in spite of the unanimous and judicially correct recommendations of the aulic council. Despite the objections that the submission had arrived late, was only in general terms and incorrectly signed, the conference recommended its acceptance. Clearly the centre of gravity in the case had moved decisively to the conference,[155] which did not consider it wise 'to insist on unnecessary subtleties in such a difficult case with such far-reaching implications for the public affairs of Europe nor to raise the impression that the Vienna government is concerned for anything more than the maintenance of the Emperor's authority, the sovereignty of the Empire and the rights of third parties'. In the belief that the imperial chancery would at once send a *Referat*

---

153   E.g. the *votum* of 16 July 1728.
154   Vienna., Staatsk. *Vortr.* K. 29 v – vi fol. 1 – 2, *Vortrag* dd. 31 July *ibid.*, fol. 12 – 16. The meetings were attended by both 'Austrians' and 'imperialists'.
155   In a report of 3 March 1731, Fabricius advised the loyal administrators to approach ministers as well as members of the aulic council with their requests: Aurich, C III a no. 163.

embodying these recommendations to the Emperor, the imperial ministers at Soissons and The Hague were informed of the recommendations, obviously in the belief that the Emperor would accept them.[156] Later the conference discovered that no *Referat* had in fact been sent to the Emperor and that no instructions had been sent to the subdelegates for weeks. Assurances had been passed to the Dutch by Sinzendorff but in fact, while the imperial government was saying one thing, the imperial subdelegate commissioners in East Frisia were doing another. On 29 July a conference, attended only by the 'Austrian' ministers, prince Eugene, Sinzendorff and Starhemberg, roundly condemned the negligence of the imperial chancery and recommended that urgent instructions be sent to The Hague and Soissons to counter the impression that the Emperor was deceiving the Dutch. As a general comment the conference recorded its opinion that the consequences would be serious if important *expeditiones* ordered by a conference were sent late or not at all. It recommended that in future the imperial chancery be required to hand over all protocols, despatches and *Referaten* to the conference president to ensure that their contents were correct. The Emperor approved this and ordered that copies of all despatches drawn up in the imperial chancery were to be made in the hand of the secretary responsible. These were then to be submitted to the Emperor for his approval before they were sent. This sharp rebuke to the imperial chancery was a sign of the rapid decline in the importance and effectiveness of this organ. It lost further standing in 1730 when revelations of corruption and leakages of documents were made. Among the documents concerned were rescripts in the Mecklenburg and East Frisian cases, rescripts to the imperial ministers in Regensburg and instructions to Kuefstein.[157] Schönborn's long absences in his diocese may have contributed to the increased inefficiency of the chancery.[158]

The imperial resolution on this *Vortrag* and the *votum* of 19 August marked a major turning point in the case. The Emperor rejected the correct but practically unfulfillable recommendations of the council. He stated that he found the *votum* well argued, but 'weighty reasons' prevented his agreeing to it. He accepted Emden's

---

[156] The recommendations were in fact not embodied in a *Referat* until 31 July, a delay of almost three months.

[157] *Relation* of the imperial chancery 7 May 1730: Vienna, Reichsk. *Vortr.* fasz. 6c fol. 456–68.

[158] Aurich, C III b no. 89, letter of the prince to Brawe senior, 17 July 1731. Brawe jun. had reported from Vienna that all *Reichssachen* were automatically communicated to Schönborn and nothing was done without his advice.

submission and ordered that any action taken by the prince or the subdelegation since the date of the submission contrary to the terms of the imperial amnesty were to be revoked. Only those demonstrably guilty of homicide and named ringleaders were excluded from the amnesty. No confiscations were to be undertaken to collect money for the compensation fund until this matter was settled. Out of his special clemency the Emperor granted the Emden party two months to put forward their grievances against the prince, the commission and the imperial decrees. The resolution was published as a verdict of the aulic council on 12 September 1729.[159]

The immediate reaction of the prince's party, apparently shared by members of the aulic council, was horror.[160] On 28 September Brawe reported that some councillors were displeased at the action of the Austrian privy council, which had intervened in judicial matters and reversed the trend of one hundred and fifty years of imperial decisions. They urged the prince to be of good cheer.[161]

The verdict seems to have made little difference to conditions in East Frisia. Arguing that the submission was meaningless, the prince's government and the subdelegates saw no reason to change their policies. The sequestration of the Emden lordships continued, the new College and the treasury remained in Aurich, the Danish troops remained on the property of the *Renitenten* and the subdelegates continued to execute for fines. This predictably led the Dutch to claim that the imperial resolution was being ignored and they renewed their agitation on behalf of the Emden party.

A conference *Vortrag* of 4 January 1730 dealt with the Dutch complaints.[162] From this point the drafting of a declaration of intent and policy on East Frisia intended for the States-General began to occupy the imperial government. The negotiations in the critical period 1729 – 32 well illustrate the manner in which Charles VI tried to reconcile his Austrian policies and the demands of his supreme judical office; it is possible to speak of a conflict between the two policies with the Emperor seeking to hold the balance between them.

---

[159]   *Merkw. RHR Concl.*, vol. VII, no. cxxii.
[160]   Aurich, C III a no. 110.
[161]   Aurich, A IV c No. 254. On 10 December he reported that Schönborn's secretary considered the verdict an affront to imperial authority. The Austrian ministry had ignored the aulic council, its verdicts and its jurisdiction under the pretence that the Emperor's particular interests demanded concessions to the Dutch. Everyone, including Schönborn, was flabbergasted and it was expected that Schönborn would vindicate the rights of his chancery and the aulic council 'rotundé' on his return and a reversal of the decision was to be expected.
[162]   Vienna, Staatsk. *Vortr.* K. 30 i fol. 3 – 34.

The conference of 4 January recommended that the Emperor give the Dutch ambassador in Vienna a formal declaration that any decision in the case would be in accordance with the provisions of the resolution of 31 August 1729 and that all outstanding points would be dealt with in the aulic council. The conference opposed the inclusion of a formal article on this in any future treaty with the United Provinces. Various drafts of the proposed declaration were considered and the conference urged the Emperor to accept nothing which might be interpreted as invalidating the verdicts of the aulic council before 31 August 1729. Bruininx presented drafts in which these verdicts were described as having been issued in *poenam renitentiae*, that is as punishment for the Estates' refusal to obey the council's earlier verdicts. This was a small point but very important. Had this been accepted, the Emperor's position would have suffered serious damage. It would have enabled the Dutch to argue that the majority of imperial decisions had not followed the full *Kognition* of the case, a full and analytical examination of the evidence, but that they had been issued because the *renitent* Estates were in the equivalent of contempt of court. The conference recommended concessions to the Dutch and the *renitent* Estates in those points grounded in the *Akkorden*, compatible with imperial law and in the matter of the removal of the Danish troops, which the 'obedient' Estates also wanted, without waiting for an examination and settlement of the grievances which could not be placed under these headings. The *Renitenten* should receive the full benefits of the amnesty.The Emperor might also include in the declaration an assurance that he had no intention of interfering with the East Frisian constitution in so far as it was based on *Akkorden* which did not conflict with the laws of the Empire. The Dutch wanted a guarantee of their garrison rights but the conference could not recommend this. Finally the ministers advised the Emperor to make no concessions until it was clear whether anything of benefit would result from negotiations with the sea powers.

The belief that he was being sacrificed introduced a note of bitterness to the communications of the prince, complaining in a letter of 4 October that he was the innocent victim of the prevailing *Konjunkturen*.[163] Indeed protests from all sides seem to have found little echo in the conferences. On imperial orders, Schönborn raised

---

[163]   *Ibid., Kl. Reichsst.* K. 405. This had long been obvious. In his report of 19 June 1726 Brawe drew attention to the importance of the *Konjunkturen*: Aurich, C III a no. 113/1. On 15 February 1727 he reported an audience with the Emperor, at which Charles VI admitted that the *Konjunkturen* had so far prevented any action in the matter: *ibid.,* A IV c no. 252.

the East Frisian case at a conference on 5 March 1730.[164] The matter was becoming increasingly complicated. Again questions were asked about the efficiency of the imperial chancery. The conference recommended:

> that the aulic council should continue to deal with this matter according to imperial law and earlier imperial orders and that the reports of count Sinzendorff should be passed to the president of the aulic council to enable him to effect the issue of a decree to the commission and its subdelegates, ordering them to stop all executions until further notice from the Emperor after a resolution based on a further major *votum* from the aulic council. This should be brought to the notice of the Emperor by means of a *Referat* or *votum*.

This looks very much as if the conference was giving indirect orders to the council, but this was in fact not so. The Emperor alone could send orders to the commission and the only organ which was constitutionally empowered to deal with this matter was the aulic council. The conference was therefore observing the correct constitutional procedure in asking the council to take steps already agreed by the Emperor. The conference was proposing that the president bring the council to do no more than confirm an earlier imperial order. The significant fact is that the council was here being asked to embody in a *votum* to the Emperor a course of action it had not initially recommended and still did not support, as shown in the *vota* of 7 March and 3/14 March,[165] in which the council adhered firmly to its earlier views. In its opinion the city of Emden had forfeited all the benefits of the amnesty as it had appealed to the Dutch in flat contradiction of imperial orders. In spite of this, in a manuscript resolution the Emperor confirmed the verdict of 12 September 1729 and ordered that rescripts be sent instantly to the subdelegates ordering them to observe it. In a second and larger *votum* the council defended itself and the commission against the charges of partiality and of co-operation with the princely government in emasculating the East Frisian constitution, which had in fact been preserved intact as the palladium of East Frisian liberties.

---

[164]   An extract from the protocol of this conference is in Vienna, RHR *Den. Rec.* K. 907 and a copy of the resolution on East Frisia *ibid.*, Staatsk. *Vortr.* K. 30 i fol. 120.

[165]   *Ibid.*, RHR *Den. Rec.* K. 907.

It had been highly presumptious of Emden to challenge the right of the Emperor to interpret the privileges of the country and to administer its constitution for the furtherance of the general good, a significant statement of constitutional theory.

The council asked the cardinal question, whether the submission had any validity, and came to the conclusion that it was empty show and that the Dutch were 'only fuel for the flames of internal disorder' in the country. The aim of the Emden party remained, as before, the annulment of all the Emperor's verdicts. In its opinion, the verdict of 12 September did not invalidate earlier verdicts, which all remained in force until further decisions were made. If this principle was abandoned, all efforts to maintain peace in the country would be frustrated. The Emperor could not allow Emden to behave as if it, alone among the Emperor's subjects, had the right to exempt itself from imperial jurisdiction and choose that of the States-General.

It seems likely that the council was still smarting from the blow it had received in the resolution of 31 August, which seems to have had little effect on its attitude. In view of the council's functions, this was correct. The purely legal considerations attending the case had not changed in spite of the verdict of 12 September, which was indeed no longer valid as Emden had ignored the conditions attached to it.

This *votum* bears a long manuscript resolution of the Emperor.[166] The verdict of 12 September 1729 was to stand in all its points but the *Renitenten* were to observe all imperial decrees issued before 3 May 1729, except those issued *loco poenae* and not with the intention of introducing better order in the country. The Emden party was warned to observe its submission to the letter, to wait quietly for a definitive verdict and to avoid all violence, recourse to foreigners and disputes. Copies of the grievances of the *Renitenten* should in the meantime be sent directly to the prince and the 'obedient' Estates for their replies.

Thus the council had avoided all reference to the contemporary political and diplomatic situation but in a further *votum* of 14 March 1730 it could not avoid it.[167] On 2 March Brawe had presented a memorial purportedly dealing with part of the treaty of Seville between England, Spain and France, Dutch accession to which was under negotiation. In one clause France and Britain confirmed all their engagements to the Dutch including the undertaking 'to procure for the Republic a full satisfaction, both regarding the commerce of the Ostend Company and the affairs of E. Frisia'. The

---

[166]   There is another copy of this in Vienna, *Kl. Reichsst.* K. 405.
[167]   *Ibid.*, RHR *Vota* K. 44.

council believed that, if true, this and other reports of Dutch interference threatened the removal of East Frisia from the body of the Empire. What attitude therefore was to be taken to the offer of aid to the Dutch from foreign powers and what advice was to be given to the Emperor?

As a result of the treaty of Seville the East Frisian case was no longer the exclusive concern of the aulic council. It now became the concern of the whole Empire, a key issue in European politics. Under the *Wahlkapitulation* all the Estates of the Empire were bound to support the Emperor and to regard the case as common to all. At issue was the Dutch claim that they could exempt East Frisia from the jurisdiction of that Empire by virtue of their so-called guarantee of the constitution. From this they also argued the right to protect a subject against his prince. The fact that the States-General were making East Frisia a topic of negotiation with foreign powers gave the Emperor all the more reason to bring the matter before the whole Empire. The only advice the council was competent to give was to ask the imperial diet for a *Reichsgutachten*, in the conviction that a great majority of the Estates would condemn the actions of the Dutch.

A critical comment on this and the earlier *votum* is contained in an anonymous and undated *Referat* on East Frisia among the miscellaneous documents on the case in the imperial chancery.[168] The writer, obviously highly placed in Vienna, referred back to the conference of 5 March 1730, at which the council had been instructed to report how far the provisions of the verdict of 12 September 1729 had been put into effect. These specific instructions had been ignored by the aulic council. Its latest *Referat* (the *votum* of 3/14 March) appeared to the writer to confine itself to a denial of the validity and adequacy of Emden's submission and to bemoaning the decline in conditions in East Frisia since the resolution of 12 September. The first eleven sheets of the *votum* were nothing more than an unnecessary rehash (*Recocta*) of matters not at issue. An attack on the Dutch right of guarantee did not answer the question put to the council, which concerned the Emperor's resolution. In the writer's view the subdelegation was obviously prejudiced in favour of the prince and too much under the influence of the Hanoverian court. Its inconsistencies were alarming. For example, Rudolf von Rheden had earlier been portrayed as a dangerous rebel deserving exclusion from the amnesty; now he was represented as a naive half-wit (*einfältiger Tropf*) who had been led astray by wicked men. The council had not dared to exclude Uffke Berends Schmidt

---

[168]   *Ibid., Kl. Reichsst.* K. 405. From the context this originated from spring 1730. The writer may have been Sinzendorff and was certainly no 'imperialist'.

from the amnesty for fear of annoying the king of Prussia, whose salt factor he was, although the commission had revealed him as a ring-leader responsible for monstrous acts of violence during the civil war.[169] Very ominous, in the writer's view, was the subdelegates' request that they be allowed to raise taxes without a diet, as the last diet had made insufficient grants. If permitted, this would raise a furore in the Empire.

In general, the writer took the view that the Dutch, the prince and the commission were trying to solve the problem by adopting extreme positions, while clearly the only way out was the middle way:

> I believe it would not be advisable to bring the Dutch to a position where they could only obtain what, in the light of their latest resolution, they consider just and right by violence and far less wise to allow the subdelegates to continue their investigation of the E. Frisian case *ad infinitum*. This would only ruin the country and the prince and might bring matters to the state where an outcry against the aulic council would arise from the whole Empire, as if H.M. were trying to raise taxes in the country by decree. This is clearly the intention of the subdelegates.

The writer then subjected the details of the council's *vota* to cogent analysis. It was important to remember, in his view, that many of the ordinances issued by the aulic council as definitive verdicts were, because of the resolution of 12 September, now only provisional. In its latest *votum* the council had recommended that all important decrees issued before 3 May 1729 would have to be obeyed to the letter before Emden's grievances could be dealt with:

> It is easy to calculate that, when five months are needed to deal with such a secondary point (*Inzidenzfrage*) and that each such point may need a *votum* running to some forty pages and when the examination of the new grievances to be presented cannot begin until all the prior requirements of the aulic council have

---

[169] The verdict of 9 August 1729 pardoned Schmidt: *Merkw.* RHR *Concl.*, vol. VII, no. cxxi. For Schmidt's career see Vienna, RHR *Den. Rec.* K. 927 (11). In an exhibit of 25 April 1729 the Prussian government claimed that Schmidt was being persecuted by the subdelegation in an effort to ruin the Prussian salt trade.

been met, no one is likely to live long enough to see the conclusion.

He considered the advice given in the third *votum*, that the question of the Dutch guarantee be brought before the Empire, 'most improper', as he believed that all hope of agreement with the Dutch was not exhausted.

In a final paragraph the writer summed up his views and gave advice. He believed the conduct of the subdelegates was open to serious objection and that the investigation of the grievances should not be placed in their hands. Great care would be needed to find a middle way, which would enable the rights of the Empire and the Emperor to be preserved without causing a breach with the Dutch. He believed that, whatever way out was chosen, either the Dutch or the Empire would be offended. If the Emperor preferred to keep the friendship of the Dutch he should adhere to the resolution of 12 September 1729. The Dutch would not have sought to protect their interests through alliance with the Seville powers had this resolution been put into effect from the first. The matter should be dealt with in the presence of the Emperor and orders be given to the council to stop wasting time with other matters and to concern itself with finding out how far the resolution had been put into effect.

Between 20 March and 31 August 1730 there was no verdict in the East Frisian case and after 31 August the case again went into suspense and no exhibits were referred. The case rested but the pressure of appeals from the prince and the *Renitenten* continued and further delay could have damaged the Emperor's position as a judge. There was a limit to the time a verdict could be held up in the interests of foreign policy. Numerous complaints were presented that decisions were being reached at the convenience of the Austrian ministry and not in accordance with law and justice. It was said that all considerations except the desire to please the Dutch had been abandoned. On 11 September and 22 December 1730 Brawe senior advised the prince to appeal against the verdict of 31 August 1730,[170] which confirmed the acceptance of the Emden submission.[171]

It was most unlikely that vague assurances would satisfy the Dutch and England. It was clear from a Dutch memorandum presented to Sinzendorff on 1 December 1730,[172] that they believed

---

[170] Vienna, RHR *Prot. Rer. Res.* xviii 75 fol. 299 – 301.
[171] Aurich, C III a no. 113/1.
[172] Vienna, *Kl. Reichsst.* K. 405.

the only way to restore peace in East Frisia would be the restoration of all privileges of the Estates under the terms of all the *Akkorden*, the grant of a full amnesty to all the *Renitenten* without exception, the restoration of the College and the Treasury to Emden and a declaration that the princes of East Frisia had never exercised unlimited powers over Emden or the Estates.

The desire to bring the Dutch into the Seville alliance led England to support them at Vienna. Matters of interest to England, including East Frisia, were handled by Robinson in negotiations with the imperial government at conferences in January and February 1731. It was constantly reaffirmed that, in trying to win over the sea powers, the Emperor must not compromise his supreme judicial authority. Sinzendorff did his best to subordinate imperial to Austrian considerations. At a meeting on 31 January 1731[173] his attitude was clearly shown: 'Not to allow inessential business to hold things up. Should not neglect other matters because of imperial affairs.'[174] The prince of East Frisia believed that the influence of the Austrian aulic chancellor was responsible for his troubles. On 30 August 1729 he wrote to Eugene and, in a milder version, to Wurmbrand complaining about Sinzendorff.[175] In a report of 1 October 1729, Brawe asserted that the latest resolution was the work of Sinzendorff, who was responsible for three decisions highly prejudicial to imperial authority in the Mecklenburg, Zwingenberg and East Frisian cases.[176]

The ministers were unanimous that, having neither funds nor allies for a war, the Emperor would have to make every concession possible. This was repeated in a *Vortrag* of 23 February.[177] The Emperor was ready to revoke all actions taken in the case since 3 May 1729, the date from which the Emden submission was held to have been effective, but the Dutch wanted a restoration of the situation of August 1721, involving the annulment of ten years' decisions of the aulic council. This was, the conference decided, unacceptable under imperial law and incompatible with the supreme judicial office. The conference could not recommend that the Emperor give the Dutch guarantees of their 'right' to keep garrisons in Emden and Leerort.

A declaration satisfactory to England was included as an annex to the Vienna treaty between the Emperor and George II of 16 March

---

[173]   *Ibid.*, Staatsk. *Vortr.* K. 32 i – ii fol. 63 – 6.
[174]   'In Sachen, so nicht essential sind, sich nicht aufhalten. Werden nicht wegen Reichssachen die anderen zurückgehen lassen.'
[175]   Aurich, C III a no. 110.
[176]   *Ibid.*, A IV c no. 254.
[177]   Vienna, Staatskanzl. *Vortr.* K. 32 i – ii fol. 87 – 104.

1731.[178] The prince was horrified, writing to Brawe on 8 May 1731[179] 'it is an unheard of procedure to make such a declaration when no reference has been made to the body to which the matter belongs and no decision made there'. This comment on the forced inactivity of the aulic council provided a new chorus to the prince's repeated complaints, that the whole trend of imperial decisions in the case had suddenly and inexplicably changed. The prince strongly and correctly suspected that an agreement was being made with the maritime powers at his cost and he placed little faith in the assurances given.[180]

After the signing of the Vienna treaty on 16 March 1731, imperial policy concentrated on finding a formula which would bring about Dutch accession to the Anglo-imperial alliance. Details of the imperial position were given in a set of instructions sent to Wenzel von Sinzendorff on 27 April 1731.[181] The Emperor was ready to change any decision of the aulic council proved contrary to the acceptable *Akkorden*. This being so, the ministers could not understand why the Emden party seemed to be doing all possible to prevent the opening of the investigation of their case in Vienna and why people who were bombarding the council with requests for a restoration of pre-1721 conditions were holding up the whole business by a trivial refusal to present their grievances to the other parties. If the Emperor simply agreed to many of their requests it would amount to an annulment of verdicts of the council without consulting the prince, which would give him grounds to challenge the decision.[182] This would only be possible in a case of *contumacia*, that is, a refusal to reply to another party's grievances. This was patently not such a case as the grievances had not been communicated. The imperial government did its best to defend the prince's interests. It considered as grotesque Gräve's argument that the *Renitenten* did not know who the 'obedient' Estates were and therefore could not hand over their grievances to them. Sinzendorff himself reported that the Dutch were well aware of the flaws in the position taken up by Emden.

[178] Naumann, p. 171.
[179] Aurich, C III a no. 128.
[180] *Ibid.*, no. 113/1, reports of 2 April and 21 May 1731, C III b no. 89: Brawe sen. reported on 2 April 1731 that Jodoci had assured him that there was no mention of East Frisia in the treaty with England and that the imperial government had given only general assurances.
[181] Vienna, *Kl. Reichsst.* K. 405.
[182] The prince only abandoned a plan to protest in the imperial diet after much advice. Eventually he issued a declaration reserving his rights: Aurich C III b no. 89.

As far as the imperial ministers could see, the main points at issue with the Dutch were the following. The Dutch wanted a total *restitutio in integrum* covering all the fines and punishments already executed. The Emperor was ready to restore everything taken after the Emden submission as a punishment for contumacy. The complaint against the resolution of 12 September 1729, which had been welcomed in the Netherlands, was that it had not been put into effect, not that it was insufficient.

The Dutch objected to a reservation clause regarding the East Frisian *Akkorden* in the imperial draft declaration, although this was aimed only at preserving imperial sovereignty over East Frisia and was accepted as such by the Dutch. The Emperor was not in a position to list those *Akkorden* he could not accept as there may well have been some unknown to him.

The Dutch insisted that the government of East Frisia be restored to what it had been before the troubles. They also insisted on treating the *Renitenten* as the injured party. Typical of the Dutch position was a resolution of the States-General of 10 May 1731.[183] Their stated aim was to restore peace and good order in East Frisia and to support a form of government based on the fundamental laws of the country. The closeness of East Frisia to the Netherlands made it vital to them to prevent any change which might prove disadvantageous to them. They found the latest imperial draft resolution quite inadequate to put an end to the unrest in the country. The accusations of partiality against the subdelegates were repeated.

They wanted an annulment of all imperial decrees since 1721, whether issued to reform supposed abuses in the country's constitution or to punish the Estates' contumacy, as the first injured their rights, the second their property. In the first category were the establishment of a new College, the transfer of the Treasury to Aurich and the confiscation of the Emden dyke directory. In the second were the contributions levied against the *Renitenten* for the maintenance of the Danish troops and the subdelegation. They wanted a confirmation of all the *Akkorden*, reserving only the Emperor's supreme judicial power and sovereignty. The Emperor's declaration, if it stood unchanged, would result in an alteration of the East Frisian constitution. They could not accept the conditions attached to the readmission of the *Renitenten* to diets. Clearly they believed that the resolutions of 12 September 1729 and 31 August 1730 had wiped the *Renitenten*'s slate clean and provided for a

---

[183] There is an extract from this in Vienna, *Kl. Reichsst.* K. 405.

return to pre-1721 conditions. They also insisted on a guarantee of their garrison rights.

A conference *Vortrag* of 1 August[184] stated that the conference believed in principle that the Emperor should do all possible to accommodate the Dutch saving imperial authority and the rights of third parties, or at least to convince neutral observers that he had done all possible to accommodate them. It would be inadvisable to act contrary to imperial law, in a manner likely to injure imperial sovereignty over East Frisia or to raise the accusation that the Emperor had sacrificed the rights of an Estate of the Empire. The conference advised the Emperor to have drawn up a list of three classes: the first of matters which could be dealt with at once by the council, the second those in which the Emperor could accommodate the Dutch without injuring his authority or the rights of a third party and the third of completely impracticable requests. Wurmbrand and Hartig agreed that this was the best method.

On the same day imperial orders were transmitted to Wurmbrand instructing him to introduce the latest Dutch proposals into the aulic council. A *votum* was sent to the Emperor on 9 August.[185] As requested, it divided the Dutch demands into three classes: those which could be agreed to without delay, those requiring addition or alteration and those incompatible with imperial honour and the supreme judicial authority. The *Akkorden* were to be observed *pro ratione decidendi* as the Dutch wished, but only those compatible with the rights of the prince and the Estates, accepted willingly by both sides at the time and not contrary to imperial law. The decrees of 1 October 1688 had confirmed the validity of these agreements 'in so far as they are not prejudicial and derogatory to Our and the Empire's sovereignty, rights and jurisdiction'. This reservation would have to be retained. If the Dutch insisted on its omission, this would be clear proof of their intention to prejudice the Empire.

The third class was discouragingly full. The council rejected the demand that all imperial verdicts issued *à l'occasion de la rénitence* since 1721 be annulled and new verdicts be reached on the grievances alone. This would be contrary to justice and the imperial constitution. The city of Emden had abused the amnesty, seeing it merely as a chance to hold up the execution of the Emperor's verdicts. It objected to the phrase 'so-called *Renitenten*' and suggested an inoffensive alternative, 'Emden and those who adhere to her'. Even if the sequester of the Emden lordships was ended, the council recommended that their obligation to contribute to a compensation fund be reserved, further that the Dutch be informed

---

[184] *Ibid.*
[185] Vienna, RHR *Den. Rec.* K. 907.

that the execution of imperial verdicts could not be suspended indefinitely to the prejudice of the prince and insisted that the city's grievances be communicated to the 'obedient' Estates as all interested parties had a right to see them. It was no longer realistic to consider all the Estates one party to the case. On this point the council believed the stubborn attitude of the Dutch ruled out all possibility of compromise.

The Dutch proposal on the compensation point was also unacceptable, as the wording of their draft suggested that in the past the *Renitenten* has been unjustly fined and oppressed. The council warned against accepting the Dutch statement that their right to keep garrisons in East Frisia had never been challenged. The council again disposed of the often repeated charge that the verdicts of 1721 had been issued before the Estates' case had been heard. In a manuscript resolution the Emperor approved this. The verdict was published on 22 August 1731.[186] This repeated the earlier assurances that the amnesty was in force and that no further fines or punishments would be levied. All money taken in fines since 3 May 1729 would be repaid and all sequestered or confiscated lands and property would be restored, reserving the liability to contribute to the compensation fund. An aulic commission was to be set up in Vienna to deal with the question of compensation and to find a compromise solution.

After some minor resolutions on the case during that winter and another in June 1732 passing on a list of grievances of the 'obedient' Estates, a name they no longer deserved, to the prince,[187] the East Frisian case again disappeared from the protocols of the aulic council until 1733. There was no further important resolution until March 1734.[188] During this quiet period activity in the conferences and diplomacy reached a climax with the issue of a 'Declaration touching E. Frisia' acceptable to the Dutch and a settlement of the Mecklenburg case and other matters to the satisfaction of the elector of Hanover which, temporarily at least, gave Charles VI a long-desired feeling of security, ended his isolation and added the

---

[186] *Ibid.*, RHR *Prot. Rer. Res.* xviii 77.

[187] *Ibid.*, 77 and 78.

[188] Among the drafts in Vienna, RHR *Relationes* K. 134 fol. 581–3 is an undated protocol containing a discussion of the Declaration, expressing the opinion that a too free reference to the *Akkorden* would be dangerous, as many had been arranged under Dutch auspices, and warning against an admission that any verdict had been issued when one party had not received a proper hearing. The case may have been discussed in the aulic council without reference to this appearing in the council's protocol of resolutions.

maritime powers to those who guaranteed the indivisibility of his lands.

A report on the progress of negotiations with the States-General was drawn up by the conference on 22 September 1731.[189] After receiving the last imperial orders and a copy of the aulic council's *votum*, Sinzendorff had continued his negotiations. From his reports and a memorial presented by Bruininx on 18 November it was clear to the conference that East Frisia was the main obstacle to agreement.[190] The Dutch insisted that all degrees of the aulic council which they regarded as having been issued as punishments for disobedience of earlier order, the so-called *Pönalitäten*, should be annulled. The conference reminded the Emperor that, in this matter, he was bound by imperial law and had to observe the rights of third parties. The great indulgence shown to the States-General was causing unfavourable comment in the Empire. The conference was therefore unanimously of the opinion that the Emperor should not give way one iota from the position he had already adopted.

The final 'Declaration touching E. Frisia' was published on 20 February 1732 when the States-General acceded to the Second Treaty of Vienna. It is a good example of how the Emperor balanced his judicial office with the requirements of foreign policy.[191] In the preamble he recognised that the Dutch were concerned only for the peace of a neighbouring territory and that their intention had never been to challenge in any way the subordination of the province of East Frisia to the Emperor and the Empire. The Emperor's declared intention was to give the Dutch new proof of his desire to accommodate their wishes as far as justice permitted, to express his true sentiments in the matter and to remove their various fears.

The actual declaration consisted of five clauses. Throughout there was only one mention of *Renitenten*. For the rest it employed the formula first suggested by the council, 'those of Emden and their adherents'. First, the Emperor confirmed that the amnesty, which he had most graciously granted, would enjoy its full effect and that fines levied against the Emden party 'because of their renitence' would not be executed. All fines taken since 3 May 1729 would be

---

[189] Vienna, Staatsk. *Vortr.* K. 34 ix – x fol. 78 – 107. On 10 August 1731 the prince received a report from The Hague that the Dutch, in conference with lord Chesterfield, were near accession to the Vienna treaty; the only point to be settled was East Frisia: Aurich, C III b no. 89.

[190] Vienna, Staatsk. *Vortr.* K. 34 xi – xii fol. 21 – 30, the record of a conference on 18 November, which produced the *Vortrag* of 21 November.

[191] There is a draft copy in Vienna, Staatsk. Vortr. K. 34 i – ii fol. 129 – 33. The version accepted by the Dutch differed slightly in its wording from the earlier version attached to the treaty of Vienna with Britain. Kappelhoff, pp. 445 – 50 prints a copy of the Declaration.

restored, reserving the obligation on the Emden party to contribute to the fund for the compensation of those who had suffered during the civil war. In this way the Emperor avoided giving way on the main point demanded by the Dutch, the annulment of the *Pönalitäten*.

In the second clause the Emperor confirmed that the city of Emden would have a further chance to put forward its grievances and to show in what way it believed the decrees of 1721 and the following years had injured it. These would then be examined quickly and decided in accordance with justice and the East Frisian *Akkorden* and all conventions and decisions sworn to by the prince on his accession but not those annulled by the august predecessors of the Emperor or prejudicial to the sovereignty of the Emperor and the Empire over East Frisia and, especially, imperial jurisdiction. Once the grievances had been communicated to the other parties designated in the resolution of 31 August 1731, one chance to reply would be given, after which the Emperor would decide upon them point by point. It continued: 'But to remove all doubts as to the true sense of this restricting clause, the Emperor at the same time declares that he is satisfied to guarantee his imperial jurisdiction against all prejudice and that his intention is not to deny the validity of the content of any accord or convention agreed to freely by parties interested in the rights of the prince and his Estates.'

Clause three confirmed the right of the Emden party to attend diets under the conditions laid down in the resolution of 31 August 1730 and the Emperor promised help to anyone improperly excluded. Clause four dealt with the question of compensation. An account of all claims was to be assembled and sent to the Emden party for its comments. The Emperor would then try to mediate a compromise, or, if this proved impossible, would decide on a fair sum. Clause five guaranteed that the financial claims of the Dutch in East Frisia would be fulfilled promptly and fully and stated that the Emperor had no wish to remove the Dutch garrisons from East Frisia.

The Dutch acceptance of the declaration, with reservations, was announced in the aulic council resolution of 6 May 1732.[192] In a bitter report of 24 March Brawe reported the common view in the council that the declaration nullified the work of years: politics rather than justice had prevailed.[193] In fact the declaration was a victory for the

---

[192] There is an extract from the Resolution in Vienna, *Kl. Reichsst*. K. 405. The Dutch urged Emden to send representatives to the aulic commission as this was likely to be the best solution to the problem.

[193] Aurich, C III a no. 113/1.

Emperor, as it involved no surrender of the principles agreed by the aulic council. The fact that the States-General had to be satisfied with the declaration drawn up in Vienna, when they had wished to make the case part of the general negotiations, was an important victory. The Emperor's stubborn refusal to abandon his imperial position and a growing Dutch fear of isolation combined to achieve this.

Conclusion

The last years of the reign of Charles VI, a period of deepening gloom and pessimism in Vienna, saw the 'imperial' content of Austrian policy relegated to a very minor position. There was no male heir, prince Eugene was dead and the country suffered lack of leadership, political uncertainty, financial weakness and military defeats in two unfortunate wars against France and the Turks. While the basis of imperial power, the Austrian lands, were threatened, the imperial idea took second place. Internationally there was a return to the situation of 1714: the alliance of the Emperor and England was designed to shut the door of the Empire in the face of France, whose diplomatic primacy in Europe was successfully reasserted in the early 1730s. The years 1731 to 1732 marked an important turning point in Charles VI's reign and in the history of Austria. By then it was clear that an attempt to revive a powerful position in the *Reich*, the 'imperial reaction', and to increase Austrian power in Europe had both failed. These years saw the beginning of a slow decline until 1740, when Austria was again on the verge of partition and extinction as a power.

The Herrenhausen alliance forced Charles VI to choose between the Empire and Austria. This was the Habsburg dilemma: had they tried to compel the Empire to do their will, they would only have forced more German rulers into the waiting arms of foreign defenders of 'German liberty'. The Emperor lacked sufficient armed power and was too often forced to resort to playing on rivalries between individual German states, a tactic of limited success. Austria's attempt to become arbiter of Germany and Europe came to nothing as she defended her very existence. Spain and the Emperor emerged from a period of intense diplomatic manoeuvring as losers and the relaxation of tension in Europe after 1732 was achieved at their expense. Austria, relying on her alliance with the sea powers, began to reduce her armed forces;[1] in the Polish

---

[1]   Wilson, p. 236.

Succession war of 1733 the Empire remained neutral, as did the Emperor's allies, the maritime powers.[2]

The creation of the Mecklenburg Provisional Administration may well have marked the high point of the brief revival of imperial consciousness and ambition which lasted for some thirty years after 1700. Thereafter the imperial branch of the Vienna government wasted away. Schönborn resigned under pressure in 1734 and after his departure the decline of the imperial chancery was swift and steep. Increasingly it lost profitable business to the *Hofkanzlei* and the salaries of imperial chancery employees were often months in arrears.[3]

Another such revival of imperial activity became very difficult after the death of Charles VI. Article I §§3 and 4 of the *Wahlkapitulation* of Charles VII promised that the Emperor would not suspend from its government any Estate, sequester the lands of any Estate or deprive any Estate of its seat and vote in the diet provisionally or under any pretext without the consent of the Empire and further restrictions were placed on the exercise of the supreme judicial office.[4]

The Mecklenburg and East Frisian cases continued to exercise the aulic council. The Mecklenburg affair persisted until 1755, when the perennial constitutional disputes were ended by the *Erbvergleich*, virtually a total victory for the knights, which remained the basis of the constitution until 1918. The East Frisian case ran its desultory course until the annexation of the country by Prussia in 1744 on the death of the last native prince. In neither was the aulic council able to achieve a satisfactory solution.

The Mecklenburg case proved especially troublesome after the establishment of an imperial commission on Christian Louis, who proved as unsatisfactory a commissioner as he had been as administrator. The hope of the council that the new commission would prove a permanent solution was soon frustrated. There were

---

[2] R. Lodge, 'English Neutrality in the War of the Polish Succession', *TRHS*, 4th series, vol. XIV (1931), pp. 141–73.

[3] Naumann, pp. 150, 176.

[4] The imperial courts were precluded from any interference in the *Kameralsachen* of any Estate of the Empire under any pretext. A projected new *Wahlkapitulation* debated by representatives of numerous princes in Offenbach included many restrictions on the supreme judicial office and the removal of what the princes saw as abuses in the operation of the aulic council: *Fabri Europäische Staats-Canzley*, vol. LXXXII (1743), pp. 648–70.

considerable delays before the interested powers, Hanover and Prussia, were satisfied with the arrangements and Christian Louis could take actual possession of his commission.[5] Attempts to effect an early removal of the Hanoverian troops were foiled by the so-called *Tumult* of Autumn 1733, when Charles Leopold called out an 'army' of peasants and townsmen, led by officers and huntsmen and actively encouraged by the clergy, to expel the commission troops.[6] Christian Louis and many of the knights fled ignominiously, to the annoyance of the council. The rising was put down with little difficulty by the Hanoverian garrisons in the country and by extra troops sent in at the beginning of the emergency, but it had important consequences for Mecklenburg. Frederick William I had been waiting for an opportunity to take an active part in the Mecklenburg case: the orders for the march of his troops had been given long in advance. Tired of waiting for the Emperor to admit him, he seized on the tumult as the required opportunity.[7] Prussian troops entered Mecklenburg after the rising had been suppressed, prevented Hanoverian attacks on Dömitz and Schwerin and sheltered fugitive rioters. It is significant that some leaders of the tumult believed the Prussians were coming to help them and there is some suspicion that Prussian agents actively stirred up the peasantry in border areas to obey Charles Leopold's summons. Once there, the Prussians refused to leave while Hanoverian forces remained and the Hanoverians, after stopping the evacuation of their troops, refused to withdraw them while the Prussians remained and while their financial claims were outstanding[8]

The influence of Hanover and Prussia on the country remained strong. In addition to the costs of the execution of 1719, the commission and the suppression of the tumult, the English crown claimed large sums advanced as loans to the knights.[9] Several verdicts of 23 March 1733 accepted claims of the knights against the duke totalling some 50,000*Rt.* in addition to the sums already liquidated. In 1734 the king of England advanced a further 50,000*Rt.* to pay for the takeover of the troops from Schwarzburg hired by Christian Louis for the security of his commission.[10] As a condition

---

5   Göttingen, Aw. 504 no. 3, Vogel to Klein, 14 January 1733.
6   For the 'Tumult' see Wick, ch. 12 and 13 *passim* and for the activity of the clergy see Sperling, pp. 34 ff.
7   Vienna, RHR *Relationes* K. 107, report of Seckendorff 29 October 1733.
8   Göttingen, Aw. 498 no. 6, report of 20 January 1734. Wick, pp. 222, 234 – 5.
9   These amounted to 30,000*Rt.* on 5 May 1733, 80,000 on 12 May 1736 and 14,000 on 21 July 1736: Vienna, RHR *Relationes* K. 107.
10 Verdict of 23 September 1734: Vienna, RHR *Prot. Rer. Res.* xviii 84.

George II insisted that the Emperor should agree to the establishment of a mortgage (*Spezialhypothek*) on a certain number of Mecklenburg *Ämter*, from the revenues of which his claims would be met. The aulic council agreed and the *Hypothek* was established on eight *Ämter* by the verdict of 18 November 1734.[11] Under this Hanover was to draw all ducal revenues from these *Ämter* and to keep a force of four hundred troops there at the expense of the *Hypothek*. This brought a sharp protest from Prussia.[12] Armed with claims for 230,747Rt. as the costs of 'putting down' the tumult, Prussia assumed a *de facto Hypothek* on a further four *Ämter*.[13] By the verdict of 15 January 1742[14] the Saxon vicariate court gave the knights a *Hypothek* on the *Amt* Doberan in settlement of their claims.[15] The accounts of the *Hypothek* which Hanover was required to submit annually, showed that in good years it produced sufficient surplus to pay off interest at five per cent and a little capital. Large amounts disappeared in the running costs of the mortgage and in payments to various Hanoverians, as under the Lüneburg Commission.[16] In 1734 the duke of Wolfenbüttel sold out his interest to Hanover. In 1765 the total unpaid amounted to 1,535,000Rt. This looked to Prussia very like a permanent Hanoverian occupation of a substantial part of the country.

The financial difficulties of Mecklenburg were well known to the aulic council. It was plain from its *vota* that the council was worried about the finances of the country. In that of 5/11 August 1723,[17] it admitted that it would take a century to pay off the *Hypothek*. It affirmed however that no alienation of Mecklenburg territory would be allowed. Hanover continued to toy with the possibility of annexation[18] and kept alive her interest in the country by the old alliance with a party among the knights. Among the conditions laid down in 1738 by the London government for the restoration of good

---

11 *Ibid.*
12 Verdict of 2 May 1735: *ibid.*, 85.
13 *Votum* of 4 July 1735, 'Novae Commissionis.': Vienna, RHR *Vota* K. 38.
14 Vienna, RHR *Den. Rec.* K. 713(1).
15 Following the death of an Emperor, in the absence of an immediate successor, the two imperial vicars, Saxony and the Palatinate, maintained their own supreme courts. According to Witte, vol. II, p. 280, the three mortgages swallowed up over half the ducal domain. In addition it had to bear the burden of pensions, appanages, Charles Leopold's *Kompetenz* and the costs of administration and of diets.
16 Vienna, RHR *Den. Rec.* K. 770(3).
17 *Ibid.*, RHR *Vota* K. 37. Mediger, *Mecklenburg*, p. 466 on the financial situation.
18 Göttingen, University library manuscript collection, Histor. 508, 'Mecklenburgensia des 18. Jahrhunderts.', fol. 1 – 36.

CONCLUSION

relations with Vienna and the fulfilment of patriotic obligations during the Turkish war was a favourable hearing in the aulic council for the knights' request for a *Spezial-Hypothek*.[19] Hanover also protected the officials appointed under the old commission against dismissal by Christian Louis, which the latter naturally regarded as an infringement of his authority.[20] Hanoverian troops remained in Mecklenburg until 1735. Christian Louis hired troops from Holstein and Schwarzburg but the cost of their maintenance was a heavy burden on his already strained finances.

The odd legal fiction that Christian Louis was not a party to the case but an impartial referee was maintained with increasing difficulty. Deeply troubled by the abiding poverty of his country and afraid for the future of his house, he found it difficult to reconcile the demands of his office as commissioner and his duties as heir presumptive.[21] The prospect of the dismemberment of his inheritance between Hanover and Prussia and a renewal of the machinations of Strelitz[22] seemed real after 1733. Christian Louis' unwillingness to take damaging decisions and his many reservations brought blistering attacks on him from the aulic council, which sought means of restricting his freedom of action. The period 1733–40 saw a large number of *vota* and verdicts of the council, which made it obvious that it did not trust the commissioner. From the beginning it had little patience with him. A spate of *vota* in the autumn and winter of 1733–4 commented on his slowness, stubborn failure to call a diet, inability to obey instructions, tendency to spend money destined for other purposes, inability to manage the economy and general untrustworthiness.[23] In a *votum* of 18 February/11 March 1735 the council put its finger on the real problem: Christian Louis behaved not as a commissioner but as a real ruler of the country. In a further *votum* of 17 August/5 September 1735 it seriously considered the possibility of giving the commission to someone else: the problem was that no one else was acceptable.

Christian Louis' relations with the Mecklenburg Estates were also poor. From the first the knights seem to have regarded him as a minor version of his brother and the towns, loyal to Charles

19 Hanover, *Cal. Br.* II E.1 no. 410a fol. 27–31: instructions to the Hanoverian government, London 8 August 1738.
20 Göttingen, Aw. 503/1, no. 8.
21 His dilemma was stated clearly in a memorandum to the Emperor of 4 October 1738: Göttingen, Aw. 509 and the Wienerische Nouvelles *ibid.*, Aw. 511.
22 *Ibid.*, Aw. 502, report of 18 December 1736 and Aw. 498 no. 38.
23 Vienna, RHR *Vota* K. 35–38.

263

Leopold even after the disastrous tumult, were very hostile.[24] What was more important, the knights were not convinced that the commissioner was able to protect them against his brother. Charles Leopold remained recalcitrant until his death in 1747. The interrogation of the ringleaders of the tumult in Hanover revealed that he had been negotiating with the French and Russian governments in an attempt to persuade them to intervene on his behalf by force.[25] An atmosphere of intrigue and conspiracy surrounded him as long as he lived. The revelation of his efforts brought him no advantage but only convinced everyone that he was completely untrustworthy. The Estates remained terrified of him: they asked the Emperor to guarantee that the commission would pass to the son of Christian Louis, Frederick, if Charles Leopold outlived his younger brother.

Christian Louis' position inside Mecklenburg improved slowly. A general pardon was issued soon after the rising in 1733 and Charles Leopold was deprived of a base of operations by the capture of Schwerin in 1735.[26] Charles Leopold fled to Wismar and, after his expulsion from there in 1741, he ended his days in Dömitz. Christian Louis' accession to the ducal throne in 1747 made life easier for him. The clergy, which had continued to read Charles Leopold's edicts until his death, transferred their allegiance to him as the new supreme bishop. He was also eventually able to win over the town magistracies[27] and continued his brother's policy of trying to protect them and the peasantry.[28] He benefited from the achievements of the Hanoverian commission, which had carried out a land survey and revised the out-dated land registers. The towns remained unreconciled to what they regarded as the unfair taxation system of the *Hufen- und Erbenmodus*.[29] After his accession,

24 See the *votum* of 6/11 August 1733: Vienna, RHR *Vota* K. 36.
25 Vienna, RHR *Relationes* K. 106, 'Des Tilly und anderer Inquisition betr'. The interrogation was conducted in Hanover to save money for Christian Louis: Göttingen, Aw. 496/2, Klein to Verpoorten, 3 January 1734. See also Wick, pp. 240 – 3.
26 *Ibid.*, p. 252. He continued to intrigue until his death. In 1741 the Russian government explored the possibility of his restoration but this was strongly opposed by Hanover: Hanover, *Cal. Br. Des.* 24 Mecklenburg no. 99, fol. 31 – 4, Mediger, *Mecklenburg*, p. 467.
27 Witte, vol. II, pp. 277 – 80.
28 He had some success in improving the position of the peasantry on the domains: Schneidewind, p. xvi. Göttingen, Aw. 498/2, exhib. of 21 February 1736 contains a copy of a lease contract of a domain farm including the condition that the peasants were not to be harshly treated.
29 The records of the renewed litigation are in Vienna, RHR *Den. Rec. K.* 705(8). The *Hufen- und Erbenmodus* was definitively established by the verdicts of 23 March 1733: Vienna, RHR *Prot. Rer. Res.* xviii 81.

Christian Louis began an offensive against the knights.[30] In 1748 he came to an agreement with Rostock under which the city left its alliance with the knighthood. Payments to the knights from the *Amt* Doberan were stopped. In 1749 the Union of the Estates was abolished under an agreement between the two dukes by which the Estates of Strelitz became a separate body.[31] A new constitutional crisis began and an aulic commission in Vienna was able to achieve nothing. The solid body of the knights was ruptured by growing friction between groups.

The crisis was finally settled after mediation by Frederick II with the signing of the *Erbvergleich* of 1755 agreed at the first diet since 1748.[32] This agreement entrenched the supremacy of the knights over the duke and the towns, confirmed their privileges and their rights over the peasants[33] and restored the constitution as under the 1701 agreement. As a result Mecklenburg remained socially, politically and economically backward. After this only minor disputes arose. In an appeal for stricter observances of his *privilegium de non appellando* in September 1769, duke Frederick complained of *Process-Sucht* as the national vice of his subjects.[34]

The aulic council was no more successful in East Frisia, though the case disappeared from the protocols of the council much sooner than that of Mecklenburg. After 1732 the case lingered on into its last phase. The accession of the sickly Charles Edzard in 1734 and the impending extinction of the house of Cirksena give the impression that the whole country was waiting for the inevitable and wished to avoid a decisive step. The case was never brought to a satisfactory judicial solution and lapsed after the Prussian annexation in 1744.

There was no significant change after 1732 but the return to pre-1721 conditions desired by the Dutch did not take place. The sequestration of the Emden lordships remained in force, the Emden party continued to be excluded from diets, the 'obedient' Estates and the Aurich College and Treasury remained in control of the country's finances and Danish troops remained billeted on the

---

[30] Wick, pp. 257 – 8.
[31] Hegel, p. 122n; Feller, pp. 159 – 60.
[32] There is a copy of this in *Fabri Europäische Staats-Canzley*, vol. CIX, pp. 169 – 376.
[33] Crull, p. 277: the period 1755 to 1820 saw the greatest incidence of *Bauernlegung* in Mecklenburg.
[34] Vienna, RHR *Privilegia de non Appellando* K. 4, Meckleburg.

former *Renitenten*.[35] The troubles left their mark on the country in the form of deep poverty; both the prince and the Estates contracted enormous debts.[36] In March 1732 the Saxon subdelegate was withdrawn and the Wolfenbüttel representative died shortly afterwards. They were not replaced. The death of George Albert in June 1734 and of Brenneysen in September of the same year removed a great deal of passion from the case and an austerity regime under Charles Edzard brought some small improvement in the prince's finances. Relations between the prince and the 'obedient' Estates soon began to fall into the same pattern of disagreement as before 1721. As then the jurisdiction of the *Hofgericht* provided a fertile source of friction.[37]

The Dutch continued to complain that the 'Declaration' had not been put into effect. In 1733 they issued another ultimatum demanding that the Emperor satisfy them in this.[38] The council refused to consider the case further until the Emden party fulfilled the conditions attached to earlier favourable resolutions.[39] It is clear from its *vota* and verdicts that the council remained hostile to Emden and its party but seemed anxious to wash its hands of the case. A resolution of 11 July 1732[40] listed the many points still unsettled in the case: the amnesty, the return of the College and Treasury to Emden, the restoration of the dismissed mayors of Norden, the restoration of the Emden garrison and dyke directory, the removal of the Danes, the restoration of all sequestered and confiscated property, the conditions to be attached to the admission of the Emden party to diets, a ruling on the use of the Salva Guardia and the jurisdiction of the *Hofgericht*. These points were still unsettled in 1744. After 1732 both parties began to comb earlier imperial decrees avidly to find justification for their own point of view. When the Saxon-Wolfenbüttel commission lapsed in 1732, it was proposed to establish an aulic commission in Vienna but this was held up by the failure of the Emden party to send correctly authorised delegates. By the resolution of 30 September 1734,[41] the council, as well as establishing the aulic commission, agreed to the restoration of the College to Emden but under strict conditions. The original recommendations of the council in its *votum*, which was

35   Klopp, vol. II pp. 556 ff.
36   Aurich, Landst. Archiv Dep. I no. 3140, extract of the diary of a deputation of the loyal Estates to Vienna.
37   Vienna, RHR *Den. Rec.* K. 924, nos. 35, 36.
38   Aurich, C III d no. 17.
39   Vienna, *Kl. Reichsst.* K. 407.
40   *Ibid.*, RHR *Prot. Rer. Res.* xviii 79.
41   *Ibid.*, 84. This verdict was the result of the large *votum* of 186 folio pages of 21 April/17 May 1734: *ibid.*, RHR *Den. Rec.* K. 907.

extremely hostile to Emden, were somewhat modified by the imperial resolution. The council blamed the city for deliberately holding up the case and drew attention to its continuing recourse to Prussia and the Dutch. It admitted that the whole case was virtually in suspense and that it was extremely complicated. An undated *Relation* on the affair among the records of the imperial chancery[42] described it as 'one of the most difficult cases by which the highest imperial courts have been exercised and fatigued for over fifty years'. The difficulties of the council were shown in a report to the prince of 30 July 1735.[43] Councillor Knorr advised Charles Edzard not to rely on a decision of the council which might divide into parties like the Vienna court. The only way out was, he believed, a compromise, possibly mediated by Hanover. If the exercise of his supreme judicial office proved politically embarrassing to the Emperor, he had adequate means available to delay a decision indefinitely.

On 12 October 1736[44] a new commission was established on the king of England as Elector of Hanover. The Hanoverian subdelegation eventually arrived in May 1738 but the whole matter was held up by a succession of minor disputes, the death of the Emperor and a dispute as to which imperial vicar was competent in East Frisia. The subdelegation left the country in January 1741 having accomplished nothing. The Dutch, apparently afraid that their already weakened influence in East Frisia was being eroded by Prussia,[45] continued to press for decisions favourable to the Emden party and for participation in the commission.[46]

Prussian preparations for annexation of the province were made early.[47] During the last years of Charles Edzard Prussia espoused the Emden cause even more eagerly than before,[48] claiming a right of interference on the basis of the *Expektanz* and the Circle

42 *Ibid.*, RHR *Relationes* K. 134 fol. 577 – 81: the arguments put forward by the *Referent* Hartig on 13 April 1734.
43 Aurich, C III a no. 208, no. 6.
44 Vienna, RHR *Prot. Rer. Res.* xviii 89.
45 Hanover, Cal. Br. 24 Österreich III no. 158 fol. 7 – 12, George II to Diede, 15 September 1732.
46 Vienna, *Kl. Reichsst.* K. 407, RHR *Den. Rec.* K. 907, *votum* of 25 October/5 November 1737.
47 F. Meinecke, *Die Idee der Staatsräson* (Munich, 1924), p. 398, quoting Frederick II's *Political Correspondence*, states that in 1741 the king proposed exchanging East Frisia, which seemed about to fall to him, for Mecklenburg.
48 E.g. the exhibits of 9 July 1743 in Vienna, RHR *Den. Rec.* K. 906(1).

Directorate.[49] Negotiations between the king and the Estates of the Emden party began in 1740,[50] with Appelle, who had long enjoyed Prussian protection and support, acting as agent during the negotiations.[51] Under an agreement signed on 14 March 1744 the Emden party agreed to accept the king of Prussia as prince, in return for which Frederick promised to observe the pre-1721 constitution and the city's rights of self-government.

Prince Charles Edzard died on 25 May 1744. Prussian patents and eagles were said to have been waiting in Emden and Greetsiehl since 1740 and needed only the addition of the date.[52] The take-over was rapid and smooth. The Danes left, the Salva Guardia melted away and the Dutch garrisons were withdrawn to avoid any clash. All imperial verdicts since 1721 were abandoned by agreement between the king and the now reunited Estates.

In retrospect the Prussian period, 1744–1810, was regarded in East Frisia as the 'good old days'. The country was treated as a favoured province: its institutions were left intact, except for reductions in Emden's rights after riots in 1749, and, in return for an annual subsidy of 40.000Rt., East Frisia was spared all recruiting. Part of the Estates' debts were taken over by the crown. Reforms in the administration of the finances were introduced and an end made of the régime of the 'blood-sucking' bailiffs and executors of the Estates.[53]

After the Prussian annexation, the constitutional case lapsed in the aulic council. The dispute between Hanover and Prussia concerning the succession, which occupied the council for some years,[54] was now sterile in the face of Frederick II's *fait accompli*.

In spite of the apparent failure of the aulic council in these two cases, the achievement of the imperial courts, especially the aulic council, was small but real. In their function of trying to preserve peace and law in a political organisation in which the bonds holding the members together were very loose, they preserved some

---

49 Exhibit of 12 February 1732 *ibid.*, *Kl. Reichsst.* K. 407.
50 For the negotiations see Klopp, vol. II, pp. 566–8 and Reimers, p. 265.
51 Aurich, Dep. I no. 4910 contains a copy of Appelle's safe conduct to visit Berlin and letters of Frederick II to the Estates. Nos. 411 and 412 contain Appelle's correspondence notes for the period August 1734 and March 1735, recording letters sent and received.
52 Klopp, vol. II, p. 571.
53 König, pp. 340–1. *Acta Borussica*, vol. IV/1, p. 591.
54 See the exchange of notes between the two governments in Hanover, *Cal. Br.* II E.l no. 233 fol. 165 and *ibid.*, 24 Österreich III no. 158 fol. 1–2. The records of the litigation are in Vienna, RHR *Den. Rec.* K. 927(8) and (9).

remnants of imperial authority.[55] Because of the existence of the imperial courts subjects were still able to find protection against injustice, excessive taxation and the whims of petty tyrants[56] and overmighty subjects were prevented from depriving their princes of their legal rights. Through the aulic council the Emperor was able to save something of his power from the wreck of imperial authority. The principle that princes could be guilty of crimes against their subjects remained firmly established. The Reformation, the Peasant Wars and the rise of absolutism, involving destruction of the Estates in many principalities, had all contributed to the gradual erosion of individual rights among the Germans but the very existence of the Empire prevented a total victory of the princes, especially in the small states.[57]

On the question of the interference of the Austrian government in political cases in the aulic council, there is no evidence that there was any interference with the legal conduct of cases under Charles VI. The political and diplomatic resorts of the Vienna government seem to have restricted themselves to deciding whether time and circumstances were favourable for the execution of verdicts of the council. It would not have helped the imperial office if the aulic council has issued scores of unenforceable verdicts. The continuing high esteem in which the imperial supreme judicial office was held in Vienna was shown in a number of reports of the state conference of 1746.[58] In considering the state of the Empire, the ministers commented: 'It is held to be best, as far as possible, to avoid foreign commitments and to direct attention to ensuring that each Estate, mighty, medium or small, obtains equal justice from the high imperial courts.' It was necessary to staff the courts, especially the aulic council, with 'able and impartial subjects, eager for justice'.

The aulic council, in coming to its decisions, looked back centuries to find a relevant law and this mirrored a major fault of the Holy Roman Empire, a tendency to look back rather than forwards. In the eighteenth century the Empire was a collection of survivals: all that was modern, forward-looking and progressive had little connexion with it. It was the tragedy of the late Empire that, although it was

---

[55] The council has been compared in some of its aspects to the UNO, the European Commission for Human Rights, the USA Supreme Court or the British Privy Council sitting as a judicial body for the Commonwealth: *The Listener*, 19 January 1967, vol. 78, pp. 92 – 3.

[56] For example, in the 1770s the aulic council deposed a number of free counts who had oppressed their subjects: Thudichum, p. 221; Sellert, p. 90; F. Hertz, 'Die Rechtsprechung der höchster Reichsgerichte im römisch-deutschen Reich und ihre politische Bedeutung', *MIÖG*, vol. 69 (1961).

[57] Feller, pp. 162 ff.

[58] Vienna, Reichsk. Vortr. fasz. 6d fol. 111 – 25. *ibid.*, no. 25, fol. 155 – 72.

obvious that something was sadly wrong with its constitution, no attempt was made to find an alternative in time. The princes were too concerned with the development of their own states and had a vested interest in preserving a weak Empire while many theorists saw in the decayed framework of the Empire the ideal constitution for Germany.[59] No social group in the Empire was strong enough to overcome the alliance of German particularism and foreign powers, which had as its aim the maintenance of German disunity. The Habsburgs were as guilty of particularism as the other princes, while clinging to the old-established theory of their supremacy. The Pragmatic Sanction was a concrete statement of an Austrian imperial idea, though this did not find legal expression until Napoleon raised a new Empire in the West and Austria adopted the imperial title in self-defence. The Habsburgs attacked the Wittelsbach Emperor Charles VII as violently as other princes, demonstrating that, when it suited them, they placed as much value on 'German liberty' as other princes. Each *Wahlkapitulation* after 1740 brought increases in the powers of the princes within their own territories while the Habsburgs increasingly used the imperial title as a means of furthering their dynastic interests. From the middle of the eighteenth century the larger princes began to refuse imperial investiture with their territories[60] and in 1745 an Englishman could say that it mattered as little who was Emperor as who was lord mayor of London.[61]

The old Empire collapsed because of faults which could only have been removed by strengthening the power of the Emperor, not by destroying it. Only in Regensburg, Wetzlar and Vienna did the Empire have any real meaning and, of these, only the aulic council and the other imperial organs in Vienna were beyond the control of the princes.[62] Previously only the Habsburgs had possessed the means to exercise imperial authority but by the eighteenth century others thought themselves capable of it. Prussia was able to challenge and defeat the rest of the Empire and Austria. The Seven Years War marked the beginning of dualism in German politics, the emergence of a competition for predominance between two powers, Austria and Prussia. In 1755 Frederick II of Prussia openly challenged the jurisdiction of the aulic council, denying its

[59] Epstein, pp. 251–2.
[60] Winter, p. 457.
[61] Hinsley, p. 172.
[62] K. Stoye, *Die politischen und religiösen Anschauungen des Freiherrn F.K. von Moser*, p. 158: the first step suggested by Moser in his scheme to regenerate the Empire was a reform of the aulic council as the imperial supreme judicial office was the most important function left to the Emperor.

competence as patently an instrument of the Vienna government. Francis I replied that this was a rusty old weapon, often turned against the aulic counil.[63]

By its very existence the aulic council swam against the tide. Even in the last years of the Empire imperial decisions in favour of subjects against their lords always roused public attention in Germany. While the preservation of internal order and external defence passed increasingly into the hands of the princes, another important aspect of the common good, the supervision of justice, remained at least partly under the control of the Emperor. Especially among mediate subjects the concept of the Empire and all that it implied could not be swept away quickly or easily. Absolutism was a local condition which could not destroy the link between the mediate subject and the Empire. The power of tradition remained strong even in the time of the Empire's deepest humiliation and prostration.[64] Although the Empire contributed little to the defence, prosperity, industry, trade or moral and cultural life of Germany, prayers were said for the Emperor in all churches in the Empire, except after 1750 in Prussia, and the life and death of the Emperor were objects of great interest among the common people.[65] Nostalgia for the Empire began before the Empire reached its end.

---

[63] Moser, *Justizverfassung*, vol. I, pp. 534 – 6.
[64] Feller, pp. 171 – 4, Epstein, pp. 595 – 6.
[65] Feller, pp. 169 – 71, Günter, 'Die Reichsidee', p. 426.

Select Bibliography

Primary Sources

Vienna, Haus- Hof- und Staatsarchiv
Reichshofrat
RHR Vota Kartons 1, 7, 20, 34 – 3, 40, 41, 44, 46, 47, 54, 55, 58, 61, 64, 65
RHR Protocollum Rerum Resolutarum, xviii, volumes 2 – 7, 9 – 14, 16,
    17, 19, 20A, 20 – 24, 26, 27, 29 – 31, 33 – 36, 38 – 43, 45 – 49, 51 – 53,
    55 – 68, 60 – 62, 64 – 66, 68 – 71, 73 – 79, 81 – 86, 88, 89, 91 – 4,
    96 – 99, 128, 129, 131, 133, 134, 151, 153, 154, 156, 159, 161, 163 – 6,
    168 – 171, 173 – 6, 178, 180, 181, 183 – 5
RHR Verfassungsakten. Faszikel 3 – 5, 8 – 14, 18 – 20, 25 – 27, 30 – 33
RHR Antiqua. Kartons 343/344, 343 II/345, 346, 347, 348, 349/350, 350/
    351, 540, 541, 542, 543, 543A, 544
RHR Relationes. Kartons 105, 106, 107, 134
RHR Privilegia de non Appelendo. Faszikel 1 – 6
RHR Denegata Recentiora. Kartons 691 (1 – 5), 692 (1, 3 – 5), 693 (1, 2),
    694 (2, 4, 5), 695 (2, 4, 5), 696 (1 – 8), 697 (1), 698 (1 – 3), 699 (1 – 3,
    5 – 9, 11, 14), 700 (2, 7, 8), 701, 702 (1), 703, 704 (1 – 4, 6), 705 (1,
    6 – 8), 706 (2, 5, 6, 9), 707 (1, 2), 708 (1 – 5), 709 (1 – 3), 710 (2, 3, 5, 6),
    711 (1), 712 (1, 5, 6, 11, 13, 17, 18), 713 (1 – 3, 7, 9, 12), 714 (3, 7, 8, 11,
    12), 715 (1, 6), 716 (3), 717 (1), 718 (1), 719 (1,3), 720 (1), 721 (1), 722
    (3), 747(2), 767 (1), 770 (1,3), 884 (2), 885 (1 – 3), 905 (1), 906 (1), 907,
    916 (10 – 12), 917 (1), 918 (1), 919 (1, 2, 6), 920 (2, 4 – 6, 8 – 11, 13), 921
    (1, 2, 4 – 6), 922 (2, 3), 923 (1, 3, 5 – 7), 924 (1), 925 (1, 2, 4), 927 (2 – 5,
    7, 8, 10, 11), 1470, 1471
Hofkanzlei
Hofkanzlei. Reich. Weisungen. Faszikel 1 – 4 (microfilm)
Staatskanzlei
Staatskanzlei. Vorträge. Kartons 22 – 24, 27 – 39
Reichskanzlei
Reichskanzlei. Vorträge. Faszikel 5c, 5d, 5e, 6a, 6b, 6c, 6d, 7c
Kleinere Reichsstände. Kartons 346 – 8, 404 – 7
Instruktionen. Faszikel 3, 5, 7, 13, 15 (microfilm)
Berichte aus dem Reich. Faszikel 19 – 24 (microfilm)
Weisungen an die Prinzipalkommission. Faszikel 4c, 5a, 5b, 5c, 6a, 6b
    (microfilm)

Hanover, Lower Saxon State Archive
Calenberg Briefschaftsarchiv
24 Österreich I no. 131, III no. 158
11 E.1 nos. 86, 131, 132, 197A, 233, 274M, 278, 342, 410A
24 Mecklenburg nos. 75, 84, 87, 99

Aurich, Lower Saxon State Archive
Princely Archive Repertorium 4
C III a nos. 110, 113/i, ii, iii, 128, 163, 174, 208, 215
C III b no. 89
C III c no. 140
C III d nos. 243B, 244, 245, 246, 247, 248, 249, 252, 253, 254
Estates' Archive Depositum I
Nos. 112, 146, 705, 706, 1355, 3138, 3139, 3140, 3141, 3244, 3257, 4910 – 4912

Göttingen, State Archive Depository
Schwerin Documents
Aw. 404, 409, 459, 460, 463, 474, 478, 491 – 500, 501/i, ii, 502 – 6, 509, 511, 512, 543

Schwerin, Mecklenburg Provincial Archive
Acta differentiarum inter duces et status provinciales
III Regnant. Carolus Leopoldus, volumes I-III, XVI – XXII
Estates' Archive
Protocols of the Small Committee, 1719 I and II, 1720 – 1723
Speziallakten. E III P. 1. 5 – P. 1. 8

Göttingen, University Library
Manuscript Collection
Histor. 508. Mecklenburgensia des 18. Jahrhunderts

Primary Printed Sources

Acta Borussica. Behördenorganisation, vol. III (Berlin, 1901)
Arneth, A. von, 'Die Relationen Venedigs über Österreich im 18. Jahrhundert', *Fontes Rerum Austriacum*, xxii (Vienna, 1863).
Bertram, F.W. von, *Breviculum praxis Imperialis aulicae* (Frankfurt, 1709)
Brenneysen, E.R. von, *Ostfriesische Historie und Landesverfassung* (2 vols., Aurich, 1720)
[Fabri] *Europäische Staats-Canzley* and *Neue Europäische Staats-canzley* (Frankfurt/Leipzig, 1697 – 1760, Ulm/Frankfurt/Leipzig, 1761 – 80)
Gerstlacher, C.F., *Handbuch der teutschen Reichsgeseze nach dem möglichst ächten Text, in sistematischer Ordung* (11 parts in 5 vols., Karlsruhe etc, 1786 – 93)
Lundorp, M.C., *Acta Publica de anno 1608* (18 vols., Frankfurt/Cologne, 1668 – 1721)
Lünig, J.C., *Teutsches Reichsarchiv* (24 parts, Leipzig, 1713 – 22)
[Moser, J.J.], *Merkwürdige Reichs-Hofrats-Conclusa* . . . (8 vols., Frankfurt, 1726 – 48).
Murray, J.J. (ed.), *A Honest Diplomat at The Hague* (Bloomington/The Hague, 1955)
Pachner von Eggenstorff, *Vollständige Sammlung aller von Anfang des noch fortwährenden Reichstags de anno 1663 bis anhero abgefassten Reichsschlüsse* (4 vols., Regensburg, 1740 – 77)

Pribram, A.F. (ed.), *Österreichische Staatsverträge. England*, vol. I (Innsbruck, 1907)

Reuss, J.A., *Beiträge zur neuesten Geschichte der Reichsgerichtlichen Verfassung und Praxis*, vol. II (Ulm, 1786)

Srbik, H. von (ed.), *Österreichische Staatsverträge. Niederlande*, vol. I (Vienna, 1912)

Uffenbach, J.C., *Tractatus singularis et methodicus de Excelsissimo consilio Caesareo-Imperiali aulico* (Vienna, 1683)

Secondary Sources

Antholz, H., *Die politische Wirksamkeit des Johannes Althusius in Emden* (Münster, 1955)

Aretin, K.O. von, (ed.), *Der Kurfürst von Mainz und die Kreisassoziationen 1648 – 1746* (Wiesbaden, 1975)

Arneth, A. von, *Prinz Eugen von Savoyen*, vol. II (Vienna, 1858)

Atkinson, C.T., *A History of Germany 1715-1815* (London, 1908)

Auer, L., 'Das Reich und der Vertrag von Sevilla 1729 – 1731', MIÖG, vol. 22 (1969)

Bader, K.S., 'Die Rechtssprechung des Reichshofrats und die Anfänge des territorialen Beamtenrechts', *Zeitschrift der Savigny-Stiftung für Rechtsgeschichte*, Germ. Abt., vol. 65 (1947)

Ballschmieter, H.-J., *Andreas Gottlieb von Bernstorff und der mecklenburgische Ständekampf, 1680 – 1720* (Cologne/Graz, 1962)

Barraclough, G., *The Origins of Modern Germany*, 2nd ed. (Oxford, 1949)

Beattie, J.M., *The English Court in the reign of George I* (Cambridge, 1967)

Beer, A., 'Zur Geschichte der Politik Karls VI', HZ, vol. 55 (1886)

Benecke, G., *Society and Politics in Germany 1500 – 1750* (London, 1974)

Biederbick, A., *Der deutsche Reichstag zu Regensburg im Jahrzehnt nach dem Spanischen Erbfolgekrieg, 1714 – 1724* (Diss. Bonn, 1937)

Bog, I., *Der Reichsmerkantilismus im 17. und 18. Jahrhundert* (Stuttgart, 1959)

Borgmann, K., *Der deutsche Religionsstreit der Jahre 1719 – 1720* (Berlin, 1937)

Braubach, M., *Versailles und Wien von Ludwig XIV bis Kaunitz* (Bonn, 1952)

—— *Diplomatie und geistiges Leben im 17. und 18. Jahrhundert* (Bonn, 1969)

—— 'Eine Satire auf den Wiener Hof aus den letzten Jahren Kaiser Karls VI', MIÖG, vol. 53 (1939)

Brennert, J., 'Reichsexekution im alten Reich', *Zeitschrift für Politik*, vol. 22 (1933)

Carsten, F.L., *Princes and Parliaments in Germany from the 15th to the 18th century* (Oxford, 1959)

Carter, A.C., *Neutrality or Commitment: the Evolution of Dutch Foreign Policy 1667 – 1795* (London, 1975)

Chance, J.F., *The Alliance of Hanover* (London, 1923)

Conrad, H., *Deutsche Rechtsgeschichte. Ein Lehrbuch* (Karlsruhe, 1954)
Conring, W., *Aurich unter den Cirksena* (Aurich, 1966)
Döhring, E., *Geschichte der Rechtspflege in Deutschland seit 1500* (Berlin, 1953)
Droysen, J.G., *Geschichte der preussischen Politik*, vol. 4 (Leipzig, 1872)
Epstein, K., *The Genesis of German Conservatism* (Princeton, 1967)
Erdmannsdörfer, B., *Deutsche Geschichte vom Westfälischen Frieden bis zum Regierungsantritt Friedrichs des Grossen* (2 vols., 1888–93)
Feller, H.R., *Die Bedeutung des Reichs und seiner Verfassung für die mittelbaren Untertanen und die Landstände im Jahrhundert nach dem Westfälischen Frieden* (Diss. Marburg, 1953)
Fellner, T. and Kretschmayr, H., *Die österreichische Zentralverwaltung* (3 parts, Vienna, 1907)
Franklin, O., *Das deutsche Reich nach Severinus de Monzambano* (Greifswald, 1872)
Gehling, T., *Ein europäischer Diplomat am Kaiserhof zu Wien* (Bonn, 1964)
Gerhard, D., *England und der Aufstieg Russlands* (Munich and Berlin, 1933)
—— (ed.), *Ständische Vertretungen in Europa im 17. und 18. Jahrhundert* (Göttingen, 1969)
Gibbs, G.C., 'Britain and the Alliance of Hanover', *EHR*, vol. 73 (1958)
Gross, L., 'Der Kampf zwischen Reichskanzlei und österreichischer Hofkanzlei um die Führung der auswärtigen Geschäfte', *Historische Vierteljahresschrift*, vol. 22 (1924/5)
—— 'Die Reichspolitik der Habsburger', *Neue Jahrbücher für deutsche Wissenschaft*, 3 (1937)
Gschliesser, O. von, *Der Reichshofrat. Bedeutung und Verfassung, Schicksal und Besetzung einer obersten Reichsbehörde 1559–1806* (Vienna, 1942)
Günter, H., 'Die Reichsidee im Wandel der Zeiten', *Historische Jahrbücher*, vol. 53 (1933)
Haan, H., 'Kaiser Ferdinand II und das Problem der Reichsabsolutismus. Die Prager Heeresreform von 1635', *HZ*, vol. 207 (1968)
Hantsch, H., *Reichsvizekanzler Friedrich Karl von Schönborn* (Augsburg, 1929)
—— *Die Geschichte Österreichs*, 3rd ed. (2 vols., Graz etc., 1962)
Hatton, R., *Diplomatic Relations between Great Britain and the Dutch Republic 1714–1721* (London, 1950)
Hatton, R., and Anderson, M.S. (eds.), *Studies in the Diplomatic History of Europe in memory of D.B. Horne* (London, 1970)
Hatton, R. and Bromley, J.S. (eds.), *William III and Louis XIV* (Liverpool, 1968)
Hegel, C., *Geschichte der mecklenburgischen Landstände bis zum Jahre 1555 mit einem Urkundenanhang* (Rostock, 1856)
Herchenhahn, J.C., *Geschichte der Entstehung, Bildung und gegenwärtigen Verfassung des kaiserlichen Reichs-Hofraths . . .* (3 vols., Mannheim, 1792–9)

Hertz, F., 'Die Rechtsprechung der höchsten Reichsgerichte im römisch-deutschen Reich und ihre politische Bedeutung', *MIÖG*, vol. 69 (1961)

Hills, G., *Rock of Contention* (London, 1974)

Hofer, E., *Die Beziehungen Mecklenburgs zu Kaiser und Reich* (Marburg, 1956)

Hofmann, H.H. (ed.), *Die Entstehung des modernen souveränen Staates* (Berlin/Cologne, 1967)

—— 'Reichsidee und Staatspolitik. Die Vorderen Reichskreise im 18. Jahrhundert', *Zeitschrift für bayerische Landesgeschichte*, vol. 33 (1970)

—— 'Heiliges Römisches Reich', *Der Staat*, vol. 9 (1970)

Holborn, H., *A History of Modern Germany*, vol. II (London, 1965)

Huber, E.R., 'Reich, Volk und Staat in der Reichsrechtswissenschaft des 17. und 18. Jahrhunderts', *Zeitschrift für die gesamte Staatswissenschaft*, vol. 102 (1942)

Jastrow, J., *Pufendorfs Lehre von der Monstrosität der Reichsverfassung* (Berlin, 1882)

Joachimsen, P. (ed.), *Der deutsche Staatsgedanke von seinen Anfängen bis auf Leibniz und Friedrich den Grossen* (Munich, 1921)

—— *Vom deutschen Volk zum deutschen Staat*, 3rd ed. (Göttingen, 1956)

Joester, I., *Enno Rudolph Brenneysen (1669–1734) und die ostfriesische Territorialgeschichtsschreibung* (Diss. Münster, 1963)

Kappelhoff, B., *Absolutistisches Regiment oder Ständeherrschaft? Landesherr und Landstände in Ostfriesland im ersten Drittel des 18. Jahrhunderts* (Hildesheim, 1982)

Kleinheyer, G., *Die kaiserlichen Wahlkapitulationen. Geschichte, Wesen und Funktion* (Karlsruhe, 1968)

Klopp, O., *Geschichte Ostfrieslands* (3 vols., Hanover, 1854–8)

König, J., *Verwaltungsgeschichte Ostfrieslands bis zum Aussterben seines Fürstenhauses* (Göttingen, 1955)

Kormann, K., 'Die Landeshoheit in ihrem Verhältnis zur Reichsgewalt im alten Deutschen Reich seit dem Westfälischen Frieden', *Zeitschrift für Politik*, vol. 7 (1914)

Koser, R., 'Brandenburg-Preussen in dem Kampfe zwischen Imperialismus und reichsständischer Libertät', *HZ*, vol. 96 (1906)

Lewitter, L.R., 'Poland, Russia and the Treaty of Vienna of 5th January 1719', *H.J.* (1970)

Lodge, R., *Great Britain and Prussia in the 18th century* (Oxford, 1923)

—— 'The Treaty of Seville (1729), *TRHS* 4th series, vol. 16 (1933)

McKay, D., *Diplomatic Relations between George I and the Emperor Charles VI 1714–9* (Diss. London, 1971)

—— 'The Struggle for Control of George I's Northern Policy 1718–9', *JMH*, vol. 45 (1973)

Mager, G., *Geschichte des Bauerntums und der Bodenkultur im Lande Mecklenburg* (Berlin, 1955)

Masur, G., 'Das Reich und die Nation im 18. Jahrhundert', *Preussisches Jahrbuch*, vol. 229 (1932)

Matthias, G., *Die Mecklenburger Frage in der ersten Hälfte des 18. Jahrhunderts und das Dekret vom 11. Mai 1728* (Diss. Halle, 1885)

Mecenseffy, G., *Karls VI Spanische Bündnispolitik 1725 – 9* (Innsbruck, 1934)

Mediger, W., *Moskaus Weg nach Europa* (Brunswick, 1952)

—— *Mecklenburg, Russland und England-Hannover 1706 – 21* (Hildesheim, 1967)

Michael, W., *Zur Entstehung der Pragmatischen Sanktion Karls VI* (Basle, 1939)

Möhlmann, G., 'Eine Beschreibung Ostfrieslands aus dem Jahre 1729', *Friesisches Jahrbuch*, vol 47 (1967)

Moser, J.J., *Von der Teutschen Justizverfassung*, vol. 1 (Frankfurt and Leipzig, 1774)

—— *Einleitung zu dem Reichs-Hof-Rats-Process* (3 vols., Frankfurt, 1731 – 7)

Murray, J.J., *George I, the Baltic and the Whig Split* (London, 1969)

—— 'Scania and the End of the Northern Alliance', *JMH*, vol. 16 (1944)

Naumann, M., *Österreich, England und das Reich* (Berlin, 1936)

Perels, K., 'Die allgemeinen Appellationsprivilegien für Brandenburg-Preussen' in *Quellen und Studien zur Verfassungsgeschichte des deutschen Reichs im Mittelalter und in der Neuzeit*, vol. 3, no. 1 (Weimar, 1908)

—— 'Die Justizverweigerung im alten Reich seit 1495', *Zeitschrift der Savigny-Stiftung für Rechtsgeschichte*, Germ. Abt., 25 (1904)

Perizonius, H.F.W., *Geschichte Ostfrieslands* (4 vols., Weener, 1868 – 9)

Pretsch, H.-J., *Graf Manteuffels Beitrag zur österreichischen Geheimdiplomatie von 1728 bis 1736* (Bonn, 1970)

Pütter, J.S., *Versuch einiger näheren Erläuterungen des Processes beyder Reichsgerichte*, 2nd ed. (Göttingen, 1768)

Randelzhofer, A., *Völkerrechtliche Aspekte des Heiligen Römischen Reiches nach 1648* (Berlin, 1967)

Ranke, E. von, *Das Fürstentum Schwarzburg-Rudolstadt zu Beginn des 18. Jahrhunderts. Der Landstreit gegen die fürstliche Willkür vor Reichkammergericht und Reichshofrat* (Diss. Halle, 1915).

Rauch, A., *Kaiser und Reich im Jahrhundert nach dem Westfälischen Frieden* (Ochsenfurt/Munich, 1933)

Reimers, H., *Ostfriesland bis zum Aussterben seines Fürstenhauses* (Bremen, 1925)

Rother, H., *Die Auseinandersetzungen zwischen Preussen und Hannover um Ostfriesland von 1690 bis 1740* (Diss. Göttingen, 1951)

Schubert, E., *König und Reich. Studien zur spätmittelalterlichen deutschen Verfassungsgeschichte* (Göttingen, 1979)

Schubert, F.H., *Die deutschen Reichstage in der Staatstheorie der Frühen Neuzeit* (Göttingen, 1966)

Sellert, W., *Über die Zuständigkeitsabgrenzung von Reichshofrat und Reichskammergericht insbesondere in Strafsachen und Angelegenheiten der freiwilligen Gerichtsbarkeit* (Aalen, 1965)

Sperling, A., *Die mecklenburgische Geistlichkeit in den Wirren unter Herzog Karl Leopold, 1713 – 47* (Diss. Rostock, 1924)

Stoye, J.W., 'Emperor Charles VI: The Early Years of the Reign', *TRHS*, 5th series, vol. 12 (1962)

Strauss, G., (ed.), *Pre-Reformation Germany* (London, 1972)

Thudichum, F., 'Das vormahlige Reichskammergericht und seine Schicksale', *Zeitschrift für das deutsche Recht*, vol. 20 (1861)

Vann, J.A. and Rowan, S.W., *The Old Reich, Essays on German Institutions 1495 – 1806* (Brussels, 1974)

Vitense, O., *Geschichte von Mecklenburg* (Gotha, 1920)

Wagner, W., (ed.), *Das Staatsrecht des Heiligen Römischen Reiches deutscher Nation* (Karlsruhe, 1968)

Wandruszka, A., *Reichspatriotismus und Reichspolitik zur Zeit des Prager Friedens von 1635* (Cologne/Graz, 1955)

Wick, P., *Versuche zur Errichtung des Absolutismus in Mecklenburg in der ersten Hälfte des 18. Jahrhunderts* (Berlin, 1964)

Williams, B., *Stanhope: a study in eighteenth century war and diplomacy* (London, 1912)

—— 'The foreign policy of England under Walpole', *EHR*, vols. 15 and 16 (1900, 1901)

Wilson, A.McC., *French Foreign Policy during the Administration of Cardinal Fleury 1726 – 43* (Cambridge, Mass., 1936)

Witte, H.N., *Mecklenburgische Geschichte* (2 vols., Wismar, 1909 – 13)

Ziekursch, J., *Die Kaiserwahl Karls VI (1711)* (Gotha, 1902)

Zwiedeneck-Südenhorst, H. von, *Die öffentliche Meinung in Deutschland im Zeitalter Ludwigs XIV* (Stuttgart, 1888)

—— 'Die Anerkennung der pragmatischen Sanktion Karls VI durch das deutsche Reich', *MIÖG* (1895).

Index

219, 227, 230ff., 261ff.
Hanover (Herrenhausen), treaty of
(1725), 190f., 202
Holland: see United Provinces

imperial diet (*Reichstag*), 17, 27,
111, 170, 176
'imperial reaction', 8, 10, 20f., 60,
183, 259

Joseph I, Holy Roman Emperor
(1705 – 11), 8
Jülich-Berg, 21 – 2, 75, 192, 197f.,
204, 210f., 225

Maria Theresa, archduchess of
Austria, 7, 187f., 213, 221
Maximilian I, Holy Roman
Emperor, 14
Mecklenburg-Schwerin, duchy of,
2, 24, chapters 3, 5, 6 and 7
passim, 260ff.
Münster, bishopric of, 73, 128, 141

Nassau-Siegen, William Hyacinth
prince of, 181f.

Ostend commercial company,
81 – 2, 147, 189, 192, 194 – 5, 204,
209, 221, 231, 247

Palatinate, 166f., 197, 213, 216
Passarowitz, peace of (1718), 117
Pragmatic Sanction, 82f., 184, 188,
209, 224
Prussia, 22, 62, 73f., 109, 113 – 16,
129, 133f., 141, 143, 147ff., 161,
167f., 185 – 6, 191, 193 – 4, 197f.,
206f., 211f., 215, 218, 232f., 267f.,
270
Pufendorf, Samuel von, 1

reform movement, imperial,
14 – 15, 29
Reich: see Empire

Reichshofrat: see aulic council
Reichskammergericht: see cameral
court
Rostock, 63 – 5, 100f., 105
Russia, 82, 102f., 106 – 9, 117, 158,
170, 182, 191, 198, 206, 210

Saxony, 83, 140, 166 – 7, 186, 196,
211f., 216, 223

Schönborn, Frederick Charles von,
imperial vice-chancellor, 10,
22 – 6, 57, 116, 151, 157, 165, 171,
178, 185, 213 – 15, 243, 245
Seville, treaty of, 222, 231, 248
Sinzendorff, Philip Ludwig von,
Austrian aulic chancellor, 25, 185,
190, 209, 243, 248n., 251
Soissons, congress of, 210, 220f.,
229
Spain, 86f., 163, 183, 186ff., 194f.,
210, 220f., 231
supreme judicial office, imperial
(*obristrichterliches Amt*), 61, 192,
244, 256, 268f.
Sweden, 75, 102, 104, 116 – 17, 162,
218

Thorn (Toruń), blood trials (1724),
192

United Provinces of the
Netherlands (Dutch Republic), 72,
78 – 9, 136, 147f., 154, 208f., 223,
240ff.

Vienna, treaties of (1725), 189f.
Vienna, treaty of (1731), 231, 251

Wahlkapitulation: see capitulation of
election
Westphalia, treaties of (1648),
16 – 18
Wittelsbachs, ambitions of, 21f.,
216